# CANADA'S TOP 100 EMPLOYERS

## (2004 EDITION)

BY

RICHARD W. YEREMA



MEDIACORP CANADA INC.
TORONTO

Thank you to all the participants in this year's competition and congratulations to those who made the list. A project such as this would not be possible without the cooperation of hundreds of Canadians from coast-to-coast-to-coast. We look forward to hearing from you for our next edition.

Of course, thanks to the New Street gang for maintaining the information that makes these projects possible, to Karen and Tony for helping transform those boxes of paper into a final book, and to Sally for ensuring our assembled words reach the reader. And, special thanks goes to Sheryl for helping complete that other project and for providing the day-to-day support that every such endeavour requires.

Richard Yerema
ry@mediacorp2.com

Canada's Top 100 Employers
Mediacorp Canada Inc.
21 New Street
Toronto, Ontario
M5R 1P7

Telephone (416) 964-6069
Fax (416) 964-3202

E-mail ct100@mediacorp2.com
Web Site http://www.CanadasTop100.com



ISBN 1-894450-17-5. Fourth edition. First edition: 2000.

Printed in Canada by Webcom

# Praise for *Canada's Top 100 Employers*:

"an instant bible to human resources professionals and job seekers"
*-The Globe and Mail (May 21, 2003)*

"a definitive...guide...to firms that lead their peers in providing a great place to work."
*-Maclean's Magazine*

The #1 selling business book of the year...
*-The Globe and Mail (Jan. 4, 2001)*

"a fountain of knowledge about Canadian workplaces, employers, workplace philosophies [and] perks"
*-The Vancouver Sun*

" these...companies are doing innovative things. They're really raising the bar."
*-The London Free Press*

"[employers in this book recognize] their employees have lives outside of work and...need time for those obligations."
*-Winnipeg Free Press*

"an updated guide on the best places to work"
*-The Globe and Mail*

"Are you tired of the 9 to 5 grind? Probably not -- if you work for one of Canada's Top 100 Employers.... Progressive companies north of the 49th parallel are going to extraordinary lengths to attract and retain quality employees."
*-CHCH-TV, Hamilton*

"showcase[s] the employers that are doing the most interesting things to attract and keep good employees"
*-The Ottawa Citizen*

"...a great way to find out which companies offer family-friendly benefits, such as job sharing and telecommuting, and which ones have earned the distinction of being named among the 10 best employers for women."
*-Canadian Living*

"...an interesting read which...bring[s] to light some innovative approaches to the workplace."
*-Kitchener-Waterloo Record*

"Canadian employers are going to extraordinary lengths to attract and retain quality employees."
*-The Edmonton Journal*

"profiles companies who do a lot for their employees."
*-The Toronto Sun*

"rate[s] firms with the best working conditions, benefits and opportunities for advancement"
*-The Ottawa Sun*

"contains in-depth profiles...on a company's benefits, working conditions and perks [and] recent developments in their business... [t]hings any employee would find most interesting."
*-Canada's HTC Career Journal*

"the book will encourage other employers to create better workplaces and conditions for their workers."
*-The Vancouver Province*

# *TABLE OF CONTENTS*

## *TABLE OF CONTENTS (Cont.)*

## *TABLE OF CONTENTS (Cont.)*

# *PREFACE TO THE FOURTH EDITION*

This fourth edition of *Canada's Top 100 Employers* features several interesting changes. For the first time this year, readers can see our editors' internal ratings that show how each employer compares in areas such as employee benefits, work atmosphere, community involvement and paid vacation allowance. These ratings make it easier for readers to see which areas a particular employer excels in — and where improvements are needed. This year's edition also includes more "Top 10 Lists" and a new branch office index that shows hiring locations across the country for each employer (previously, only head offices were shown). In addition, more than a third of the employers in last year's edition were replaced in this new edition.

To develop this year's list, we started by reviewing the recruitment histories of over 51,000 employers across Canada that we track for our job-searching periodicals, including our flagship newspaper *Canada Employment Weekly*. Much of the work we do at Mediacorp involves monitoring weekly recruitment at thousands of Canadian employers, reporting new job announcements and recording which employers are the most active in their field or region.

From this initial group, invitations were sent to over 6,000 of the fastest-growing employers, plus several hundred other companies and organizations in areas that we wanted to look at more closely this year. Employers were asked to complete an extensive application process that included a thorough review of their operations and human resource practices. Our objective at this stage was really to uncover the best employee perks and HR benefits in each industry. We looked for the really interesting and novel things that set these employers apart from others in their field.

This year's edition shows readers the internal grades assigned to employers in the seven key human resources areas we review: (1) Physical Workplace; (2) Work Atmosphere & Social; (3) Health, Financial & Family Benefits; (4) Vacation & Time Off; (5) Employee Communications; (6) Performance Management; and (7) Training & Skills Development. The new grading system lets readers quickly identify what's remarkable about each employer — and where there's room for improvement. These grades are assigned relative to other employers in the book.

In addition to these criteria, we also describe (and grade) each employer's charitable efforts and involvement in the community. In our book's first edition, we observed a strong correlation between charitable work and how an employer treats its own employees. Employers who take a broader view of their responsibilities to the community, it turns out, are almost always better places to work.

In choosing the finalists, our editorial team considered how each employer compares to others in its industry. This book includes large and small employers from a range of industries, offering very different benefits and working conditions. The common thread that runs through all the finalists is that each is a leader in its industry. From software innovators to city governments, the employers chosen as this year's Top 100 stand out from others in their industry in attracting and retaining quality employees.

## *PREFACE (Cont.)*

In reviewing the applicants for a book such as this, it is inevitable that some outstanding employers will be passed over. We encourage them to stay interested in this subject — and our annual competition. Several of the new employers featured in this year's edition were applicants that were previously unsuccessful.

As well, evaluating something as personal as working conditions necessarily requires subjective choices and judgements on our part. For these, we ask the reader's indulgence and understanding. (The expanded "Top Ten" lists at the back of the book are intended to address — if only partially — some of the particular concerns of individual readers.)

Perhaps the most interesting trend we've seen this year is that many employers are breaking away from their industries and becoming agents of change on their own when it comes to being great employers. Previous applicants have returned to us and said "We've really improved, can you take another look?" They've been improving things like paid vacation allowance, personal days off and family-friendly benefits because they now can see what other employers are doing — and how important these benefits are to Canadians.

Another interesting trend we've noticed this year is the effect of being included in the "Canada's Top 100 Employers" list. Besides a dramatic increase in the number of resumes they receive, these employers quickly take on the role of industry leaders when it comes to being an employer of choice. When we review their HR programs for the next edition, inevitably they have improved most of the areas where we previously noted some weakness. It makes the choices tougher for our editors, but the results are wonderful for readers. These employers are creating a process of self-improvement that is continually raising the bar for other employers in their industry.

*-Richard Yerema, Editor* *-Tony Meehan, Publisher*

**ADACEL INC.**
**7900, boulevard Taschereau**
**Édifice E**
**Brossard, QC J4X 1C2**

**Tel. 450-672-3888**
**Fax 450-672-4434**
**careers@adacelcanada.com**
**http://www.adacelinc.com**

**INDUSTRY: SEARCH & NAVIGATION EQUIPMENT MANUFACTURERS**

*Highlights:*

- Get four weeks of paid vacation allowance in your first year — one of the most progressive vacation policies offered by any employer in Québec.
- Build your career at a growing high technology company that has nearly tripled its employee count in the past two years.
- Work for an employer that offers excellent international opportunities (in the USA, United Kingdom and Australia) — and smooths your transfer between countries with a special benefit matching program.

## *Employer Background*

Adacel Inc. is a leading developer of air traffic control systems and training simulators. The company designs and installs air traffic control systems for civil aviation and defence applications. In addition, Adacel's three-dimensional 360-degree tower and radar simulators are used in air traffic controller training in over 40 countries on five continents, making the company a world leader in the field.

Adacel develops its products to rigorous military standards. The company recently provided its air traffic management software to Lockheed Martin for the U.S. Federal Aviation Administration's oceanic air traffic management upgrading project. In addition, the company has supplied training simulators to the FAA, NASA, Nav Canada and a number of training colleges in the United States.

Adacel Inc. is a wholly-owned subsidiary of Australia-based Adacel Technologies Limited. Founded in 1987, the publicly-traded parent company is one of Australia's leading developers of advanced software and systems for aviation, telecommunications, defence and e-business applications. The parent company markets proprietary software, systems and training products in Australia, the United Kingdom, North America and Asia. In Canada, Adacel has offices in Brossard, Dorval and Barrie, Ontario.

**Workforce at a Glance:** Number of full-time employees: **154**. At this location: **151**. Worldwide: **400**. New jobs created in Canada in past year: **53**. Percentage of employees who are women: **20**. Of managers: **5**. Percentage of employees who are visible minorities: **12**. Of managers: **2**. Resumes received by their human resources staff in past year: 3,000. Average employee age: **35**. Years longest-serving employee has worked there: **4.5**.

### *Physical Workplace* — *Rating: B+*

Adacel's physical workplace is rated as **average**. The company's Canadian head office is in the Montréal suburb of Brossard, only 15 minutes' drive from downtown and 20 minutes from the nearest ski hill.

**Physical Workplace at a Glance:** Their **employee lounge and rest areas** feature: comfortable couches; table tennis; hockey nets in the underground garage. For **food and refreshment**, Adacel offers: free coffee and tea; outdoor eating area; barbeque. Nearby **amenities** include: variety of restaurants; major shopping mall; fitness facility; park/wilderness area (St. Lawrence Maritime Park). For **commuters**, Adacel offers: nearby public transit; free onsite car parking; secure bicycle parking. Other work area **amenities** include: open-concept workstations; plant life that is tended professionally.

### *Work Atmosphere & Social* — *Rating: A*

Adacel's work atmosphere is rated as **above-average**. Employees at Adacel enjoy casual dress daily and can listen to radio or music while they are working. There is also a company-subsidized social committee, which has operated since 1998.

During the year, employees enjoy a variety of events, such as the "*Sugaring-Off*" maple sugar party held every spring, summer barbeques, Friday early-bird golf games, a weekly breakfast club, Friday socials at a nearby pub, a Halloween dress-up contest, birthday celebrations, a Christmas party and a separate holiday event for the children of employees. The social club also operates a snack bar on an honour system along with "all the java you can drink".

Adacel regularly celebrates corporate milestones with draws for movie tickets, dinner certificates and even weekend getaways.

### *Health, Financial & Family Benefits* — *Rating: B+*

Adacel's health benefits plan is rated as **average**.

**Health Benefits at a Glance:** Adacel's health plan includes the following coverage: dental (80% of eligible costs, to $2,500 each year); prescription drug; extended health benefits; physiotherapy; massage therapy; alternative therapies; personal and family counselling.

The company's salary and financial benefits are rated as **above-average**. To keep pay-levels competitive, Adacel participates in outside salary surveys every 12 months. Individual salaries are reviewed every 12 months. The company offers a group RSP that allows employees to contribute up to 5% of their salary, with matching employer contributions.

**Financial Benefits at a Glance:** Adacel provides a variety of financial benefits, including: life and disability insurance; share purchase plan; referral bonuses for some employees (to $1,000); year-end bonuses.

Adacel's family-friendly benefits are rated as **average**. Employees with preschool children have access to a daycare facility located nearby. Other family-friendly benefits include: flexible start and finish hours.

### *Vacation & Time Off* — *Rating: A+*

Adacel's vacation and time off are rated as **exceptional**. New employees receive 4 weeks of vacation allowance after their first year. Employees at Adacel also receive 5 paid personal days off each year, in addition to their regular vacation allowance. The company also offers a shutdown period from Christmas to New Year's. Employees at the company can also apply for unpaid leaves of absence. (Employees celebrating 10 years on the job can take a 13-week unpaid leave.)

### *Employee Communications* — *Rating: B+*

Adacel's internal communications program is rated as **average**. The company has an intranet site, which keeps employees informed about news and human resource policies that affect their work. As a smaller employer, employees regularly attend "brainstorming" meetings and open communications are encouraged at all levels within the company.

### *Performance Management* — *Rating: A*

Adacel's performance management program is rated as **above-average**. The company operates a well-designed performance management program. Once a year, employees and managers meet for review sessions. (Managers receive training in how to conduct effective reviews.) Objectives are set for the coming year and employees receive a completed copy of their evaluation.

### *Training & Skills Development* — *Rating: B+*

Adacel's training and skills development program is rated as **average**. The company provides tuition subsidies for courses related to an employee's current position (100% of tuition). The company assists employees' career development with: reimbursement for professional association dues; in-house training.

### *Community Involvement* — *Rating: B+*

Adacel's community involvement program is rated as **average**. A good corporate citizen, Adacel actively supports a variety of local charitable initiatives.

Last year, employees raised funds for the local United Way campaign, with Adacel matching their donations. The employee social committee also organized a successful food drive for the St. Vincent de Paul Society at the company's Christmas party.

**ADVANCED BOOK EXCHANGE INC.**
**410 Garbally Road, Suite 4**
**Victoria, BC V8T 2K1**

**Tel. 250-412-3200**
**Fax 250-475-6014**
**personnel@abebooks.com**
**http://www.abebooks.com**

abebooks™

**INDUSTRY: OTHER RETAILERS**

*Highlights:*

- Build your career at one of the Internet's most successful retailers that has developed a profitable — and sustainable — business that is growing by over 50% per year.
- Work for an enlightened employer that chose the city where its head office is located — beautiful Victoria, BC — after asking employees where they wanted to live.
- Get three weeks of paid vacation allowance to start, plus three paid personal days off each year at this employer.

***Employer Background***

Advanced Book Exchange Inc. (Abebooks) is an Internet-based network of independent booksellers that specializes in rare and used books.

From an idea scratched on a notepad in 1995, the privately-held company has grown to become one the most interesting Canadian business success stories from the dot.com era. Profitable since its inception, the company provides one of the best examples of successful Internet retailing — its revenues are growing by 50% a year!

Victoria-based Abebooks is based on a simple idea — use the power of the Internet to create the world's biggest used bookseller. Without physically handling a book, the company brings together booksellers and customers from around the world. Abebooks' retail network consists of over 10,000 booksellers worldwide and a virtual inventory of over 40 million used, rare and out-of-print books. Their user-friendly website lets you find an 1844 edition of "A Christmas Carol" by Charles Dickens ($42,000) or a first edition of George Orwell's "1984" ($415) without leaving your house.

The privately-held company provides booksellers with the software and technical support to create and manage their inventory lists. The booksellers pay a monthly listing fee (which varies with the number of titles they advertise) and a small commission on each sale through the Abebooks site (between 10,000 and 15,000 books are sold on the site every day). The company's business model works because everyone wins — the retailer, the customer and Abebooks.

In 2001, the company acquired Germany-based Justbooks GmbH and has since launched customized websites for Germany, France and the United Kingdom. Recently, the company entered into partnership agreements with Amazon, Barnes & Noble, e-Bay and Biblioquest (Australia), reaching millions of additional customers.

**Workforce at a Glance:** Number of full-time employees: **88**. Worldwide: **103**. New jobs created in Canada in past year: **1**. Percentage of employees who are women: **57**. Of managers: **61**. Percentage of employees who are visible minorities: **7**. Of managers: **4**. Resumes received by their human resources staff in past year: **450**. Weeks of vacation their HR manager took last year: **4**. Average employee age: **33**. Years longest-serving employee has worked there: **6**. Person you should get to know first: **Leslie in Payroll makes new employees feel welcome on their very first day**. Car the president drives: **2003 Toyota Prius**.

### *Physical Workplace* — *Rating: A*

Abebooks' physical workplace is rated as **above-average**. The location offers great mountain views and is only minutes away from the Selkirk Waterway boardwalk as well as nearby cycling trails. The custom-designed head office was built after consulting employees about the city where they wanted to locate the office. Not surprisingly, employees chose beautiful Victoria — which was also recently chosen by the magazine Condé Nast Traveller as the most charming city in the Americas.

Employees also provided feedback when furnishing the head office interior, from carpet colours to artwork. Abebooks recently established a "*Cool Office Committee*" to review and make recommendations for future workplace improvements.

**Physical Workplace at a Glance:** Their **employee lounge and rest areas** feature: comfortable couches; foosball. For **food and refreshment**, Abebooks offers: free snacks (including popcorn, pastries, fresh fruit every week); free coffee and tea; free soft drinks. Nearby **amenities** include: variety of restaurants; major shopping mall; fitness facility; dog daycare facility; park/wilderness area (Galloping Goose Trail). For **commuters**, Abebooks offers: transit subsidies; nearby public transit; free onsite car parking. Other **work area amenities** include: open-concept workstations; access to natural light for all employees.

### *Work Atmosphere & Social* — *Rating: A*

Abebooks' work atmosphere is rated as **above-average**. Employees at Abebooks enjoy casual dress daily. Employees enjoy a variety of social events during the year, including a summer fun day, a family day at a nearby lake, cooking contests between departments, golfing, bowling, a Halloween party and a Christmas party for employees and their guests. The company also holds draws for tickets to professional hockey games — and even the chance to stay in the CEO's house when he's away. There is also a company-subsidized social committee.

### *Health, Financial & Family Benefits* — *Rating: B+*

Abebooks' health benefits plan is managed by Equitable Life and is rated as **average**.

**Health Benefits at a Glance:** Abebooks' health plan includes the following coverage: dental (80% of eligible costs, to $2,000 each year); eyecare (to $200 every 2 years); extended health benefits; physiotherapy; massage therapy; alternative therapies; personal and family counselling; prescription drug.

The company's salary and financial benefits are rated as **average**. To keep pay-levels competitive, Abebooks participates in outside salary surveys every 12 months. Individual salaries are reviewed every 12 months.

**Financial Benefits at a Glance:** Abebooks provides a variety of financial benefits, including: life and disability insurance; discounts on surplus company computer equipment; share purchase plan; year-end bonuses (to $800 for non-executives).

Abebooks' family-friendly benefits are rated as **average**. Family-friendly benefits include: shortened work week (fewer hours); flexible start and finish hours.

***Vacation & Time Off*** ***Rating: A***

Abebooks' vacation and time off are rated as **above-average**. New employees receive 3 weeks of vacation allowance after their first year. Employees at Abebooks also receive 3 paid personal days off each year, in addition to their regular vacation allowance.

***Employee Communications*** ***Rating: A***

Abebooks' internal communications program is rated as **above-average**. To solicit feedback from employees, the company operates a traditional suggestion box program and an email suggestion box. An employee satisfaction survey is conducted by having employees complete questionnaires every 12 months. An outside consultant compiles the survey results for Abebooks' management team. In addition, the employee-owned company operates an online information service for employees and hosts quarterly shareholder meetings at a nearby golf course.

***Performance Management*** ***Rating: A***

Abebooks' performance management program is rated as **above-average**. The company operates a well-designed performance management program. Once a year, employees and managers meet for review sessions. (Managers receive training in how to conduct effective reviews.) At the annual meetings, employees and managers review past performance and develop objectives for the upcoming year. Informal reviews are held every few months to monitor progress.

***Training & Skills Development*** ***Rating: B+***

Abebooks' training and skills development program is rated as **average**. The company assists employees' career development with: in-house training. Abebooks provides each employee with financial support for one training opportunity every year. (Some technical employees may receive additional support.)

***Community Involvement*** ***Rating: B+***

Abebooks' community involvement program is rated as **average**. A good corporate citizen, Abebooks actively supports a variety of local charitable initiatives. Last year, employees provided food donations to the Mustard Seed Food Bank and supported the local Lions Club as well as a local Christmas Hamper program for seniors. Employees take part in the selection of charitable groups assisted by the company.

Algorithmics
*Incorporated*

**ALGORITHMICS INCORPORATED**
**185 Spadina Avenue**
**Toronto, ON M5T 2C6**

**Tel. 416-217-1500**
**Fax 416-971-6677**
**careers@algorithmics.com**
**http://www.algorithmics.com**

**INDUSTRY: SOFTWARE COMPANIES**

***Highlights:***

- Get three weeks of paid vacation allowance to start, plus two paid personal days off each year — and receive a special two-week paid sabbatical every five years.
- Get rewarded for outstanding work with additional vacation days, gift certificates, baseball tickets and paid weekend vacations — one group of employees received a company-paid ski trip to Whistler!
- Work in Toronto's funky Queen Street West area in a beautifully renovated loft that includes an onsite café and a rooftop patio with great views.

## *Employer Background*

Algorithmics Incorporated develops risk management software for the financial services industry. The company's software helps large financial services companies manage risks associated with complex financial transactions. Founded in 1989, Algorithmics' software is used by over 140 clients in 26 countries, including 40 of the 100 largest financial institutions in the world.

In addition to its Toronto head office, Algorithmics has locations in 15 cities around the world, including all major financial centres.

**Workforce at a Glance:** Number of full-time employees: **255**. Worldwide: **488**. Percentage of employees who are women: **30**. Of managers: **20**. Percentage of employees who are visible minorities: **44**. Of managers: **28**. Resumes received by their human resources staff in past year: **13,000**. Weeks of vacation their HR manager took last year: **2**. Average employee age: **33**. Years longest-serving employee has worked there: **11**. Car the president drives: **rides a bike to work**.

## *Physical Workplace* — *Rating: A+*

Algorithmics' physical workplace is rated as **exceptional**. The head office is located in a renovated six-storey warehouse near the city's Chinatown and fashion districts. Steps from the trendy Queen & Spadina intersection, the loft-style building offers a comfortable work environment with high ceilings, hardwood floors and exposed brick walls.

**Physical Workplace at a Glance:** Their **onsite fitness facility** features: free memberships; treadmills; stationary bikes; rowing machines; weights; shower facilities. Their

**employee lounge and rest areas** feature: comfortable couches; music; television; pool table; electronic piano. For **food and refreshment**, Algorithmics offers: free snacks (including fresh fruit every morning); free coffee and tea; outdoor eating area. The company has an onsite cafeteria that features: subsidized meals (a turkey sandwich costs $2.00); healthy menu items; special diet menus. Nearby **amenities** include: variety of restaurants; local shops and services; Toronto's famous Kensington Market. For **commuters**, Algorithmics offers: nearby public transit; secure bicycle parking. Other **work area amenities** include: open-concept workstations; ergonomic workstation design; wireless connectivity throughout office; plant life that is tended professionally; windows that open.

### *Work Atmosphere & Social* — *Rating: A*

Algorithmics' work atmosphere is rated as **above-average**. Employees at Algorithmics enjoy casual dress daily and can listen to radio or music while they are working. There is also a company-subsidized social committee, called the '*Algo Social Committee*'.

The committee organizes a variety of employee events every year, including golf tournaments, bowling nights, restaurant and pub nights and trips to major sporting events. With more than 40 PhDs on staff, Algoritmics relies on the social committee to keep life interesting for its highly-educated workforce.

Each Christmas, the company treats employees to an evening of dinner and dancing at a unique local venue, such as the Art Gallery of Ontario. The company also hosts a children's Christmas party, complete with food and entertainment. During the year, catered parties with live music are held in the employee lounge to celebrate company achievements and new software releases.

### *Health, Financial & Family Benefits* — *Rating: A*

Algorithmics' health benefits plan is managed by Manulife Financial and is rated as **above-average**. There is no waiting period before new employees are eligible for coverage.

**Health Benefits at a Glance:** Algorithmics' health plan includes the following coverage: dental (100% of eligible costs, to $2,000 each year); orthodontics (50% of eligible costs with a lifetime maximum of $2,000); eyecare (to $200 every 2 years); extended health benefits; prescription drug; nutrition planning; massage therapy; physiotherapy; alternative therapies; personal and family counselling; employee assistance plan (EAP) for substance abuse/mental health.

The company's salary and financial benefits are rated as **above-average**. To keep pay-levels competitive, Algorithmics participates in outside salary surveys every 12 months. Individual salaries are reviewed every 12 months. The company offers a group RSP that allows employees to contribute up to 4% of their salary, with matching employer contributions.

**Financial Benefits at a Glance:** Algorithmics provides a variety of financial benefits, including: life and disability insurance; share purchase plan; signing bonuses for some employees; referral bonuses for some employees (from $2,000 to $10,000); year-end bonuses.

Algorithmics' family-friendly benefits are rated as **average**. Employees with pre-school children have access to a daycare facility located nearby. Other family-friendly benefits include: flexible start and finish hours; telecommuting and working from home.

***Vacation & Time Off*** **Rating: A**

Algorithmics' vacation and time off are rated as **above-average**. New employees receive 3 weeks of vacation allowance after their first year, which increases to 4 weeks after 5 years of service. The maximum vacation allowance is 4 weeks for long-serving employees. Employees at Algorithmics also receive 2 paid personal days off each year, in addition to their regular vacation allowance. Employees at the company can also apply for unpaid leaves of absence. (Recently, one employee took a six-month leave to travel through South America.)

In addition, employees celebrating 5 years with the company receive a two-week paid leave in addition to their regular vacation allowance. (This unique bonus is available on each 5th anniversary thereafter.)

***Employee Communications*** **Rating: B+**

Algorithmics' internal communications program is rated as **average**. The company has an intranet site, which keeps employees informed about news and human resource policies that affect their work. To solicit feedback from employees, the company operates a traditional suggestion box program and an email suggestion box. Employees also meet with senior management for quarterly "town hall" meetings, where workplace and business issues are discussed.

***Performance Management*** **Rating: A+**

Algorithmics' performance management program is rated as **exceptional**. The company operates a thorough performance management program. Every 6 months, employees and managers meet for review sessions. (Managers receive training in how to conduct effective reviews.) As part of the review process, employees also have the opportunity to provide confidential feedback on their manager's performance.

Algorithmics recognizes exceptional employee performance with additional vacation days, gift certificates, restaurant dinners, tickets to sporting events and company-paid weekend vacations. (Last year, a deserving group of employees enjoyed a Whistler ski trip!)

***Training & Skills Development*** **Rating: A**

Algorithmics' training and skills development program is rated as **above-average**. The company provides tuition subsidies for courses related to an employee's current position (100% of tuition to $2,000). Commendably, Algorithmics also offers subsidies for courses not related to an employee's current job. The company assists employees' career development with: reimbursement for professional association dues; in-house training. Algorithmics' in-house training program includes a range of courses, from technical to personal interest courses.

***Community Involvement*** **Rating: A**

Algorithmics' community involvement program is rated as **above-average**. A very good corporate citizen, Algorithmics actively supports a variety of local and national charitable initiatives. Employees take part in the selection of charitable groups assisted by the company. Last year, the company contributed to approximately 7 charitable groups, including: the United Way, the St. Bart's Food Bank, the Heart and Stroke Foundation, the Brain Tumor Foundation and the Adopt-a-Family program.

Alias®

**ALIAS SYSTEMS**
**210 King Street East**
**Toronto, ON M5A 1J7**

**Tel. 416-362-9181**
**Fax 416-369-6142**
**imhouse@aw.sgi.com**
**http://www.aliaswavefront.com**

**INDUSTRY: SOFTWARE COMPANIES**

***Highlights:***

- Design Oscar-winning software that brought Gollum to life in Lord of the Rings and had Spider-Man climbing the walls.
- Work in a hip downtown warehouse-style loft for a software company that actually has a viable business model.
- Kick back after a game of *Ratchet & Clank* with fellow co-workers who hold tequila parties, wear costumes at Halloween and have a sinister hockey team called the *Black Squirrels.*

## *Employer Background*

Alias Systems (a division of Silicon Graphics Limited) develops advanced animation and graphics software for entertainment, design and manufacturing applications. Founded in 1983, the company's award-winning animation software (including the industry-leading Maya program) is used around the world in motion picture, advertising, video game and industrial design applications.

Alias' software is behind many recent blockbuster films, including The Lord of the Rings, Star Wars, Spider-Man and The Matrix. On the industrial design side, the company's software was recently used by French automaker Renault to develop the Megane II, recently named "European Car of the Year."

In 1995, Alias became a division of Mountain View, California-based Silicon Graphics Limited. The Toronto-based subsidiary has offices in the United States, Europe and Asia to serve its lengthy customer list, which includes Disney, Sony Pictures, General Motors, Boeing, and Nike, to name a few.

Alias continues to grow with the launch of innovative new software products — the company filed for 33 patents last year. Alias' long term business strategy is to make its software ubiquitous in an ever-growing number of industries around the world.

**Workforce at a Glance:** At this location: **350**. Worldwide: **486**. New jobs created in Canada in past year: **37**. Percentage of employees who are women: **35**. Of managers: **30**. Resumes received by their human resources staff in past year: **5,000**. Weeks of vacation their HR manager took last year: **4**. Average employee age: **35**. Years longest-serving employee has worked there: **16**. Person you should get to know first: **Maria in Facilities (she knows everybody and everything — and has a secret stash of snacks)**. Car the president drives: **Jaguar**. Where it's parked in the lot: **with everyone else**.

## *Physical Workplace* *Rating: A*

Alias' physical workplace is rated as **above-average**. Prior to selecting its the head office location, Alias surveyed its employees about their preferences for location and work environments. An employee committee worked closely with the company in selecting the final location.

Based on these consultations, the company selected an old warehouse (the building originally housed a dairy) in Toronto's "downtown east" design district, near the Toronto Sun building. The renovated workspace offers exposed brick, timber beams, high ceilings, oversized ironwork and original hardwood floors. The open workspace provides a highly interactive work environment that encourages the creativity needed for Alias' products.

**Physical Workplace at a Glance:** Their **employee lounge and rest areas** feature: comfortable couches; television; music; pool table; board games; meditation or religious observance room; video games (including Ratchet & Clank for Playstation 2). For **food and refreshment**, Alias offers: free coffee and tea; free meals for employees working late; self-serve cafés on every floor. Nearby **amenities** include: Toronto's newly-restored Distillery area; variety of restaurants; fitness facility; park/wilderness area (St. James Park). For **commuters**, Alias offers: nearby public transit; secure bicycle parking. Other **work area amenities** include: open-concept workstations; ergonomic workstation design; windows that open; plant life that is tended professionally.

## *Work Atmosphere & Social* *Rating: A+*

Alias' work atmosphere is rated as **exceptional**. Employees at Alias enjoy casual dress daily and can listen to radio or music while they are working. The company lets employees bring their pets to work. There is also a company-subsidized social committee, called the '*D2 Department of Diversions*', which has operated since 1999.

The social committee hosts a variety of events during the year, including a summer deck party, company picnic (held at Ontario Place last year), tequila party, Halloween party (with costume contest), winter holiday party at Christmas, monthly breakfasts, free family movie screenings, and wine and cheese parties to celebrate new product launches. Last year, employees celebrated the company's first Oscar, which was awarded for Alias' groundbreaking film animation software.

Employees also operate their own hockey team (*The Black Squirrels*), as well as baseball and ultimate frisbee teams that compete in local leagues.

## *Health, Financial & Family Benefits* *Rating: A*

Alias' health benefits plan is managed by Maritime Life and is rated as **exceptional**. Alias pays 100% of the premiums associated with the plan. There is no waiting period before new employees are eligible for coverage.

**Health Benefits at a Glance:** Alias' health plan includes the following coverage: dental (100% of eligible costs, to $2,500 each year); orthodontics (50% of eligible costs with a lifetime maximum of $2,500); eyecare (to $150 every 2 years); prescription drug; extended health benefits; nutrition planning; massage therapy; physiotherapy; alternative therapies; personal and family counselling; employee assistance plan (EAP) for substance abuse/mental health; travel insurance.

The company's salary and financial benefits are rated as **average**. To keep pay-levels competitive, Alias participates in outside salary surveys every 12 months. Individual salaries are reviewed every 12 months. The company offers a group RSP that allows employees to contribute up to a maximum of $4,800 per year, with matching employer contributions at the rate of 25¢ for each employee dollar contributed.

> **Financial Benefits at a Glance:** Alias provides a variety of financial benefits, including: life and disability insurance; share purchase plan; discounted company products; on-the-spot awards for exceptional performance; long service awards; awards to celebrate patent approvals; signing bonuses for some employees; referral bonuses for some employees (from $500 to $2,000).

Alias' family-friendly benefits are rated as **above-average**. Employees with preschool children have access to a daycare facility located nearby. For employees who take maternity leave, Alias provides a generous top-up to 65% of salary for the first 25 weeks of their leave. Other family-friendly benefits include: flexible start and finish hours; telecommuting and working from home.

***Vacation & Time Off*** — ***Rating: A***

Alias' vacation and time off are rated as **above-average**. New employees receive 3 weeks of vacation allowance after their first year, which increases to 4 weeks after 5 years of service. Employees at Alias also receive 1 paid personal day off each year, in addition to their regular vacation allowance. Impressively, employees can apply to take a paid sabbatical after only four years on the job. Employees at the company can also apply for unpaid leaves of absence. (One employee recently took a six month leave of absence to travel the world.)

***Employee Communications*** — ***Rating: B+***

Alias' internal communications program is rated as **average**. To keep employees informed about new developments, Alias publishes an in-house newsletter (called *WaveLength*). The company also has an intranet site, which keeps employees informed about news and human resource policies that affect their work. To solicit feedback from employees, the company operates an email suggestion box. An employee satisfaction survey is conducted every 12 months. An outside consultant compiles the survey results for Alias' management team.

***Performance Management*** — ***Rating: A***

Alias' performance management program is rated as **above-average**. The company operates a well-designed performance management program. Once a year, employees and managers meet for review sessions. (Managers receive training in how to conduct effective reviews.) Alias recognizes exceptional performance with cash awards as well as theatre tickets and gift certificates.

Under Alias' performance management program, employees have an opportunity to complete self-assessments and set their own future training needs. Employees can also provide confidential feedback on their manager's performance through an annual employee survey.

*Training & Skills Development* *Rating: A*

Alias' training and skills development program is rated as **above-average**. The company provides tuition subsidies for courses related to an employee's current position (100% of tuition). Commendably, Alias also offers subsidies for courses not related to an employee's current job (100% of tuition). The company assists employees' career development with: reimbursement for professional association dues; career planning; mentoring; in-house training.

Many of the company's in-house training programs focus on leadership development, including career management, development and employee coaching. Alias also provides "lunch and learn" sessions, a self-study library and software training for employees.

*Community Involvement* *Rating: B+*

Alias' community involvement program is rated as **average**. A good corporate citizen, Alias actively supports a variety of charitable initiatives.

Last year, the company contributed to 11 charitable groups, including the YMCA Corporate Challenge, Heart & Stroke Foundation, CHUM City Wish Christmas Toy Drive, Second Harvest food bank, and Toronto's Hospital for Sick Children.

**ALTAGAS SERVICES INC.**
**355 - 4th Avenue SW**
**Suite 1700**
**Calgary, AB T2P 0J1**

**Tel. 403-691-7776**
**Fax 403-508-7256**
**careers@altagas.ca**
**http://www.altagas.ca**

# AltaGas

**INDUSTRY: NATURAL GAS UTILITIES**

*Highlights:*

- Get three weeks of paid vacation allowance in your first year, plus eight paid personal days off each year.
- Pursue your training and educational goals at this employer with generous tuition subsidies and paid time off to attend classes.
- Celebrate five years at this employer with an all-expense-paid weekend for two at a nearby resort.

## *Employer Background*

AltaGas Services Inc. is a pipeline and energy services company that transports natural gas from the field to markets. Founded in 1994, the diversified energy company is active in natural gas gathering and processing, extraction, transmission, distribution and energy services, as well as marketing wholesale electricity.

AltaGas acquires and integrates underused midstream oil and gas businesses and makes the investment required to upgrade the facilities. In addition to Alberta, AltaGas has pipeline and processing facilities in Saskatchewan and Montana. The company also distributes natural gas to customers in Inuvik, Northwest Territories, which represents the first such commercial agreement in Canada's far north. Last year, the publicly-traded company had revenues of over $484 million.

**Workforce at a Glance:** Number of full-time employees: **333**. At this location: **141**. New jobs created in Canada in past year: **11**. Percentage of employees who are women: **36**. Of managers: **33**. Percentage of employees who are visible minorities: **8**. Of managers: **6**. Resumes received by their human resources staff in past year: **3,500**. Weeks of vacation their HR manager took last year: **4**. Average employee age: **37**. Years longest-serving employee has worked there: **9**. Person you should get to know first: **Michelle in Office Services, creator of a unique orientation kit that arrives in a new trash can**.

## *Physical Workplace* — *Rating: B+*

AltaGas' physical workplace is rated as **average**. The company's head office occupies six floors of a downtown office tower. The building is connected to the city's covered walkway system, which provides all-weather access to a wide selection of restaurants, shops and services. Inside the head office, employees are greeted by fresh-cut flowers (delivered weekly) and original artwork (on loan from a local gallery) in common areas.

**Physical Workplace at a Glance:** For **food and refreshment**, AltaGas offers: free snacks (including the employee-sponsored "Treat Fridays"); free coffee and tea; outdoor eating area. Nearby **amenities** include: variety of restaurants; major shopping mall; IMAX theatre; live theatre; outdoor market; fitness facility; park/wilderness area (Prince's Island Park and Millennium Park). For **commuters**, AltaGas offers: nearby public transit; secure bicycle parking; nearby bicycle path network; shower and locker facilities. Other **work area amenities** include: open-concept workstations; ergonomic workstation design.

### *Work Atmosphere & Social* — *Rating: A*

AltaGas' work atmosphere is rated as **above-average**. Employees at AltaGas enjoy business casual dress daily and can listen to radio or music while they are working. The company has an on-site concierge service. There is also a company-subsidized social committee, which has operated since 1994.

The social club organizes a variety of fun activities during the year, including a Calgary Stampede breakfast, whitewater rafting, laser tag, bowling, curling and golfing. Across the company, AltaGas employees also celebrate individual and corporate milestones with evening dinners, movie matinees, birthday parties, summer barbeques, weekend getaways, nights at the ballet and baseball games. Employees also have their own lunchtime running and power-walking club.

Every year, the company also hosts a Stampede lunch, an evening Christmas party, a holiday event for employees' children, and a service awards banquet (employees celebrating five years at the company receive an all-expense-paid weekend for two at a nearby resort).

### *Health, Financial & Family Benefits* — *Rating: A*

AltaGas' health benefits plan is managed by Manulife Financial and is rated as **above-average**. Full-time and part-time employees who work more than 24 hours per week are covered by the plan.

**Health Benefits at a Glance:** AltaGas' health plan includes the following coverage: dental (90% of eligible costs, with no annual maximum); orthodontics (50% of eligible costs with a lifetime maximum of $2,500); eyecare (to $200 every 2 years); prescription drug; massage therapy; physiotherapy; alternative therapies; extended health benefits; personal and family counselling; employee assistance plan (EAP) for substance abuse/mental health.

The company's salary and financial benefits are rated as **above-average**. To keep pay-levels competitive, AltaGas participates in outside salary surveys every 12 months. Individual salaries are reviewed every 12 months. The company offers a group RSP that allows employees to contribute up to 4.8% of their salary, with matching employer contributions. Through the company's RSP provider and legal counsel, employees also receive preferred rates on lines of credit and real estate legal fees.

**Financial Benefits at a Glance:** AltaGas provides a variety of financial benefits, including: life and disability insurance; share purchase plan; signing bonuses for some employees; year-end bonuses.

AltaGas' family-friendly benefits are rated as **above-average**. Employees with pre-school children have access to a daycare facility located nearby. For employees who take maternity leave, AltaGas provides a top-up to 100% of salary for the first 6 weeks of their leave. Other family-friendly benefits include: flexible start and finish hours; shortened work week (fewer hours); telecommuting and working from home; reduced summer hours.

### *Vacation & Time Off* — *Rating: A+*

AltaGas' vacation and time off are rated as **exceptional**. New employees receive 3 weeks of vacation allowance after their first year, which increases to 4 weeks after 10 years of service. The maximum vacation allowance is 5 weeks for long-serving employees. Employees at AltaGas also receive 8 paid personal days off each year, in addition to their regular vacation allowance. Employees at the company can also apply for unpaid leaves of absence.

### *Employee Communications* — *Rating: A*

AltaGas' internal communications program is rated as **above-average**. To keep employees informed about new developments, AltaGas publishes an in-house newsletter. The company also has an intranet site, which keeps employees informed about news and human resource policies that affect their work. To solicit feedback from employees, the company operates an email suggestion box. AltaGas also hosts employee surveys to capture feedback on job-related subjects. Recently, the company commissioned an outside consultant to conduct a survey on the company's short term incentive plan.

### *Performance Management* — *Rating: A*

AltaGas' performance management program is rated as **above-average**. The company operates a formal performance management program. Once a year, employees and managers meet for review sessions. (Managers receive training in how to conduct effective reviews.) The reviews form the basis for the company's short-term incentive program.

All employees have the opportunity to provide confidential feedback through regular employee surveys. Departing employees can also provide direct feedback through an exit interview process.

### *Training & Skills Development* — *Rating: A*

AltaGas' training and skills development program is rated as **above-average**. The company provides tuition subsidies for courses related to an employee's current position (100% of tuition). Commendably, AltaGas also offers subsidies for courses not related to an employee's current job (100% of tuition). The company assists employees' career development with: reimbursement for professional association dues; career planning; in-house training. The company also allows employees to take courses during work hours and even pays full salary during while apprentices are attending class.

*Community Involvement* *Rating: A*

AltaGas' community involvement program is rated as **above-average**. A very good corporate citizen, AltaGas actively supports a variety of local and national charitable initiatives. The company's donations committee represents employees from across the company. Employees take part in the selection of charitable groups assisted by the company. Last year, the company contributed to approximately 40 charitable groups, including: the United Way; Calgary Corporate Challenge; Heart and Stroke Foundation; Adopt-a-Family; Toy Mountain; Canadian Cancer Society; Lung Association; the MS Society; Child Find Alberta.

**AMEX CANADA INC.**
**101 McNabb Street**
**Markham, ON L3R 4H8**

**Tel. 905-474-8000**
**Fax 905-474-8952**
**http://www.americanexpress.ca**

**INDUSTRY: LOAN COMPANIES, PERSONAL**

*Highlights:*

- Take up to four weeks of paid vacation allowance after your first year thanks to a generous "personal days off" program and a flexible benefits plan that lets you trade unused benefits for more vacation days.
- Shape up your body — and your lifestyle — with this employer's extensive wellness program, which covers everything from daily exercise to relaxation training.
- Take a paid leave of absence (for up to six months) when you volunteer at the charitable organization of your choice.

***Employer Background***

Amex Canada Inc., issuer of the familiar American Express cards, is a leading provider of financial and travel-related services.

Amex Canada is a subsidiary of New York-based American Express Company. Founded in 1850, the parent company is is a leading global travel and financial and services provider. In addition to credit cards and travellers' cheques, the company offers a wide range of insurance and other financial products and services.

In Canada, Amex is the industry leader in travelers' cheques and is a significant player in the credit card and direct banking markets. Building on its success in these fields, the company is developing new co-branded products for its customers. An example is the new Tiger Woods credit card, which includes membership rewards and golfing privileges at courses across the country. The company has also entered into a new partnership with TD Canada Trust to supply corporate credit cards to its commercial customers.

Amex continues to create jobs in Canada. The company's call centre in Markham, which serves customers across Canada and the United States, is expected to create 250 jobs this year.

**Workforce at a Glance:** Number of full-time employees: **3,416**. At this location: **2,335**. Worldwide: **75,459**. New jobs created in Canada in past year: **83**. Percentage of employees who are women: **68**. Of managers: **54**. Percentage of employees who are visible minorities: **46**. Of managers: **21**. Resumes received by their human resources staff in past year: **1,455**. Weeks of vacation their HR manager took last year: **3**. Average employee age: **36**. Years longest-serving employee has worked there: **37**. Person you should get to know first: **Petti in the cafeteria somehow always remembers your breakfast order**.

### *Physical Workplace* — *Rating: A+*

Amex Canada's physical workplace is rated as **exceptional**. The majority of Amex's employees work at the company's recently renovated 3-storey head office in Markham, located just north of Toronto. The head office features a spectacular onsite fitness centre that offers a wellness program that is one of the most extensive in the country. The program gives employees a range of great exercise options (from yoga to pilates), along with useful lifestye seminars (such as relaxation training) and even an annual health expo.

**Physical Workplace at a Glance:** Their **onsite fitness facility** features: subsidized memberships; weights; rowing machines; stairmasters; stationary bikes; treadmills; instructor-led classes; shower facilities. Their **employee lounge and rest areas** feature: comfortable couches; meditation or religious observance room. For **food and refreshment**, Amex Canada offers: kitchen area with vending machines; outdoor eating area; barbeque. Nearby **amenities** include: major shopping mall; variety of restaurants; the restored area of Old Unionville; park/wilderness area (Clark Young Woods); recreation centre (Milliken Mills). For **commuters**, Amex Canada offers: free onsite car parking; nearby public transit. Other **work area amenities** include: plant life that is tended professionally; access to natural light for all employees; open-concept workstations; ergonomic workstation design; wireless connectivity throughout office; onsite store with dry cleaning service.

### *Work Atmosphere & Social* — *Rating: B+*

Amex Canada's work atmosphere is rated as **average**. Employees at Amex Canada enjoy business casual dress daily and can listen to radio or music while they are working.

Each year, Amex employees are invited to a day-long company meeting at a nearby hotel. The day includes presentations by senior management and is followed by drinks, dinner and live entertainment. During the summer, Amex employees compete in the "*Extreme Games*", held on the company's expansive head office grounds.

### *Health, Financial & Family Benefits* — *Rating: A+*

Amex Canada's health benefits plan is managed by Maritime Life and is rated as **exceptional**. Their health benefits plan is flexible, meaning that employees can tailor individual plans to their personal circumstances. Amex Canada pays 100% of the premiums associated with the plan. Full-time and part-time employees who work more than 20 hours per week are covered by the plan. There is no waiting period before new employees are eligible for coverage.

**Health Benefits at a Glance:** Amex Canada's health plan includes the following coverage: dental (100% of eligible costs, to $1,500 each year); orthodontics (50% of eligible costs with a lifetime maximum of $1,500); eyecare; extended health benefits; prescription drug; nutrition planning; physiotherapy; massage therapy; alternative therapies; wellness program through onsite fitness centre; personal and family counselling; employee assistance plan (EAP) for substance abuse/mental health.

The company's salary and financial benefits are rated as **exceptional**. To keep pay-levels competitive, Amex Canada participates in outside salary surveys every 6 months. Individual salaries are reviewed every 12 months. The company offers a group RSP that allows employees to contribute up to 3% of their salary, with matching employer contributions. The company also operates a traditional pension plan.

**Financial Benefits at a Glance:** Amex Canada provides an extensive set of financial benefits, including: life and disability insurance; subsidized auto insurance; subsidized home insurance; discounted car leases; discounted home Internet access; discounted company products; share purchase plan; signing bonuses for some employees; referral bonuses for some employees (to $1,000); year-end bonuses (from $1,000 to $20,000 for non-executives).

Amex Canada's family-friendly benefits are rated as **above-average**. Employees with pre-school children have access to a daycare facility located nearby. The company also provides an adoption benefit of up to $2,800 per child. Other family-friendly benefits include: reduced summer hours; compressed work week (same hours, fewer days); shortened work week (fewer hours); telecommuting and working from home; flexible start and finish hours.

***Vacation & Time Off*** **Rating: A**

Amex Canada's vacation and time off are rated as **above-average**. New employees receive 2.25 weeks of vacation allowance after their first year, which increases to 3 weeks after 3 years of service. The maximum vacation allowance is 6 weeks for long-serving employees. Employees at Amex Canada also receive 4 paid personal days off each year, in addition to their regular vacation allowance. Employees can also purchase up to 5 additional vacation days each year by waiving unused benefits under the company's flexible benefits plan. Employees at the company can also apply for unpaid leaves of absence.

***Employee Communications*** **Rating: A**

Amex Canada's internal communications program is rated as **above-average**. To keep employees informed about new developments, Amex Canada publishes an in-house newsletter. The company also has an intranet site (called *Amexweb*), which keeps employees informed about news and human resource policies that affect their work. To solicit feedback from employees, the company operates an email suggestion box. An employee satisfaction survey is conducted by having employees complete an online questionnaire every 6 months. An outside consultant compiles the survey results for Amex Canada's management team.

***Performance Management*** **Rating: A**

Amex Canada's performance management program is rated as **above-average**. The company operates a formal performance management program. Every 6 months, employees and managers meet for review sessions. (Managers receive training in how to conduct effective reviews.) At the annual review, employees work with their managers to establish a career development plan for the upcoming year. An informal review is held during the year to monitor progress. Employees also have the opportunity to provide confidential feedback on their manager's performance.

### *Training & Skills Development* — *Rating: A+*

Amex Canada's training and skills development program is rated as **exceptional**. The company provides tuition subsidies for courses related to an employee's current position (100% of tuition). Commendably, Amex Canada also offers subsidies for courses not related to an employee's current job (100% of tuition). The company assists employees' career development with: reimbursement for professional association dues; career planning; mentoring; in-house training. The company's in-house training program includes a variety of courses, from computer training to management development.

### *Community Involvement* — *Rating: A+*

Amex Canada's community involvement program is rated as **exceptional**. An outstanding corporate citizen, Amex Canada actively supports a variety of charitable initiatives. Through the company's admirable paid-sabbatical program, employees can apply for up to 6 months of paid leave to work for a registered charity of their choosing. Under the program, employees can also apply for a company donation of up to $1,000 for the charitable organization. (Amex also offers paid time off for employee volunteers who don't take leaves of absence.)

Amex Canada has also been increasing the support it provides to young people in Canada. Recently, the company developed a new program (called "*Dream Big*") in partnership with the Tiger Woods Foundation and Junior Achievement Canada. Designed for high school seniors, the program helps students plan their futures through interactive discussions and activities. In another unique educational program (called the "*Creative Arts Learning Partnership*"), Amex Canada connects arts organizations with elementary school teachers across the country, providing young people with an early understanding of the importance of art and culture in the community.

**ATS AUTOMATION TOOLING SYSTEMS INC.**
**250 Royal Oak Road**
**PO Box 32100, Preston Centre**
**Cambridge, ON N3H 5M2**

**Tel. 519-653-6500**
**Fax 519-653-6533**
**http://www.atsautomation.com**

**INDUSTRY: SPECIAL INDUSTRY MACHINERY MANUFACTURERS**

*Highlights:*

- Build your career at a growing employer in the manufacturing industry that combines space-age technology with a very human work atmosphere.
- Educate your children with this employer's unique scholarship program, which awards 75 annual scholarships (worth $1,000 each) to employees' children who attend college or university.
- Vanquish the inventors of baseball in a summer employee tournament that pits this employer's Canadian and US divisions against one another.

## *Employer Background*

ATS Automation Tooling Systems Inc. designs and builds automated manufacturing systems. Founded in 1978, the company's automated and robotic manufacturing systems are used by automotive, healthcare, microelectronic and high-tech manufacturers around the world. With over 10,000 installations, ATS' systems manufacture everything from auto parts to hand-held razors.

Based in Cambridge, Ontario, ATS has 28 facilities around the world. In addition to Cambridge, ATS has manufacturing facilities in Stratford, Kitchener, Bowmanville, Burlington and Mississauga, Ontario. Thanks to recent acquisitions, the company also has subsidiaries in France and Germany. ATS is publicly-traded and posted revenues of $549 million last year.

**Workforce at a Glance:** Number of full-time employees: **1,897**. At this location: **1,006**. Worldwide: **3,360**. New jobs created in Canada in past year: **188**. Percentage of employees who are women: **23**. Of managers: **8**. Average employee age: **38**. Years longest-serving employee has worked there: **25**.

## *Physical Workplace* — *Rating: A*

ATS' physical workplace is rated as **above-average**. The majority of the company's Canadian employees work at its Cambridge head office. The custom-built facility is located in a new industrial park with easy access to major highways. (A new onsite fitness facility will be completed this year.)

**Physical Workplace at a Glance:** For **food and refreshment**, ATS offers: free coffee and tea; outdoor eating area. The company has an onsite cafeteria that features: healthy menu items. Nearby **amenities** include: variety of restaurants; major shopping mall; outdoor walking trails; park/wilderness area (Riverside Park); recreation centre (YMCA). For **commuters**, ATS offers: free onsite car parking; nearby public transit. Other **work area amenities** include: open-concept workstations; air-conditioned manufacturing areas; ergonomic workstation design.

***Work Atmosphere & Social*** ***Rating: A+***

ATS' work atmosphere is rated as **exceptional**. Employees at ATS enjoy business casual dress daily and can listen to radio or music while they are working. There is also a company-subsidized social committee, which has operated since 1997.

The committee organizes a variety of fun social events for employees. Every summer, the company hosts a huge family picnic with food, drinks, softball, volleyball and children's entertainment. During the Christmas season, employees and their guests are treated to a dinner dance, which also includes an employee awards ceremony. There is also a separate holiday party for employees' children. ATS subsidizes employee baseball, hockey and volleyball teams that compete in local leagues. (Every summer, baseball teams from the Canadian and U.S. divisions gather for a company-wide tournament.)

True to the German roots of its founders, ATS observes an interesting tradition each time it opens a new plant around the world. Employees enjoy food and refreshments while a tree is hoisted to the highest part of the plant. Called "*Richfest*", the old German custom is said to bring good luck and adds a delightfully human touch to the space-age efficiency that characterizes ATS facilities.

***Health, Financial & Family Benefits*** ***Rating: A***

ATS' health benefits plan is managed by Clarica Life and is rated as **above-average**. Full-time and part-time employees who work more than 20 hours per week are covered by the plan. New employees must wait 30 days before they can enroll in the plan.

> **Health Benefits at a Glance:** ATS' health plan includes the following coverage: dental (80% of eligible costs, with no annual maximum); eyecare (to $100 every 2 years); extended health benefits; prescription drug; massage therapy; physiotherapy; alternative therapies; personal and family counselling; employee assistance plan (EAP) for substance abuse/mental health.

The company's salary and financial benefits are rated as **above-average**. To keep pay-levels competitive, ATS participates in outside salary surveys every 12 months. Individual salaries are reviewed every 12 months. The company offers a group RSP that allows employees to contribute up to 3% of their salary, with matching employer contributions. The company also operates a traditional pension plan.

> **Financial Benefits at a Glance:** ATS provides a variety of financial benefits, including: life and disability insurance; discounted car leases; share purchase plan; profit-sharing plan; referral bonuses for some employees (from $250 to $1,000).

ATS' family-friendly benefits are rated as **above-average**. Employees with preschool children have access to a daycare facility located nearby. The company also operates a scholarship program to assist employees' children attending college or university in Canada. Under the program, ATS awards 75 scholarships each year worth $1,000 apiece. (Students can receive the scholarship for up to 4 consecutive years while they are at school.) Other family-friendly benefits include: free family coverage on health plan.

***Vacation & Time Off*** **Rating: B+**

ATS' vacation and time off are rated as **average**. New employees receive 2 weeks of vacation allowance after their first year, which increases to 3 weeks after 5 years of service. The maximum vacation allowance is 4 weeks for long-serving employees. Employees at the company can also apply for unpaid leaves of absence. (Recently, one employee took a 2 year leave to work in Australia.)

***Employee Communications*** **Rating: A**

ATS' internal communications program is rated as **above-average**. To keep employees informed about new developments, ATS publishes an in-house newsletter. The company also has an intranet site, which keeps employees informed about news and human resource policies that affect their work. An employee satisfaction survey is conducted every 24 months. An outside consultant compiles the survey results for ATS' management team.

***Performance Management*** **Rating: A**

ATS' performance management program is rated as **above-average**. The company operates a thorough performance management program. Once a year, employees and managers meet for review sessions. (Managers receive training in how to conduct effective reviews.) New employees receive their first review after three months on the job. Afterwards, employees and managers meet once a year to discuss past performance and set goals for the upcoming year. The process also encourages employees to provide direct feedback to their managers throughout the year.

***Training & Skills Development*** **Rating: A**

ATS' training and skills development program is rated as **above-average**. The company provides tuition subsidies for courses related to an employee's current position (100% of tuition). Commendably, ATS also offers subsidies for courses not related to an employee's current job (50% of tuition). The company assists employees' career development with: reimbursement for professional association dues; in-house training. The company offers a variety of in-house courses, from computer skills improvement to supervisor training.

***Community Involvement*** **Rating: A**

ATS' community involvement program is rated as **above-average**. A very good corporate citizen, ATS actively supports a variety of local and national charitable initiatives. Some of the organizations assisted by ATS last year include: United Way, Heart & Stroke Foundation, Canadian National Institute for the Blind, Canadian Cancer Society, Canadian Lung Association, Cambridge Women's Crisis Centre, Big Brothers and Big Sisters, and Conestoga College.

**BANFF CENTRE, THE**
**PO Box 1020, Station 19**
**Banff, AB T1L 1H5**

**Tel. 403-762-6177**
**Fax 403-762-6677**
**jobs@banffcentre.ca**
**http://www.banffcentre.ca**

# THE BANFF CENTRE

**INDUSTRY: COLLEGES & UNIVERSITIES**

*Highlights:*

- Work and live in one of this country's most spectacular natural settings, Banff National Park — a UNESCO World Heritage Site.
- Develop yourself at an employer that's also a renowned educational institution — and get special employee tuition subsidies.
- Keep in shape at a wonderful onsite fitness facility that offers swimming, pilates classes and even an indoor rock climbing wall (real rock climbing is nearby).

## *Employer Background*

The Banff Centre is one of Canada's most unique post-secondary educational and cultural institutions. Founded as a summer drama school in 1933, The Banff Centre maintains the spirit of a small cultural retreat in the mountains. At the same time, the Centre is an internationally renowned school for the arts, an institute for professional growth, a forum for mountain culture and a world-class conference facility.

The Centre has four operating divisions. The principal division, Arts Programming, offers accomplished artists an opportunity to pursue professional development and individual growth throughout their careers. The curriculum encompasses music and dance, writing, new media and visual arts, theatre, Aboriginal arts and other forms of artistic expression outside traditional categories.

The Leadership Development division provides popular leadership training for professionals working in the business, government, Aboriginal and non-profit sectors.

The Mountain Culture division offers a forum for the international mountain community to share experiences and ideas related to the natural and cultural development of mountain places.

Finally, the Conference Hosting division provides meeting and accommodation facilities to organizations from around the world. Over 30,000 conference guests use the facilities each year, and the resulting income helps support the Centre's arts programming. It also helps make The Banff Centre one of Canada's most self-sufficient public institutions — 75% of its revenues are from non-government sources.

**Workforce at a Glance:** Number of full-time employees: **488**. New jobs created in Canada in past year: **41**. Percentage of employees who are women: **48**. Of managers:

55. Percentage of employees who are visible minorities: **8**. Of managers: **4**. Resumes received by their human resources staff in past year: **6,586**. Years longest-serving employee has worked there: **37**.

## *Physical Workplace* — *Rating: A+*

The Banff Centre's physical workplace is rated as **exceptional**. One of the most attractive aspects of working at The Banff Centre is its location in Banff National Park, a UNESCO world heritage site. Situated on 17 hectares, the campus is nestled on the slope of Tunnel Mountain, overlooking the town of Banff. There is plenty of green space for quiet contemplation, as well as spectacular views.

**Physical Workplace at a Glance:** Their **onsite fitness facility** features: subsidized memberships; treadmills; stationary bikes; stairmasters; rowing machines; weights; basketball court; indoor rock climbing wall; shower facilities; sauna; swimming pool; instructor-led classes (pilates and power yoga). Their **employee lounge and rest areas** feature: comfortable couches; fireplace; music; pool table; outdoor amphitheatre. For **food and refreshment**, The Banff Centre offers: free coffee and tea; free soft drinks; outdoor eating area; barbeque; coffee shop (The Kiln Cafe). The Centre has an onsite cafeteria that features: subsidized meals (a complete meal costs $3.21); healthy menu items. Nearby **amenities** include: variety of restaurants; fitness facility; park/wilderness area (it's inside Banff National Park!). For **commuters**, The Banff Centre offers: free onsite car parking; secure bicycle parking. Other **work area amenities** include: open-concept workstations; access to natural light for all employees; ergonomic workstation design; windows that open.

## *Work Atmosphere & Social* — *Rating: A*

The Banff Centre's work atmosphere is rated as **above-average**. Employees at The Banff Centre enjoy business casual dress daily and can listen to radio or music while they are working. There is also a Centre-subsidized social committee, called the '*Healthy Initiatives Partnership*'.

The Centre regularly hosts fun employee events and celebrations, including ice cream days on the patio, movie nights, a golf tournament, an annual scavenger hunt, a staff variety night, a Christmas party, a curling bonspiel and an employee craft sale. The Banff Centre also hosts an annual awards ceremony to honour employees reaching milestones of continued service.

## *Health, Financial & Family Benefits* — *Rating: A*

The Banff Centre's health benefits plan is managed by Great-West Life and is rated as **above-average**. Full-time and part-time employees who work more than 20 hours per week are covered by the plan.

**Health Benefits at a Glance:** The Banff Centre's health plan includes the following coverage: dental (80% of eligible costs, with no annual maximum); orthodontics (50% of eligible costs with a lifetime maximum of $2,000); eyecare (to $35 every year); prescription drug; nutrition planning; massage therapy; physiotherapy; alternative therapies; extended health benefits; personal and family counselling; employee assistance plan (EAP) for substance abuse/mental health.

The Centre's salary and financial benefits are rated as **average**. To keep pay-levels competitive, The Banff Centre participates in outside salary surveys every

12 months. Individual salaries are reviewed every 12 months. The Centre operates a traditional pension plan where The Banff Centre makes a contribution equal to 4.9% of each employee's salary to their plan each year.

**Financial Benefits at a Glance:** The Banff Centre provides a variety of financial benefits, including: life and disability insurance; discounted company products (e.g. a free pass to the annual "Festival of the Arts").

The Banff Centre's family-friendly benefits are rated as **above-average**. Employees with pre-school children have access to a daycare facility located nearby. For employees who take maternity leave, The Banff Centre provides a top-up to 70% of salary for the first 6 weeks of their leave. Other family-friendly benefits include: free family coverage on health plan; flexible start and finish hours; shortened work week (fewer hours); compressed work week (same hours, fewer days).

***Vacation & Time Off*** ***Rating: B+***

The Banff Centre's vacation and time off are rated as **average**. New employees receive 2 weeks of vacation allowance after their first year, which increases to 3 weeks after 3 years of service. The maximum vacation allowance is 5 weeks for long-serving employees. (Professional and management employees start with 3 weeks vacation, which increases to a maximum of 5 weeks.) Employees at the Centre can also apply for unpaid leaves of absence.

***Employee Communications*** ***Rating: A***

The Banff Centre's internal communications program is rated as **above-average**. To keep employees informed about new developments, The Banff Centre publishes an in-house newsletter (called *The Rough Copy*). The Centre also has an intranet site, which keeps employees informed about news and human resource policies that affect their work. The Centre regularly conducts in-house employee surveys. Recently, employees were asked for their feedback on an employee assistance plan and a new performance recognition program.

***Performance Management*** ***Rating: B+***

The Banff Centre's performance management program is rated as **average**. The Centre operates a formal performance management program. Once a year, employees and managers meet for review sessions. (Managers receive training in how to conduct effective reviews.) The new program ensures that employees can provide confidential feedback to the Employee Relations Manager.

***Training & Skills Development*** ***Rating: A***

The Banff Centre's training and skills development program is rated as **above-average**. The Centre provides tuition subsidies for courses related to an employee's current position (100% of tuition). The Centre assists employees' career development with: reimbursement for professional association dues; career planning; in-house training; mentoring.

The Banff Centre's informal mentoring program involves many senior employees who regularly assist new employees. The Centre also encourages its faculty members to lead in-house employee training programs.

***Community Involvement*** ***Rating: B+***

The Banff Centre's community involvement program is rated as **average**. A good member of the community, The Banff Centre actively supports a variety of charitable initiatives.

As a non-profit employer, the Centre supports many local initiatives in Banff and the Bow Valley area by providing services and volunteers in lieu of financial donations. Examples include the Centre's support for local Canada Day celebrations as well as a popular local festival ("*One Hot Summer*") that introduces new residents to activities and events in the community.

BMO Financial Group
Groupe financier

**BANK OF MONTREAL**
**1 First Canadian Place**
**PO Box 150**
**Toronto, ON M5X 1H3**

**Tel. 416-867-5000**
**Fax 866-263-8691**
**staffing.partners@bmo.com**
**http://www.bmo.com**

**INDUSTRY: COMMERCIAL BANKS**

*Highlights:*

- Receive cash prizes (to $1,000) and get extra days off in exchange for excellent performance.
- Get an extra week of paid vacation allowance if you take your vacation in the less popular winter season.
- Get financial support from a special fund designed to assist employees who encounter unforeseen personal difficulties.

## *Employer Background*

Bank of Montreal is Canada's oldest bank and one of the leading financial institutions in North America. Established in 1817, Bank of Montreal (BMO) provides financial products and services to Canadians across the country. Through its network of branches and related companies, the bank offers personal and commercial banking, wealth management and investment banking services.

In addition to its vast Canadian business, BMO has a growing presence south of the border. Over the past few years, the bank has made significant acquisitions in the United States. Today, BMO serves over 1.5 million U.S. clients directly and through its Chicago-based subsidiary, Harris Bank.

One of North America's largest financial institutions, BMO has over $252 billion in assets and annual revenues of nearly $8 billion.

**Workforce at a Glance:** Number of full-time employees: **25,500**. Worldwide: **34,500**. New jobs created in Canada in past year: **500**. Percentage of employees who are women: **69**. Of managers: **50**. Percentage of employees who are visible minorities: **19**. Of managers: **19**. Average employee age: **40**.

## *Physical Workplace* — *Rating: B+*

BMO's physical workplace is rated as **average**. BMO employees work in a variety of locations and settings across the country, from small towns to the largest cities. Head office employees work at Toronto's landmark First Canadian Place office tower. The country's tallest building is located in the heart of the financial district, providing employees with convenient access to the city's underground walking network. BMO also operates a major data centre in Toronto's east end and an information technology research and development centre ("E-Development Loft") in the city's trendy fashion district.

**Physical Workplace at a Glance:** Their **employee lounge and rest areas** feature: multipurpose quiet and religious observance room. For **food and refreshment**, BMO offers: a kitchen area and lunchroom. Nearby **amenities** include: variety of restaurants; major shopping mall; fitness facility. For **commuters**, BMO offers: nearby public transit; secure bicycle parking. Other **work area amenities** include: open-concept workstations; ergonomic workstation design.

***Work Atmosphere & Social*** ***Rating: B+***

BMO's work atmosphere is rated as **average**. Unique for its sheer size, BMO organizes one of the most impressive employee social events in this book. Each year, the bank reserves Paramount Canada's Wonderland for employees and their families. Employees in the Greater Toronto Area (and those who want to make the trip) enjoy a day at the theme park and a chance to win great prizes, such as a home computer system. Other fun perks offered by BMO include discounts on company-sponsored events, such as live theatre and sporting competitions.

***Health, Financial & Family Benefits*** ***Rating: A***

BMO's health benefits plan is managed by Great-West Life and Clarica Life and is rated as **exceptional**. Their health benefits plan is flexible, meaning that employees can tailor individual plans to their personal circumstances. Full-time and part-time employees are covered by the plan. There is no waiting period before new employees are eligible for coverage.

The bank also operates a unique financial grant program (the Sir Vincent Meredith Fund), to assist employees facing unexpected financial difficulties due to personal reasons.

**Health Benefits at a Glance:** BMO's health plan includes the following coverage: dental (90% of eligible costs, to $1,700 each year); orthodontics (50% of eligible costs with a lifetime maximum of $1,500); eyecare (to $250 every 2 years); prescription drug; extended health benefits; massage therapy; physiotherapy; personal and family counselling; employee assistance plan (EAP) for substance abuse/mental health.

The bank's salary and financial benefits are rated as **above-average**. To keep pay-levels competitive, BMO participates in outside salary surveys every 12 months. Individual salaries are reviewed every 12 months. BMO operates a traditional pension plan where it contributes 1.25% of an employee's salary every year.

**Financial Benefits at a Glance:** BMO provides a variety of financial benefits, including: share purchase plan (with matching company contributions); life and disability insurance; free banking services; discount on products from BMO suppliers (including cellular phones, computers and vacation travel); signing bonuses for some employees; year-end bonuses.

BMO's family-friendly benefits are rated as **above-average**. For employees who take maternity leave, BMO provides a top-up to 95% of salary for the first 6 weeks of their leave. Other family-friendly benefits include: flexible start and finish hours; shortened work week (fewer hours); compressed work week (same hours, fewer days); telecommuting and working from home; reduced summer hours.

### *Vacation & Time Off* *Rating: B+*

BMO's vacation and time off are rated as **average**. New employees receive 2 weeks of vacation allowance after their first year, which increases to 3 weeks after 3 years of service. The maximum vacation allowance is 5 weeks for long-serving employees. Employees who take their vacation in the winter receive an additional week of paid vacation.

The bank also operates an interesting personal days off program. Through this program, managers can grant short paid leaves of absence for employees to use as needed. The length of each leave is determined on a case-by-case basis. Employees can also apply for unpaid leaves of absence for personal reasons on an individual basis.

### *Employee Communications* *Rating: A*

BMO's internal communications program is rated as **above-average**. To keep employees informed about new developments, BMO publishes an in-house newsletter (called *First Bank News*). The bank also has an intranet site, which keeps employees informed about news and human resource policies that affect their work.

In addition, employees receive regular email updates as well as divisional and specialized newsletters. BMO also operates an interesting employee suggestion box program. The online initiative ("Ideanet") sends employee suggestions directly to those with the expertise to evaluate and the authority to implement them.

### *Performance Management* *Rating: A*

BMO's performance management program is rated as **above-average**. The bank operates a comprehensive performance management program. Once a year, employees and managers meet for review sessions. (Managers receive training in how to conduct effective reviews.)

As part of the review process, managers also provide employees with year-round coaching, career counselling and feedback. Employees also have access to a variety of online tools for assistance throughout the process. Employees can provide confidential feedback on their manager's performance through the annual employee survey.

### *Training & Skills Development* *Rating: A+*

BMO's training and skills development program is rated as **exceptional**. The bank provides tuition subsidies for courses related to an employee's current position (100% of tuition). Commendably, BMO also offers subsidies for courses not related to an employee's current job (100% of tuition). The bank assists employees' career development with: reimbursement for professional association dues; mentoring; online training; in-house training.

BMO offers a wide range of in-house programs to employees at its impressive training centre in the Toronto suburb of Scarborough. The training centre features a variety of classrooms and a residential wing, which includes a relaxation area, healthclub and dining hall with menus for special diets. Employees from across the country can enroll in a variety of courses, including personal development, management, sales and marketing, risk management, information technology, project management and professional programs. (The bank also offers a financial services MBA in partnership with Dalhousie University.)

BMO is also a leader in addressing barriers to advancement for women, Aboriginal Canadians, visible minorities and people with disabilities. Over the past decade, committees of employees, managers, executives and outside consultants have worked together to help design equitable workplace strategies. (Employers looking to build workplaces that reflect the diversity of their communities would be well advised to review BMO's detailed reports.)

BMO is also a leader in addressing barriers to advancement for women, Aboriginal Canadians, visible minorities and people with disabilities. Over the past decade, committees of employees, managers, executives and outside consultants have worked together to help design equitable workplace strategies. (Employers looking to build workplaces that reflect the diversity of their communities would be well advised to review BMO's detailed reports.)

***Community Involvement*** ***Rating: A+***

BMO's community involvement program is rated as **exceptional**. An outstanding member of the community, BMO actively supports a variety of local and national charitable initiatives. Employees at BMO receive paid time off (1 day each year) to volunteer at local charities.

As one of Canada's largest corporate donors, BMO supports over 2,000 community and charitable organizations. The bank has an outstanding volunteer grants program that matches employee and retiree volunteering with cash donations (to $1,500 per year).

BMO employees also operate their own foundation ("Fountain of Hope") to raise money for charities across Canada — last year, employees raised over $3 million. The bank pays for all of the foundation's administrative costs to ensure that all donations go to charity.

bhpbilliton

**BHP BILLITON DIAMONDS INC.**
**4920 - 52nd Street**
**Suite 1102**
**Yellowknife, NT X1A 3T1**

**Tel. 867-669-9292**
**Fax 867-669-9943**
**ekati.hr@bhpbilliton.com**
**http://www.bhpbilliton.com**

**INDUSTRY: MINING, NONMETALLIC MINERALS**

***Highlights:***

- Work in one of this book's most unique environments, where herds of Bathurst caribou roam past your workplace and employees are treated to never-ending summer days and spectacular aurora borealis displays in the winter.
- Discover a diamond mine that doubles as a tundra oasis, with a full gymnasium, golfing simulators and an all-you-can-eat cafeteria.
- Fly your family members in from Yellowknife for an annual Family Day celebration they won't soon forget.

## *Employer Background*

BHP Billiton Diamonds Inc. operates Canada's first diamond mine. The development of the Ekati Diamond Mine is a legendary story of determination and tenacity that has unfolded over the last two decades in one of Canada's most remote regions.

In 1985, geologist Charles Fipke found diamond indicator minerals in the Lac de Gras area of the Northwest Territories, 300 km northeast of Yellowknife. In 1989, he staked the first diamond claims in the area on a shoestring budget. Over the next two years, Fipke's company, Dia Met Minerals Ltd., and its new partner, BHP, continued his prospecting work. In November 1991, the two companies announced their findings to the world — there were diamonds in Canada's north — and triggered the largest mineral claim rush in North American history.

In 1994, BHP undertook the huge task of building a working mine where no roads or infrastructure existed. With offices in Yellowknife, Kelowna and Vancouver, BHP Billiton Diamonds Inc. is the Canadian subsidiary of Australian-based BHP Billiton Limited, one of the world's largest mining companies. With mining operations around the world, BHP was able to adapt its expertise to the unique technical, environmental and social challenges of building a mine in the Canadian sub-artic.

Construction of the mine was an accomplishment in itself. In the fall of 1998, less than two years after work began, BHP's state-of-the-art Ekati Diamond Mine officially opened and produced its first diamond. Today, the mine produces 9,000 carats of diamonds every day — enough to fill about two coffee cans.

Located only 200 km south of the Arctic Circle and without road access, attracting and retaining skilled workers is a daunting challenge for BHP. Yet, last year, the company received over 6,000 applications to work at the site. This enviable record stems from the company's commitment to being "the employer of choice in the mining industry." How BHP accomplishes this is what makes it one of Canada's best employers.

**Workforce at a Glance:** Number of full-time employees: **767**. At this location: **752**. Worldwide: **38,000**. New jobs created in Canada in past year: **110**. Percentage of employees who are women: **14**. Of managers: **5**. Percentage of employees who are visible minorities: **54**. Of managers: **3**. Resumes received by their human resources staff in past year: **6,000**. Weeks of vacation their HR manager took last year: **3**. Average employee age: **38**. Years longest-serving employee has worked there: **30**. Person you should get to know first: **Christine can help you secure a great room.** Car the president drives: **1985 Lexus**. Where it's parked in the lot: **with everyone else**.

## *Physical Workplace* — *Rating: A+*

BHP Billiton's physical workplace is rated as **exceptional**. Located above the treeline in a sub-arctic environment, the Ekati mining complex has a natural beauty all its own. From Bathurst caribou herds that pass nearby to never-ending summer days and spectacular aurora borealis displays in the winter, BHP offers one of the most amazing work environments in this book.

BHP's mine is really a small community that offers a variety of work environments. In addition to open-pit mining and ore processing activities, there is an internal road network, airport strip, power station, maintenance facilities, water and wastewater treatment plants, security and emergency services and a permanent camp where employees live.

Since most Ekati employees work a two-week-in/two-week-out rotation, the permanent camp facility is designed to accommodate about 400 people. To reach the site, employees (and contractors) are provided with company-paid flights from Yellowknife and communities across the Northwest Territories.

The permanent camp includes seven three-storey residential wings, where employees have their own rooms with windows and private bathrooms. In the centre of the complex, employees have shared access to a 24-hour dining facility, an employee lounge, a fully-equipped fitness facility and laundry facilities.

**Physical Workplace at a Glance:** Their **onsite fitness facility** features: free memberships; subsidized memberships; treadmills; stationary bikes; stairmasters; rowing machines; weights; basketball court; floor hockey; volleyball; badminton; squash courts; running track; golf simulators (2); driving range; putting green; instructor-led classes; seasonal tundra walking trail; shower facilities. Their **employee lounge and rest areas** feature: comfortable couches; music; television; pool table; foosball; table hockey; table tennis; board games; computers with Internet access; laundry facilities. The company has an onsite cafeteria that features: free meals; healthy menu items; special diet menus; fresh pastries; pizza; sandwiches; soft and hard ice cream (and it's all you can eat).

## *Work Atmosphere & Social* — *Rating: A*

BHP Billiton's work atmosphere is rated as **above-average**. Employees at BHP Billiton enjoy casual dress daily and can listen to radio or music while they are working. There is also a company-subsidized social committee, called the '*Klub Koala*', which has operated since 1998.

Throughout the year, employees celebrate milestones and significant events with special dinners and local entertainment. The company hosts a variety of events every year, including a Christmas party, a separate Christmas party for employees' children, a summer golf day and a winter hockey tournament. The company also sponsors employee volleyball, softball and hockey (called the *Diamond Diggers*) teams.

For families of employees, BHP hosts a popular family day every year. The company brings family members from Yellowknife and surrounding communities for a full-day of activities at the mine.

***Health, Financial & Family Benefits*** ***Rating: A***

BHP Billiton's health benefits plan is managed by Sun Life and is rated as **above-average**.

> **Health Benefits at a Glance:** BHP Billiton's health plan includes the following coverage: dental; orthodontics; eyecare (to $350 every 2 years); prescription drug; extended health benefits; physiotherapy; massage therapy; personal and family counselling; employee assistance plan (EAP) for substance abuse/mental health.

The company's salary and financial benefits are rated as **above-average**. To keep pay-levels competitive, BHP Billiton participates in outside salary surveys every 12 months. Individual salaries are reviewed every 12 months. The company operates a traditional pension plan.

> **Financial Benefits at a Glance:** BHP Billiton provides a variety of financial benefits, including: life and disability insurance; discounted diamond purchase plan; fuel subsidies (for Yellowknife and community-based employees); northern travel allowance (to $9,000).

BHP Billiton's family-friendly benefits are rated as **above-average**. For employees who take maternity leave, BHP Billiton provides a top-up to 100% of salary for the first 6 weeks of their leave. Other family-friendly benefits include: compressed work week (same hours, fewer days).

***Vacation & Time Off*** ***Rating: A+***

BHP Billiton's vacation and time off are rated as **exceptional**. Employees who work a regular workweek receive four weeks of paid vacation. Employees who work a two-week rotation schedule receive two weeks. Employees at the company can also apply for unpaid leaves of absence.

***Employee Communications*** ***Rating: A***

BHP Billiton's internal communications program is rated as **above-average**. To keep employees informed about new developments, BHP Billiton publishes an in-house newsletter (called *The Diamond Pipe*). The company also has an intranet site, which keeps employees informed about news and human resource policies that affect their work. To solicit feedback from employees, the company operates a traditional suggestion box program. An employee satisfaction survey is conducted every 12 months. An outside consultant compiles the survey results for BHP Billiton's management team. The company also publishes a variety of unique publications every year, including a company calendar, which serves as a photo journal of life at the mine, and even a colouring book for employees' children.

### *Performance Management* — *Rating: A*

BHP Billiton's performance management program is rated as **above-average**. The company operates a well-designed performance management program. Once a year, employees and managers meet for review sessions. (Managers receive training in how to conduct effective reviews.) BHP Billiton uses a 360-degree feedback process to gather additional performance-related information from co-workers, supervisors and employees.

As part of the review process, BHP Billiton's succession planning process helps identify the company's top performers for future leadership roles. The company also recognizes outstanding employees with annual safety performance, employee appreciation and environmental stewardship awards.

### *Training & Skills Development* — *Rating: A*

BHP Billiton's training and skills development program is rated as **above-average**. The company provides tuition subsidies for courses related to an employee's current position (80% of tuition). The company assists employees' career development with: extensive orientation and safety training; reimbursement for professional association dues; career planning; in-house training.

Employees can take advantage of a variety of in-house training initiatives, including literacy improvement, leadership development, career planning, computer-based learning and apprenticeship programs. As part of one of the world's largest mining groups, BHP Billiton also provides employees with an opportunity to gain international experience at other company-owned facilities around the world.

### *Community Involvement* — *Rating: A+*

BHP Billiton's community involvement program is rated as **exceptional**. An outstanding corporate citizen, BHP Billiton actively supports a variety of local charitable initiatives. Employees take part in the selection of charitable groups assisted by the company.

From the opening of its mine, the company has worked closely with Aboriginal people and the territorial government to ensure that benefits from the mine flow back to northern communities. Wherever possible, BHP ensures that northern and Aboriginal suppliers are used. The company has also exceeded its employment commitments to northern and Aboriginal communities: over 70% of staff are northern residents and 44% are Aboriginal.

BHP has also taken care to minimize the mine's impact on the fragile arctic ecosystem. The company continually monitors the air, water, land and wildlife around its claim block and reports its findings to the territorial government. BHP also funds Aboriginal studies to integrate traditional knowledge of the region with the company's environmental management program. Ongoing research and reclamation work ensures that the site will be safe for residents and wildlife when mining ends.

BHP is an active supporter of charities in many of the communities that send employees to the mine. The employee-run charitable program encourages staff to volunteer with organizations in their communities. The company provides donations in support of community social programs, youth education, arts and culture and environmental protection.

BIOWARE CORP

BIOWARE CORP.
10508 - 82nd Avenue
Suite 302
Edmonton, AB T6E 6H2

Tel. 780-430-0164
Fax 780-439-6374
http://www.bioware.com

**INDUSTRY: SOFTWARE COMPANIES**

*Highlights:*

- Get three weeks of paid vacation allowance to start, a paid break between Christmas and New Years — and an extra week off when you release a new product.
- Feed your video gaming addiction by working on some of the industry's top-selling games — including the blockbuster "*Star Wars: Knights of the Old Republic*" — at an employer that also offers discounted video game consoles and employee Playdium passes.
- Build your career at a growing employer that's built partnerships with the leading players in the video game industry, creating career advancement opportunities and great new jobs.

***Employer Background***

BioWare Corp. develops computer video games. The Edmonton-based software company creates interactive video games for the PC and console platforms, including Microsoft Xbox.

Founded in 1995, the privately-held Canadian company is fulfilling its mission statement to "entertain the world" — over 7 million copies of its games have been sold worldwide. International versions of its games have been created for French, Spanish, German, Italian, Portuguese, Polish, Korean, Chinese and Japanese markets.

BioWare has released 10 major products since its first game in 1996, and has received numerous industry and consumer awards. The company's games include "Shattered Steel", the "Baldur's Gate" series, "Neverwinter Nights" and the "MDK2" series.

BioWare's latest release, "Star Wars: Knights of the Old Republic", is currently receiving rave reviews and is experiencing exceptional sales worldwide. The Star Wars game is the first developed in association with California-based Lucas Arts Entertainment Company. The blue-chip partnership is another success for a Canadian software developer that has become a major employer of gamers in this country.

**Workforce at a Glance:** Number of full-time employees: **139**. New jobs created in Canada in past year: **18**. Percentage of employees who are women: **8**. Resumes received by their human resources staff in past year: **2,350**. Weeks of vacation their HR manager took last year: **2**. Average employee age: **29**. Years longest-serving employee has worked there: **7**.

## *Physical Workplace* — *Rating: A*

BioWare's physical workplace is rated as **above-average**. The head office is located in Edmonton's trendy Old Strathcona neighbourhood. The downtown location provides easy access to numerous shops and services as well as the Edmonton River Valley park, with trails for jogging and cycling.

**Physical Workplace at a Glance:** Their **employee lounge and rest areas** feature: comfortable couches; music; television; video games (of course); foosball; table tennis; pool table. For **food and refreshment**, BioWare offers: free snacks (including muffins, fruit, bagels, yogurt); free coffee and tea; outdoor eating area; barbeque. Nearby **amenities** include: variety of restaurants; local shops and services; Kinsmen Recreation Centre (free memberships); Chapters bookstore and Starbucks coffee shop downstairs; park/wilderness area (Edmonton River Valley Park). For **commuters**, BioWare offers: free onsite car parking; nearby public transit; secure bicycle parking.

## *Work Atmosphere & Social* — *Rating: A+*

BioWare's work atmosphere is rated as **exceptional**. Employees at BioWare enjoy casual dress daily and can listen to radio or music while they are working. The company lets employees bring their pets to work.

Employees enjoy several company-sponsored events during the year, including summer barbeques, morning breakfasts, monthly birthday celebrations, movie days, family days with skating, skiing and snowboarding, an employee Christmas dinner and dance, as well as a separate party for employees' children (with gifts from Santa).

BioWare also purchases tickets for employees to attend the city's famous "*Klondike Days*" festival, a local Playdium entertainment facility (obviously for research purposes), as well as Edmonton Oilers and Edmonton Eskimos hockey and football tickets.

## *Health, Financial & Family Benefits* — *Rating: B+*

BioWare's health benefits plan is managed by Manulife Financial and is rated as **average**. New employees must wait 90 days before they can enroll in the plan.

**Health Benefits at a Glance:** BioWare's health plan includes the following coverage: dental (100% of eligible costs, to $1,500 each year); eyecare; extended health benefits; prescription drug; massage therapy; physiotherapy; alternative therapies; personal and family counselling.

The company's salary and financial benefits are rated as **above-average**. To keep pay-levels competitive, BioWare participates in outside salary surveys. To ensure its pay levels are competitive, Bioware monitors industry trends and works closely with the University of Alberta.

**Financial Benefits at a Glance:** BioWare provides a variety of financial benefits, including: life and disability insurance; share purchase plan; profit-sharing plan; discounted home computers; discounted company products; $100 towards video game consoles (or other electronic gadgets).

### *Vacation & Time Off* *Rating: A+*

BioWare's vacation and time off are rated as **exceptional**. New employees receive 3 weeks of vacation allowance after their first year. When a new product ships, employees who worked on the project receive a bonus week of vacation. Each year, BioWare also provides employees with a paid holiday shutdown from Christmas to New Year's.

### *Employee Communications* *Rating: A*

BioWare's internal communications program is rated as **above-average**. The company has an intranet site, which keeps employees informed about news and human resource policies that affect their work. To solicit feedback from employees, the company operates an email suggestion box. An in-house employee satisfaction survey is conducted by having employees complete an online questionnaire every 12 months.

### *Performance Management* *Rating: A*

BioWare's performance management program is rated as **above-average**. The company operates a thorough performance management program. Every 6 months, employees and managers meet for review sessions. (Managers receive training in how to conduct effective reviews.) At the reviews, employees work with their supervisor, producers and senior managers, to establish future training goals. The final written appraisals are reviewed by senior managers, including the company's joint-CEOs. Employees also have the opportunity to provide confidential feedback on their manager's performance through the annual online survey.

### *Training & Skills Development* *Rating: A*

BioWare's training and skills development program is rated as **above-average**. The company provides tuition subsidies for courses related to an employee's current position. The company assists employees' career development with: reimbursement for professional association dues; educational conference subsidies; onsite library; mentoring; in-house training. The company's in-house training program covers a range of subject areas, from computer modelling to balancing creative expression with new technology.

### *Community Involvement* *Rating: A*

BioWare's community involvement program is rated as **above-average**. A very good corporate citizen, BioWare actively supports a variety of local charitable initiatives. Employees take part in the selection of charitable groups assisted by the company. Employees at BioWare receive paid time off to volunteer at local charities.

Last year, the company sponsored the Snowflake Gala, which raised money for the Stollery Children's Hospital Foundation. In addition to donating money to the event, BioWare sponsored a children's activity tent, which included Xbox kiosks and Christmas gifts for children. The company also donated money to the Royal Alexandra Hospital to help establish a children's recreation and learning centre.

In a unique initiative, BioWare also supports the University of Alberta's computer science department. The company provides financial support to the department, and assists with teaching new programming languages and developing new games.

# BLAKE, CASSELS & GRAYDON LLP

BLAKE, CASSELS & GRAYDON LLP
199 Bay Street
Suite 2800, PO Box 25, Commerce Court West
Toronto, ON M5L 1A9

Tel. 416-863-2400
Fax 416-863-2653
toronto@blakes.com
http://www.blakes.com

**INDUSTRY: LAW FIRMS**

*Highlights:*

- Build your career at one of the country's most established law firms, which is growing and creating career opportunities across Canada as well as overseas.
- Develop yourself at an employer that takes employee training seriously — this employer holds a national training awareness week each January — and offers lunch-hour workshops on a variety of subjects.
- Give back to your community at this employer, which provides lawyers to community pro bono programs that assist low income clients who can't afford legal services.

## *Employer Background*

Blake Cassels & Graydon LLP is one of Canada's leading law firms.

Established in 1856, Blakes is a leading corporate law firm, serving blue-chip clients across the country and around the world. As one of the country's oldest law firms, Blakes' expertise is often called upon to support in-house counsel as well as provide advice to other law firms.

Blakes has over 500 lawyers in offices in Toronto, Ottawa, Montréal, Calgary and Vancouver. The firm also has offices in London and Beijing, and recently formed a marketing alliance with three U.S. law firms to help expand its capabilities in the rapidly developing Chinese market.

**Workforce at a Glance:** Number of full-time employees: **940**. At this location: **645**. Worldwide: **945**. New jobs created in Canada in past year: **58**. Percentage of employees who are women: **79**. Of managers: **68**. Resumes received by their human resources staff in past year: **2,000**. Average employee age: **39**. Years longest-serving employee has worked there: **30**. Car the president drives: **prefers to take the subway**.

## *Physical Workplace* — *Rating: A*

Blakes' physical workplace is rated as above-average. The firm occupies 11 storeys of one the tallest buildings in downtown Toronto. The building is connected to the city's underground walking network, which gives employees convenient access to numerous restaurants and shops as well as the city's subway system.

**Physical Workplace at a Glance:** Their **employee lounge and rest areas** feature: comfortable couches; newspapers and magazines; card tables; sleep room; shower facilities. For **food and refreshment**, Blakes offers: kitchen areas; free coffee and tea. The firm has an onsite cafeteria that features: subsidized meals (soup and bagel combo costs $2.00); healthy menu items. Nearby **amenities** include: variety of restaurants; major shopping mall; park/wilderness area (Toronto Islands); recreation centre (CityCore Golf & Driving Range). For **commuters**, Blakes offers: nearby public transit; secure bicycle parking. Other **work area amenities** include: open-concept workstations; access to natural light for all employees; ergonomic workstation design; plant life that is tended professionally.

### *Work Atmosphere & Social* — *Rating: A*

Blakes' work atmosphere is rated as **above-average**. Employees at Blakes enjoy business casual dress daily and can listen to radio or music while they are working. The firm has an on-site concierge service.

Employees enjoy a variety of activities throughout the year, including a Christmas holiday dinner dance (with a separate Christmas party for employees' children), a winter ski day, an employee picnic in the summer, a golf day (with other fun activities) and an annual employee awards celebration. Blakes also sponsors employee basketball, hockey, touch-football and softball teams that compete in local leagues.

### *Health, Financial & Family Benefits* — *Rating: B+*

Blakes' health benefits plan is rated as **average**. **Health Benefits at a Glance:** Blakes' health plan includes the following coverage: dental; orthodontics; extended health benefits; prescription drug; nutrition planning; massage therapy; physiotherapy; alternative therapies; personal and family counselling; employee assistance plan (EAP) for substance abuse/mental health.

The firm's salary and financial benefits are rated as **above-average**. To keep pay-levels competitive, Blakes participates in outside salary surveys every 12 months. Individual salaries are reviewed every 12 months.

**Financial Benefits at a Glance:** Blakes provides a variety of financial benefits, including: life and disability insurance; subsidized auto insurance; discounted company products (free legal services); signing bonuses for some employees; referral bonuses for some employees (to $250).

Blakes' family-friendly benefits are rated as **average**. Employees with pre-school children have access to a daycare facility located nearby. Other family-friendly benefits include: reduced summer hours; telecommuting and working from home; compressed work week (same hours, fewer days); shortened work week (fewer hours); job sharing; flexible start and finish hours.

### *Vacation & Time Off* — *Rating: A*

Blakes' vacation and time off are rated as **above-average**. New employees receive 3 weeks of vacation allowance after their first year, which increases to 4 weeks after 5 years of service. The maximum vacation allowance is 6 weeks for long-serving employees. Employees at the firm can also apply for unpaid leaves of absence. (One employee recently took a 6 month leave to travel overseas.)

### *Employee Communications* *Rating: B+*

Blakes' internal communications program is rated as **average**. To keep employees informed about new developments, Blakes publishes an in-house newsletter. The firm also has an intranet site, which keeps employees informed about news and human resource policies that affect their work.

### *Performance Management* *Rating: A*

Blakes' performance management program is rated as **above-average**. The firm operates a well-designed performance management program. Once a year, employees and managers meet for review sessions. (Managers receive training in how to conduct effective reviews.) Prior to the annual meetings, employees complete online self-evaluations and managers complete corresponding online assessments. These written reviews form the basis for discussions at the review meetings. Employees also have the opportunity to provide confidential feedback on their manager's performance.

### *Training & Skills Development* *Rating: A+*

Blakes' training and skills development program is rated as **exceptional**. The firm provides tuition subsidies for courses related to an employee's current position (75% of tuition). Commendably, Blakes also offers subsidies for courses not related to an employee's current job (75% of tuition). The firm assists employees' career development with: reimbursement for professional association dues; mentoring; career planning; in-house training.

Blakes' in-house training program ranges from lunch hour sessions to professional education courses. These courses include financial planning, health and wellness, software and technical training, management training, conflict resolution, time management and language training. To encourage ongoing employee education, the firm also operates a "*National Training Week*" every January that includes several firm-wide training initiatives.

### *Community Involvement* *Rating: A*

Blakes' community involvement program is rated as **above-average**. A very good corporate citizen, Blakes actively supports a variety of charitable initiatives. Employees take part in the selection of charitable groups assisted by the firm. Employees at Blakes receive paid time off (1 day each year) to volunteer at local charities.

Every year, the firm supports charities, arts organizations and community initiatives across the country. Last year, the firm supported local United Campaigns across the country, the Hospital for Sick Children in Toronto and the Alberta Children's Hospital in Calgary. Blakes also provides lawyer volunteers for Pro-Bono Law Ontario, which offers free legal services to those in need.

The firm also operates a generous national scholarship program. Through this program, Blakes provides renewable scholarships (to $10,000 each) to students who have completed their first year at law school. The firm also supports fundraising campaigns and sponsors teaching programs at law schools across the country, including the University of Toronto, McGill University, Queen's University, Osgoode Hall and the University of British Columbia.

**BLAST RADIUS INC.**
**1146 Homer Street**
**Vancouver, BC V6B 2X6**

**Tel. 604-647-6500**
**Fax 604-682-3616**
**careers@blastradius.com**
**http://www.blastradius.com**

**INDUSTRY: INFORMATION TECHNOLOGY CONSULTING FIRMS**

*Highlights:*

- Get a one-month paid sabbatical after only four years on the job with this employer.
- Work for a thoughtful employer that offers rewards for exceptional performance that are customized to each employee's needs — such as a trip for one employee's boyfriend to Amsterdam!
- Work in a renovated heritage building in Vancouver's Yaletown district that also features a micro-brewery.

## *Employer Background*

Blast Radius Inc. is an IT consulting firm that develops sophisticated websites that integrate new technologies with companies' overall business strategies. Founded in 1996, Blast Radius develops large-scale websites that automate marketing, sales and customer service functions. The company provides clients with a wide range of consulting services, from content development to follow-up support. Blast Radius primarily serves customers in the financial services, media and entertainment, retail, travel and transportation industries. The company's impressive client list includes such well-known leaders as Nike, Nintendo, BMW, Universal Studios and Aeroplan.

With its strong focus on developing long-term relationships, the company survived the recent technology meltdown and has continued to grow. Last year, the company increased its annual revenues by 20% to over $22 million by establishing a new XML product division and expanding its European presence with Nintendo Europe.

In addition to its Vancouver head office, the company has offices in Toronto, Los Angeles, New York and Amsterdam.

**Workforce at a Glance:** Number of full-time employees: **157**. At this location: **101**. Worldwide: **183**. New jobs created in Canada in past year: **36**. Percentage of employees who are women: **27**. Of managers: **22**. Percentage of employees who are visible minorities: **27**. Of managers: **17**. Resumes received by their human resources staff in past year: **5,979**. Average employee age: **32**. Years longest-serving employee has worked there: **7**. Car the president drives: **walks to work**.

## *Physical Workplace* — *Rating: A*

Blast Radius' physical workplace is rated as **above-average**. Located in Vancouver's historic Yaletown district, the head office is within walking distance to the False Creek waterfront and the seawall that leads to the city's famous Stanley Park. The head office is located in a renovated heritage building with exposed brick and wood beams throughout. (The building is also home to a microbrewery, making for lively office parties.)

**Physical Workplace at a Glance:** Their **employee lounge and rest areas** feature: music; television; video games; table tennis. For **food and refreshment**, Blast Radius offers: free coffee and tea; outdoor eating area; barbeque; subsidized meals (to $15) when working late. Nearby **amenities** include: variety of restaurants; local shops and services; fitness facility; grocery stores and organic food market; park/wilderness area (David Lamm Park); recreation centre (Roundhouse Community Centre). For **commuters**, Blast Radius offers: nearby public transit; secure bicycle parking; shower facilities. Other **work area amenities** include: open-concept workstations; ergonomic workstation design; access to natural light for all employees; plant life that is tended professionally; windows that open.

## *Work Atmosphere & Social* — *Rating: A+*

Blast Radius' work atmosphere is rated as **exceptional**. Employees at Blast Radius enjoy casual dress daily and can listen to radio or music while they are working. The company lets employees bring their pets to work. There is also a company-subsidized social committee, called the '*The Fun Squad*'.

The Fun Squad organizes a variety of events throughout the year, including a summer barbeque, a pool party dinner at a local hotel, a Halloween costume contest and a Christmas party for employees and their guests. The Christmas party includes an awards ceremony with a variety of interesting categories, such as the "*Sense of Humour Under Pressure*" award.

Blast Radius also sponsors employee sporting activities, including afternoon volleyball, basketball and floor hockey. The company subsidizes an ultimate frisbee team (called the "*Potty Mouths*") and a beach volleyball team that both compete in local leagues.

## *Health, Financial & Family Benefits* — *Rating: B+*

Blast Radius' health benefits plan is managed by Great-West Life and is rated as **above-average**. Full-time and part-time employees who work more than 30 hours per week are covered by the plan. New employees must wait 90 days before they can enroll in the plan.

**Health Benefits at a Glance:** Blast Radius' health plan includes the following coverage: dental (80% of eligible costs, to $1,000 each year); orthodontics (50% of eligible costs, to $1,000 each year); eyecare (to $200 every 2 years); extended health benefits; prescription drug; nutrition planning; massage therapy; physiotherapy; alternative therapies; personal and family counselling.

The company's salary and financial benefits are rated as **average**. To keep pay-levels competitive, Blast Radius participates in outside salary surveys every 6 months. Individual salaries are reviewed every 6 months.

**Financial Benefits at a Glance:** Blast Radius provides a variety of financial benefits, including: life and disability insurance; discounted products from company suppliers and clients; quarterly performance bonuses; referral bonuses for some employees (from $1,000 to $2,500).

Blast Radius' family-friendly benefits are rated as **average**. Employees with pre-school children have access to a daycare facility located nearby. Other family-friendly benefits include: telecommuting and working from home; flexible start and finish hours.

*Vacation & Time Off* *Rating: A*

Blast Radius' vacation and time off are rated as **above-average**. New employees receive 3 weeks of vacation allowance after their first year, which increases to 4 weeks after 5 years of service. Employees at Blast Radius also receive 3 paid personal days off each year, in addition to their regular vacation allowance. Employees at the company can also apply for unpaid leaves of absence.

Blast Radius also operates an exceptional paid-sabbatical program. After only four years on the job, employees can apply to take a one month paid sabbatical.

*Employee Communications* *Rating: A*

Blast Radius' internal communications program is rated as **above-average**. To keep employees informed about new developments, Blast Radius publishes an in-house newsletter, which is available online. The company also has an intranet site, which keeps employees informed about news and human resource policies that affect their work. To solicit feedback from employees, the company operates an email suggestion box. An in-house employee satisfaction survey is conducted periodically.

As a result of employee feedback, the company recently established an in-house "Cultural Task Force" to address the employee morale issues that arose during the high-tech sector's recent economic downturn.

*Performance Management* *Rating: A+*

Blast Radius' performance management program is rated as **exceptional**. The company operates a well-designed performance management program. Every 6 months, employees and managers meet for review sessions. (Managers receive training in how to conduct effective reviews.) Employees and managers establish annual goals and meet for mid-year progress reviews. The review process forms the basis for salary increases and succession planning. Employees also have the opportunity to provide confidential feedback on their manager's performance.

Blast Radius recognizes exceptional employee performance with awards such as weekends at Whistler, Sony Playstations and digital cameras. (Generally, the awards are matched to the employee's interests or needs at the time.) Recently, one employee who was working for an extended period in Amsterdam received a surprise guest — the employee's boyfriend was flown over for a visit, courtesy of the company.

*Training & Skills Development* *Rating: B+*

Blast Radius' training and skills development program is rated as **average**. The company provides tuition subsidies for courses related to an employee's current position. The company assists employees' career development with: reimbursement for professional association dues; mentoring; in-house training.

As part of the company's in-house training program, employees also host monthly workshops on job-related and life skills. These workshops range from XML language training to wine tasting and writing skills.

*Community Involvement* *Rating: A*

Blast Radius' community involvement program is rated as **above-average**. A very good corporate citizen, Blast Radius actively supports a variety of local and national charitable initiatives. Employees take part in the selection of charitable groups assisted by the company. Last year, the company contributed to approximately 5 charitable groups, including: the United Way, the Canadian National Institute for the Blind, the Society for the Prevention of Cruelty to Animals and a local food bank.

**BOEHRINGER INGELHEIM (CANADA) LTD.**
**5180 South Service Road**
**Burlington, ON L7L 5H4**

**Tel. 905-639-0333**
**Fax 905-637-9659**
**hr@bur.boehringer-ingelheim.com**
**http://www.boehringer-ingelheim.ca**

**INDUSTRY: PHARMACEUTICAL & DRUG MANUFACTURERS**

*Highlights:*

- Get more free time at an employer that offers three weeks of paid vacation allowance to start (increasing to four weeks after only three years) and a great "earned days off" program that lets you take off every second Friday.
- Spend more time with your family thanks to this employer's progressive family-friendly benefits, which include generous maternity leave top-up (93% of salary for 18 weeks) and several alternative work arrangements.
- Take care of yourself better with this employer's excellent health plan and generous financial benefits.

## *Employer Background*

Boehringer Ingelheim (Canada) Ltd. is a leading pharmaceutical company. The company is active in the research and development of pharmaceutical treatments for a range of illnesses. Through its Vetmedica division, the company also develops a variety of veterinary medicines

Boehringer Ingelheim Canada is a subsidiary of Germany-based Boehringer Ingelheim Gmbh. Established in 1885, the parent company is one of world's leading pharmaceutical companies and operates in 44 countries. The privately-held company is also one of the world's leading research and development firms, investing over $1.3 billion in developing new drugs last year.

Founded in 1972, the Canadian subsidiary is one of this country's fastest growing pharmaceutical research firms. In addition to its Burlington head office, the company has a second facility in Laval.

**Workforce at a Glance:** Number of full-time employees: **567**. At this location: **236**. Worldwide: **31,843**. New jobs created in Canada in past year: **40**. Percentage of employees who are women: **51**. Of managers: **47**. Resumes received by their human resources staff in past year: **1,831**. Weeks of vacation their HR manager took last year: **3.5**. Average employee age: **40**. Years longest-serving employee has worked there: **33**. Person you should get to know first: **Mike in Building Services will ensure your office gets set-up perfectly**. Car the president drives: **BMW**. Where it's parked in the lot: **reserved spot in front**.

### *Physical Workplace* — *Rating: A*

Boehringer Ingelheim's physical workplace is rated as **above-average**. The company's suburban head office is located in a park-like setting and features a large indoor atrium that serves as a gathering place for employees.

**Physical Workplace at a Glance:** Their **employee lounge and rest areas** feature: television; board games; sleep room. For **food and refreshment**, Boehringer Ingelheim offers: free coffee and tea; outdoor eating area; barbeque. The company has an onsite cafeteria that features: subsidized meals (a turkey sandwich costs $2.90); special diet menus; healthy menu items. Nearby **amenities** include: variety of restaurants; major shopping mall; fitness facility (with subsidized memberships); park/wilderness area (Spencer Smith Park). For **commuters**, Boehringer Ingelheim offers: free onsite car parking; convenient highway access; nearby public transit; secure bicycle parking; shower facilities. Other **work area amenities** include: open-concept workstations; modern laboratories; ergonomic workstation design; corporate training centre; access to natural light for all employees; plant life that is tended professionally; relaxing indoor water fountain.

### *Work Atmosphere & Social* — *Rating: A*

Boehringer Ingelheim's work atmosphere is rated as **above-average**. Employees at Boehringer Ingelheim enjoy business casual dress daily. There is also a company-subsidized social committee, called the '*SociaLink*', which has operated since 1990.

Employees enjoy a variety of events throughout the year, including a Christmas dinner dance for employees and their spouses, a separate Christmas party for employees' children, an employee golf tournament, a summer gourmet barbeque and occasional parties to celebrate significant accomplishments.

The company also celebrates individual milestones through its long-service awards program. Employees celebrating 10 years on the job receive a bonus equal to half their monthly salary. Employee who reach their 25th anniversary receive the equivalent of a full month's salary.

Boehringer Ingelheim Canada also sponsors employee hockey teams in Burlington and Laval. In addition to competing in local leagues, these teams compete against each other (and a team from its Connecticut subsidiary) in an annual intra-company hockey tournament.

### *Health, Financial & Family Benefits* — *Rating: A+*

Boehringer Ingelheim's health benefits plan is rated as **exceptional**. Boehringer Ingelheim pays 100% of the premiums associated with the plan. There is no waiting period before new employees are eligible for coverage.

**Health Benefits at a Glance:** Boehringer Ingelheim's health plan includes the following coverage: dental (80% of eligible costs, to $1,500 each year); orthodontics (50% of eligible costs with a lifetime maximum of $2,000); eyecare (to $150 every 2 years); prescription drug; extended health benefits; nutrition planning; massage therapy; physiotherapy; alternative therapies; personal and family counselling; employee assistance plan (EAP) for substance abuse/mental health.

The company's salary and financial benefits are rated as **exceptional**. To keep pay-levels competitive, Boehringer Ingelheim participates in outside salary surveys every 12 months. Individual salaries are reviewed every 12 months. The company operates a traditional pension plan where Boehringer Ingelheim makes a contribution equal to 4% of each employee's salary to their plan each year. The company also provides a group RSP (with matching employer contributions) and an employee savings plan.

> **Financial Benefits at a Glance:** Boehringer Ingelheim provides an extensive set of financial benefits, including: life and disability insurance; signing bonuses for some employees; referral bonuses for some employees (from $200 to $2,500); year-end bonuses.

Boehringer Ingelheim's family-friendly benefits are rated as **above-average**. Employees with pre-school children have access to a daycare facility located nearby. For employees who take maternity leave, Boehringer Ingelheim provides a generous top-up to 90% of salary for the first 18 weeks of their leave. Other family-friendly benefits include: flexible start and finish hours; telecommuting and working from home.

### *Vacation & Time Off* — *Rating: A*

Boehringer Ingelheim's vacation and time off are rated as **above-average**. New employees receive 3 weeks of vacation allowance after their first year, which increases to 4 weeks after 3 years of service. The maximum vacation allowance is 6 weeks for long-serving employees. Each year, Boehringer Ingelheim also provides employees with a paid holiday shutdown from Christmas to New Year's. Employees at the company can also apply for unpaid leaves of absence.

Boehringer Ingelheim also operates an interesting "earned days off" program. When the workload permits, employees can work an extra 20 minutes each day and take off every second Friday.

### *Employee Communications* — *Rating: A+*

Boehringer Ingelheim's internal communications program is rated as **exceptional**. To keep employees informed about new developments, Boehringer Ingelheim publishes an in-house newsletter (called *Focus*), which is available online. The company also has an intranet site (called *Navigator*), which keeps employees informed about news and human resource policies that affect their work. To solicit feedback from employees, the company operates an email suggestion box. An employee satisfaction survey is conducted by having employees complete an online questionnaire every 24 months. An outside consultant compiles the survey results for Boehringer Ingelheim's management team. The company also invites all employees to attend the company's annual meeting. This company-wide event is held offsite and includes business updates, guest speakers and video links with the company's management in Germany and employees around the world.

### *Performance Management* — *Rating: A*

Boehringer Ingelheim's performance management program is rated as **above-average**. The company operates a comprehensive performance management program. Once a year, employees and managers meet for review sessions. (Managers receive training in how to conduct effective reviews.) At the reviews, employees and managers review past accomplishments and set personal goals and training objectives for the upcoming year. Boehringer Ingelheim recognizes exceptional performance with gift certificates, restaurant dinners and European vacations (for sales employees).

Employees also have the opportunity to provide confidential feedback on their manager's performance through the review process and the annual employee satisfaction survey.

***Training & Skills Development*** ***Rating: A***

Boehringer Ingelheim's training and skills development program is rated as **above-average**. The company provides tuition subsidies for courses related to an employee's current position (100% of tuition). Commendably, Boehringer Ingelheim also offers subsidies for courses not related to an employee's current job. The company assists employees' career development with: reimbursement for professional association dues; job-rotation; in-house training. The company's onsite training program includes a variety of courses, from work-life balance to finance and accounting.

***Community Involvement*** ***Rating: A***

Boehringer Ingelheim's community involvement program is rated as **above-average**. A very good corporate citizen, Boehringer Ingelheim actively supports a variety of local and national charitable initiatives. Employees take part in the selection of charitable groups assisted by the company. Last year, the company contributed to approximately 14 charitable groups, including: Halton Woman's Place, the Carpenter Hospice, the Canadian Lung Association, the Canadian Cancer Society and the Easter Seals Society.

**CAE INC.**
**8585, chemin de la Côte-de-Liesse**
**St-Laurent, QC H4L 4X4**

**Tel. 514-341-6780**
**Fax 514-340-5335**
**hr@cae.com**
**http://www.cae.com**

**INDUSTRY: OTHER ELECTRICAL EQUIPMENT & SUPPLIES MANUFACTURERS**

***Highlights:***

- Develop yourself at an employer that takes training so seriously that they've built a training centre with 11 classrooms and three lecture halls.
- Build an international career with an employer where science and technology shape almost every aspect of their work, employee benefits and even community involvement programs.
- Work for an employer that makes your non-working life easier by providing onsite employee banking, dry cleaning and a subsidized cafeteria (where turkey sandwiches cost only $1.50).

***Employer Background***

CAE Inc. is a leading manufacturer of advanced flight simulation systems and marine automation technology.

Founded in 1947, Montréal-based CAE is the world's leading manufacturer of advanced flight simulators. The publicly-traded company supplies 80% of the world's aircraft simulators. CAE's simulators are used by military organizations, training schools and commercial airlines in over 50 countries. CAE supplies leading airlines such as Air Canada, Delta, Air China, Lufthansa and KLM, to name a few.

CAE also develops sophisticated marine automation technology for commercial shiplines and naval forces around the world. The company's advanced technology is used on more than 500 large vessels in a range of applications, from engine control to video monitoring systems.

Recently, CAE has expanded its business by providing complementary training services. Building on its existing customer base, this has become a significant growth area for the company.

With operations in 18 countries, CAE is one of Canada's leading exporters and one of the country's leading research and development companies, investing an astounding 10% of its revenues in R&D each year. CAE had revenues of over $1 billion last year.

**Workforce at a Glance:** Number of full-time employees: **3,968**. Worldwide: **6,162**. Percentage of employees who are visible minorities: **16**. Of managers: **10**. Resumes received by their human resources staff in past year: **31,250**. Average employee age: **38**.

### *Physical Workplace* — *Rating: A*

CAE's physical workplace is rated as **above-average**. The company recently added a major new building to its massive head office complex. The company has also renovated most of its older facilities, updating workstations (50 each month), renovating the cafeteria and updating the air conditioning systems. In addition, CAE employs two full-time health and safety specialists to address workplace safety and comfort issues. (New initiatives include an expanded onsite medical facility with three full-time employees.)

**Physical Workplace at a Glance:** Their **employee lounge and rest areas** feature: comfortable couches; meditation or religious observance room. For **food and refreshment**, CAE offers: outdoor eating area; barbeque. The company has an onsite cafeteria that features: subsidized meals (a turkey sandwich costs $1.50); healthy menu items; salad bar. Nearby **amenities** include: fitness facility (with subsidized memberships); tennis courts; baseball diamond; ice rink; variety of restaurants; major shopping mall. For **commuters**, CAE offers: free onsite car parking; nearby public transit; secure bicycle parking; shower facilities. Other **work area amenities** include: open-concept workstations; ergonomic workstation design; state-of-the-art manufacturing facilities; plant life that is tended professionally; boutique with dry cleaning service; onsite bank with ATM.

### *Work Atmosphere & Social* — *Rating: A*

CAE's work atmosphere is rated as **above-average**. Employees at CAE enjoy business casual dress daily and can listen to radio or music while they are working. There is also a company-subsidized social committee, called the '*CAE Social & Recreation Club*', which has operated since 1963.

The club organizes events for employees throughout the year, including summer barbeques, horseback riding, whitewater rafting, golf tournaments, baseball, soccer, paintball and skiing. The company also subsidizes employee baseball and hockey teams that compete in local leagues.

Every year, CAE hosts a huge Christmas party (with games and presents for employees' children) and an annual open house in the summer ("*CAE Day*"), complete with plant tours and entertainment for employees and their families.

### *Health, Financial & Family Benefits* — *Rating: A*

CAE's health benefits plan is rated as **above-average**. CAE pays 100% of the premiums associated with the plan. There is no waiting period before new employees are eligible for coverage.

**Health Benefits at a Glance:** CAE's health plan includes the following coverage: dental (90% of eligible costs, with no annual maximum); orthodontics (50% of eligible costs with a lifetime maximum of $1,500); eyecare (to $185 every 2 years); extended health benefits; prescription drug; massage therapy; physiotherapy; personal and family counselling; employee assistance plan (EAP) for substance abuse/mental health.

The company's salary and financial benefits are rated as **above-average**. To keep pay-levels competitive, CAE participates in outside salary surveys every 12 months. Individual salaries are reviewed every 12 months. The company operates a traditional pension plan.

**Financial Benefits at a Glance:** CAE provides a variety of financial benefits, including: life and disability insurance; group RRSP; share purchase plan (with matching company contributions); referral bonuses for some employees (to $1,000).

CAE's family-friendly benefits are rated as **above-average**. Employees with pre-school children have access to a daycare facility located nearby. For employees who take maternity leave, CAE provides a top-up to 75% of salary for the first 18 weeks of their leave. Employees can also take time during the day (with pay) to attend to family emergencies. Other family-friendly benefits include: flexible start and finish hours.

### *Vacation & Time Off* — *Rating: B+*

CAE's vacation and time off are rated as **average**. New employees receive 2 weeks of vacation allowance after their first year, which increases to 3 weeks after 3 years of service. The maximum vacation allowance is 4 weeks for employees who spend 10 years with the company. Each year, CAE also provides employees with a paid holiday shutdown from Christmas to New Year's. Employees at the company can also apply for unpaid leaves of absence.

### *Employee Communications* — *Rating: A*

CAE's internal communications program is rated as **above-average**. To keep employees informed about new developments, CAE publishes an in-house newsletter, which is published in French, English and German. The company also has an intranet site, which keeps employees informed about news and human resource policies that affect their work. (A web kiosk is available for manufacturing employees who do not have internet access in their work areas.) The company also publishes a variety of divisional and project-related newsletters.

### *Performance Management* — *Rating: A*

CAE's performance management program is rated as **above-average**. The company operates a formal performance management program. Once a year, employees and managers meet for review sessions. (Managers receive training in how to conduct effective reviews.) At the reviews, individual performance is evaluated and training goals are set for the upcoming year. The reviews form the basis for training, promotions and salary increases.

### *Training & Skills Development* — *Rating: A+*

CAE's training and skills development program is rated as **exceptional**. The company provides tuition subsidies for courses related to an employee's current position. The company assists employees' career development with: mentoring; in-house training. CAE operates an impressive training centre (which features eleven classrooms and three lecture halls), where employees can take a range of in-house courses, from basic computer software instruction to advanced flight training.

### *Community Involvement* — *Rating: A+*

CAE's community involvement program is rated as **exceptional**. An outstanding corporate citizen, CAE actively supports a variety of local charitable initiatives. Employees are strong supporters of the annual United Way campaign, raising over $362,000 last year.

The company encourages Canadian students to share the company's passion for science and technology. The company collaborates on research and development projects with local universities, investing over $500,000 annually. In addition, the company is a major sponsor of the annual Canadian Engineering Competition and the Québec Engineering Competition and Engineering Games.

A good environmental citizen, CAE recently introduced a tough new recycling program with the goal of recycling 70% of its waste. (As part of this initiative, employees now carry their own coffee mugs to work.)

**CANADIAN BROADCASTING CORPORATION**
**250 Lanark Avenue**
**PO Box 3220, Station C**
**Ottawa, ON K1Z 6R5**

CBC Radio-Canada

**Tel. 613-724-1200**
**Fax 613-724-5664**
**resume@ottawa.cbc.ca**
**http://www.cbc.ca**

**INDUSTRY: TELEVISION BROADCASTING COMPANIES**

*Highlights:*

- Build your career at a revitalized national institution, which has been consolidating its regional offices and is building a new head office in downtown Ottawa.
- Develop your skills at an employer well-known in the media industry for providing exceptional training, from journalism ethics to technical and production skills.
- Work at the only employer in this book to offer career opportunities for people in both of Canada's official languages and eight Aboriginal languages.

## *Employer Background*

Canadian Broadcasting Corporation (CBC) is the largest cultural institution in the country. The CBC is the only broadcasting company to provide coast-to-coast-to-coast services in English and French (through Société Radio-Canada), as well as eight Aboriginal languages.

The Crown corporation was established by the Federal government in 1936 — largely in response to American programming expanding into Canada's airwaves. Today, the public broadcaster develops and presents a wide range of programming that "informs, enlightens and entertains" through two national television networks, four national radio networks; two specialty news channels; three specialty television services; an international short-wave radio service; and interactive Internet sites.

In addition to its head office in Ottawa, the CBC has major broadcast facilities in St. John's, Halifax, Moncton, Québec, Montréal, Toronto, Winnipeg, Regina, Edmonton, Vancouver and Yellowknife.

**Workforce at a Glance:** Number of full-time employees: **8,835**. New jobs created in Canada in past year: **416**. Percentage of employees who are women: **44**. Of managers: **46**. Percentage of employees who are visible minorities: **5**. Of managers: **3**. Weeks of vacation their HR manager took last year: **4**. Average employee age: **41**. Years longest-serving employee has worked there: **40**. Car the president drives: **Chrysler Concord**. Where it's parked in the lot: **reserved spot in front**.

## *Physical Workplace* — *Rating: A*

CBC's physical workplace is rated as **above-average**. Employees at the public broadcaster work in a variety of settings across Canada, from the National Broadcasting Centre in Toronto to stations in the high arctic. Over the past number of years, the CBC has consolidated many of its local operations into regional facilities. The Ottawa head office is the latest example, with five offices moving into a new downtown facility this year.

**Physical Workplace at a Glance:** The Corporation has an onsite cafeteria that features: subsidized meals (a turkey sandwich costs $3.00); healthy menu items. Nearby **amenities** include: variety of restaurants; coffee shops. For **commuters**, CBC offers: free onsite car parking; nearby public transit. Other **work area amenities** include: open-concept workstations; ergonomic workstation design; access to natural light for all employees; views overlooking the Ottawa River; plant life that is tended professionally; instructor-led fitness classes (held in studios) and onsite shower facilities.

### *Work Atmosphere & Social* — *Rating: A*

CBC's work atmosphere is rated as **above-average**. Employees at CBC enjoy casual dress daily and can listen to radio or music while they are working. There is also a Corporation-subsidized social committee.

Across the country, the broadcaster hosts employee Christmas parties, summer picnics, golf tournaments and celebrations to launch the new television season. The CBC also hosts an annual awards celebration for employees who have completed lengthy terms of service.

### *Health, Financial & Family Benefits* — *Rating: A*

CBC's health benefits plan is managed by Great-West Life and is rated as **above-average**. CBC pays 100% of the premiums associated with the plan. Full-time and part-time employees are covered by the plan.

**Health Benefits at a Glance:** CBC's health plan includes the following coverage: dental (95% of eligible costs, to $2,500 each year); orthodontics (50% of eligible costs with a lifetime maximum of $2,000); eyecare (to $240 every 2 years); extended health benefits; prescription drug; massage therapy; physiotherapy; alternative therapies; personal and family counselling; employee assistance plan (EAP) for substance abuse/mental health.

The Corporation's salary and financial benefits are rated as **above-average**. To keep pay-levels competitive, CBC participates in outside salary surveys every 12 months. Individual salaries are reviewed every 12 months. The Corporation operates a traditional pension plan.

**Financial Benefits at a Glance:** CBC provides a variety of financial benefits, including: life and disability insurance; discounted company products; subsidized auto insurance; subsidized home insurance; low-interest home loans; referral bonuses for some employees.

CBC's family-friendly benefits are rated as **average**. For employees who take maternity leave, CBC provides a top-up to 93% of salary for the first 2 weeks of their leave. Other benefits include: compressed work week (same hours, fewer days); flexible start and finish hours; telecommuting and working from home.

### *Vacation & Time Off* — *Rating: A*

CBC's vacation and time off are rated as **above-average**. New employees receive 3 weeks of vacation allowance after their first year. The maximum vacation allowance is 7 weeks for long-serving employees. Employees at the Corporation can also apply for unpaid leaves of absence.

### *Employee Communications* — *Rating: A*

CBC's internal communications program is rated as **above-average**. To keep employees informed about new developments, CBC publishes an in-house newsletter. The Corporation also has an intranet site, which keeps employees informed about news and human resource policies that affect their work. An employee satisfaction survey is conducted every 24 months. An outside consultant compiles the survey results for CBC's management team. The CBC's HR department also conducts regular in-house employee satisfaction surveys on a variety of workplace-related issues.

### *Performance Management* — *Rating: A*

CBC's performance management program is rated as **above-average**. The Corporation operates a comprehensive performance management program. Once a year, employees and managers meet for review sessions. (Managers receive training in how to conduct effective reviews.) At the annual meetings, managers and employees review past performance and develop training plans for the upcoming year. In addition to mid-year progress reviews, managers provide informal coaching throughout the year. The reviews form the basis for succession planning and future salary increases.

### *Training & Skills Development* — *Rating: A+*

CBC's training and skills development program is rated as **exceptional**. The Corporation provides tuition subsidies for courses related to an employee's current position (100% of tuition). The Corporation assists employees' career development with: reimbursement for professional association dues; mentoring; in-house training.

The CBC's in-house training program includes a tremendous variety of courses, including journalism, television production, technical training, new digital technology, information technology, language training, management, administration and creativity classes. In the broadcast industry, the CBC has a reputation for training exceptionally competent personnel.

### *Community Involvement* — *Rating: B+*

CBC's community involvement program is rated as **average**. A good member of the community, CBC actively supports a variety of charitable initiatives. Across the country, employees support numerous community events every year, including local food drives and regional United Way campaigns.

As a Crown corporation, it is difficult for the broadcaster to spend public funds on charitable organizations. Many of the Corporation's employees play active roles in supporting charitable groups in their fields.

**CARA OPERATIONS LIMITED**
**6303 Airport Road**
**Mississauga, ON L4V 1R8**

**Tel. 905-405-6500**
**Fax 905-405-6604**
**careers@cara.com**
**http://www.cara.com**

**INDUSTRY: RESTAURANTS & FOODSERVICE**

*Highlights:*

- Build your career at a leader in the hospitality field that offers its employees extensive training — and advancement opportunities across nine different divisions.
- Give back to your community by working at a thoughtful employer that has an exceptional community involvement program and donates money from the sale of its dinners each holiday season to local charities.
- Help educate your kids at an employer that offers 50 major academic scholarships every year to employees' children who are interested in attending college or university.

## *Employer Background*

Cara Operations Limited operates several leading national restaurant chains and provides institutional food services (including catering and distribution) across Canada.

Established in 1883 as The Canada Railway News Company Limited, Cara Operations has grown into one of the largest integrated foodservice companies in the country. The publicly-traded company has annual sales of over $1.8 billion, more than 1,100 franchised and company-owned restaurant locations, and over 38,850 full- and part-time employees.

Cara's portfolio of restaurants includes well-known banners such as Swiss Chalet, Harvey's, Second Cup, Kelsey's, Montana's, Milestone's and Outback Steakhouse, as well as airport terminal restaurants across Canada. Cara's food distribution businesses consists of the Airport Services Division and the Summit Food Service Distributors Inc. subsidiary.

**Workforce at a Glance:** Number of full-time employees: **9,728**. At this location: **313**. New jobs created in Canada in past year: **4,558**. Percentage of employees who are women: **52**. Of managers: **28**. Resumes received by their human resources staff in past year: **36,500**. Weeks of vacation their HR manager took last year: **2**. Average employee age: **39**. Years longest-serving employee has worked there: **48**.

## *Physical Workplace* — *Rating: A*

Cara's physical workplace is rated as **above-average**. Located across from Toronto's international airport, Cara Operations' head office was recently renovated. The open-concept design also features meeting rooms that can be used as private workspaces when needed.

**Physical Workplace at a Glance:** For **food and refreshment**, Cara offers: free coffee and tea; kitchen areas. The company has an onsite cafeteria that features: subsidized meals; and the "*ToAst! Café*", which serves complimentary Second Cup coffee and menu items from Swiss Chalet and Harvey's. Nearby **amenities** include: variety of restaurants; major shopping mall; fitness facility. For **commuters**, Cara offers: free onsite car parking; nearby public transit. Other **work area amenities** include: open-concept workstations; ergonomic workstation design; plant life that is tended professionally.

### *Work Atmosphere & Social* — *Rating: A*

Cara's work atmosphere is rated as **above-average**. Employees at Cara enjoy business casual dress daily. There is also a company-subsidized social committee, which has operated since 1998.

During the year, the company welcomes new employees over afternoon snacks and drinks at its quarterly meetings. Cara also closes early on the last Thursday of each month for a catered social event — when the weather is warm the event is held outdoors so employees can enjoy a Harvey's barbeque.

Cara also organizes several social events every year, including a family picnic (with games, prizes and gifts for employees' children) and a Christmas holiday gala that includes dinner, dancing and a ceremony to recognize long-serving employees.

### *Health, Financial & Family Benefits* — *Rating: A*

Cara's health benefits plan is managed by Great-West Life and is rated as **above-average**. New employees must wait 30 days before they can enroll in the plan.

**Health Benefits at a Glance:** Cara's health plan includes the following coverage: dental (100% of eligible costs, to $2,000 each year); orthodontics (50% of eligible costs with a lifetime maximum of $2,000); extended health benefits; prescription drug; massage therapy; physiotherapy; alternative therapies; personal and family counselling; employee assistance plan (EAP) for substance abuse/mental health.

The company's salary and financial benefits are rated as **above-average**. To keep pay-levels competitive, Cara participates in outside salary surveys every 12 months. Individual salaries are reviewed every 12 months. The company offers a group RSP that allows employees to contribute up to 5% of their salary, with matching employer contributions.

**Financial Benefits at a Glance:** Cara provides a variety of financial benefits, including: life and disability insurance; discounted car leases; discounted home computers; discounted company products; signing bonuses for some employees; year-end bonuses.

Cara's family-friendly benefits are rated as **average**. Family-friendly benefits include: reduced summer hours; flexible start and finish hours.

To help offset the tuition costs paid by some of its employees, Cara provides 40 scholarships (worth $1,000 each) and 10 additional scholarships (worth $3,500 each) to employees' children interested in post-secondary studies.

### *Vacation & Time Off* — *Rating: B+*

Cara's vacation and time off are rated as **average**. New employees receive 2 weeks of vacation allowance after their first year, which increases to 3 weeks after 5 years of service. The maximum vacation allowance is 5 weeks for long-serving employees. Employees at the company can also apply for unpaid leaves of absence.

### *Employee Communications* — *Rating: B+*

Cara's internal communications program is rated as **average**. Cara keeps employees informed about new company developments through internal newsletters, email updates and bulletin board postings. The company also hosts quarterly meetings in the cafe, where head office employees enjoy free food and have the opportunity to raise issues with senior management. Senior managers host similar meetings at locations across the country.

### *Performance Management* — *Rating: A*

Cara's performance management program is rated as **above-average**. The company operates a well-designed performance management program. Once a year, employees and managers meet for review sessions. (Managers receive training in how to conduct effective reviews.) To prepare for the annual review, each employee completes a written self-assessment, which is compared to their manager's assessment. Afterwards, employees and managers meet to compare the assessments and establish objectives for the upcoming year. The reviews form the basis for employee training, promotions and salary increases.

Across the company, Cara does a good job of rewarding employees for excellent work. In addition to bonuses, promotions and pay increases, the company's Swiss Chalet and Milestone's divisions recognize top performers with a leased car — last year's "MVP" from Swiss Chalet received a Mercedes convertible for a year.

### *Training & Skills Development* — *Rating: A+*

Cara's training and skills development program is rated as **exceptional**. The company provides tuition subsidies for courses related to an employee's current position (100% of tuition). The company assists employees' career development with: in-house training.

The company's extensive in-house training program (called "*Cara College*") offers management and leadership training workshops across the country. Many of the company's divisions provide technical training at their own facilities, including The Swiss Chalet Academy and Harvey's Continuous Development Centre.

The company also operates an internal job posting program, which lets employees know about new job opportunities across all of Cara's operations — Swiss Chalet, Harvey's, Second Cup, Kelsey's, Montana's, Outback, Milestone's, Cara Air Terminal/Airport Services and Summit Food distribution

Cara also works closely with the University of Guelph's School of Hospitality & Tourism Management and the Canadian Academy of Travel & Tourism. The company has committed $1 million over the next four years for scholarships and research initiatives at universities and colleges across Canada.

***Community Involvement*** ***Rating: A+***

Cara's community involvement program is rated as **exceptional**. An outstanding corporate citizen, Cara actively supports a variety of local and national charitable initiatives.

A member of the Canadian Centre for Philanthropy's "*Imagine*" program, Cara contributes 1% of its pre-tax earnings to charities and non-profit organizations. Last year, the company donated over $650,000 to charities nationwide. The company focuses its giving on health-related organizations, including the Smart Risk Foundation, the Concerned Kids Charity and Safe Kids Canada, to name only a few.

Each year, Cara organizes a popular golf tournament to raise money for research programs at a local hospital. Last year's event attracted 300 participants and raised over $100,000 for the Women's College Hospital Foundation. In addition, employees select (and participate in) a variety of fundraising initiatives for different charities, including the Canadian Breast Cancer Foundation and the Daily Bread Food Bank.

Cara's divisions operate their own charitable programs across the country. During the Christmas season, Swiss Chalet outlets donate 50 cents from each holiday dinner to a local charity — the company raised $60,000 through the program last year. The Kelsey's division hosts an annual golf tournament, sponsors minor hockey teams and operates its own foundation ("*Kelsey's for Kids*"), which has raised over $1 million since its inception.

Carlson Wagonlit Travel®

**CARLSON WAGONLIT TRAVEL**
**10 Carlson Court**
**Suite 800**
**Toronto, ON M9W 6L2**

**Tel. 416-679-6443**
**Fax 416-798-1779**
**cwthr-canada@carlson.com**
**http://www.carlsonwagonlit.ca**

**INDUSTRY: TRAVEL AGENCY & TOUR OPERATORS**

***Highlights:***

- Work for an employer that treats employee feedback seriously — this employer improved its vacation policy and added new referral bonuses recently after employee input.
- Get three weeks of paid vacation allowance at this employer and two paid personal days off each year — plus a unique "month off" program where you also get paid for the first week of a month-long leave.
- Give back to your community at an employer that values employee community service — each year, this employer awards a free vacation to the employee who does the most community service.

## *Employer Background*

Carlson Wagonlit Travel is a leading travel management company. Founded in 1994, the company provides individual travel services as well as complete travel and conference management services for some of the country's largest companies.

For its corporate clients, the company provides travel management services, including travel bookings, hotel reservations and car rentals. The company's conference management business includes complete organizational services for meetings, conferences and special events for customers across the country.

Carlson Wagonlit's personal travel business serves individuals through over 300 retail locations across Canada. The company helps individual customers design personally tailored vacations to destinations around the world. Carlson Wagonlit also operates centralized call centres to provide around-the-clock support for all its clients.

Worldwide, Carlson Wagonlit Travel operates through a network of over 3,000 locations in 141 countries. The company is co-owned by Minneapolis-based Carlson Companies, Inc. and Paris-based Accor Group.

**Workforce at a Glance:** Number of full-time employees: **692**. Worldwide: **20,000**. Percentage of employees who are women: **84**. Of managers: **82**. Percentage of employees who are visible minorities: **35**. Of managers: **15**. Resumes received by their human resources staff in past year: **2,000**. Average employee age: **38**. Years longest-serving employee has worked there: **38**.

***Physical Workplace*** ***Rating: A***

Carlson Wagonlit's physical workplace is rated as **above-average**. Appropriately, for a travel company, Carlson Wagonlit's head office is located close to Toronto's Pearson International Airport (the company operates a shuttle between the two).

Prior to moving to the new location, the company surveyed its employees about where the office should be located. In a thoughtful gesture, the company agreed to subsidize the travel expenses for any employee whose transportation costs increased as a result of the move.

**Physical Workplace at a Glance:** Their **employee lounge and rest areas** feature: comfortable couches; sleep room. For **food and refreshment**, Carlson Wagonlit offers: free snacks; free coffee and tea. The company has an onsite cafeteria. Nearby **amenities** include: variety of restaurants; major shopping mall; fitness facility in the building (with subsidized memberships); airport. For **commuters**, Carlson Wagonlit offers: nearby public transit; transit subsidies; free onsite car parking. Other **work area amenities** include: open-concept workstations; ergonomic workstation design.

***Work Atmosphere & Social*** ***Rating: A+***

Carlson Wagonlit's work atmosphere is rated as **exceptional**. Employees at Carlson Wagonlit enjoy casual dress on Fridays and can listen to radio or music while they are working. There is also a company-subsidized social committee, which has operated since 1999.

Employees enjoy a variety of social events throughout the year, including monthly birthday celebrations, impromptu celebrations for employee weddings and new babies (new parents also receive a resource kit from the company), a summer picnic, a Halloween costume party and a holiday potluck celebration at Christmas.

Carlson Wagonlit also operates an admirable fund that lets employees help co-workers in need. Employees can donate money to the fund, which is used to assist employees whenever they are facing difficult circumstances (e.g. a serious illness in the family). Employees can also donate unused vacation allowance (up to 5 days) to co-workers who need additional time away from the office.

***Health, Financial & Family Benefits*** ***Rating: A***

Carlson Wagonlit's health benefits plan is rated as **above-average**. Their health benefits plan is flexible, meaning that employees can tailor individual plans to their personal circumstances. New employees must wait 90 days before they can enroll in the plan.

**Health Benefits at a Glance:** Carlson Wagonlit's health plan includes the following coverage: dental; orthodontics; eyecare (to $200 every 2 years); extended health benefits; prescription drug; nutrition planning; massage therapy; physiotherapy; alternative therapies; personal and family counselling; employee assistance plan (EAP) for substance abuse/mental health.

The company's salary and financial benefits are rated as **above-average**. To keep pay-levels competitive, Carlson Wagonlit participates in outside salary surveys every 12 months. Individual salaries are reviewed every 12 months. The company offers a group RSP that allows employees to contribute up to 6% of their salary, with matching employer contributions at the rate of 50¢ for each employee dollar contributed.

> **Financial Benefits at a Glance:** Carlson Wagonlit provides a variety of financial benefits, including: life and disability insurance; discounted car leases; discounted company products; signing bonuses for some employees; referral bonuses for some employees (from $250 to $1,000); year-end bonuses (from $1,000 to $20,000 for non-executives).

Carlson Wagonlit's family-friendly benefits are rated as **average**. Employees with pre-school children have access to a daycare facility located nearby. Other family-friendly benefits include: telecommuting and working from home; shortened work week (fewer hours); flexible start and finish hours.

***Vacation & Time Off*** — ***Rating: A***

Carlson Wagonlit's vacation and time off are rated as **above-average**. New employees receive 3 weeks of vacation allowance after their first year, which increases to 4 weeks after 5 years of service. The maximum vacation allowance is 6 weeks for long-serving employees. Employees at Carlson Wagonlit also receive 2 paid personal days off each year, in addition to their regular vacation allowance. Employees at the company can also apply for unpaid leaves of absence. (One employee recently took a 3 month leave for language studies in Spain.)

In addition to its unpaid leave program, Carlson Wagonlit operates a unique "months off program". Under this program, employees can take four weeks off (for any reason) and receive full pay for one week of their leave.

***Employee Communications*** — ***Rating: A+***

Carlson Wagonlit's internal communications program is rated as **exceptional**. To keep employees informed about new developments, Carlson Wagonlit publishes an in-house newsletter. The company also has an intranet site, which keeps employees informed about news and human resource policies that affect their work. An employee satisfaction survey is conducted every 12 months. An outside consultant compiles the survey results for Carlson Wagonlit's management team.

The company recently launched a new feedback program (called "*Great Ideas*"), which awards employees with gift certificates when their suggestions are adopted. As a result of this program, the company has introduced several meaningful new initiatives, including a new referral bonus program (to $1,000) and an extra week of vacation for employees after their 5th year at the company.

The feedback program provides an interesting contrast to many employee surveys. All too often, these surveys ask a multitude of questions on everything other than what's important to employees (e.g. more vacation allowance). Carlson Wagonlit's initiative provides a useful example of how to encourage employees to raise matters that are important to them, not management.

*Performance Management* *Rating: A*

Carlson Wagonlit's performance management program is rated as **above-average**. The company operates a comprehensive performance management program. Every 6 months, employees and managers meet for review sessions. (Managers receive training in how to conduct effective reviews.) During the review, employees and managers review past performance set new goals for the upcoming year. Carlson Wagonlit recognizes exceptional performance with travel coupons (to $1,000), paid vacations to a 5-star resort, restaurant dinners, movie tickets and certificates for massages.

*Training & Skills Development* *Rating: A*

Carlson Wagonlit's training and skills development program is rated as **above-average**. The company provides tuition subsidies for courses related to an employee's current position (100% of tuition). Commendably, Carlson Wagonlit also offers subsidies for courses not related to an employee's current job (50% of tuition). The company assists employees' career development with: reimbursement for professional association dues; career planning; in-house training. The company's in-house training program includes a variety of courses, ranging from technical skills to leadership training.

*Community Involvement* *Rating: A*

Carlson Wagonlit's community involvement program is rated as **above-average**. A very good corporate citizen, Carlson Wagonlit actively supports a variety of local and national charitable initiatives. In the community, Carlson Wagonlit provides support to the United Way, Goodwill and local food banks. To encourage employee involvement, the company also awards a free vacation every year to its top community service employee.

# Cascades

**CASCADES INC.**
**404, boulevard Marie-Victorin**
**Kingsey Falls, QC J0A 1M0**

**Tel. 819-363-5100**
**Fax 819-363-5155**
**info@cascades.com**
**http://www.cascades.com**

**INDUSTRY: PAPER & PAPER PRODUCT MANUFACTURERS**

*Highlights:*

- Get three weeks paid vacation allowance in your first year — and spend part of it at one of the company's condos in Miami or Mount Tremblant.
- Enjoy small town life — and get a $5,000 cheque (plus annual property tax rebates) from this employer when you build a new home there.
- Skate and golf to your heart's content: this employer hosts a summer golf tournament with over 500 players and a winter hockey tournament with over 70 teams from across Canada.

## *Employer Background*

Cascades Inc. is a leading manufacturer of specialized packaging and paper products. From humble beginnings as a small waste collection business, Kingsey Falls-based Cascades has grown to become one the world's leading paper companies, manufacturing a variety of packaging products, tissue paper and fine papers.

Founded in 1964, Cascades operates through three primary sectors, including: packaging products; tissue paper; and fine paper. The packaging products division manufactures containerboard and corrugated packaging products, boxboard cartons and specialty packaging products. The tissue paper segment manufactures bathroom paper, facial tissues, napkins, paper towels and other consumer products. The fine paper division manufactures coated and uncoated paper and specialty graphic arts papers.

Cascades is also one of the largest integrated recycling companies in Canada. The company operates an extensive waste paper collection program that includes large and small companies, government offices, universities and schools across Québec and Eastern Ontario. Through this impressive program, the company recycles over one million tons of paper every year, which is enough to save approximately 20 million trees.

The publicly-traded company has manufacturing facilities in Canada, the United States, Mexico, the United Kingdom, France, Germany and Sweden. Cascades has annual revenues of over $3 billion.

**Workforce at a Glance:** Number of full-time employees: **10,761**. At this location: **85**. Worldwide: **14,063**. Percentage of employees who are women: **15**. Of managers: **10**. Percentage of employees who are visible minorities: **5**. Of managers: **3**. Resumes received by their human resources staff in past year: **5,000**. Weeks of vacation their HR manager took last year: **4**. Average employee age: **39**. Years longest-serving employee has worked there: **37**. Person you should get to know first: **Éric will take you on a tour of the Kingsey Fall production facilities**.

## *Physical Workplace* — *Rating: A*

Cascades' physical workplace is rated as **above-average**. The company is the driving force behind the economic and social development of Kingsey Falls. Employing over half of the town's residents, Cascades' massive operation includes over a dozen facilities, including research and development, manufacturing, maintenance, water treatment, transportation and head office operations.

**Physical Workplace at a Glance:** Their **onsite fitness facility** features: free memberships; treadmills; stationary bikes; stairmasters; rowing machines; weights; instructor-led classes; full-time fitness and health instructor; shower facilities. Their **employee lounge and rest areas** feature: music; television. For **food and refreshment**, Cascades offers: free snacks (including fruit, vegetables and dip); outdoor eating area. Nearby **amenities** include: variety of restaurants; local shops and services; park/wilderness area (Marie-Victorin Park with walking, cycling and canoeing); recreation centre (Sportplex Centre). For **commuters**, Cascades offers: free onsite car parking; secure bicycle parking; within a 15 minute walk for many employees. Other **work area amenities** include: open-concept workstations; ergonomic workstation design; plant life that is tended professionally.

## *Work Atmosphere & Social* — *Rating: A+*

Cascades' work atmosphere is rated as **exceptional**. Employees at Cascades enjoy business casual dress daily and can listen to radio or music while they are working. The company has an on-site concierge service. There is also a company-subsidized social committee, called the '*Social Club Cascades Inc.*', which has operated since 1997.

Every year, the company hosts a number of social events, including an employee Christmas party, a summer pool party, a special party for its administrative staff, and a unique event for new employees, the initiation party. Cascades also owns and operates its own maple sugar shack, where it hosts a springtime celebration for customers and employees.

The company also subsidizes employee hockey, badminton and volleyball teams. In addition, Cascades organizes several employee sports tournaments every year. These include a golf tournament with over 575 participants, an annual hockey tournament that includes over 70 teams from across Canada, as well as summer baseball, floor hockey and volleyball tournaments.

## *Health, Financial & Family Benefits* — *Rating: A+*

Cascades' health benefits plan is rated as **exceptional**. Cascades's health plan also covers employees in their retirement.

**Health Benefits at a Glance:** Cascades' health plan includes the following coverage: dental (80% of eligible costs, with no annual maximum); orthodontics (50% of eligible costs with a lifetime maximum of $1,000); eyecare (to $300 every 2 years); extended health benefits; prescription drug; massage therapy; physiotherapy; personal and family counselling; employee assistance plan (EAP) for substance abuse/mental health.

The company's salary and financial benefits are rated as **exceptional**. To keep pay-levels competitive, Cascades participates in outside salary surveys every 24 months. Individual salaries are reviewed every 12 months. The company offers a group RSP that allows employees to contribute up to 4% of their salary, with matching employer contributions. The company also operates a traditional pension plan where the company makes an annual contribution of up to 5% of an employee's salary, without any contribution from the employee.

**Financial Benefits at a Glance:** Cascades provides an extensive set of financial benefits, including: life and disability insurance; residential subsidy (to $5,000 for building a new home); municipal tax subsidy (a portion of real estate taxes are reimbursed every year); discounted company products; discounted home computers; share purchase plan; profit-sharing plan.

Cascades' family-friendly benefits are rated as **exceptional**. Employees with pre-school children have access to a subsidized daycare facility located onsite. The daycare facility has 75 spaces, employs 18 childcare workers and has a 4-month waiting list for new spaces. For employees who take maternity leave, Cascades provides a top-up to 95% of salary for the first 15 weeks of their leave.

### *Vacation & Time Off* — *Rating: A*

Cascades' vacation and time off are rated as **above-average**. New employees receive 3 weeks of vacation allowance after their first year, which increases to 4 weeks after 5 years of service. The maximum vacation allowance is 7 weeks for long-serving employees. Employees at the company can also apply for unpaid leaves of absence. (Recently, an employee took a one year leave to complete a law degree.)

As part of its benefits plan, employees also have the opportunity to reserve company-owned condominiums and enjoy their vacation in nearby Mont-Tremblant or Miami, Florida.

### *Employee Communications* — *Rating: A+*

Cascades' internal communications program is rated as **exceptional**. To keep employees informed about new developments, Cascades publishes an in-house newsletter (called *The Cascadeur*). To solicit feedback from employees, the company operates a traditional suggestion box program and an email suggestion box. An employee satisfaction survey is conducted every 24 months. An outside consultant compiles the survey results for Cascades' management team.

### *Performance Management* — *Rating: A*

Cascades' performance management program is rated as **above-average**. The company operates a comprehensive performance management program. Once a year, employees and managers meet for review sessions. (Managers receive training in how to conduct effective reviews.) The review process encourages open communication between employees and managers.

*Training & Skills Development* — *Rating: A+*

Cascades' training and skills development program is rated as **exceptional**. The company provides tuition subsidies for courses related to an employee's current position. Commendably, Cascades also offers subsidies for courses not related to an employee's current job. The company assists employees' career development with: reimbursement for professional association dues; mentoring; in-house training. The company's in-house training program includes a variety of courses, including finance, language, information technology, coaching and technical training.

*Community Involvement* — *Rating: A*

Cascades' community involvement program is rated as **above-average**. A very good corporate citizen, Cascades actively supports a variety of charitable initiatives. Employees take part in the selection of charitable groups assisted by the company. Last year, the company contributed to approximately 200 charitable groups, including: the United Way, Sherbrooke Universtiy, Université du Québec à Trois-Rivières, Ryerson University and numerous local charities in the communities where the company operates.

**CERIDIAN CANADA LTD.**
**125 Garry Street**
**Winnipeg, MB R3C 3P2**

**Tel. 204-975-5918**
**Fax 204-975-5998**
**http://www.ceridian.ca**

**INDUSTRY: OUTSOURCED PAYROLL PROCESSING**

*Highlights:*

- Get recognized by your co-workers for a job well done and receive a company-paid vacation to a southern destination.
- Work for an employer where managers get the interior offices and employees take the window offices with nice views and better light.
- Develop yourself at a company that takes employee training seriously, offering more than 200 in-house courses in both official languages.

## *Employer Background*

Ceridian Canada Ltd. provides payroll and human resources management services to organizations across the country. Founded in 1998, the company serves over 40,000 organizations in virtually every industry. Impressively, the company processes payrolls for over 2.6 million Canadians – approximately 17% of the working population.

Ceridian Canada is a subsidiary of Minneapolis, Minnesota-based Ceridian Corporation. With roots dating back to 1957, the parent company serves more than 135,000 organizations across North America and the United Kingdom. The publicly-traded company has revenues of over $1 billion annually. In Canada, Ceridian has offices in over a dozen cities from coast to coast.

**Workforce at a Glance:** Number of full-time employees: **1,124**. At this location: **272**. New jobs created in Canada in past year: **21**. Percentage of employees who are women: **68**. Of managers: **46**. Resumes received by their human resources staff in past year: **600**. Weeks of vacation their HR manager took last year: **3**. Average employee age: **38**. Years longest-serving employee has worked there: **25**.

## *Physical Workplace* — *Rating: B+*

Ceridian's physical workplace is rated as **average**. The company's head office in Winnipeg is only a short walk to the city's riverside trail and the popular Forks Market. Inside the head office, managers' offices are located in the interior while employee workstations are located around the perimeter for better access to natural light and views of the surrounding city.

**Physical Workplace at a Glance:** Their **employee lounge and rest areas** feature: comfortable couches; music. For **food and refreshment**, Ceridian offers: free coffee and tea. Nearby **amenities** include: variety of restaurants; major shopping mall; park/ wilderness area (Riverwalk and The Forks); recreation centre (YMCA). For **com-**

**muters**, Ceridian offers: subsidized car parking; nearby public transit; secure bicycle parking. Other **work area amenities** include: open-concept workstations; ergonomic workstation design; access to natural light for all employees; plant life that is tended professionally.

### *Work Atmosphere & Social* — *Rating: A*

Ceridian's work atmosphere is rated as **above-average**. Employees at Ceridian enjoy business casual dress daily and can listen to radio or music while they are working. Throughout the year, employees enjoy a number of subsidized events throughout the year, including a year-end party (called the *T4 Party*), seasonal social events, pizza lunches and birthday celebrations.

### *Health, Financial & Family Benefits* — *Rating: A*

Ceridian's health benefits plan is managed by Great-West Life and is rated as **above-average**. Their health benefits plan is flexible, meaning that employees can tailor individual plans to their personal circumstances. Full-time and part-time employees who work more than 18 hours per week are covered by the plan. New employees must wait 90 days before they can enroll in the plan.

**Health Benefits at a Glance:** Ceridian's health plan includes the following coverage: dental (100% of eligible costs, to $2,000 each year); orthodontics (60% of eligible costs with a lifetime maximum of $3,000); eyecare (to $200 every 2 years); extended health benefits; prescription drug; massage therapy; physiotherapy; alternative therapies; personal and family counselling; employee assistance plan (EAP) for substance abuse/mental health; wellness committee.

The company's salary and financial benefits are rated as **above-average**. To keep pay-levels competitive, Ceridian participates in outside salary surveys every 6 months. Individual salaries are reviewed every 6 months. The company operates a traditional pension plan.

**Financial Benefits at a Glance:** Ceridian provides a variety of financial benefits, including: life and disability insurance; low-interest home loans; discounted home computers; share purchase plan; profit-sharing plan; referral bonuses for some employees (from $500 to $1,000); year-end bonuses.

Ceridian's family-friendly benefits are rated as **above-average**. Employees with pre-school children have access to a daycare facility located nearby. For employees who take maternity leave, Ceridian provides a top-up to 95% of salary for the first 6 weeks of their leave. The company also provides an adoption benefit of up to $5,000 per child. Other family-friendly benefits include: reduced summer hours; telecommuting and working from home; compressed work week (same hours, fewer days); flexible start and finish hours.

### *Vacation & Time Off* — *Rating: A*

Ceridian's vacation and time off are rated as **above-average**. New employees receive 3 weeks of vacation allowance after their first year, which increases to 4 weeks after 10 years of service. The maximum vacation allowance is 5 weeks for long-serving employees. Employees at the company can also apply for unpaid leaves of absence.

### *Employee Communications* *Rating: A*

Ceridian's internal communications program is rated as **above-average**. To keep employees informed about new developments, Ceridian publishes an in-house newsletter (called *Masterfile*), which is available online. The company also has an intranet site, which keeps employees informed about news and human resource policies that affect their work. An in-house employee satisfaction survey is conducted by having employees complete an online questionnaire every 12 months.

### *Performance Management* *Rating: A*

Ceridian's performance management program is rated as **above-average**. The company operates a thorough performance management program. Every 3 months, employees and managers meet for review sessions. (Managers receive training in how to conduct effective reviews.) Ceridian uses a 360-degree feedback process to gather additional performance-related information from co-workers, supervisors and employees. Ceridian recognizes exceptional performance with gift certificates and unique awards.

The company also operates a unique peer recognition program. Employees can nominate co-workers for the annual "*President's Club Award*", which includes a paid vacation to a southern destination.

### *Training & Skills Development* *Rating: A*

Ceridian's training and skills development program is rated as **above-average**. The company provides tuition subsidies for courses related to an employee's current position (100% of tuition to $2,000). Commendably, Ceridian also offers subsidies for courses not related to an employee's current job. The company assists employees' career development with: reimbursement for professional association dues; in-house training; online training; career planning. Employees can develop personalized career development plans using a career planning tool available on the company's intranet site. The company's extensive in-house training program includes over 200 courses, with most available in English and French.

### *Community Involvement* *Rating: A*

Ceridian's community involvement program is rated as **above-average**. A very good corporate citizen, Ceridian actively supports a variety of local and national charitable initiatives. Every year, Ceridian employees support charitable groups, arts organizations and local United Way campaigns across the country. Employees take part in the selection of charitable groups assisted by the company. Employees at Ceridian receive paid time off to volunteer at local charities.

**CGI GROUP INC.**
**1130, rue Sherbrooke ouest**
**5e étage**
**Montréal, QC H3A 2M8**

**Tel. 514-841-3200**
**Fax 514-841-3435**
**http://www.cgi.com**

**INDUSTRY: INFORMATION TECHNOLOGY CONSULTING FIRMS**

*Highlights:*

- Build your technology career at Canada's largest (and fastest growing) IT consulting firm — this employer is within striking distance of becoming one of the world's largest players in its field.
- Get three weeks paid vacation allowance to start — plus have your previous work experience considered in setting your overall vacation entitlement.
- Develop yourself at an employer that provides generous tuition subsidies and extensive in-house training — a key strength in an industry that depends on brains.

## *Employer Background*

CGI Group Inc. is the largest full-service information technology consulting company in Canada. Founded in 1976, the company is primarily focused on large-scale systems integration and outsourcing contracts. CGI targets niche markets where it has specialized expertise, including financial services and telecommunications (its two largest sectors), manufacturing, retail, distribution and government, including public utilities and healthcare.

CGI is North America's fourth-largest information technology consulting company. The Montréal-based company maintains over 60 offices across Canada, the United States and Europe, providing a full range of information technology services to over 3,500 clients worldwide.

With annual revenues of over $2.1 billion, the publicly-traded company has an impressive record of continuous growth. Last year, CGI acquired Montréal-based Cognicase Inc. and nearly doubled its employees. The company also landed several major new contracts, including a partnership with Canada Post to manage its new "*Innovapost*" service.

**Workforce at a Glance:** Number of full-time employees: **16,077**. At this location: **6,694**. Worldwide: **19,518**. New jobs created in Canada in past year: **7,559**. Percentage of employees who are women: **34**. Of managers: **31**. Percentage of employees who are visible minorities: **10**. Of managers: **5**. Resumes received by their human resources staff in past year: **10,400**. Average employee age: **39**.

## *Physical Workplace* — *Rating: B+*

CGI's physical workplace is rated as **average**. Over the past year, many of Montréal's 6,600 employees have moved into the company's new 25-storey CGI

E-Commerce Place, situated close to the company's corporate office downtown. (Previously, the employees were dispersed across 15 offices around Montréal.)

**Physical Workplace at a Glance:** Their **onsite fitness facility** features: subsidized memberships; weights; instructor-led classes (including pilates, yoga and boxing). For **food and refreshment**, CGI offers: free coffee and tea. Nearby **amenities** include: variety of restaurants; local shops and services; major shopping mall; park/ wilderness area (Mont Royal and the McGill University grounds). For **commuters**, CGI offers: nearby public transit. Other **work area amenities** include: open-concept workstations; ergonomic workstation design; temperature control at individual workstations (at the new E-Commerce Place); plant life that is tended professionally; comfortable couches.

## *Work Atmosphere & Social* — *Rating: B+*

CGI's work atmosphere is rated as **average**. There is a company-subsidized social committee that has operated since 1976. Each year, the social club organizes several events for employees, including a summer golf tournament and an employee Christmas party. The company sponsors two employee hockey teams (called "*Thunder*" and "*Storm*") and enters an ice canoe racing team in the famous Québec Winter Carnival.

## *Health, Financial & Family Benefits* — *Rating: A*

CGI's health benefits plan is rated as **above-average**. Their health benefits plan is flexible, meaning that employees can tailor individual plans to their personal circumstances.

**Health Benefits at a Glance:** CGI's health plan includes the following coverage: dental; eyecare; extended health benefits; prescription drug; nutrition planning; massage therapy; physiotherapy; alternative therapies; personal and family counselling; employee assistance plan (EAP) for substance abuse/mental health.

The company's salary and financial benefits are rated as **above-average**. To keep pay-levels competitive, CGI participates in outside salary surveys every 6 months. Individual salaries are reviewed every 12 months.

**Financial Benefits at a Glance:** CGI provides a variety of financial benefits, including: life and disability insurance; discounted car leases; share purchase plan (with matching company contributions); profit-sharing plan; referral bonuses for some employees (to $2,000).

CGI's family-friendly benefits are rated as **average**. Employees with pre-school children have access to a daycare facility located nearby. Other family-friendly benefits include: telecommuting and working from home; compressed work week (same hours, fewer days); shortened work week (fewer hours); flexible start and finish hours.

## *Vacation & Time Off* — *Rating: A*

CGI's vacation and time off are rated as **above-average**. New employees receive 3 weeks of vacation allowance after their first year, which increases to 4 weeks after 10 years of service. The maximum vacation allowance is 5 weeks for long-serving employees. (CGI also considers work experience outside the company when establishing vacation allowance for new employees.) Employees at the company can also apply for unpaid leaves of absence.

*Employee Communications* *Rating: A*

CGI's internal communications program is rated as **above-average**. To keep employees informed about new developments, CGI publishes an in-house newsletter (called *Perspectives*). The company also has an intranet site, which keeps employees informed about news and human resource policies that affect their work. An in-house employee satisfaction survey is conducted every 12 months.

*Performance Management* *Rating: A*

CGI's performance management program is rated as **above-average**. The company operates a well-designed performance management program. Once a year, employees and managers meet for review sessions. (Managers receive training in how to conduct effective reviews.) Informal meetings take place throughout the year. Employees also receive feedback after each assignment.

*Training & Skills Development* *Rating: A*

CGI's training and skills development program is rated as **above-average**. The company provides tuition subsidies for courses related to an employee's current position (100% of tuition). Commendably, CGI also offers subsidies for courses not related to an employee's current job (100% of tuition). The company assists employees' career development with: reimbursement for professional association dues; mentoring; in-house training; IT reference materials.

*Community Involvement* *Rating: B+*

CGI's community involvement program is rated as **average**. A good corporate citizen, CGI actively supports a variety of local charitable initiatives. Across Canada, CGI supports a variety of community initiatives, including local United Way campaigns. Many of the company's executives also serve on the boards of charitable organizations.

**CO-OPERATIVE TRUST COMPANY OF CANADA**
**333 - 3rd Avenue North**
**Saskatoon, SK S7K 2M2**

**Tel. 306-956-1890**
**Fax 306-652-7614**
**hr@co-operativetrust.ca**
**http://www.co-operativetrust.ca**

**INDUSTRY: CREDIT UNIONS**

*Highlights:*

- Get three weeks of paid vacation allowance in your first year — plus five paid personal days off.
- Keep your career on track even while you're on maternity leave — this employer interviews employees who are taking maternity leave for internal promotions.
- Work for an employer that allows an employee committee to set the questions for their annual employee satisfaction survey.

## *Employer Background*

Co-operative Trust Company of Canada provides financial products and services to credit unions across the country. Founded in 1952, Saskatoon-based Co-operative Trust Company of Canada was originally set up to provide trustee services and long-term mortgages to credit unions across Saskatchewan. In 1967, the company expanded to serve credit unions and their members across the country.

Today, Co-operative Trust provides credit unions with a complete line of financial services, including deposits, mortgages, lease financing, credit cards, and personal and corporate trust services. The company has over $10 billion in assets under management and a track record of innovation in the financial services industry — from electronic mortgage applications to the first mutual funds for credit union members.

Co-operative Trust serves over 76,000 customers through 650 credit unions across Canada. The company's products are marketed to individuals through member brokers and electronic banking services.

**Workforce at a Glance:** Number of full-time employees: **201**. New jobs created in Canada in past year: **7**. Percentage of employees who are women: **80**. Of managers: **42**. Percentage of employees who are visible minorities: **3**. Resumes received by their human resources staff in past year: **300**. Weeks of vacation their HR manager took last year: **4**. Average employee age: **38**. Years longest-serving employee has worked there: **42**. Car the president drives: **2003 Nissan Murano SE**. Where it's parked in the lot: **reserved spot in front**.

## *Physical Workplace* — *Rating: B+*

Co-operative Trust's physical workplace is rated as **average**. The majority of Co-operative Trust's employees work at its head office in downtown Saskatoon.

The location is adjacent to a riverside park and directly across the river from the University of Saskatchewan.

**Physical Workplace at a Glance:** For **food and refreshment**, Co-operative Trust offers: outdoor eating area; top floor cafeteria (location chosen by employees) offers great views of the surrounding city. The company has an onsite cafeteria that features: subsidized meals (a turkey sandwich costs $4.75). Nearby **amenities** include: variety of restaurants; major shopping mall; fitness facility; park/wilderness area (Kinsmen Park and the Riverbank Park); recreation centre (YMCA). For **commuters**, Co-operative Trust offers: nearby public transit; free onsite car parking; subsidized car parking; secure bicycle parking. Other **work area amenities** include: open-concept workstations; access to natural light for all employees; ergonomic workstation design; shower facilities for those who bicycle to work.

## *Work Atmosphere & Social* — *Rating: B+*

Co-operative Trust's work atmosphere is rated as **average**. Employees at Co-operative Trust enjoy business casual dress daily. There is also a company-subsidized social committee.

The committee helps to organize a variety of events throughout the year, including a Christmas dinner and dance, a summer family barbeque, an annual staff meeting and dinner, and quarterly coffee-and-cake parties to recognize long-serving employees. The company also subsidizes softball and beach volleyball teams, a women's golf league and an annual employee hockey tournament.

## *Health, Financial & Family Benefits* — *Rating: A*

Co-operative Trust's health benefits plan is managed by Co-operators Life and is rated as **above-average**. Full-time and part-time employees are covered by the plan.

**Health Benefits at a Glance:** Co-operative Trust's health plan includes the following coverage: dental (85% of eligible costs, to $1,000 each year); orthodontics (50% of eligible costs, to $1,000 each year); eyecare (to $200 every 2 years); prescription drug; extended health benefits; physiotherapy; massage therapy; alternative therapies; personal and family counselling; employee assistance plan (EAP) for substance abuse/mental health.

The company's salary and financial benefits are rated as **above-average**. To keep pay-levels competitive, Co-operative Trust participates in outside salary surveys every 12 months. Individual salaries are reviewed every 12 months. The company operates a traditional pension plan where Co-operative Trust makes a contribution equal to 6% of each employee's salary to their plan each year.

**Financial Benefits at a Glance:** Co-operative Trust provides a variety of financial benefits, including: life and disability insurance; low-interest home loans; subsidized home insurance; discounted company products; year-end bonuses (from $1,600 to $10,000 for non-executives).

Co-operative Trust's family-friendly benefits are rated as **above-average**. Employees with pre-school children have access to a daycare facility located nearby. For employees who take maternity leave, Co-operative Trust provides a top-up to 100% of salary for the first 2 weeks of their leave. The company also ensures that employees absent from the office on maternity leave are interviewed for internal promotions. Other family-friendly benefits include: flexible start and finish hours; shortened work week (fewer hours); compressed work week (same hours, fewer days); telecommuting and working from home; reduced summer hours.

### *Vacation & Time Off* — *Rating: A*

Co-operative Trust's vacation and time off are rated as **above-average**. New employees receive 3 weeks of vacation allowance after their first year, which increases to 4 weeks after 10 years of service. The maximum vacation allowance is 6 weeks for long-serving employees. Employees at Co-operative Trust also receive 5 paid personal days off each year, in addition to their regular vacation allowance. Employees at the company can also apply for unpaid leaves of absence.

### *Employee Communications* — *Rating: A*

Co-operative Trust's internal communications program is rated as **above-average**. To keep employees informed about new developments, Co-operative Trust publishes an in-house newsletter. The company also has an intranet site, which keeps employees informed about news and human resource policies that affect their work. To solicit feedback from employees, the company operates an email suggestion box. An employee satisfaction survey is conducted periodically. An outside consultant compiles the survey results for Co-operative Trust's management team. The company also conducts an employee satisfaction survey every year. In a thoughtful initiative, an employee committee works closely with an outside consultant to design and manage the survey. This inclusive approach helps to ensure that the survey deals with the issues that are important to employees.

### *Performance Management* — *Rating: B+*

Co-operative Trust's performance management program is rated as **average**. The company operates a formal performance management program. Once a year, employees and managers meet for review sessions. (Managers receive training in how to conduct effective reviews.) Employees can provide feedback through the company's annual survey and a new 360-degree feedback process.

### *Training & Skills Development* — *Rating: B+*

Co-operative Trust's training and skills development program is rated as **average**. The company provides tuition subsidies for courses related to an employee's current position (100% of tuition). Co-operative Trust offers bonuses to employees who successfully complete certain professional accreditation programs and courses. The company assists employees' career development with: in-house training; reimbursement for professional association dues.

### *Community Involvement* — *Rating: A+*

Co-operative Trust's community involvement program is rated as **exceptional**. An outstanding corporate citizen, Co-operative Trust actively supports a variety of local and national charitable initiatives. The company is a member of the *Imagine* program operated by the Canadian Centre for Philanthropy. The program commits members to donating 1% of their pre-tax profits to charities. Employees take part in the selection of charitable groups assisted by the company. Employees at Co-operative Trust receive paid time off to volunteer at local charities. Last year, the company contributed to approximately 75 charitable groups.

**CO-OPERATORS LIFE INSURANCE COMPANY**
**1920 College Avenue**
**Regina, SK S4P 1C4**

the co-operators
A Better Place For You™

**Tel. 306-347-6200**
**Fax 306-347-6806**
**cooplife_hr@cooperators.ca**
**http://www.cooperators.ca**

**INDUSTRY: LIFE INSURANCE COMPANIES**

*Highlights:*

- Work for an employer that offers a 36-hour work week and a popular "earned days off" program that lets you work a little longer each day in exchange for every second Friday off.
- Take advantage of great alternative work options and generous maternity top-up payments (100% for 15 weeks) designed to assist employees with young families.
- Make a difference in your community at an employer that gives you a paid day off every year to volunteer at a local charity.

## *Employer Background*

Co-operators Life Insurance Company (part of Guelph, Ontario-based The Co-operators Group Limited) provides individual and group life insurance and retirement products. The story of Regina-based Co-operators Life Insurance Company is the stuff of Prairie legend. The company started in 1945, when 16 Saskatchewan Wheat Pool employees began selling small life insurance policies to the hard-scrabble farmers who sold their grain to the Pool.

From humble beginnings, Co-op Life has grown into one of Canada's leading life insurance companies, providing financial security to over 500,000 policyholders nationwide. The company sells a variety of life and health insurance products to individuals and group policyholders. Most recently, Co-op Life has become one of Canada's leading providers of travel insurance.

These are challenging times for providers of life insurance and group benefits. New competitors, such as Canada's large banks, are aggressively courting customers to develop market share. Demutualization — the transformation of policyholder-owned insurers into public companies owned by shareholders — has also sharpened competition in the industry.

True to its prairie roots, Co-op Life has overcome these challenges by staying close to the customers who built the company. The insurance company sells its policies through a unique distribution system of franchised agents, independent brokers and a joint venture with CUMIS Insurance, which sells life insurance policies to 4.5 million credit union members.

Co-op Life manages assets of nearly $1 billion and posted record revenues of over $552 million last year.

**Workforce at a Glance:** Number of full-time employees: **534**. At this location: **507**. New jobs created in Canada in past year: **38**. Percentage of employees who are women: **79**. Of managers: **53**. Percentage of employees who are visible minorities: **6**. Of managers: **1.6**. Resumes received by their human resources staff in past year: **863**. Average employee age: **38**.

### *Physical Workplace* — *Rating: A*

Co-op Life's physical workplace is rated as **above-average**. Located in downtown Regina, the head office includes two five-storey buildings connected by a large lobby and employee lounge. The company recently renovated much of its space and retained an ergonomic consultant to review all work areas. All employee work areas are wheelchair accessible.

**Physical Workplace at a Glance:** Their **onsite fitness facility** features: subsidized memberships; treadmills; stationary bikes; stairmasters; weights; instructor-led classes (aerobics); music and television; shower facilities. Their **employee lounge and rest areas** feature: comfortable couches; sleep room; internet kiosks. For **food and refreshment**, Co-op Life offers: outdoor eating area. The company has an onsite cafeteria that features: subsidized meals (turkey sandwich costs $1.90); healthy menu items; special diet menus. Nearby **amenities** include: variety of restaurants; major shopping mall; park/wilderness area (Wascana Park). For **commuters**, Co-op Life offers: nearby public transit; subsidized car parking; secure bicycle parking. Other **work area amenities** include: open-concept workstations; ergonomic workstation design.

### *Work Atmosphere & Social* — *Rating: B+*

Co-op Life's work atmosphere is rated as **average**. Employees at Co-op Life enjoy business casual dress daily and can listen to radio or music while they are working. (In the summer, employees can wear casual dress shorts to work.) There is also a company-subsidized social committee, which has operated since 1960.

The committee organizes numerous social events throughout the year, including a golf tournament, a Christmas party (with a separate party for employees' children) and summer barbeques. The company also has an annual staff meeting that includes a day of presentations by management and an evening of socializing over food and games.

### *Health, Financial & Family Benefits* — *Rating: A*

Co-op Life's health benefits plan is managed by the company itself and is rated as **above-average**. Their health benefits plan is flexible, meaning that employees can tailor individual plans to their personal circumstances. There is no waiting period before new employees are eligible for coverage.

**Health Benefits at a Glance:** Co-op Life's health plan includes the following coverage: dental (80% of eligible costs, to $2,500 each year); orthodontics (50% of eligible costs, to $2,500 each year); eyecare (to $150 every 2 years); prescription drug; extended health benefits; physiotherapy; massage therapy; personal and family counselling; employee assistance plan (EAP) for substance abuse/mental health.

The company's salary and financial benefits are rated as **above-average**. To keep pay-levels competitive, Co-op Life participates in outside salary surveys every 6 months. Individual salaries are reviewed every 24 months. The company operates a traditional pension plan where Co-op Life makes a contribution equal to 7.5% of each employee's salary to their plan each year.

**Financial Benefits at a Glance:** Co-op Life provides a variety of financial benefits, including: life and disability insurance; share purchase plan; profit-sharing plan; discounted company products; year-end bonuses (from $12,000 to $13,300 for non-executives).

Co-op Life's family-friendly benefits are rated as **above-average**. Employees with pre-school children have access to a daycare facility located nearby. For employees who take maternity leave, Co-op Life provides a generous top-up to 100% of salary for the first 15 weeks of their leave. Other family-friendly benefits include: flexible start and finish hours; shortened work week (fewer hours); compressed work week (same hours, fewer days); telecommuting and working from home.

### *Vacation & Time Off* — *Rating: A*

Co-op Life's vacation and time off are rated as **above-average**. New employees receive 3 weeks of vacation allowance after their first year, which increases to 4 weeks after 10 years of service. The maximum vacation allowance is 6 weeks for long-serving employees. Employees at the company can also apply for unpaid leaves of absence.

Employees at Co-op Life also take advantage of a 36-hour work week, as well as an enlightened "earned days off" program. By working a little longer each day, employees are able to take every second Friday off.

### *Employee Communications* — *Rating: A*

Co-op Life's internal communications program is rated as **above-average**. To keep employees informed about new developments, Co-op Life publishes an in-house newsletter (called *The LifeLine*). The company also has an intranet site, which keeps employees informed about news and human resource policies that affect their work. An employee satisfaction survey is conducted every 36 months. An outside consultant compiles the survey results for Co-op Life's management team.

### *Performance Management* — *Rating: B+*

Co-op Life's performance management program is rated as **average**. The company operates a formal performance management program. Once a year, employees and managers meet for review sessions. (Managers receive training in how to conduct effective reviews.) Along with generous bonuses, top performing employees can receive corporate box seats to "Regina Pats" hockey games.

In addition to the annual reviews, the company welcomes all new employees with an orientation workshop that includes presentations by senior management. The company is also one of the few far-sighted employers in this book that conducts exit interviews with departing employees.

***Training & Skills Development*** ***Rating: A+***

Co-op Life's training and skills development program is rated as **exceptional**. The company provides tuition subsidies for courses related to an employee's current position (100% of tuition). Commendably, Co-op Life also offers subsidies for courses not related to an employee's current job (100% of tuition). Co-op Life offers bonuses to employees who successfully complete certain professional accreditation programs and courses. The company assists employees' career development with: reimbursement for professional association dues; career planning; in-house training. Employees also receive paid time off to study for upcoming exams. Employees who complete at least two courses receive a $75 dinner certificate.

***Community Involvement*** ***Rating: A+***

Co-op Life's community involvement program is rated as **exceptional**. An outstanding corporate citizen, Co-op Life actively supports a variety of local and national charitable initiatives. Co-op Life is a member of the Imagine initiative, donating 1% of its pre-tax profits to charitable causes. Employees take part in the selection of charitable groups assisted by the company. Employees at Co-op Life receive paid time off (1 day each year) to volunteer at local charities. Last year, Co-op Life's employees volunteered over 2,000 hours on charitable projects in the community (about 3.7 hours per employee).

Throughout the year, the company and its employees support numerous community organizations, including the Regina Symphony Orchestra, the Regina Folk Festival, local hospitals, a sexual assault centre, AIDS Regina, the Salvation Army, the United Way and many others. (The company made contributions to over 70 charitable groups last year.)

In addition, the company regularly purchases tickets to local events, including Globe Theatre productions and the Saskatchewan Roughriders, and distributes the tickets to its employees.

**CUETS**

CREDIT UNION ELECTRONIC TRANSACTION SERVICES

**CREDIT UNION ELECTRONIC TRANSACTION SERVICES INC.**
**2055 Albert Street**
**7th Floor, North Tower**
**Regina, SK S4P 3G8**

**Tel. 306-566-1269**
**Fax 306-566-7906**
**humanresources@cuets.ca**
**http://www.cuets.ca**

**INDUSTRY: DATA PROCESSING & PREPARATION SERVICES**

*Highlights:*

- Take three full weeks of paid vacation allowance during your first year (most require you to work a year first).
- Get four weeks of paid vacation allowance after only two years on the job — plus the ability to buy (or sell) an extra week of vacation each year.
- Continue your studies with this employer's generous tuition subsidies — available even to part-time employees.

## *Employer Background*

CUETS manages credit cards and electronic transactions for credit unions, banks and other financial services providers.

Founded in 1981, CUETS serves 98% of credit unions across Canada and is expanding beyond its traditional base to other financial services providers. The company provides customer service and transaction processing services for the new MasterCard issued by President's Choice Financial.

With the exploding use of debit cards and other forms of e-commerce, CUETS has seen its business expand dramatically. The company created 53 new positions last year. In addition to the Regina head office, CUETS operates a bilingual customer service centre in Winnipeg.

**Workforce at a Glance:** Number of full-time employees: **400**. At this location: **296**. New jobs created in Canada in past year: **53**. Percentage of employees who are women: **70**. Of managers: **55**. Percentage of employees who are visible minorities: **10**. Of managers: **10**. Resumes received by their human resources staff in past year: **2,000**. Weeks of vacation their HR manager took last year: **4**. Average employee age: **34**. Years longest-serving employee has worked there: **21**. Car the president drives: **Pick-up truck (hey, it's Saskatchewan)**. Where it's parked in the lot: **with everyone else**.

## *Physical Workplace* — *Rating: A*

CUETS' physical workplace is rated as **above-average**. Located near the downtown core, the head office was recently renovated to feature more open-concept work areas to ensure employees have plenty of natural light. Managers work in open offices and all employees have access to quiet rooms.

**Physical Workplace at a Glance:** Their **employee lounge and rest areas** feature: comfortable couches; music; television; pool table; shuffleboard (practice for the Saskatchewan tradition of curling). For **food and refreshment**, CUETS offers: free coffee and tea; outdoor eating area; barbeque. The company has an onsite cafeteria that features: healthy menu items; special diet menus. Nearby **amenities** include: fitness facility (with subsidized memberships); variety of restaurants; one of the city's best pubs; park/wilderness area (Victoria Park and Wascana Park). For **commuters**, CUETS offers: nearby public transit; free onsite car parking; secure bicycle parking. Other **work area amenities** include: ergonomic workstation design; plant life that is tended professionally.

### *Work Atmosphere & Social* — *Rating: B+*

CUETS' work atmosphere is rated as **average**. Employees at CUETS enjoy business casual dress daily. There is also a company-subsidized social committee, which has operated since 1993.

Throughout the year, CUETS organizes numerous events to celebrate holidays and employee accomplishments. In addition to a Christmas party (where the company provides employees with cab fare home), there are celebrations at local pubs, themed events (e.g. Wacky Hat day), holiday celebrations, dinner events and a spring employee convention that includes business speakers as well an evening of dining and entertainment.

### *Health, Financial & Family Benefits* — *Rating: B+*

CUETS' health benefits plan is managed by Maritime Life and is rated as **average**. Full-time and part-time employees who work more than 15 hours per week are covered by the plan.

**Health Benefits at a Glance:** CUETS' health plan includes the following coverage: dental; orthodontics; eyecare (to $200 every 2 years); prescription drug; nutrition planning; massage therapy; physiotherapy; alternative therapies; extended health benefits; personal and family counselling.

The company's salary and financial benefits are rated as **average**. To keep pay-levels competitive, CUETS participates in outside salary surveys every 12 months. Individual salaries are reviewed every 12 months. The company operates a traditional pension plan. The company also completes its own marketplace survey every 4 months. CUETS operates a traditional pension plan.

**Financial Benefits at a Glance:** CUETS provides a variety of financial benefits, including: life and disability insurance; discounted home computers; low-interest home loans; referral bonuses for some employees (from $300 to $500); year-end bonuses (to $10,000 for non-executives).

CUETS' family-friendly benefits are rated as **average**. Employees with preschool children have access to a daycare facility located nearby. Other family-friendly benefits include: flexible start and finish hours; shortened work week (fewer hours); telecommuting and working from home.

### *Vacation & Time Off* — *Rating: A*

CUETS' vacation and time off are rated as **above-average**. New employees receive 3 weeks of vacation allowance after their first year, which increases to 4 weeks after 2 years of service. The maximum vacation allowance is 5 weeks for long-serving employees. Employees can also purchase (or sell) one additional week of vacation each year. Employees at the company can also apply for unpaid leaves of absence.

*Employee Communications* *Rating: A*

CUETS' internal communications program is rated as **above-average**. To keep employees informed about new developments, CUETS publishes an in-house newsletter. The company also has a well-developed intranet site, which keeps employees informed about news and human resource policies that affect their work. To solicit feedback from employees, the company operates an email suggestion box. An employee satisfaction survey is conducted every 12 months. An outside consultant compiles the survey results for CUETS' management team.

*Performance Management* *Rating: B+*

CUETS' performance management program is rated as **average**. The company operates a comprehensive performance management program. Once a year, employees and managers meet for review sessions. (Managers receive training in how to conduct effective reviews.)

*Training & Skills Development* *Rating: A*

CUETS' training and skills development program is rated as **above-average**. The company provides tuition subsidies for courses related to an employee's current position (100% of tuition). Commendably, CUETS also offers subsidies for courses not related to an employee's current job (100% of tuition). The company assists employees' career development with: in-house training; mentoring; career planning; reimbursement for professional association dues.

CUETS also provides tuition subsidies (50% of tuition) for part-time employees. In addition, employees can take advantage of full tuition subsidies for French language courses.

*Community Involvement* *Rating: A+*

CUETS' community involvement program is rated as **exceptional**. An outstanding corporate citizen, CUETS actively supports a variety of local and national charitable initiatives. Employees take part in the selection of charitable groups assisted by the company. Employees at CUETS receive paid time off to volunteer at local charities. Last year, the company contributed to approximately 15 charitable groups, including: the United Way, Canadian Cancer Society, Computers for Kids Canada and the Salvation Army.

Employees also volunteer and host fundraising events for numerous community initiatives every year. (In a recent employee survey, CUETS' strong community involvement program was cited as a key workplace benefit.

**CRYSTAL DECISIONS, INC.**
**840 Cambie Street**
**Vancouver, BC V6B 4J2**

**Tel. 604-681-3435**
**Fax 604-691-2934**
**http://www.crystaldecisions.com**

crystal decisions

A SEAGATE COMPANY

**INDUSTRY: SOFTWARE COMPANIES**

*Highlights:*

- Take a ski break at this employer's cabin in Whistler — available to employees for only $20 per night.
- Build your career at a fast-growing Canadian software company whose products are used by millions of people around the world — and have won the respect of the industry's largest players.
- Develop yourself at an employer that believes strongly in continuing education — employees can receive between $5,000 and $10,000 for part-time and full-time studies.

## *Employer Background*

Crystal Decisions, Inc. develops industry-leading reporting, analysis and information delivery software. Founded in 1984, the company's software enables businesses (as well as their employees and customers) to easily access, manage and make sense of large amounts of data. The company's software is used by millions of people in thousands of companies worldwide.

Crystal Reports, the company's award-winning flagship tool, is used as a key component of nearly 345 software packages from companies such as Microsoft, PeopleSoft, and SAP. Developing successful alliances with these industry giants has led to extraordinary growth for Crystal Decisions.

Last year, Crystal Decisions passed a significant milestone when it reached 14 million registered customers. The privately-held company posted annual revenues of over $341 million — the best year in its history — and recorded its tenth consecutive quarter of growth. In an industry that has been short on good news lately, Crystal Decisions' success is even more remarkable.

**Workforce at a Glance:** Number of full-time employees: **924**. At this location: **893**. Worldwide: **1,627**. New jobs created in Canada in past year: **78**. Percentage of employees who are women: **33**. Of managers: **28**. Resumes received by their human resources staff in past year: **21,434**. Weeks of vacation their HR manager took last year: **3**. Average employee age: **33**. Years longest-serving employee has worked there: **17**. Person you should get to know first: **if you ask him nicely, Rob in Facilities will set up your desk with all the extras**.

## *Physical Workplace* — *Rating: A+*

Crystal Decisions' physical workplace is rated as **exceptional**. When choosing its current location, the company surveyed employees about where they would like to work. As a result, the company located its head office near the trendy Yaletown district. The office is only a short walk away from the popular Robson Street area and the False Creek waterfront, where employees can go for a lunch-hour jog (or rollerblade) along the seawall.

The downtown location makes it easy for Crystal Decisions' employees to avoid taking the car to work — the overwhelming majority bus, bike or carpool to the office. (Employees regularly participate in Vancouver's "*Commuter Challenge*", a week-long competition that encourages alternative transportation to reduce congestion and pollution.)

**Physical Workplace at a Glance:** Their **onsite fitness facility** features: free memberships; treadmills; stationary bikes; stairmasters; rowing machines; weights; instructor-led classes (e.g. pilates and yoga); shower facilities. Their **employee lounge and rest areas** feature: sleep room; comfortable couches; fireplace; television; video games (latest game is Gran Turismo); pool table; table hockey; foosball; cappuccino machine. For **food and refreshment**, Crystal Decisions offers: free snacks (including daily fresh fruit, herbal teas, hot chocolate, breakfast cereal and soup); free coffee and tea; outdoor eating area; barbeque. Nearby **amenities** include: variety of restaurants; major shopping mall; fitness facility; park/wilderness area (David Lam Park and the False Creek Seawall); recreation centre (The Roundhouse Community Centre). For **commuters**, Crystal Decisions offers: nearby public transit; transit subsidies; secure bicycle parking. Other **work area amenities** include: open-concept workstations; access to natural light for all employees; ergonomic workstation design; windows that open; plant life that is tended professionally.

## *Work Atmosphere & Social* — *Rating: A+*

Crystal Decisions' work atmosphere is rated as **exceptional**. Employees at Crystal Decisions enjoy casual dress daily and can listen to radio or music while they are working.

Every few months, individual departments host their own "*Fun Day*" for employees. In the past, employees have used the day to attend local wine festivals, enjoy a day of skiing, and even volunteer in the community (stocking shelves at a food bank or painting houses for Habitat for Humanity). Throughout the year, employees are treated to free lunches to celebrate birthdays and other special occasions.

Crystal Decisions also hosts regular social events, including an annual Christmas party (the aptly-named "*Crystal Ball*"), annual sales meetings (with live music), quarterly social events and regular barbeques. Last year, the company even rented six movie theatres for a special advance screening of the latest Harry Potter film.

## *Health, Financial & Family Benefits* — *Rating: A*

Crystal Decisions' health benefits plan is managed by Great-West Life and is rated as **above-average**. Full-time and part-time employees who work more than 20 hours per week are covered by the plan. New employees must wait 90 days before they can enroll in the plan.

**Health Benefits at a Glance:** Crystal Decisions' health plan includes the following coverage: dental (90% of eligible costs, to $2,500 each year); orthodontics (50% of eligible costs, to $2,000 each year); eyecare (to $250 every 2 years); prescription drug; extended health benefits; massage therapy; physiotherapy; personal and family counselling.

The company's salary and financial benefits are rated as **above-average**. To keep pay-levels competitive, Crystal Decisions participates in outside salary surveys every 12 months. Individual salaries are reviewed every 6 months. The company offers a group RSP that allows employees to contribute up to 6% of their salary, with matching employer contributions.

**Financial Benefits at a Glance:** Crystal Decisions provides a variety of financial benefits, including: share purchase plan; life and disability insurance; discounted home computers; discounted home Internet access; discounted company products; no fee personal banking; discounted meals at local restaurants; discounted Microsoft products; referral bonuses for some employees (from $1,000 to $2,500).

Crystal Decisions' family-friendly benefits are rated as **average**. Employees with pre-school children have access to a daycare facility located nearby. Other family-friendly benefits include: flexible start and finish hours; shortened work week (fewer hours); compressed work week (same hours, fewer days); telecommuting and working from home.

### *Vacation & Time Off* — *Rating: A*

Crystal Decisions' vacation and time off are rated as **above-average**. New employees receive 3 weeks of vacation allowance after their first year, which increases to 4 weeks after 10 years of service. The maximum vacation allowance is 5 weeks for long-serving employees. For short getaways, Crystal Decisions owns a cabin in Whistler where employees can rent a room for only $20 a night. Employees at the company can also apply for unpaid leaves of absence. (One employee is currently on an 18-month leave to complete a Master's degree at Cambridge University in England.)

### *Employee Communications* — *Rating: B+*

Crystal Decisions' internal communications program is rated as **average**. The company has an intranet site, which keeps employees informed about news and human resource policies that affect their work. To solicit feedback from employees, the company operates an email suggestion box. An employee satisfaction survey is conducted by having employees complete an online questionnaire every 12 months. An outside consultant compiles the survey results for Crystal Decisions' management team.

### *Performance Management* — *Rating: A*

Crystal Decisions' performance management program is rated as **above-average**. The company operates a well-designed performance management program. Every 6 months, employees and managers meet for review sessions. (Managers receive training in how to conduct effective reviews.) Employees have the opportunity to provide confidential feedback on their manager's performance through the annual employee satisfaction survey.

Crystal Decisions recognizes exceptional performance with quarterly bonuses and company-paid dinners with the president. The company's sales employees have an opportunity to win trips to exotic locations, such as last year's annual sales meeting in Maui and weekends for two at a luxury West Coast resort. As a special bonus, the company's six top-ranking sales employees each received a convertible Mercedes sportscar last year!

***Training & Skills Development*** ***Rating: A+***

Crystal Decisions' training and skills development program is rated as **exceptional**. The company provides tuition subsidies for courses related to an employee's current position (100% of tuition). Commendably, Crystal Decisions also offers subsidies for courses not related to an employee's current job (100% of tuition). The company assists employees' career development with: reimbursement for professional association dues; in-house training. Employees can apply for up to $5,000 of company assistance for part-time studies and $10,000 for full-time studies.

***Community Involvement*** ***Rating: A+***

Crystal Decisions' community involvement program is rated as **exceptional**. An outstanding corporate citizen, Crystal Decisions actively supports a variety of local charitable initiatives. Employees take part in the selection of charitable groups assisted by the company. Last year, the company contributed to approximately 40 charitable groups, including: the United Way, Fruit for Kids (donations go to a local school breakfast club), the Red Cross, the Canadian Breast Cancer Society, Big Brothers and Big Sisters, the Vancouver Food Bank and Habitat for Humanity, to name a few.

The company also operates a unique program (*Crystal Community*) to encourage employees to volunteer their talents and time. Through this program, the company has donated 188 computers to local schools — and employees have donated their time and expertise to rebuild the computers for each school's needs.

**DALSA CORPORATION**
**605 McMurray Road**
**Waterloo, ON N2V 2E9**

**Tel. 519-886-6000**
**Fax 519-886-3972**
**hr@dalsa.com**
**http://www.dalsa.com**

**INDUSTRY: ELECTRONIC COMPONENT MANUFACTURERS**

***Highlights:***

- Work for an employer with several international locations (including Germany and Japan) — and a generous assistance plan that makes it possible to relocate.
- Enjoy a tremendous range of social activities at this employer, from lunches with live music to a mid-winter beach party.
- Improve your language skills, if you're not a native English speaker, with company-paid ESL classes during working hours.

## *Employer Background*

Dalsa Corporation manufactures image sensors, digital camera systems and semiconductor wafers. The company's advanced digital sensors are used in everything from automotive airbag systems to factory-line control systems.

Dalsa markets its sensors on their own (as electronic semiconductor components) and as part of larger camera and industrial control systems. These systems perform a variety of tasks, from detecting manufacturing defects to capturing images for high-definition video cameras used by the movie industry. Dalsa's camera technology can even be found on the Canadarm2, where it assists the construction of the International Space Station.

Founded in 1980, the publicly-traded company serves manufacturers, end-users and scientific and research communities around the world. In addition to its Waterloo head office, Dalsa has locations in Bromont (Québec), Colorado, Arizona, Germany and Japan.

Through recent acquisitions and strong demand for its technology, Dalsa's revenues jumped to over $112 million last year.

**Workforce at a Glance:** Number of full-time employees: **564**. At this location: **241**. Worldwide: **697**. New jobs created in Canada in past year: **75**. Percentage of employees who are women: **45.7**. Of managers: **16**. Percentage of employees who are visible minorities: **4**. Of managers: **5**. Resumes received by their human resources staff in past year: **6,403**. Average employee age: **37**. Years longest-serving employee has worked there: **39**.

## *Physical Workplace* — *Rating: B+*

Dalsa's physical workplace is rated as **average**. Located in Canada's technology triangle, Dalsa's Waterloo head office is situated in an industrial park near the city's main expressway. (The company holds an option on 50 acres of land adjacent to the park for a new head office.)

> **Physical Workplace at a Glance:** For **food and refreshment**, Dalsa offers: free coffee and tea; lunch hour visits from the popular "lunch-lady" who sells homemade soup, sandwiches and pastries (a turkey sandwich cost $3.00). Nearby **amenities** include: variety of restaurants; major shopping mall; park/wilderness area (RIM Park); recreation centre. For **commuters**, Dalsa offers: free onsite car parking; nearby public transit; secure bicycle parking; shower facilities. Other **work area amenities** include: open-concept workstations; access to natural light for all employees; ergonomic workstation design; large windows in manufacturing areas; plant life that is tended professionally.

## *Work Atmosphere & Social* — *Rating: A+*

Dalsa's work atmosphere is rated as **exceptional**. Employees at Dalsa enjoy business casual dress daily and can listen to radio or music while they are working. There is also a company-subsidized social committee.

The committee organizes events for employees and their families throughout the year. These include lunches with live entertainment (including music, comedians and hypnotists), curling and golf tournaments, a mid-winter beach party day (complete with tropical drinks and ice cream), summer barbeques and specially catered luncheons to celebrate the cultural diversity of Dalsa's workforce. The committee also arranges for discounted tickets to amusement parks, the local symphony and other entertainment venues.

Dalsa sponsors a year-end luncheon (to celebrate successes and recognize outstanding employees), departmental celebrations, lunch-and-learn courses (including gardening classes), an annual company-paid dinner and dance, and a popular children's Christmas party. In addition, Dalsa sponsors employee sports teams that compete in local baseball, basketball and hockey leagues (their hockey team is aptly named "*The Chargers*").

## *Health, Financial & Family Benefits* — *Rating: A*

Dalsa's health benefits plan is managed by Canada Life and is rated as **above-average**. Their health benefits plan is flexible, meaning that employees can tailor individual plans to their personal circumstances. New employees must wait 90 days before they can enroll in the plan.

> **Health Benefits at a Glance:** Dalsa's health plan includes the following coverage: dental (90% of eligible costs, to $2,000 each year); orthodontics (50% of eligible costs with a lifetime maximum of $2,000); eyecare (to $250 every 2 years); prescription drug; extended health benefits; physiotherapy; massage therapy; alternative therapies; personal and family counselling; employee assistance plan (EAP) for substance abuse/mental health.

The company's salary and financial benefits are rated as **above-average**. To keep pay-levels competitive, Dalsa participates in outside salary surveys every 6 months. Individual salaries are reviewed every 12 months. The company offers a group RSP that allows employees to contribute up to 6% of their salary, with matching employer contributions. **Financial Benefits at a Glance:** Dalsa provides a variety of financial benefits, including: share purchase plan; profit-sharing plan; life and disability insurance.

Dalsa's family-friendly benefits are rated as **average**. Employees with pre-school children have access to a daycare facility located nearby. Other family-friendly benefits include: flexible start and finish hours; shortened work week (fewer hours); compressed work week (same hours, fewer days).

***Vacation & Time Off*** ***Rating: B+***

Dalsa's vacation and time off are rated as **average**. New employees receive 2 weeks of vacation allowance after their first year, which increases to 3 weeks after 5 years of service. The maximum vacation allowance is 4 weeks for long-serving employees. (Vacation entitlement increases by 1 day for every year of service until the maximum of 4 weeks is reached.) Employees at the company can also apply for unpaid leaves of absence. (One employee recently took a 6 month leave to travel through Europe)

***Employee Communications*** ***Rating: B+***

Dalsa's internal communications program is rated as **average**. To keep employees informed about new developments, Dalsa publishes an in-house newsletter (called *Insight*). The company also has a well-developed intranet site (called *Vision Portal*), which keeps employees informed about news and human resource policies that affect their work. To gather employee feedback, Dalsa operates a traditional suggestion box that goes directly to senior management. Employee feedback has led to numerous improvements, including construction of new washrooms and changes in the employee benefits plan.

***Performance Management*** ***Rating: A***

Dalsa's performance management program is rated as **above-average**. The company operates a well-designed performance management program. Every 6 months, employees and managers meet for review sessions. (Managers receive training in how to conduct effective reviews.) Employees provide direct feedback on their positions in one-on-one sessions with their managers.

Performance excellence is recognized through a variety of peer, individual and team awards. Based on employee nominations, Dalsa's "Employee of the Year" award is particularly generous — winners receive a recognition plaque and $2,000.

***Training & Skills Development*** ***Rating: A***

Dalsa's training and skills development program is rated as **above-average**. The company provides tuition subsidies for courses related to an employee's current position (100% of tuition). Commendably, Dalsa also offers subsidies for courses not related to an employee's current job (50% of tuition). The company assists employees' career development with: reimbursement for professional association dues; career planning; in-house training. The company's extensive in-house training program includes a variety of courses, from technical to first-aid training.

Dalsa also has a generous relocation assistance plan, which allows employees from its international locations to work at the Waterloo head office (and vice versa).

*Community Involvement* *Rating: A*

Dalsa's community involvement program is rated as **above-average**. A very good corporate citizen, Dalsa actively supports a variety of local charitable initiatives. Employees take part in the selection of charitable groups assisted by the company. Last year, the company contributed to approximately 35 charitable groups, including: the Grand River Hospital Foundation, the Kitchener-Waterloo Symphony and Opera, the Butterfly Learning Centre (a non-profit daycare centre), the United Way, the University of Waterloo's Research Chair in Sensor Technology, and the Waterloo Food Bank.

Dalsa is a strong supporter of local high school, college and university co-op education programs. In a unique initiative, the company also provides ESL classes for new employees (whose first language is not English) during working hours in partnership with community organizations.

**DIAGNOSTIC CHEMICALS LIMITED**
**16 McCarville Street**
**Charlottetown, PE C1E 2A6**

**Tel. 902-566-1396**
**Fax 902-566-2498**
**employment@dclchem.com**
**http://www.dclchem.com**

**INDUSTRY: PHARMACEUTICAL & DRUG MANUFACTURERS**

*Highlights:*

- Work in one of Canada's most popular vacation destinations, where residents enjoy a high quality of life and no traffic congestion.
- Build your career at a Canadian success story — a high-tech PEI employer that's succeeding in global markets, creating new jobs and opportunity for its employees.

## *Employer Background*

Diagnostic Chemicals Limited (DCL) is a pharmaceutical company that develops innovative biochemical and diagnostic products.

The company has two main operating businesses: the BioVectra DCL Division, which produces innovative biopharmaceuticals and provides manufacturing services for the pharmaceutical industry; and the Diagnostic Division, which produces chemistry reagents for blood testing and point-of-care membrane test strips for human and veterinary healthcare.

DCL was incorporated in 1970 by Dr. J. Regis Duffy, then Dean of Science at the University of Prince Edward Island. The company was formed to create opportunities on PEI for its highly educated workforce. Today, the company manufactures more than 400 products and sells to customers across Canada, the United States, Mexico, the United Kingdom, Europe, the Middle East, Hong Kong and Taiwan — over 90% of its sales are exports.

DCL continues to build on a history of success rooted in the quality and dedication of its PEI staff. The company boasts a low turnover rate and continues to expand. In addition to its main 95,000 square-foot manufacturing plant, DCL recently opened a 33,500 square-foot state-of-the-art biopharmaceutical manufacturing facility in Charlottetown.

**Workforce at a Glance:** Number of full-time employees: **169**. Worldwide: **185**. New jobs created in Canada in past year: **19**. Percentage of employees who are women: **49**. Of managers: **49**. Percentage of employees who are visible minorities: **35**. Of managers: **35**. Resumes received by their human resources staff in past year: **500**. Average employee age: **36**. Years longest-serving employee has worked there: **29**.

## *Physical Workplace* — *Rating: B+*

DCL's physical workplace is rated as **average**. In addition to its state-of-the-art laboratories and manufacturing facilities, the most remarkable feature about

DCL is its location on beautiful Prince Edward Island. The province is one of Canada's most popular vacation destinations and offers residents a high quality of life, with great beaches, golfing, sailing, cycling and no traffic congestion.

**Physical Workplace at a Glance:** Their **employee lounge and rest areas** feature: music; outdoor volleyball net. For **food and refreshment**, DCL offers: free coffee and tea; outdoor eating area. Nearby **amenities** include: fitness facility (with subsidized memberships); variety of restaurants; major shopping mall; park/wilderness area (walking trails). For **commuters**, DCL offers: free onsite car parking; convenient highway access. Other **work area amenities** include: windows that open.

### *Work Atmosphere & Social* — *Rating: B+*

DCL's work atmosphere is rated as **average**. Employees at DCL enjoy business casual dress daily and can listen to radio or music while they are working. There is also a company-subsidized social committee, which has operated since 1975.

With input from all employees, the company's social committee organizes an annual Christmas party and a company-wide lunch every June to recognize fellow staff for years of continued service. Last year, DCL also hosted an employee lunch and celebration for the opening of its new manufacturing facility.

### *Health, Financial & Family Benefits* — *Rating: B+*

DCL's health benefits plan is rated as **average**.

**Health Benefits at a Glance:** DCL's health plan includes the following coverage: dental; eyecare (to $175 every 2 years); prescription drug; extended health benefits; physiotherapy; personal and family counselling.

The company's salary and financial benefits are rated as **above-average**. To keep pay-levels competitive, DCL participates in outside salary surveys every 12 months. Individual salaries are reviewed every 12 months. The company operates a traditional pension plan where DCL makes a contribution equal to 5% of each employee's salary to their plan each year.

**Financial Benefits at a Glance:** DCL provides a variety of financial benefits, including: profit-sharing plan; group RSP; life and disability insurance; year-end bonuses.

DCL's family-friendly benefits are rated as **average**. Employees with pre-school children have access to a daycare facility located nearby. Other family-friendly benefits include: flexible start and finish hours; shortened work week (fewer hours).

### *Vacation & Time Off* — *Rating: B+*

DCL's vacation and time off are rated as **average**. New employees receive 2 weeks of vacation allowance after their first year, which increases to 3 weeks after 5 years of service. The maximum vacation allowance is 5 weeks for long-serving employees. (For the first five years, vacation increases at the rate of one day every year.) Employees at the company can also apply for unpaid leaves of absence.

### *Employee Communications* — *Rating: B+*

DCL's internal communications program is rated as **average**. The company has an intranet site, which keeps employees informed about news and human resource policies that affect their work. To solicit feedback from employees, the company operates a traditional suggestion box program.

### *Performance Management* — *Rating: A*

DCL's performance management program is rated as **above-average**. The company operates a formal performance management program. Once a year, employees and managers meet for review sessions. (Managers receive training in how to conduct effective reviews.) Employees provide reverse feedback as part of their manager's performance evaluation.

### *Training & Skills Development* — *Rating: A*

DCL's training and skills development program is rated as **above-average**. The company provides tuition subsidies for courses related to an employee's current position (100% of tuition). Commendably, DCL also offers subsidies for courses not related to an employee's current job (100% of tuition). The company assists employees' career development with: reimbursement for professional association dues; in-house training.

### *Community Involvement* — *Rating: A*

DCL's community involvement program is rated as **above-average**. A very good corporate citizen, DCL actively supports a variety of local and national charitable initiatives. Employees take part in the selection of charitable groups assisted by the company. Last year, the company also contributed to approximately 8 charitable groups, including: the United Way, the Canadian Cancer Society, the Canadian Diabetes Association, Big Brothers and Big Sisters, Adopt-a-Family at Christmas, and the local food bank.

DCL employees also volunteer as mentors in support of the Prince Edward Island Science and Technology website.

DOFASCO

Our product is steel. Our strength is people.

*...our home is Hamilton.*

**DOFASCO INC.**
**PO Box 2460**
**Hamilton, ON L8N 3J5**

**Tel. 905-548-7100**
**Fax 905-548-7437**
**hresources@dofasco.ca**
**http://www.dofasco.ca**

**INDUSTRY: STEEL & UNFINISHED METAL MANUFACTURERS**

*Highlights:*

- Invest in your future with a generous company-wide profit-sharing program that's been operating since 1938!
- Shape up at this employer's 100 acre fitness facility that's open to employees, retirees and their families.
- Deck the halls at the largest Christmas party in this book — last year, more than 30,000 employees, retirees and their families celebrated in style at a local sports coliseum.

## *Employer Background*

Dofasco Inc. is one of North America's leading steel manufacturers. Established in 1912, the company makes a wide range of primary steel products, including hot- and cold-rolled products and coated steel used in the automotive, construction, energy and manufacturing industries.

Dofasco serves customers throughout North America. In addition to Hamilton, the company has facilities in Kitchener, Concord (north of Toronto), Ohio, Kentucky and Monterrey, Mexico.

Last year, Dofasco shipped over 4.1 million tons of steel and posted revenues of over $3.5 billion.

**Workforce at a Glance:** Number of full-time employees: **7,385**. Percentage of employees who are women: **9**. Of managers: **8**. Resumes received by their human resources staff in past year: **7,512**. Weeks of vacation their HR manager took last year: **7**. Average employee age: **46**.

## *Physical Workplace* — *Rating: B+*

Dofasco's physical workplace is rated as **average**. Located on Hamilton Harbour in the north end of the city, the company's manufacturing complex covers over 730 acres. (The huge facility offers a free shuttle service between company buildings.)

Dofasco's manufacturing areas have come a long way since the early days of steelmaking. Today, many employees work in air-conditioned control rooms, where they control highly automated manufacturing processes. In all work areas, health and safety is paramount. (To foster safety awareness, the company hosts an annual health and safety fair with over 85 exhibits and demonstrations.)

The head office building includes an extensive collection of Canadian art and houses the administration, human resources, research and development, environment and energy, medical, and health and safety departments.

**Physical Workplace at a Glance:** The company has an onsite cafeteria that features: subsidized meals (a turkey sandwich costs $1.75). Nearby **amenities** include: variety of restaurants; major shopping mall; recreation centre (F.H. Sherman Learning & Recreation Centre). For **commuters**, Dofasco offers: free onsite car parking; convenient highway access; nearby public transit; secure bicycle parking. Other **work area amenities** include: open-concept workstations; ergonomic workstation design; plant life that is tended professionally; onsite credit union.

## *Work Atmosphere & Social* — *Rating: A*

Dofasco's work atmosphere is rated as **above-average**. Employees at Dofasco enjoy business casual dress daily and can listen to radio or music while they are working.

The company's annual Christmas party is a vast affair, where over 30,000 employees, retirees and children enjoy a day of festivities at Hamilton's Copps Coliseum. In the summer, Dofasco hosts a huge Canada Day celebration with food and refreshments, all-day entertainment and evening fireworks. In addition, the company regularly celebrates business accomplishments and employee milestones.

## *Health, Financial & Family Benefits* — *Rating: A+*

Dofasco's health benefits plan is rated as **exceptional**. A unique benefit for employees and retirees (and their families) is the company's F.H. Sherman Learning and Recreation Centre, located in nearby Stoney Creek. The 100-acre facility is home to more than 60 sports leagues and recreation clubs for children and adults. The building features two skating rinks, a double gymnasium, indoor basketball courts, seven baseball diamonds, batting cages, soccer fields, a running track, tennis courts, a golf driving range, mini-golf and a children's summer camp.

**Health Benefits at a Glance:** Dofasco's health plan includes the following coverage: dental; orthodontics; eyecare (to $175 every 2 years); extended health benefits; prescription drug; nutrition planning; massage therapy; personal and family counselling; health testing clinic; a wellness program that includes Weight Watchers at Work; stress management, smoking cessation and fitness classes.

The company's salary and financial benefits are rated as **exceptional.** To keep pay-levels competitive, Dofasco participates in outside salary surveys every 12 months. Individual salaries are reviewed every 12 months. The company operates a traditional pension plan. In addition, Dofasco has a generous profit sharing program that has been operating since 1938. (Eligible employees received an average of $7,426 last year.)

**Financial Benefits at a Glance:** Dofasco provides an extensive set of financial benefits, including: life and disability insurance; discounted customer products (including automobiles and home appliances); share purchase plan.

Dofasco's family-friendly benefits are rated as **above-average**. Employees with pre-school children have access to a daycare facility located nearby. Dofasco also sponsors numerous programs for employees' children at its recreation complex, including sports teams and summer camps. Other family-friendly benefits include: flexible start and finish hours; shortened work week (fewer hours); compressed work week (same hours, fewer days); telecommuting and working from home; job-sharing.

### *Vacation & Time Off* — *Rating: B+*

Dofasco's vacation and time off are rated as **average**. New employees receive 2 weeks of vacation allowance after their first year, which increases to 3 weeks after 4 years of service. The maximum vacation allowance is 8 weeks for long-serving employees. Employees at the company can also apply for unpaid leaves of absence.

### *Employee Communications* — *Rating: A*

Dofasco's internal communications program is rated as **above-average**. To keep employees informed about new developments, Dofasco publishes an in-house newsletter. The company also has a well-developed intranet site, which keeps employees informed about news and human resource policies that affect their work. Every three months, the company gathers feedback through a small survey sent to one-quarter of its employees. An outside consultant tabulates the survey's results, which are presented to management and shared with employees.

### *Performance Management* — *Rating: A*

Dofasco's performance management program is rated as **above-average**. The company operates a thorough performance management program. (Managers receive training in how to conduct effective reviews.) During their first year, employees receive performance reviews every three months. Afterwards, employees and managers meet once a year to discuss performance and set goals for the upcoming year. Managers also provide ongoing coaching throughout the year.

All department managers receive budgets to reward excellent job performance and celebrate employee milestones and accomplishments.

### *Training & Skills Development* — *Rating: A+*

Dofasco's training and skills development program is rated as **exceptional**. The company provides tuition subsidies for courses related to an employee's current position (100% of tuition). Commendably, Dofasco also offers subsidies for courses not related to an employee's current job (100% of tuition). The company assists employees' career development with: reimbursement for professional association dues; career planning; mentoring; in-house training.

Impressively, Dofasco invested over $15 million in training last year. The company has two training centres and even publishes its own course calendar for its in-house training program. As additional encouragement, Dofasco rewards employees who upgrade their skills through a unique "pay for skills" program.

The company also operates an award-winning workplace literacy program and provides three annual post-secondary scholarships ($2,500 each) to employees' children.

*Community Involvement* *Rating: A+*

Dofasco's community involvement program is rated as **exceptional**. An outstanding corporate citizen, Dofasco actively supports a variety of local and national charitable initiatives. The company has received recognition from the Canadian Centre for Philanthropy for its charitable efforts. Last year, the company donated nearly $3 million to 160 charitable organizations. An employee-run donations committee makes all funding decisions, which focus on healthcare, education, arts and culture, social services and community development. Employees at Dofasco receive paid time off to volunteer at local charities.

Recent charitable contributions include a MRI machine donated to the Hamilton General Hospital, funds to build a hiking trail along the Niagara Escarpment and Lake Ontario as well as support for the Art Gallery of Hamilton.

Dofasco is also committed to minimizing the environmental impacts of steel manufacturing. The company recently received ISO 4001 certification in recognition of its environmental management systems. Dofasco was also the first company in Canada to sign a voluntary environmental management agreement with the federal and provincial governments.

**ECOTRUST CANADA**
**1238 Homer Street**
**Suite 200**
**Vancouver, BC V6B 2Y5**

**Tel. 604-682-4141**
**Fax 604-682-1944**
**info@ecotrustcan.org**
**http://www.ecotrustcan.org**

**INDUSTRY: MANAGEMENT CONSULTING FIRMS**

*Highlights:*

- Work for a small employer that offers big employer benefits, including great maternity top-up (75% of salary for 26 weeks) and three weeks of paid vacation allowance for new employees.
- Take off and go skiing for a day (when conditions are perfect) thanks to an enlightened "personal days off" program that's based on mutual trust and respect.
- Make a difference in the larger community at an employer that's on the front lines of creating sustainable economic development — one project at a time.

## *Employer Background*

Ecotrust Canada is a non-profit organization that supports the development of a sustainable economy in the coastal temperate rainforests of British Columbia. Founded in 1994, Ecotrust aims to develop a "conservation economy" — an economy based on ecological improvement rather than degradation. Ecotrust is guided by the principle that long-term economic sustainability and conservation are mutually dependent. This enlightened (and often misunderstood) view highlights how healthy and diverse local economies lead to greater environmental protection.

Ecotrust provides services to help individuals and organizations bring economic, social and ecological prosperity to coastal communities. The small non-profit organization primarily serves conservation entrepreneurs, local communities and First Nations communities.

Ecotrust's services fall into two categories: information services and economic development. The information services branch provides mapping and information products, land use planning, networking services, onsite training and technical support services. Ecotrust's economic development services branch provides business loans, strategic planning, market research and analysis.

Over the past year, Ecotrust has participated in several major environmental projects, including: the launch of an eco-forestry operation for the Tsleil-Waututh First Nation; the establishment of a sustainable shellfish operation for the Nuu-chah-nulth Nations; and the provision of almost $3 million in business loans to conservation entrepreneurers.

In addition to its Vancouver head office, Ecotrust has an economic development office on Vancouver Island.

**Workforce at a Glance:** Number of full-time employees: **18**. At this location: **13**. New jobs created in Canada in past year: **3**. Percentage of employees who are women: **38**. Of managers: **43**. Percentage of employees who are visible minorities: **10**. Resumes received by their human resources staff in past year: **500**. Weeks of vacation their HR manager took last year: **3**. Average employee age: **38**. Years longest-serving employee has worked there: **8**. Person you should get to know first: **Caroline, who knows everything about the organization**.

## *Physical Workplace* — *Rating: A*

Ecotrust's physical workplace is rated as **above-average**. Ecotrust's head office is located in the city's historic Yaletown warehouse district, within walking distance to the popular False Creek waterfront. The downtown location allows employees to take public transit, bicycle or walk to work — no employees commute to the office by car. Prior to selecting this location, Ecotrust surveyed employees to find out their views on everything from neighbourhood preferences to natural lighting considerations.

**Physical Workplace at a Glance:** Their **employee lounge and rest areas** feature: comfortable couches; table tennis. For **food and refreshment**, Ecotrust offers: free coffee and tea; a kitchen area. Nearby **amenities** include: variety of restaurants; local shops and services; fitness facility; park/wilderness area (False Creek); recreation centre (The Roundhouse Community Centre). For **commuters**, Ecotrust offers: nearby public transit; secure bicycle parking; shower and change room. Other **work area amenities** include: open-concept workstations; ergonomic workstation design; windows that open; plant life that is tended professionally.

## *Work Atmosphere & Social* — *Rating: A+*

Ecotrust's work atmosphere is rated as **exceptional**. Employees at Ecotrust enjoy casual dress daily and can listen to radio or music while they are working. The organization lets employees bring their pets to work.

Ecotrust celebrates special events throughout the year, including an annual retreat, a Christmas wine and cheese party, a summer barbeque, employee birthdays and length-of-service celebrations. Compared to many of the employers in this book, Ecotrust's social events resemble small family gatherings. Last year's summer barbeque was held at the President's home, where employees enjoyed a home-cooked meal.

One of the best features of Ecotrust's work environment is that employees are free to manage their own schedules so long as the work gets done. When the snow is good at Whistler, it's not uncommon for some Ecotrust employees to spend a day on the slopes and then make the work time up later.

Once a year, all Ecotust employees attend a retreat, where they discuss the organization's progress and individual projects. Last year, employees attended a traditional feast with the Namgis First Nation in Alert Bay. These events — in the communities they serve — remind Ecotrust employees of the natural legacy they are working to protect.

## *Health, Financial & Family Benefits* — *Rating: A*

Ecotrust's health benefits plan is managed by Pacific Blue Cross and is rated as **above-average**.

> **Health Benefits at a Glance:** Ecotrust's health plan includes the following coverage: dental (100% of eligible costs, to $1,500 each year); orthodontics (50% of eligible costs with a lifetime maximum of $1,500); eyecare (to $150 every 2 years); prescription drug; extended health benefits; physiotherapy; massage therapy; alternative therapies; personal and family counselling; employee assistance plan (EAP) for substance abuse/mental health.

The organization's salary and financial benefits are rated as **average**. To keep pay-levels competitive, Ecotrust participates in outside salary surveys every 24 months. Individual salaries are reviewed every 12 months. The organization offers a group RSP that allows employees to contribute up to 6% of their salary, with matching employer contributions. **Financial Benefits at a Glance:** Ecotrust provides a variety of financial benefits, including: life and disability insurance.

Ecotrust's family-friendly benefits are rated as **above-average**. Employees with pre-school children have access to a daycare facility located nearby. For employees who take maternity leave, Ecotrust provides a generous top-up to 75% of salary for the first 26 weeks of their leave. Other family-friendly benefits include: flexible start and finish hours; shortened work week (fewer hours); compressed work week (same hours, fewer days); telecommuting and working from home.

## *Vacation & Time Off* — *Rating: A*

Ecotrust's vacation and time off are rated as **above-average**. New employees receive 3 weeks of vacation allowance after their first year, which increases to 4 weeks after 4 years of service. Employees at Ecotrust also receive 3 paid personal days off each year, in addition to their regular vacation allowance. Employees at the organization can also apply for unpaid leaves of absence. (Recently, one employee took a 16-month leave to complete a post-graduate degree.)

## *Employee Communications* — *Rating: B+*

Ecotrust's internal communications program is rated as **average**. To keep employees informed about new developments, Ecotrust publishes an in-house newsletter (called *Notes from the Front*). To solicit feedback from employees, the organization operates an email suggestion box. To gather additional feedback, Ecotrust recently conducted a survey of employees, clients and donors. An outside consultant managed the process and reported the results to Ecotrust's management.

## *Performance Management* — *Rating: A*

Ecotrust's performance management program is rated as **above-average**. The organization operates a thorough performance management program. Once a year, employees and managers meet for review sessions. (Managers receive training in how to conduct effective reviews.)

As part of the process, employees prepare written self-assessments of their own performance and outline their needs for future training and development, as well as salary expectations. Employees and managers discuss the assessments and develop joint performance reports outlining objectives for the upcoming year. Employees can provide feedback on their manager's performance to Ecotrust's Operations Manager.

### *Training & Skills Development* — *Rating: A*

Ecotrust's training and skills development program is rated as **above-average**. The organization provides tuition subsidies for courses related to an employee's current position (100% of tuition). Commendably, Ecotrust also offers subsidies for courses not related to an employee's current job (100% of tuition). The organization assists employees' career development with: reimbursement for professional association dues; in-house training. The company's in-house training program covers a variety of subjects, from geographic information systems (GIS) to professional fundraising.

### *Community Involvement* — *Rating: A*

Ecotrust's community involvement program is rated as **above-average**. A very good member of the community, Ecotrust actively supports a variety of local charitable initiatives. Employees take part in the selection of charitable groups assisted by the organization. Employees at Ecotrust receive paid time off to volunteer at local charities.

Beyond its raison d'être, Ecotrust helps community organizations in their fundraising efforts and provides grants for local programs. Last year, Ecotrust supported the Raincoast Education Society, the Qqs Camps, the Kitlope Rediscovery Camps and the annual All-Native Basketball Tournament.

**ENMAX CORPORATION**
**141 - 50th Avenue SE**
**Calgary, AB T2G 4S7**

**Tel. 403-514-3000**
**Fax 403-514-2165**
**jobs@enmax.com**
**http://www.enmax.com**

**INDUSTRY: ELECTRIC UTILITIES**

*Highlights:*

- Get three weeks of paid vacation allowance in your first year — plus 12 paid personal days off each year.
- Build your career at a growing energy retailer that's actively investing in tomorrow's technologies (such as large-scale wind farms) to deliver clean, environmentally sustainable electricity.
- Work in a spectacular head office that's a showpiece facility, in terms of both employee comfort and efficient energy use.

## *Employer Background*

Enmax Corporation is an electrical and natural gas distribution and transmission company. The company provides electricity, natural gas and related services to over 400,000 residential, commercial and industrial customers, primarily in Calgary and Southern Alberta.

Originally established in 1805 (as the City of Calgary Electric System), the company operates within Alberta's deregulated utilities market. Founded in 2001 and wholly-owned by the City of Calgary, Enmax operates through two primary subsidiaries: Enmax Energy Corporation (retail energy services) and Enmax Power Corporation (distribution and transmission).

Besides relying on traditional methods of power generation, the company is taking a leading role in generating electricity through wind power. In partnership with Calgary-based Vision Quest Windelectric, the company recently completed construction of Canada's largest "wind farm" south of Fort Macleod, Alberta. The project includes 114 wind turbines and generates enough energy to power 32,500 homes.

Enmax posted revenues of over $1 billion last year. In addition to its Calgary head office, Enmax has locations in Red Deer and Lethbridge.

**Workforce at a Glance:** Number of full-time employees: **1,385**. New jobs created in Canada in past year: **111**. Percentage of employees who are women: **38**. Of managers: **33**. Resumes received by their human resources staff in past year: **9,992**. Average employee age: **39**.

## *Physical Workplace* — *Rating: A+*

Enmax's physical workplace is rated as **exceptional**. Its head office is located in a newly renovated building in Calgary. In designing the office, the company gathered employee feedback through online surveys and an employee advisory group. Enmax also published a special newsletter to keep employees informed as construction progressed.

The remarkable head office is a showpiece facility that once served as a factory warehouse (that was scheduled for demolition). The state-of-the-art facility has been completely rebuilt and now features environmentally friendly materials throughout (from flooring to furniture), as well as motion-sensitive lighting and climate control systems.

**Physical Workplace at a Glance:** Their **onsite fitness facility** features: free memberships; treadmills; stationary bikes; stairmasters; weights; onsite massage therapy; instructor-led classes; sauna. Their **employee lounge and rest areas** feature: comfortable couches; television. For **food and refreshment**, Enmax offers: free coffee and tea; onsite Tim Hortons and Starbucks. The company has an onsite cafeteria that features: subsidized meals (a turkey sandwich costs $2.75); healthy menu items; special diet menus. Nearby **amenities** include: variety of restaurants; major shopping mall; park/wilderness area (Sandy Beach in Brittannia); recreation centre (Talisman Centre). For **commuters**, Enmax offers: nearby public transit; free onsite car parking; secure bicycle parking. Other **work area amenities** include: open-concept workstations; access to natural light for all employees; ergonomic workstation design; onsite dry cleaning service; onsite ATM.

## *Work Atmosphere & Social* — *Rating: A*

Enmax's work atmosphere is rated as **above-average**. Employees at Enmax enjoy business casual dress daily. Employees enjoy a variety of social events throughout the year, including an employee Christmas party (with a separate event for employees' children), a Calgary Stampede breakfast, summer golf tournament, fishing derby and parties for retirees.

## *Health, Financial & Family Benefits* — *Rating: A*

Enmax's health benefits plan is managed by Blue Cross and is rated as **above-average**. Their health benefits plan is flexible, meaning that employees can tailor individual plans to their personal circumstances. There is no waiting period before new employees are eligible for coverage.

**Health Benefits at a Glance:** Enmax's health plan includes the following coverage: dental (100% of eligible costs, to $1,500 each year); orthodontics (50% of eligible costs with a lifetime maximum of $1,500); eyecare (to $300 every 2 years); extended health benefits; prescription drug; massage therapy; physiotherapy; personal and family counselling; employee assistance plan (EAP) for substance abuse/mental health; smoking cessation plan.

The company's salary and financial benefits are rated as **above-average**. To keep pay-levels competitive, Enmax participates in outside salary surveys every 12 months. Individual salaries are reviewed every 12 months. The company operates a traditional pension plan.

**Financial Benefits at a Glance:** Enmax provides a variety of financial benefits, including: life and disability insurance; signing bonuses for some employees; referral bonuses for some employees (to $750); year-end bonuses.

Enmax's family-friendly benefits are rated as **above-average**. For employees who take maternity leave, Enmax provides a top-up to 90% of salary for the first 6 weeks of their leave. Other family-friendly benefits include: flexible start and finish hours; shortened work week (fewer hours).

***Vacation & Time Off*** ***Rating: A+***

Enmax's vacation and time off are rated as **exceptional**. New employees receive 3 weeks of vacation allowance after their first year, which increases to 4 weeks after 8 years of service. The maximum vacation allowance is 7 weeks for long-serving employees. Employees at Enmax also receive 12 paid personal days off each year, in addition to their regular vacation allowance. Employees book these days in advance and are encouraged to schedule at least one day off every month.

***Employee Communications*** ***Rating: A***

Enmax's internal communications program is rated as **above-average**. To keep employees informed about new developments, Enmax publishes an in-house newsletter (called *Buzz*). The company also has an intranet site (called *Intramax*), which keeps employees informed about news and human resource policies that affect their work. An employee satisfaction survey is conducted every 12 months. An outside consultant compiles the survey results for Enmax's management team.

***Performance Management*** ***Rating: A***

Enmax's performance management program is rated as **above-average**. The company operates a comprehensive performance management program. Every 4 months, employees and managers meet for review sessions. (Managers receive training in how to conduct effective reviews.) Employees can also provide confidential feedback on their manager's performance through an annual survey. At the reviews, employees work closely with their managers to discuss career goals and establish future training needs. The review process forms the basis for salary increases.

***Training & Skills Development*** ***Rating: A***

Enmax's training and skills development program is rated as **above-average**. The company provides tuition subsidies for courses related to an employee's current position (100% of tuition). Commendably, Enmax also offers subsidies for courses not related to an employee's current job (100% of tuition). The company assists employees' career development with: reimbursement for professional association dues; mentoring; career planning; in-house training.

***Community Involvement*** ***Rating: A***

Enmax's community involvement program is rated as **above-average**. A very good corporate citizen, Enmax actively supports a variety of local charitable initiatives.

Enmax supports charitable and community initiatives in four key areas: youth and education; community development; sports and recreation; and arts and culture. The company also provides special support to the Kids Cancer Care Foundation of Alberta. Every year, employees also volunteer for charities through a number of local initiatives, including the Enmax High-Wire Gala (in support of children living with cancer and the "*Paint-the-Town*" program (to help paint senior citizens' homes).

ENVIRONICS COMMUNICATIONS

**ENVIRONICS COMMUNICATIONS INC.**
**33 Bloor Street East**
**Toronto, ON M4W 3H1**

**Tel. 416-920-9000**
**Fax 416-920-1822**
**communicate@environicspr.com**
**http://www.environicspr.com**

**INDUSTRY: PUBLIC RELATIONS FIRMS**

***Highlights:***

- Get a $4,000 paid vacation anywhere in the world when you spend four years at this employer — plus a $3,000 Canadian vacation on your eighth anniverary.
- Get three weeks of paid vacation allowance after your first year — plus five paid personal days off.
- Work for an employer that allows you to volunteer your public relations expertise for charitable organizations on company time.

## *Employer Background*

Environics Communications, Inc. is a full-service public relations firm. Founded in 1994, the firm is one Canada's largest and most recognized communications firms

Environics manages public relations campaigns for some of the country's largest organizations, including Pfizer Canada, Xerox Canada, Johnson & Johnson Canada, Goodyear Canada and Mackenzie Financial. The firm creates public relations campaigns ranging from creative local campaigns (some even featuring sumo-wrestlers) to complete communication strategies for multi-billion dollar mergers

In addition to its Toronto head office, Environics has offices in Montréal, Washington, DC, and Stamford, Connecticut.

**Workforce at a Glance:** Number of full-time employees: **51**. At this location: **44**. Worldwide: **67**. New jobs created in Canada in past year: **5**. Percentage of employees who are women: **70**. Of managers: **66**. Percentage of employees who are visible minorities: **8**. Resumes received by their human resources staff in past year: **1,000**. Weeks of vacation their HR manager took last year: **4**. Average employee age: **33**. Years longest-serving employee has worked there: **9**. Car the president drives: **Jaguar X Type**. Where it's parked in the lot: **with everyone else**.

## *Physical Workplace* — *Rating: A*

Environics' physical workplace is rated as **above-average**. The firm's downtown head office is located only a few blocks away from Toronto's trendy Yorkville area, one of the city's most popular destinations.

**Physical Workplace at a Glance:** Their **employee lounge and rest areas** feature: comfortable couches; television. For **food and refreshment**, Environics offers: free snacks (including chocolate bars, cookies, popcorn and granola bars); free coffee and tea; free soft drinks. Nearby **amenities** include: variety of restaurants; local shops and services; fitness facility; park/wilderness area (Rosedale Valley Ravine). For **commuters**, Environics offers: nearby public transit; secure bicycle parking. Other **work area amenities** include: ergonomic workstation design; access to natural light for all employees.

*Work Atmosphere & Social* *Rating: A*

Environics' work atmosphere is rated as **above-average**. Employees at Environics enjoy casual dress daily and can listen to radio or music while they are working. The firm lets employees bring their pets to work.

Employees enjoy numerous events throughout the year, including celebrations for employee weddings and new babies, catered lunches, restaurant dinners, rock concerts and sporting events. In addition to sponsoring an employee baseball team (named *Dash-30-Dash* — you need to be a PR flack to get this one), the company also rents a corporate box from time to time so employees can enjoy a Toronto Maple Leafs hockey game in style.

Environics also hosts an annual retreat where employees from different cities gather for a day of meetings and an evening on the town.

*Health, Financial & Family Benefits* *Rating: A*

Environics' health benefits plan is managed by Desjardins Financial and is rated as **above-average**. There is no waiting period before new employees are eligible for coverage.

**Health Benefits at a Glance:** Environics' health plan includes the following coverage: dental (100% of eligible costs, to $2,000 each year); orthodontics (50% of eligible costs with a lifetime maximum of $1,500); eyecare (to $200 every 2 years); extended health benefits; prescription drug; nutrition planning; massage therapy; physiotherapy; alternative therapies; personal and family counselling.

The firm's salary and financial benefits are rated as **above-average**. To keep pay-levels competitive, Environics participates in outside salary surveys every 24 months. Individual salaries are reviewed every 12 months.

**Financial Benefits at a Glance:** Environics provides a variety of financial benefits, including: life and disability insurance; discounted home Internet access; discounted home computers; profit-sharing plan; referral bonuses for some employees (to $500); year-end bonuses (from $1,000 to $20,000 for non-executives).

Environics' family-friendly benefits are rated as **average**. Employees with preschool children have access to a daycare facility located nearby. Other family-friendly benefits include: flexible start and finish hours; shortened work week (fewer hours); telecommuting and working from home; reduced summer hours.

*Vacation & Time Off* *Rating: A*

Environics' vacation and time off are rated as **above-average**. New employees receive 3 weeks of vacation allowance after their first year, which increases to 4 weeks after 5 years of service. The maximum vacation allowance is 4 weeks for long-serving employees. Employees at Environics also receive 5 paid personal days off each year, in addition to their regular vacation allowance. Employees at the firm can also apply for unpaid leaves of absence. (Recently, one employee took a 4 month leave to travel the world)

Environics also provides a unique vacation benefit for employees celebrating 5 years with company. On their fifth anniversary, employees receive $1,000 for airline tickets and $3,000 in spending money for a trip to anywhere in the world — in addition to their regular vacation allowance. On their eighth anniversary with the company, employees receive extra time off and a $3,000 holiday anywhere in Canada.

***Employee Communications*** ***Rating: A***

Environics' internal communications program is rated as **above-average**. To solicit feedback from employees, the firm operates an email suggestion box. An in-house employee satisfaction survey is conducted every 12 months.

***Performance Management*** ***Rating: A***

Environics' performance management program is rated as **above-average**. The firm operates a thorough performance management program. Once a year, employees and managers meet for review sessions. Environics uses a 360-degree feedback process to gather additional performance-related information from co-workers, supervisors and employees. As part of the review process, employees and managers develop a written report outlining employees' strengths and future goals.

***Training & Skills Development*** ***Rating: A***

Environics' training and skills development program is rated as **above-average**. The firm provides tuition subsidies for courses related to an employee's current position (100% of tuition). The firm assists employees' career development with: reimbursement for professional association dues; mentoring; in-house training. As part of its in-house training program, Environics hosts monthly educational sessions (with guest speakers) for all employees.

***Community Involvement*** ***Rating: A***

Environics' community involvement program is rated as **above-average**. A very good corporate citizen, Environics actively supports a variety of charitable initiatives. Last year, the firm donated money to the Canadian Breast Cancer Foundation and several local hospitals.

In addition, Environics encourages employee volunteerism by allowing employees to donate their public relations expertise to particular charities on company time. (The firm also assists these charities with cash donations.) Recently, employees have assisted the Nature Conservancy of Canada and Frontier College.

**EPCOR UTILITIES INC.**
**10065 Jasper Avenue**
**Epcor Centre**
**Edmonton, AB T5J 3B1**

**Tel. 780-412-7777**
**Fax 780-412-7602**
**http://www.epcor.ca**

**INDUSTRY: COMBINED ELECTRIC & OTHER UTILITIES**

*Highlights:*

- Build your career at a growing employer in the energy industry that offers stability and career advancement opportunities as it continues to expand across Canada.
- Work for a progressive employer where over 75% of your co-workers view the company's extensive volunteer program one of the best perks of working there.
- Take advantage of a unique "personal days off" program that lets you take the paid time off (3 days per year) in hourly increments to run errands or deal with personal emergencies.

## *Employer Background*

Epcor Utilities Inc. provides electricity, water and gas to customers in western Canada and Ontario, as well as technology solutions to municipalities across the country. The company sells the "essential elements for living" — power, water and natural gas — to customers in Alberta, British Columbia, Ontario and Washington State.

Founded in 1995 through the amalgamation of Edmonton's power and water utilities, the creation of Epcor was the first strategic coupling of power and water utilities in Canada. (The City of Edmonton continues to be Epcor's sole shareholder.) Through its recent acquisition of Toronto-based Union Energy Inc., Epcor also supplies energy products and services to over 900,000 customers in Ontario.

Epcor's generating division operates major electricity generating plants in Alberta, British Columbia and Washington State. In addition to using fuels such as natural gas and coal, the company uses non-traditional fuels to generate electricity. At its large Clover Bar generating station in Edmonton, a portion of the plant uses methane gas from a nearby landfill to generate electricity.

The company's water services division supplies drinking water to nearly one million people in Edmonton and 40 surrounding communities. Last year, Epcor completed the installation of the world's largest ultraviolet water treatment system in Edmonton. This state-of-the-art technology has been the subject of considerable interest from municipalities across Canada.

Epcor also provides meter reading, traffic control and street lighting systems to municipalities across the country. The company recenly won a contract to replace Calgary's traffic signals with new energy-efficient lights that consume 90% less energy.

**Workforce at a Glance:** Number of full-time employees: **3,250**. At this location: **1,962**. Percentage of employees who are women: **33**. Of managers: **28**. Resumes received by their human resources staff in past year: **35,000**. Average employee age: **41**. Years longest-serving employee has worked there: **37**.

## *Physical Workplace* — *Rating: B+*

Epcor's physical workplace is rated as **average**. Epcor's work environment varies considerably, depending on the employee's area of responsibility. Employees who work in operations, construction or maintenance are often outside or work in plant settings. (At all sites, workplace safety is paramount.) Epcor's head office in Edmonton is home to over 1,200 employees. Located in a modern 20-storey office tower (that uses solar roof panels for heat generation), the office boasts spectacular views of the North Saskatchewan River and is connected to the city's pedestrian walkway network, which provides all-weather access to restaurants, shops and services.

**Physical Workplace at a Glance:** Their **employee lounge and rest areas** feature: comfortable couches; television; outdoor patio. Nearby **amenities** include: variety of restaurants; major shopping mall; fitness facility; park/wilderness area (the North Saskatchewan River Vally Park is Canada's longest urban park); recreation centre (YMCA). For **commuters**, Epcor offers: nearby public transit; free onsite car parking; secure bicycle parking; shower facilities. Other **work area amenities** include: open-concept workstations; ergonomic workstation design; onsite health and safety consultants; plant life that is tended professionally.

## *Work Atmosphere & Social* — *Rating: A*

Epcor's work atmosphere is rated as **above-average**. Employees at Epcor enjoy business casual dress daily and can listen to radio or music while they are working. There is also a company-subsidized social committee, which has operated since 1958.

Epcor hosts a variety of social events, including a huge Christmas celebration for employees and their guests (over 1,600 attended last year), summer barbeques and celebrations for significant accomplishments. Epcor also sponsors an employee team in Edmonton's annual "Corporate Challenge", which includes running, badminton, basketball, bowling, race walking, slo-pitch, table tennis, team triathlon, track and field, volleyball and a scavenger hunt (Epcor employees placed second in their division last year).

## *Health, Financial & Family Benefits* — *Rating: A*

Epcor's health benefits plan is managed by Sun Life and is rated as **above-average**. Their health benefits plan is flexible, meaning that employees can tailor individual plans to their personal circumstances. Full-time and part-time employees who work more than 20 hours per week are covered by the plan.

**Health Benefits at a Glance:** Epcor's health plan includes the following coverage: dental; orthodontics (50% of eligible costs with a lifetime maximum of $2,000); eyecare (to $200 every 2 years); extended health benefits; prescription drug; nutrition planning; massage therapy; physiotherapy; alternative therapies; personal and family counselling; employee assistance plan (EAP) for substance abuse/mental health.

The company's salary and financial benefits are rated as **above-average**. To keep pay-levels competitive, Epcor participates in outside salary surveys every 12 months. Individual salaries are reviewed every 12 months. The company operates a traditional pension plan where Epcor makes a contribution equal to 5% of each employee's salary to their plan each year.

**Financial Benefits at a Glance:** Epcor provides a variety of financial benefits, including: life and disability insurance; signing bonuses for some employees; year-end bonuses (to $50,000 for non-executives).

Epcor's family-friendly benefits are rated as **above-average**. For employees who take maternity leave, Epcor provides a top-up to 95% of salary for the first 6 weeks of their leave. Other family-friendly benefits include: flexible start and finish hours; shortened work week (fewer hours); compressed work week (same hours, fewer days); telecommuting and working from home.

***Vacation & Time Off*** ***Rating: A***

Epcor's vacation and time off are rated as **above-average**. New employees receive 3 weeks of vacation allowance after their first year, which increases to 4 weeks after 7 years of service. The maximum vacation allowance is 6 weeks for long-serving employees. Employees at Epcor also receive 3 paid personal days off each year, in addition to their regular vacation allowance. Epcor's "personal days off" program is interesting in that it provides the time off in 24 hourly increments. Employees can take an hour or two at various times to attend to errands or deal with personal emergencies. Employees at the company can also apply for unpaid leaves of absence.

***Employee Communications*** ***Rating: A***

Epcor's internal communications program is rated as **above-average**. To keep employees informed about new developments, Epcor publishes an in-house newsletter (called *The Essential Spirit*). The company also has an intranet site, which keeps employees informed about news and human resource policies that affect their work. To solicit feedback from employees, the company operates an email suggestion box. An employee satisfaction survey is conducted every 12 months. An outside consultant compiles the survey results for Epcor's management team.

***Performance Management*** ***Rating: A+***

Epcor's performance management program is rated as **exceptional**. The company operates a formal performance management program. Once a year, employees and managers meet for review sessions. (Managers receive training in how to conduct effective reviews.) Epcor uses a 360-degree feedback process to gather additional performance-related information from co-workers, supervisors and employees.

At the reviews, employees and managers jointly develop individual performance plans that focus on technical, behavioural and operational competence.

Employees and managers meet twice a year to monitor progress. All Epcor employees — including the CEO — take part in the performance management program.

### *Training & Skills Development* *Rating: A+*

Epcor's training and skills development program is rated as **exceptional**. The company provides tuition subsidies for courses related to an employee's current position (100% of tuition). Commendably, Epcor also offers subsidies for courses not related to an employee's current job (100% of tuition). Epcor offers bonuses to employees who successfully complete certain professional accreditation programs and courses. The company assists employees' career development with: reimbursement for professional association dues; career planning; in-house training; online training.

### *Community Involvement* *Rating: A+*

Epcor's community involvement program is rated as **exceptional**. An outstanding corporate citizen, Epcor actively supports a variety of local and national charitable initiatives. A member of the Canadian Centre for Philanthropy's "*Imagine*" program, Epcor donates at least 1% of its annual pre-tax profits to charities that focus on community, health and education.

Last year, the company provided support to Stollery Children's Hospital, Edmonton City Centre Church (for a nutritional food program), the Science Alberta Foundation (for an interactive science program that tours elementary schools), the University of Alberta and the United Way.

Epcor also supports a variety of cultural venues and events, including the Epcor Centre for the Performing Arts, the Epcor Environment Gallery at the Odyssium and the Edmonton International Street Performer's Festival.

To promote volunteerism, Epcor operates an outstanding program (called *Essential Volunteers*) to encourage employees to volunteer their time with charities and community groups of their own choosing. For every 50 hours an employee volunteers, Epcor donates $150 to the organization. Under the innovative program, over 100 organizations received support last year. In a recent survey, more than 75% of Epcor employees cited the volunteer program as a key benefit of working at the company — an excellent example of how good employers can build community involvement into the working lives of their employees.

**ERNST & YOUNG LLP**
**222 Bay Street, Ernst & Young Tower**
**PO Box 251, Toronto-Dominion Centre**
**Toronto, ON M5K 1J7**

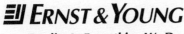

ERNST & YOUNG
*Quality In Everything We Do*

**Tel. 416-864-1234**
**Fax 416-864-1174**
**http://www.ey.com/can**

**INDUSTRY: ACCOUNTING, AUDITING & BOOKKEEPING FIRMS**

*Highlights:*

- Work for an employer that explicitly states that its employees come before clients — satisfied employees provide better service to clients, which is better for everyone.
- Build your career at an employer that applies the "continuous improvement" model to all its recruitment and retention programs — this employer recently fine-tuned its health benefits plan, maternity leave program and even its pension plan.
- Reward yourself with an employer that offers a wide range of cash bonuses — referral bonuses, signing bonuses, year-end bonuses and even bonuses for course completions.

## *Employer Background*

Ernst & Young LLP is one of Canada's leading professional services firms, providing audit, advisory, tax, corporate finance and other services to the nation's leading corporations.

Ernst & Young has a long history in Canada that dates back to 1864, when the venerable firm of Clarkson, Gordon & Co. was established. Ernst & Young LLP is part of the worldwide partnership of Ernst & Young International Ltd., which was created in 1989 through the merger of Arthur Young (which included Clarkson Gordon) and Ernst & Whinney.

As a member of Ernst & Young International, the Canadian partnership offers professional services in more than 140 countries and employs 106,000 people worldwide. In Canada, Ernst & Young has 16 locations from coast-to-coast.

**Workforce at a Glance:** Number of full-time employees: **3,077**. At this location: **1,416**. Worldwide: **106,000**. Percentage of employees who are women: **55**. Of managers: **47**. Percentage of employees who are visible minorities: **17**. Of managers: **13**. Resumes received by their human resources staff in past year: **15,546**. Average employee age: **37**.

## *Physical Workplace* — *Rating: A*

Ernst & Young's physical workplace is rated as **above-average**. The firm's head office occupies 12 floors of a modern office tower in the heart of the Toronto's financial district. The building is connected to the city's underground walking network, providing employees with convenient access numerous restaurants, shops and entertainment options.

**Physical Workplace at a Glance:** Their **employee lounge and rest areas** feature: comfortable couches; television. For **food and refreshment**, Ernst & Young offers: free coffee and tea. The firm has an onsite cafeteria that features: subsidized meals (a turkey sandwich costs $3.50); healthy menu items; special diet menus; and great views of Lake Ontario. Nearby **amenities** include: major shopping mall; variety of restaurants; fitness facility (with subsidized memberships). For **commuters**, Ernst & Young offers: nearby public transit; secure bicycle parking. Other **work area amenities** include: open-concept workstations; ergonomic workstation design; healthcare room; plant life that is tended professionally.

## *Work Atmosphere & Social* — *Rating: A*

Ernst & Young's work atmosphere is rated as **above-average**. Employees at Ernst & Young enjoy business casual dress daily and can listen to radio or music while they are working. The firm has an on-site concierge service.

Throughout the year, Ernst & Young subsidizes a variety of employee activities. These include annual ski and golf days (held on company time), bicycle and winery tours in Niagara, celebrations to recognize individual accomplishments, and a huge holiday dinner dance. Ernst & Young also subsidizes employee hockey, volleyball and basketball teams. (The women's volleyball team captured the Chartered Accountant's league championship last year.)

The firm also supports a variety of arts organizations (including the Toronto Symphony Orchestra, Canadian Opera Company and National Ballet of Canada) and purchases blocks of tickets for its employees.

## *Health, Financial & Family Benefits* — *Rating: A+*

Ernst & Young's health benefits plan is managed by Manulife Financial and is rated as **exceptional**. Their health benefits plan is flexible, meaning that employees can tailor individual plans to their personal circumstances. Full-time and part-time employees who work more than 20 hours per week are covered by the plan.

Ernst & Young also operates an explicit "people come first" strategy. "We are now having the courage to say our people come first, and our clients come second," says Jim Freer, Vice Chair, Human Resources (Americas). "Our clients realize that... when we focus our attention on treating our people well... they, as clients, receive better attention." Because of this enlightened view, the firm recently made changes to its benefits plan (including more flexible health coverage, an increase in maternity top-up payments and higher company contributions to the pension plan) to make sure employees' needs were being met.

**Health Benefits at a Glance:** Ernst & Young's health plan includes the following coverage: dental (80% of eligible costs, to $1,500 each year); orthodontics (50% of eligible costs with a lifetime maximum of $2,000); eyecare (to $200 every 2 years); extended health benefits; prescription drug; massage therapy; physiotherapy; personal and family counselling; employee assistance plan (EAP) for substance abuse/ mental health.

The firm's salary and financial benefits are rated as **exceptional**. To keep pay-levels competitive, Ernst & Young participates in outside salary surveys every 12 months. Individual salaries are reviewed every 12 months. The firm operates a traditional pension plan. Ernst & Young contributes up to 14% of an employees annual salary, depending on years of service.

> **Financial Benefits at a Glance:** Ernst & Young provides an extensive set of financial benefits, including: life and disability insurance; low-interest home loans; discounted car leases; discounted home computers; discounted cellular phones; free tax return preparation; profit-sharing plan; signing bonuses for some employees; referral bonuses for some employees; year-end bonuses.

Ernst & Young's family-friendly benefits are rated as **exceptional**. Employees with pre-school children have access to a daycare facility located nearby. For employees who take maternity leave, Ernst & Young provides a generous top-up to 100% of salary for the first 17 weeks of their leave. The firm also provides an adoption benefit of up to $5,000 per child. Other family-friendly benefits include: flexible start and finish hours; shortened work week (fewer hours); compressed work week (same hours, fewer days); telecommuting and working from home; reduced summer hours.

Recognizing that many employees work for extended periods at out-of-town locations, Ernst & Young also makes its sophisticated videoconferencing facilities available to travelling employees for "virtual" family reunions.

### *Vacation & Time Off* — *Rating: A*

Ernst & Young's vacation and time off are rated as **above-average**. New employees receive 3 weeks of vacation allowance after their first year, which increases to 4 weeks after 5 years of service. The maximum vacation allowance is 5 weeks for long-serving employees. Employees at the firm can also apply for unpaid leaves of absence. (Recently, one employee took a leave to extend a vacation and study art in Paris.)

### *Employee Communications* — *Rating: A+*

Ernst & Young's internal communications program is rated as **exceptional**. The firm has a well-developed intranet site, which keeps employees informed about news and human resource policies that affect their work. An employee satisfaction survey is conducted every 12 months. An outside consultant compiles the survey results for Ernst & Young's management team. Ernst & Young publishes four electronic newsletters on its intranet site that offer employees news from around the world — and across the hall. The company recently introduced a new bilingual weekly newsletter (called *Canadian Connection*) and a new feedback feature (called *Ask E&Y Canada*) on the company's intranet site.

Ernst & Young also operates a unique People Advisory Committee, which consists of employees who represent the firm in terms of ethnicity, gender, work experience, location and practice area. The group meets quarterly with senior management to discuss workplace issues. The firm also operates a special Ethnic Diversity Task Force and a new Gender Equity Advisory Group, which deal with initiatives targeted in these fields.

***Performance Management*** ***Rating: A+***

Ernst & Young's performance management program is rated as **exceptional**. The firm operates a comprehensive performance management program. Once a year, employees and managers meet for review sessions. (Managers receive training in how to conduct effective reviews.) Ernst & Young uses a 360-degree feedback process to gather additional performance-related information from co-workers, supervisors and employees.

As part of the review process, employees complete personal evaluations to review past performance and set future goals. Managers and employees meet informally to discuss progress during the year. Employees can also provide confidential feedback on their manager's performance through the company's intranet site.

***Training & Skills Development*** ***Rating: A+***

Ernst & Young's training and skills development program is rated as **exceptional**. The firm provides tuition subsidies for courses related to an employee's current position (100% of tuition). Commendably, Ernst & Young also offers subsidies for courses not related to an employee's current job (50% of tuition). Ernst & Young offers bonuses (such as $1,000 cash payments) to employees who successfully complete certain professional accreditation programs and courses. The firm assists employees' career development with: reimbursement for professional association dues; mentoring; career planning; in-house training; online training.

***Community Involvement*** ***Rating: A***

Ernst & Young's community involvement program is rated as **above-average**. A very good corporate citizen, Ernst & Young actively supports a variety of charitable initiatives. Across the country, the firm supports local United Way campaigns as well as numerous hospitals, cultural events and community organizations. In support of higher education, the firm operates a generous program that matches employee donations (to $5,000) to colleges and universities across Canada.

**EXPORT DEVELOPMENT CANADA**
**151 O'Connor Street**
**Ottawa, ON K1A 1K3**

**Tel. 613-598-2500**
**Fax 613-598-2578**
**hrrh@edc.ca**
**http://www.edc.ca**

**INDUSTRY: BUSINESS LEASING & FINANCE COMPANIES**

*Highlights:*

- Work for a dynamic Crown corporation where you'll deal with transactions in over 200 countries.
- Get excellent maternity leave (95% of salary for 17 weeks) as well as a variety of family-friendly work arrangements.
- Work for an employer that gives out hundreds of large scholarships each year (totalling over $1 million) to students interested in international trade.

## *Employer Background*

Export Development Canada is a federal Crown corporation that provides trade finance and risk management services to Canadian exporters in markets around the world.

Founded in 1944, EDC provides a range of financial services to assist Canadian exporters in overseas markets. These services include credit insurance, bonding and guarantees, political risk insurance and buyer loans. The Crown-owned corporation is a profit-making business, operated on a commercial basis.

As Canada's international trade expands, EDC's services are increasingly in demand. Last year, the company served over 7,223 exporters — a 14% increase over the previous year.

**Workforce at a Glance:** Number of full-time employees: **1,010**. At this location: **964**. Worldwide: **1,014**. New jobs created in Canada in past year: **27**. Percentage of employees who are women: **51**. Of managers: **36**. Resumes received by their human resources staff in past year: **11,759**. Weeks of vacation their HR manager took last year: **4**. Years longest-serving employee has worked there: **42**. Car the president drives: **walks to work**.

## *Physical Workplace* — *Rating: B+*

EDC's physical workplace is rated as **average**. Most of EDC's employees work at its head office in downtown Ottawa. The office tower is near the grounds of Parliament Hill and the historic Rideau Canal.

**Physical Workplace at a Glance:** Their **onsite fitness facility** features: free memberships; instructor-led classes. Nearby **amenities** include: variety of restaurants; major shopping mall; the popular Byward Market; local shops and services; park/wilderness area (Confederation Park and the Rideau Canal); recreation centre (YMCA).

For **commuters**, EDC offers: nearby public transit; transit subsidies; subsidized car parking; secure bicycle parking. Other **work area amenities** include: open-concept workstations; access to natural light for all employees.

## *Work Atmosphere & Social* — *Rating: A*

EDC's work atmosphere is rated as **above-average**. Employees at EDC enjoy business casual dress daily. There is also a company-subsidized social committee, called the '*Recreational Committee*', which has operated since 1980.

The social committee organize lunch-hour seminars and fun activities throughout the year, including a summer recreation day, an annual dinner/dance, and a Christmas party for employees' children. EDC also sponsors employees sports activities, including squash, touch football, tennis, ultimate frisbee, volleyball and hockey.

## *Health, Financial & Family Benefits* — *Rating: B+*

EDC's health benefits plan is rated as **average**.

**Health Benefits at a Glance:** EDC's health plan includes the following coverage: dental; eyecare; prescription drug; physiotherapy; massage therapy; alternative therapies; extended health benefits; fitness club subsidies (for regional offices); employee assistance plan (EAP) for substance abuse/mental health.

The company's salary and financial benefits are rated as **average**. The company operates a traditional pension plan.

**Financial Benefits at a Glance:** EDC provides a variety of financial benefits, including: life and disability insurance; discounted home computers (to $1,500); group RSP; year-end bonuses.

EDC's family-friendly benefits are rated as **above-average**. Employees with pre-school children have access to a daycare facility located nearby. For employees who take maternity leave, EDC provides a generous top-up to 95% of salary for the first 17 weeks of their leave. Other family-friendly benefits include: flexible start and finish hours; shortened work week (fewer hours); compressed work week (same hours, fewer days).

## *Vacation & Time Off* — *Rating: A*

EDC's vacation and time off are rated as **above-average**. New employees receive 3 weeks of vacation allowance after their first year, which increases to 4 weeks after 8 years of service. The maximum vacation allowance is 5 weeks for long-serving employees. Employees at the company can also apply for unpaid leaves of absence.

## *Employee Communications* — *Rating: A+*

EDC's internal communications program is rated as **exceptional**. To keep employees informed about new developments, EDC publishes an in-house newsletter (called *Link*), which is bilingual. The company also has an intranet site, which keeps employees informed about news and human resource policies that affect their work. An employee satisfaction survey is conducted every 12 months. An outside consultant compiles the survey results for EDC's management team.

In addition to the annual opinion survey, employees can provide confidential feedback through an employee committee ("*Sounding Board*") and an administrators' advisory committee. EDC also publishes a periodic magazine ("*ExportWise*") and hosts an annual conference for all employees.

***Performance Management*** ***Rating: A***

EDC's performance management program is rated as **above-average**. The company operates a thorough performance management program. Once a year, employees and managers meet for review sessions. As part of the review process, managers provide ongoing coaching and feedback as well as mid-year reviews.

Exceptional performance is recognized through individual and team awards, including lunches, dinners, movies and a range of recreational activities. Employees also have the opportunity to nominate their colleagues for special recognition awards.

***Training & Skills Development*** ***Rating: A***

EDC's training and skills development program is rated as **above-average**. The company provides tuition subsidies for courses related to an employee's current position (100% of tuition). The company assists employees' career development with: career planning; in-house training; reimbursement for professional association dues; management succession planning.

***Community Involvement*** ***Rating: A+***

EDC's community involvement program is rated as **exceptional**. An outstanding corporate citizen, EDC actively supports a variety of local and national charitable initiatives. Employees take part in the selection of charitable groups assisted by the company. Employees at EDC receive paid time off to volunteer at local charities. Last year, the company also contributed to approximately 12 charitable groups, including: the United Way, Toy Mountain, the Ottawa Snowsuit Fund (a winter clothing drive), and sponsorship of the Canadian Woman Entrepreneurer of the Year Award.

EDC also supports university students across the country through a number of programs. In addition to hiring co-op and summer students, EDC recently established a $1 million scholarship as part of its youth education and employment strategy. Annual scholarships ($3,000 to $5,000 each) are awarded to undergraduate and graduate students across Canada interested in international business, finance or international relations, a unique charitable program that also strengthens EDC's mission of enhancing Canada's international trade.

FAIRMONT HOTELS & RESORTS
100 Wellington Street West
Suite 1600, Canadian Pacific Tower, TD Centre
Toronto, ON M5K 1B7

Tel. 416-874-2600
Fax 416-874-2799
pathfinder@fairmont.com
http://www.fairmont.com

**INDUSTRY: HOTEL & RESORT OPERATORS**

***Highlights:***

- Develop your career in an industry not known for long-term careers — this employer is the exception, with a strong focus on hiring, training and nurturing employees throughout their working life.
- Work in some of Canada's most spectacular places, from the historic Chateau Frontenac in Québec to the beautiful Chateau Lake Louise in Alberta.
- Become popular again with friends and family with discounted employee rates at this employer's hotels and resorts around the world.
- Work for an enlightened employer that wrote the book on operating a profitable recycling program in the hospitality industry.

## *Employer Background*

Fairmont Hotels & Resorts is North America's largest operator of luxury hotels and resorts. Established in 1887 as Canadian Pacific Hotels, Fairmont Hotels & Resorts has 41 properties worldwide (including 20 in Canada). The company's unique collection of upscale city hotels and resorts are located across Canada, the United States, Mexico, Bermuda, Barbados and the United Arab Emirates.

Across Canada, many of Fairmont's historic properties have become tourist attractions themselves. The company's landmark properties include Le Château Frontenac (a world heritage site in Québec City), Château Laurier in Ottawa and the Fairmont Banff Springs, to name a few. The company has also developed many new resorts in the tradition of its historic properties, such as the Fairmont Château Whistler and Fairmont Tremblant.

Fairmont Hotels & Resorts is an operating subsidiary of publicly-traded Fairmont Hotels & Resorts Incorporated. The Toronto-based parent company also owns Delta Hotels, which manages and franchises downtown hotels and resort properties across Canada.

**Workforce at a Glance:** Number of full-time employees: **9,334**. At this location: **296**. Worldwide: **17,898**. Percentage of employees who are women: **50**. Of managers: **49**. Resumes received by their human resources staff in past year: **600**. Average employee age: **38**.

### *Physical Workplace* — *Rating: A+*

Fairmont's physical workplace is rated as **exceptional**. The majority of Fairmont's employees work in some of the world's most spectacular places. From the Canadian Rockies to the Caribbean, each hotel is unique in its setting and employee amenities. Depending on the location, employees enjoy subsidized accommodations, complimentary meals at employee restaurants (with menus for special diets), computer rooms and employee quiet rooms. At some resorts, employees can take advantage of healthclub and golf memberships, ski passes and organized recreational activities.

Fairmont's head office is located in downtown Toronto just steps from its world-famous Royal York Hotel. The location is close to public transit, commuter rail and major highways.

> **Physical Workplace at a Glance:** Their **employee lounge and rest areas** feature: music; television. For **food and refreshment**, Fairmont offers: free snacks; kitchen area; free coffee and tea. Nearby **amenities** include: variety of restaurants; major shopping mall; fitness facility; recreation centre (Wellington Club). For **commuters**, Fairmont offers: nearby public transit; convenient highway access. Other **work area amenities** include: open-concept workstations; wireless connectivity throughout office; ergonomic workstation design; plant life that is tended professionally.

### *Work Atmosphere & Social* — *Rating: A*

Fairmont's work atmosphere is rated as **above-average**. Employees at Fairmont enjoy business casual dress daily and can listen to radio or music while they are working. The building manager operates a concierge service for all tenants. There is also a company-subsidized social committee, called the '*Service Plus Committee*', which has operated since 1994.

The committee organizes a variety of social events throughout the year, including a summer picnic, a boat cruise, cultural awareness days and a winter holiday party.

### *Health, Financial & Family Benefits* — *Rating: A*

Fairmont's health benefits plan is managed by Great-West Life and is rated as **above-average**. New employees must wait 90 days before they can enroll in the plan.

> **Health Benefits at a Glance:** Fairmont's health plan includes the following coverage: dental (100% of eligible costs, to $1,500 each year); orthodontics (50% of eligible costs with a lifetime maximum of $1,500); eyecare (to $250 every 2 years); prescription drug; extended health benefits; nutrition planning; physiotherapy; massage therapy; alternative therapies; personal and family counselling; employee assistance plan (EAP) for substance abuse/mental health.

The company's salary and financial benefits are rated as **above-average**. To keep pay-levels competitive, Fairmont participates in outside salary surveys every 12 months. Individual salaries are reviewed every 12 months. The company operates a traditional pension plan.

> **Financial Benefits at a Glance:** Fairmont provides a variety of financial benefits, including: life and disability insurance; discounted car leases; discounted home

Internet access; discounted rates (for family and friends) at hotel properties across Canada and around the world; referral bonuses for some employees (from $100); year-end bonuses (from $5,800 to $66,000 for non-executives).

Fairmont's family-friendly benefits are rated as **above-average**. Employees with pre-school children have access to a daycare facility located nearby. For employees who take maternity leave, Fairmont provides a top-up to 70% of salary for the first 6 weeks of their leave. Other family-friendly benefits include: flexible start and finish hours; telecommuting and working from home.

***Vacation & Time Off*** ***Rating: B+***

Fairmont's vacation and time off are rated as **average**. New employees receive 2 weeks of vacation allowance after their first year, which increases to 3 weeks after 3 years of service. The maximum vacation allowance is 6 weeks for long-serving employees. Employees at the company can also apply for unpaid leaves of absence.

***Employee Communications*** ***Rating: A***

Fairmont's internal communications program is rated as **above-average**. To keep employees informed about new developments, Fairmont publishes an in-house newsletter (called *Dialogue*). The company also has an intranet site (called *myFairmont*), which keeps employees informed about news and human resource policies that affect their work. An employee satisfaction survey is conducted every 12 months. An outside consultant compiles the survey results for Fairmont's management team.

***Performance Management*** ***Rating: A***

Fairmont's performance management program is rated as **above-average**. The company operates a formal performance management program. Once a year, employees and managers meet for review sessions. Employees also have the opportunity to provide feedback on their manager's performance. Fairmont also operates an extensive leadership management training program for managers.

The company recognizes exceptional employee performance through several awards. At the hotel properties, employees of the month are chosen via employee and customer feedback. From these winners, each hotel selects an employee of the year who receives free accommodations for two at any Fairmont hotel in the world.

***Training & Skills Development*** ***Rating: A+***

Fairmont's training and skills development program is rated as **exceptional**. The company provides tuition subsidies for courses related to an employee's current position (100% of tuition). Commendably, Fairmont also offers subsidies for courses not related to an employee's current job. The company assists employees' career development with: reimbursement for professional association dues; career planning.

As a service-driven business, Fairmont recognizes that attracting and promoting top talent is vital to its success. The company operates an extensive in-house training program with courses ranging from food preparation to finance. Fairmont also offers apprenticeship training and a unique summer work experience program at resort properties.

Fairmont works closely with hospitality industry associations and post-secondary institutions (such as the University of Guelph's hospitality program) to develop customized training programs for its employees.

***Community Involvement*** ***Rating: A+***

Fairmont's community involvement program is rated as **exceptional**. An outstanding corporate citizen, Fairmont actively supports a variety of local, national and international charitable initiatives.

As the world's first "green" hotel operator, the scope of Fairmont's recycling and conservation efforts is breathtaking. The company's environmental program focuses on waste management, energy and water conservation, and the use of earth-friendly products. At some properties, over 80% of what was previously thrown away as garbage (from food to furniture) is now recycled or reused. The company's ambitious (and profitable) program has succeeded largely because of employee involvement and commitment.

Fairmont's employee-run recycling program has been so successful that its hotels now compete for the coveted title of "Environmental Hotel of the Year". For employers in any industry, this is an excellent example of how to involve employees in making a positive environmental impact. (Fairmont's "Green Partnership Guide" is distributed to hotel management schools and other hotel chains around the world.)

Fairmont's focus on the environment has led to the creation of a unique charitable donations program. Through the company's enlightened "Adopt-a-Shelter" initiative, each hotel donates linens, lamps, furniture and other unused items to local women's shelters across North America.

Recently, Fairmont introduced a separate program to protect endangered species in the areas where it operates. This program raises funds for the conservation of beluga whales in the St. Lawrence River, right-whales off the coast of New Brunswick, grizzly bears and wolves in Alberta, sea turtles in Acapulco and bluebirds in Bermuda.

**FRANK RUSSELL CANADA LTD.**
**100 King Street West**
**Suite 5900, 1 First Canadian Place**
**Toronto, ON M5X 1E4**

**Tel. 416-362-8411**
**Fax 416-640-6195**
**hrcanada@russell.com**
**http://www.russell.com**

**INDUSTRY: INVESTMENT ADVISORS**

*Highlights:*

- Get an exceptional paid vacation allowance of four weeks in your first year — the best in Canada's financial services industry.
- Celebrate ten years on the job with an additional eight week paid sabbatical.
- Work at this employer's other offices around the world for a few months — or even a few years — through a well-developed international work experience program.

## *Employer Background*

Frank Russell Canada Ltd. provides investment management services to institutional and individual investors.

Frank Russell Canada is a subsidiary of Tacoma, Washington-based Frank Russell Company. Established in 1936, the parent company is one of the world's top investment management firms, managing over $2.5 trillion for major corporations, institutions, governments and individual investors. The company has offices in London, Paris, Sydney, Auckland, Tokyo, New York, Tacoma and Toronto.

Frank Russell opened its Toronto office in 1985. Today, the Canadian subsidiary manages assets for institutional and, more recently, individual investors. The company operates a nationwide retail investment program ("Sovereign Investment Program") for individuals through partnerships with TD Canada Trust, Royal Bank and Scotiabank.

Despite one of the longest bear markets in recent memory, Frank Russell continues to experience growth in Canada.

**Workforce at a Glance:** Number of full-time employees: **79**. Worldwide: **1,265**. New jobs created in Canada in past year: **5**. Percentage of employees who are women: **58**. Of managers: **58**. Percentage of employees who are visible minorities: **43**. Of managers: **43**. Resumes received by their human resources staff in past year: **1,000**. Weeks of vacation their HR manager took last year: **5**. Average employee age: **36**. Years longest-serving employee has worked there: **19**. Person you should get to know first: **Renata has been with the company since 1985 and knows the scoop (incriminating and otherwise) on everyone**.

## *Physical Workplace* — *Rating: B+*

Frank Russell's physical workplace is rated as **average**. Located in a modern office building in Toronto's financial district, Frank Russell's head office sits above the city's extensive underground walking network. When designing the interior of the head office, a design committee gathered feedback from employees about the new office space. Occupying nearly the entire 59th floor, the office also provides spectacular views of Lake Ontario and the surrounding city.

**Physical Workplace at a Glance:** Their **employee lounge and rest areas** feature: music; television; comfortable couches. For **food and refreshment**, Frank Russell offers: free coffee and tea; free soft drinks; outdoor eating area; kitchen area. Nearby **amenities** include: variety of restaurants; major shopping mall; fitness facility (with subsidized memberships). For **commuters**, Frank Russell offers: nearby public transit. Other **work area amenities** include: open-concept workstations; ergonomic workstation design; plant life that is tended professionally.

## *Work Atmosphere & Social* — *Rating: B+*

Frank Russell's work atmosphere is rated as **average**. Employees at Frank Russell enjoy casual dress on Fridays and can listen to radio or music while they are working. The company has an on-site concierge service.

Throughout the year, Frank Russell celebrates employee milestones and birthdays, and hosts impromptu celebrations for business accomplishments and various special events. The company also hosts an annual summer picnic at a different location every year (on company time) and a Christmas party for employees and their spouses.

## *Health, Financial & Family Benefits* — *Rating: A*

Frank Russell's health benefits plan is managed by Great-West Life and is rated as **above-average**. Frank Russell pays 100% of the premiums associated with the plan. New employees must wait 90 days before they can enroll in the plan.

Employees at Frank Russell receive a comprehensive employee benefits package that includes dental, orthodontics, eyecare, prescription drugs, extended health, nutrition planning, physiotherapy, massage therapy, alternative therapies, counselling, healthclub subsidies (to $1,000 annually) and flexible work arrangements.

**Health Benefits at a Glance:** Frank Russell's health plan includes the following coverage: dental (100% of eligible costs, to $4,000 each year); orthodontics (50% of eligible costs with a lifetime maximum of $2,000); eyecare (to $200 every 2 years); prescription drug; extended health benefits; nutrition planning; massage therapy; physiotherapy; alternative therapies; personal and family counselling; employee assistance plan (EAP) for substance abuse/mental health; healthclub subsidies (to $1,000 annually).

The company's salary and financial benefits are rated as **exceptional**. To keep pay-levels competitive, Frank Russell participates in outside salary surveys every 24 months. Individual salaries are reviewed every 12 months. The company operates a traditional pension plan where Frank Russell makes a contribution equal to 15% of each employee's salary to their plan each year. If this amount is greater than the maximum allowed for an annual RRSP contribution, then the remainder is paid to the employee as a cash bonus.

**Financial Benefits at a Glance:** Frank Russell provides an extensive set of financial benefits, including: life and disability insurance; discounted company products; project bonuses; share purchase plan (almost all employees own equity in the company); year-end bonuses.

Frank Russell's family-friendly benefits are rated as **average**. Employees with pre-school children have access to a daycare facility located nearby. Other family-friendly benefits include: flexible start and finish hours; telecommuting and working from home; free family coverage on health plan.

### *Vacation & Time Off* — *Rating: A+*

Frank Russell's vacation and time off are rated as **exceptional**. New employees receive 4 weeks of vacation allowance after their first year, which increases to 5 weeks after 10 years of service. In addition, it's not uncommon for the office to shut down early prior to long weekends in the summer. Employees at the company can also apply for unpaid leaves of absence.

Employees reaching their 10th anniversary with the company receive a fully-paid 8 week sabbatical, in addition to their regular vacation allowance.

### *Employee Communications* — *Rating: B+*

Frank Russell's internal communications program is rated as **average**. To keep employees informed about new developments, Frank Russell publishes an in-house newsletter. The company also has an intranet site (called *Soundings*), which keeps employees informed about news and human resource policies that affect their work. To solicit feedback from employees, the company operates a traditional suggestion box program and an email suggestion box.

### *Performance Management* — *Rating: A*

Frank Russell's performance management program is rated as **above-average**. The company operates a thorough performance management program. Once a year, employees and managers meet for review sessions. (Managers receive training in how to conduct effective reviews.) Prior to each review, employees and managers prepare written assessments of progress towards last year's goals. Employees can also provide written feedback on the review process and their managers.

Performance excellence is recognized through a variety of individual and team awards. Individual recipients are honoured at special breakfasts and luncheons with cash awards (to $525), certificates and crystal gift plaques. Team awards include an extra vacation day for all members.

### *Training & Skills Development* — *Rating: A*

Frank Russell's training and skills development program is rated as **above-average**. Commendably, Frank Russell offers subsidies for courses not related to an employee's current job (90% of tuition). The company assists employees' career development with: reimbursement for professional association dues. The company also offers paid study days (from one to five days, depending on the course).

Employees can also take advantage of a formal international assignment program, which is an important part of the company's overall business strategy. Through this program, employees have the opportunity to work temporarily at other offices around the world for up to five years.

***Community Involvement*** ***Rating: B+***

Frank Russell's community involvement program is rated as **average**. A good corporate citizen, Frank Russell actively supports a variety of charitable initiatives.

Every year, the company actively supports the local United Way campaign. Employees host silent auctions, email bingo, raffles and book sales to raise money (and have fun). The company also gives employees paid time off to volunteer for the United Way's "Helping Hands Day". During the Christmas season, an employee committee raises donations, food, clothing and gifts for families in need.

**FULLER LANDAU LLP**
**151 Bloor Street West**
**12th Floor**
**Toronto, ON M5S 1S4**

**Tel. 416-645-6500**
**Fax 416-645-6501**
**http://www.fullerlandau.com**

**INDUSTRY: ACCOUNTING, AUDITING & BOOKKEEPING FIRMS**

*Highlights:*

- Work hard and get weekly performance awards (chosen by your co-workers), special tax season cash bonuses and even an all-expense-paid vacation.
- Play hard at an employer that gives you paid time off to unwind and celebrates the end of tax season with a huge bash.
- Pocket an automatic $5,000 salary increase when you successfuly complete the Chartered Accountant's final exam.

## *Employer Background*

Fuller Landau LLP is a chartered accounting and business consulting firm. Established in 1948, the firm has a long history of serving mid-sized entrepreneurial clients.

Fuller Landau provides a complete range of accounting and professional services, including audit; tax; corporate recovery and insolvency; corporate finance; mergers and acquisitions; business valuations; litigation; information technology; human resources consulting; and personal financial planning services. The firm has offices in Toronto and Montréal.

**Workforce at a Glance:** Number of full-time employees: **133**. At this location: **60**. New jobs created in Canada in past year: **20**. Percentage of employees who are women: **49**. Of managers: **12**. Percentage of employees who are visible minorities: **20**. Of managers: **5**. Resumes received by their human resources staff in past year: **2,157**. Weeks of vacation their HR manager took last year: **3**. Average employee age: **39**. Years longest-serving employee has worked there: **50**. Car the president drives: **1999 Saab**. Where it's parked in the lot: **with everyone else**.

## *Physical Workplace* — *Rating: A*

Fuller Landau's physical workplace is rated as **above-average**. The firm's Toronto head office is located in a 15-storey building on Toronto's upscale Bloor Street West shopping area, steps away from the University of Toronto and the trendy Yorkville district.

**Physical Workplace at a Glance:** For **food and refreshment**, Fuller Landau offers: free snacks (including fresh fruit, chocolate bars, cereal bars and almonds); free coffee and tea; free soft drinks. Nearby **amenities** include: variety of restaurants;

local shops and services; movie theatres; Royal Ontario Museum; fitness facility (with subsidized memberships); park/wilderness area (Queen's Park). For **commuters**, Fuller Landau offers: nearby public transit; subsidized car parking. Other **work area amenities** include: open-concept workstations; ergonomic workstation design; access to natural light for all employees; plant life that is tended professionally.

*Work Atmosphere & Social* *Rating: A*

Fuller Landau's work atmosphere is rated as **above-average**. Employees at Fuller Landau enjoy business casual dress daily and can listen to radio or music while they are working. There is also a firm-subsidized social committee, called the '*Fuller Fun Committee*'.

The committee organizes a variety of fun activities and events every year, including an "end of tax season" party, quarterly socials at a local pub, a unique summer car rally (with barbeque) and a Christmas cocktail party. Throughout the year, the firm also celebrates significant events in employees' personal and professional lives, such as weddings, new babies, birthdays, employment anniversaries and completing the Chartered Accountant's final examination.

*Health, Financial & Family Benefits* *Rating: A*

Fuller Landau's health benefits plan is managed by Canada Life and is rated as **above-average**. New employees must wait 90 days before they can enroll in the plan.

**Health Benefits at a Glance:** Fuller Landau's health plan includes the following coverage: dental (90% of eligible costs, to $2,000 each year); orthodontics (50% of eligible costs with a lifetime maximum of $1,500); extended health benefits; prescription drug; massage therapy; physiotherapy; alternative therapies; personal and family counselling.

The firm's salary and financial benefits are rated as **above-average**. To keep pay-levels competitive, Fuller Landau participates in outside salary surveys every 12 months. Individual salaries are reviewed every 12 months.

**Financial Benefits at a Glance:** Fuller Landau provides a variety of financial benefits, including: life and disability insurance; performance awards (to $3,500); new businees referral bonuses (to 10% of annual billings); referral bonuses for some employees (from $500 to $2,000); year-end bonuses (from $300 to $8,500 for non-executives).

Fuller Landau's family-friendly benefits are rated as **average**. Employees with pre-school children have access to a daycare facility located nearby. Other family-friendly benefits include: reduced summer hours; flexible start and finish hours.

*Vacation & Time Off* *Rating: A*

Fuller Landau's vacation and time off are rated as **above-average**. New employees receive 3 weeks of vacation allowance after their first year, which increases to 4 weeks after 5 years of service. Fuller Landau also provides employees with one paid day off each year specifically for relaxing and fun activities.

### *Employee Communications* — *Rating: A*

Fuller Landau's internal communications program is rated as **above-average**. To keep employees informed about new developments, Fuller Landau publishes an in-house newsletter (called *The WIC*). An employee satisfaction survey is conducted every 12 months. An outside consultant compiles the survey results for Fuller Landau's management team.

### *Performance Management* — *Rating: A+*

Fuller Landau's performance management program is rated as **exceptional**. The firm operates a well-designed performance management program. Once a year, employees and managers meet for review sessions. (Managers receive training in how to conduct effective reviews.) Fuller Landau uses a 360-degree feedback process to gather additional performance-related information from co-workers, supervisors and employees. As part of this process, employees can select co-workers who are familiar with their work to provide feedback.

At the annual reviews, employees and their managers set performance goals for the upcoming year. In addition, employees meet with their managers for formal mid-year updates. The review process forms the basis for future training and salary increases.

Fuller Landau recognizes exceptional performance with weekly awards that are made by co-workers — recipients can win an annual paid vacation. At the end of tax season (traditionally the firm's busiest time), employees can also receive special cash bonuses (to $3,500) for exceptional performance.

### *Training & Skills Development* — *Rating: A*

Fuller Landau's training and skills development program is rated as **above-average**. The firm provides tuition subsidies for courses related to an employee's current position (100% of tuition). Commendably, Fuller Landau also offers subsidies for courses not related to an employee's current job (50% of tuition). The firm assists employees' career development with: reimbursement for professional association dues; mentoring; monthly training sessions; weekly lunchtime seminars. Fuller Landau also provides an automatic $5,000 salary increase to employees when they complete the Chartered Accountant's final exam.

### *Community Involvement* — *Rating: A*

Fuller Landau's community involvement program is rated as **above-average**. A very good corporate citizen, Fuller Landau actively supports a variety of local and national charitable initiatives. Last year, the firm contributed to approximately 15 charitable groups, including: the United Way, the Canadian Liver Foundation, the Easter Seals Society, the Arthritis Society, the AIDS Committee of Toronto, Jewish Family Services and the Chinese Martyrs Catholic Church.

For employees who provide 20 hours of volunteer service with a registered charity, the company matches their efforts with a $150 donation in their name. In a unique initiative last year, the company also hosted a huge Christmas party for children at a downtown elementary school, where over 680 children enjoyed a day of fun activities.

GENERAL DYNAMICS CANADA, LTD.
3785 Richmond Road
Ottawa, ON K2H 5B7

Tel. 613-596-7000
Fax 613-596-7637
info@gdcanada.com
http://www.gdcanada.com

# GENERAL DYNAMICS
Canada

**INDUSTRY: ROCKET & SPACE VEHICLE MANUFACTURERS**

*Highlights:*

- Build your career at an employer that's poised for substantial growth as Canada modernizes its armed forces and takes on significant peace-keeping duties overseas.
- Work for a benevolent employer that gives out free turkeys to employees at Christmas and organizes family events for employees throughout the year.
- Stick handle your way to the top at a hockey-oriented employer that boasts no fewer than six in-house hockey teams and offers employees free tickets to Ottawa Senators' hockey games.

## *Employer Background*

General Dynamics Canada, Ltd. is a leading defence contractor. Designed to rigorous military standards, the company's high-tech electronics equipment includes complete communication systems for land, air and maritime applications.

In addition to its manufacturing operations, General Dynamics Canada places significant emphasis on research and development. The company's products include the world's first digital tank firing control system, portable air traffic control systems (that operate from a single airplane) and advanced remote-controlled land mine detection systems. General Dynamics Canada supplies equipment to armed forces in over 20 countries.

Established in 1948, General Dynamics Canada is a subsidiary of Virginia-based General Dynamics Corporation. The parent company is a leading defense contractor, manufacturing nuclear submarines, destroyers, amphibious assault vehicles, large commercial vessels, aircraft and defense systems for governments around the world. In Canada, General Dynamics has locations in Ottawa and Calgary.

**Workforce at a Glance:** Number of full-time employees: **1,255**. At this location: **792**. New jobs created in Canada in past year: **64**. Percentage of employees who are women: **30**. Of managers: **9**. Percentage of employees who are visible minorities: **12**. Of managers: **4**. Resumes received by their human resources staff in past year: **10,000**. Weeks of vacation their HR manager took last year: **3**. Average employee age: **43**. Years longest-serving employee has worked there: **40**. Car the president drives: **Lexus**. Where it's parked in the lot: **reserved spot in front**.

### *Physical Workplace* — *Rating: A*

General Dynamics' physical workplace is rated as **above-average**. The company's suburban head office in Ottawa is situated on a campus-like setting and is comprised of three buildings connected by enclosed walkways. There is also a large lawn area (with a baseball diamond) for employee gatherings.

**Physical Workplace at a Glance:** Their **onsite fitness facility** features: subsidized memberships; treadmills; stationary bikes; stairmasters; weights; instructor-led classes; outdoor basketball, volleball and baseball; shower facilities. For **food and refreshment**, General Dynamics offers: outdoor eating area; barbeque. The company has an onsite cafeteria that features: subsidized meals (a turkey sandwich costs $3.25); healthy menu items; cultural theme days with special menu items. Nearby **amenities** include: variety of restaurants; major shopping mall; park/wilderness area (Andrew Haydon Park); recreation centre (Nepean Sportsplex). For **commuters**, General Dynamics offers: free onsite car parking; nearby public transit. Other **work area amenities** include: open-concept workstations; ergonomic workstation design; plant life that is tended professionally.

### *Work Atmosphere & Social* — *Rating: A*

General Dynamics' work atmosphere is rated as **above-average**. Employees at General Dynamics enjoy business casual dress daily and can listen to radio or music while they are working. There is also a company-subsidized social committee, which has operated since 1965.

The committee organizes a variety of events and activities throughout the year, including employee golf tournaments, family trips to amusement parks, subsidized tickets to professional hockey games, monthly movie nights and an annual awards dinner for long-serving employees.

Each Christmas, the company gives a free turkey to every employee. The company also hosts a Christmas party for employees, with a separate event for employees' children. General Dynamics also sponsors 6 competitive employee hockey teams, as well as recreational softball, soccer and hockey teams that compete in local leagues.

### *Health, Financial & Family Benefits* — *Rating: A*

General Dynamics' health benefits plan is rated as **above-average**. Their health benefits plan is flexible, meaning that employees can tailor individual plans to their personal circumstances. There is no waiting period before new employees are eligible for coverage.

**Health Benefits at a Glance:** General Dynamics' health plan includes the following coverage: dental; orthodontics (50% of eligible costs with a lifetime maximum of $2,000); eyecare (to $200 every 2 years); extended health benefits; prescription drug; nutrition planning; massage therapy; physiotherapy; personal and family counselling; employee assistance plan (EAP) for substance abuse/mental health.

The company's salary and financial benefits are rated as **above-average**. To keep pay-levels competitive, General Dynamics participates in outside salary surveys. Individual salaries are reviewed every 12 months. The company operates a traditional pension plan.

**Financial Benefits at a Glance:** General Dynamics provides a variety of financial benefits, including: life and disability insurance; discounted car leases; subsidized auto insurance; performance bonuses; referral bonuses for some employees (to $2,000).

General Dynamics' family-friendly benefits are rated as **above-average**. Employees with pre-school children have access to a daycare facility located nearby. For employees who take maternity leave, General Dynamics provides a top-up to 70% of salary for the first 18 weeks of their leave. Other family-friendly benefits include: compressed work week (same hours, fewer days); shortened work week (fewer hours); flexible start and finish hours.

To help some of its employees with their children's tuition costs, General Dynamics awards 6 academic scholarships each year to employees' children who are attending college or university.

***Vacation & Time Off*** ***Rating: A***

General Dynamics' vacation and time off are rated as **above-average**. New employees receive 3 weeks of vacation allowance after their first year, which increases to 4 weeks after 10 years of service. The maximum vacation allowance is 5 weeks for long-serving employees. Employees at the company can also apply for unpaid leaves of absence. (One employee recently took a 2 year leave to be with their spouse, who was working overseas.)

***Employee Communications*** ***Rating: A***

General Dynamics' internal communications program is rated as **above-average**. To keep employees informed about new developments, General Dynamics publishes an in-house newsletter (called *Connected*). The company also has an intranet site, which keeps employees informed about news and human resource policies that affect their work. To solicit feedback from employees, the company operates an email suggestion box. An employee satisfaction survey is conducted every 36 months. An outside consultant compiles the survey results for General Dynamics' management team.

***Performance Management*** ***Rating: A***

General Dynamics' performance management program is rated as **above-average**. The company operates a formal performance management program. Once a year, employees and managers meet for review sessions. (Managers receive training in how to conduct effective reviews.) General Dynamics uses a 360-degree feedback process to gather additional performance-related information from co-workers, supervisors and employees. At the annual meetings, past performance is reviewed and goals are set for the upcoming year. General Dynamics recognizes exceptional performance with tickets to professional hockey games and financial bonuses. Managers also receive bonuses for meeting their review responsibilities.

***Training & Skills Development*** ***Rating: A***

General Dynamics' training and skills development program is rated as **above-average**. The company provides tuition subsidies for courses related to an employee's current position (100% of tuition). Commendably, General Dynamics also offers subsidies for courses not related to an employee's current job (100% of tuition). The company assists employees' career development with: reimbursement for professional association dues; industry seminars; in-house training.

***Community Involvement*** ***Rating: A***

General Dynamics' community involvement program is rated as **above-average**. A very good corporate citizen, General Dynamics actively supports a variety of local and national charitable initiatives. Employees at General Dynamics receive paid time off to volunteer at local charities. Last year, the company contributed to approximately 30 charitable groups.

Last year, the company supported the United Way, Canadian Blood Services, the Canadian Cancer Society and the Queensway-Carleton Hospital. The company also sponsors employee dragonboat and volleyball teams that compete in charity fundraising events.

**GENNUM CORPORATION**
**PO Box 489, Station A**
**Burlington, ON L7R 3Y3**

**Tel. 905-632-2996**
**Fax 905-632-2055**
**career@gennum.com**
**http://www.gennum.com**

**INDUSTRY: ELECTRONIC COMPONENT MANUFACTURERS**

*Highlights:*

- Work hard and become eligible for an incredible annual performance award of up to $12,000 in cash.
- Take part in a generous share purchase plan that is so popular 90% of employees are shareholders.
- Work for an established business with an entrepreneurial flare and an enviable record of success in niche markets.

## *Employer Background*

Gennum Corporation manufactures silicon integrated circuits and thin-film hybrid microcircuit components used in hearing aids, high-end video broadcast systems, and data communications. Founded in 1973, the publicly-traded company's success is based on a strategy of focusing on niche markets and becoming the leading supplier in these markets.

Gennum's hearing instrument products include a wide range of components used by manufacturers of analog and digital hearing aids — impressively, the company's integrated circuits are found in almost two-thirds of the world's analog hearing aids.

The company's high-performance circuits are also used by professional video equipment manufacturers for video processing, image transmission and conversion applications. Gennum's newest line of business is the development of integrated circuits for high-speed data communications. The company was recently awarded a major contract to design and manufacture complex integrated circuits for a leading communications company.

Gennum serves an international customer base from its head office in Burlington, a design centre in Ottawa and subsidiaries in Japan and the United Kingdom.

**Workforce at a Glance:** Number of full-time employees: **505**. At this location: **493**. Worldwide: **518**. New jobs created in Canada in past year: **42**. Percentage of employees who are women: **50**. Of managers: **14**. Resumes received by their human resources staff in past year: **5,000**. Weeks of vacation their HR manager took last year: **3**. Average employee age: **39**. Years longest-serving employee has worked there: **29**.

### *Physical Workplace* — *Rating: B+*

Gennum's physical workplace is rated as **average**. Gennum's Burlington head office is located in a commercial area with easy access to major highways. The head office campus has three separate buildings, totaling 175,000 square feet of office and manufacturing space. Gennum recently opened a new 68,000-square-foot building to house its technical, sales and marketing, and administrative employees.

**Physical Workplace at a Glance:** For **food and refreshment**, Gennum offers: free coffee and tea; kitchen areas; outdoor eating area. Nearby **amenities** include: variety of restaurants; major shopping mall; fitness facility; park/wilderness area (Spencer Smith Park); recreation centre (Tansley Woods Recreation Centre). For **commuters**, Gennum offers: free onsite car parking; nearby public transit; secure bicycle parking. Other **work area amenities** include: open-concept workstations; high-technology industrial areas; ergonomic workstation design; plant life that is tended professionally.

### *Work Atmosphere & Social* — *Rating: A*

Gennum's work atmosphere is rated as **above-average**. Employees at Gennum enjoy business casual dress daily and can listen to radio or music while they are working. There is also a company-subsidized social committee.

Every year the committee organizes a variety of fun events, including an employee summer picnic, winery and brewery tours, a golf tournament, informal musical concerts by employees, a boat cruise, and paintball competitions.

Gennum also sponsors an employee Christmas party (with a separate children's party), a summer barbeque, departmental social events and retirement parties. The company also subsidizes employee baseball, soccer, basketball and hockey teams.

### *Health, Financial & Family Benefits* — *Rating: A*

Gennum's health benefits plan is managed by Sun Life and is rated as **above-average**. New employees must wait 30 days before they can enroll in the plan.

**Health Benefits at a Glance:** Gennum's health plan includes the following coverage: dental (80% of eligible costs, to $1,500 each year); orthodontics (50% of eligible costs, to $1,500 each year); eyecare (to $250 every 2 years); prescription drug; extended health benefits; physiotherapy; massage therapy; alternative therapies; personal and family counselling; employee assistance plan (EAP) for substance abuse/mental health.

The company's salary and financial benefits are rated as **exceptional**. To keep pay-levels competitive, Gennum participates in outside salary surveys every 12 months. Individual salaries are reviewed every 12 months. The company offers a group RSP that allows employees to contribute up to 5% of their salary, with matching employer contributions.

**Financial Benefits at a Glance:** Gennum provides an extensive set of financial benefits, including: share purchase plan (over 90% of employees are shareholders); discounted car leases; life and disability insurance; discounted home computers; discounted home Internet access; referral bonuses for some employees (from $1,000 to $4,000); year-end bonuses.

Gennum's family-friendly benefits are rated as **average**. Employees with preschool children have access to a daycare facility located nearby. Other family-friendly benefits include: flexible start and finish hours; shortened work week (fewer hours); compressed work week (same hours, fewer days); telecommuting and working from home; reduced summer hours.

### *Vacation & Time Off* — *Rating: B+*

Gennum's vacation and time off are rated as **average**. New employees receive 2 weeks of vacation allowance after their first year, which increases to 3 weeks after 3 years of service. The maximum vacation allowance is 5 weeks for long-serving employees. Each year, Gennum also provides employees with a paid holiday shutdown from Christmas to New Year's. Employees at the company can also apply for unpaid leaves of absence.

### *Employee Communications* — *Rating: A*

Gennum's internal communications program is rated as **above-average**. The company has an intranet site (called *InfoGen*), which keeps employees informed about news and human resource policies that affect their work. An employee satisfaction survey is conducted by having employees complete an online questionnaire every 12 months. An outside consultant compiles the survey results for Gennum's management team.

### *Performance Management* — *Rating: A+*

Gennum's performance management program is rated as **exceptional**. The company operates a comprehensive performance management program. Every 6 months, employees and managers meet for review sessions. (Managers receive training in how to conduct effective reviews.) Managers also provide ongoing feedback and coaching throughout the year.

Gennum has an excellent program of performance incentives. Each year, one employee receives a significant cash award for outstanding contribution to the company — in the past, this award has been as much as $12,000. The reward is unique in that all employees have the opportunity to participate. Outstanding employees also compete for the annual "President's Award", which includes a $3,000 cash award. Individual departments recognize employees through gift certificates and cash awards.

### *Training & Skills Development* — *Rating: A*

Gennum's training and skills development program is rated as **above-average**. The company provides tuition subsidies for courses related to an employee's current position (100% of tuition). Commendably, Gennum also offers subsidies for courses not related to an employee's current job. The company assists employees' career development with: reimbursement for professional association dues; in-house training. The company's in-house training program includes a variety of courses, including leadership development, communication skills, health and safety, and computer training.

***Community Involvement*** ***Rating: A+***

Gennum's community involvement program is rated as **exceptional**. An outstanding corporate citizen, Gennum actively supports a variety of local charitable initiatives. Employees take part in the selection of charitable groups assisted by the company. Employees at Gennum receive paid time off to volunteer at local charities.

Gennum concentrates its charitable activities in the areas of health, welfare, culture and education. The company supports a number of organizations in the Burlington area, including the United Way, the McMaster University Science and Engineering Camp, the Burlington Arts Centre, the Burlington Drury Lane Theatre Company, a local hospital and a regional cancer centre.

GEORGIAN

YOUR COLLEGE · YOUR FUTURE

**GEORGIAN COLLEGE**
**1 Georgian Drive**
**Barrie, ON L4M 3X9**

**Tel. 705-722-1968**
**Fax 705-722-1503**
**resume@georgianc.on.ca**
**http://www.georgianc.on.ca**

**INDUSTRY: COLLEGES & UNIVERSITIES**

*Highlights:*

- Take advantage of tremendous family-friendly benefits offered by this employer, including outstanding maternity leave top-up (93% of salary for 52 weeks), onsite daycare and a range of alternative work options.
- Build your career at a growing college that provides a wonderful quality of life in Ontario's Muskoka region, offering teaching opportunities on campuses as far afield as India and Bahrain.
- Get three weeks paid vacation allowance to start (nine weeks if you're a faculty member) and additional paid time off for the Christmas holidays.

*Employer Background*

Situated less than two hours drive north of Toronto, Georgian College is a community college serving one of Ontario's fastest-growing regions. For over 30 years, the College has been an important contributor to the growth and economic development of the Georgian Bay region of Ontario. The College serves the counties of Grey, Bruce, Dufferin and Simcoe, as well as the municipalities of Muskoka and Parry Sound — a vast area comprising 30,000 square kilometres.

Georgian offers courses to over 5,000 full-time and 25,000 part-time students. The College has more than 50 post-secondary certificate, diploma and post-diploma programs in the arts, health sciences, business, engineering technology and hospitality. Georgian also offers a wide range of skills development programs.

Georgian has over 1,240 full- and part-time employees at campuses across the region. There are three main campuses (Barrie, Orillia and Owen Sound) and five satellite campuses (Bracebridge, Collingwood, Midland, Orangeville and Parry Sound). The main campus in Barrie recently opened a new student residence, an expanded fitness centre and a new Centre for Technology-Enhanced Learning.

Recently, Georgian also opened a satellite campus in India's Punjab state. The campus has 100 students enrolled in a three-year computer analyst program. This ongoing project provides opportunities for Georgian faculty to teach for a semester in India. The College has signed a similar agreement to develop an international campus in Bahrain.

**Workforce at a Glance:** Number of full-time employees: **603**. At this location: **462**. New jobs created in Canada in past year: **113**. Percentage of employees who are women: **76**. Of managers: **58**. Resumes received by their human resources staff in past year: **6,834**. Weeks of vacation their HR manager took last year: **7**. Average employee age: **47**. Years longest-serving employee has worked there: **33**. Person you should get to know first: **Erin at the Barrie campus knows where everything is — and the best way to get there**. Car the president drives: **Ford Explorer**. Where it's parked in the lot: **reserved spot in front**.

## *Physical Workplace* — *Rating: A+*

Georgian's physical workplace is rated as **exceptional**. The College's central campus in Barrie is situated on 140 acres and is home to its main facilities. An outdoor fitness trail winds through the campus and a recently expanded athletic centre, with a tournament-sized gymnasium and fitness facility, is available for students and employees alike.

**Physical Workplace at a Glance:** Their **onsite fitness facility** features: subsidized memberships; stairmasters; treadmills; stationary bikes; rowing machines; weights; gymnasium; climbing wall; instructor-led classes; sauna; whirlpool; shower facilities. Their **employee lounge and rest areas** feature: comfortable couches; fireplace; music; television; video games; pool table; meditation or religious observance room. For **food and refreshment**, Georgian offers: outdoor eating area; fully licensed pub (called *The Last Class*). The College has an onsite cafeteria that features: subsidized meals (a turkey sandwich costs $2.99); healthy menu items; special diet menus. Nearby **amenities** include: variety of restaurants; major shopping mall; hospital; golf course; park/wilderness area (Lake Simcoe). For **commuters**, Georgian offers: subsidized car parking; nearby public transit. Other **work area amenities** include: open-concept workstations; ergonomic workstation design; windows that open; plant life that is tended professionally; onsite bank with ATM.

## *Work Atmosphere & Social* — *Rating: A*

Georgian's work atmosphere is rated as **above-average**. Employees at Georgian enjoy business casual dress daily and can listen to radio or music while they are working.

Employees enjoy a variety of subsidized events during the year, including a Christmas party for employees' children, a variety show (with proceeds donated to student bursaries), wine tasting nights, and numerous departmental gatherings to celebrate birthdays, weddings and new babies. Georgian also hosts an annual event (called *Georgian Day*), where employees attend lectures and workshops and enjoy a game of golf, or another recreational activity, to close the day.

## *Health, Financial & Family Benefits* — *Rating: A*

Georgian's health benefits plan is managed by Sun Life and is rated as **above-average**. Depending on an employee's position, the College pays for 75% or 100% of the premiums. New employees must wait 30 days before they can enroll in the plan.

**Health Benefits at a Glance:** Georgian's health plan includes the following coverage: dental (100% of eligible costs, to $2,000 each year); orthodontics (50% of eligible costs with a lifetime maximum of $2,000); eyecare (to $300 every 2 years); extended health benefits; prescription drug; physiotherapy; massage therapy; alternative therapies; personal and family counselling; employee assistance plan (EAP) for substance abuse/mental health.

The College's salary and financial benefits are rated as **above-average**. To keep pay-levels competitive, Georgian participates in outside salary surveys every 24 months. Individual salaries are reviewed every 12 months. The College operates a traditional pension plan where Georgian makes a contribution equal to 7.6% of each employee's salary to their plan each year.

**Financial Benefits at a Glance:** Georgian provides a variety of financial benefits, including: life and disability insurance; discounted home computers; year-end bonuses (from $400 to $3,000 for non-executives).

Georgian's family-friendly benefits are rated as **exceptional**. Employees with pre-school children have access to a subsidized daycare facility located onsite. The daycare facility has 99 spaces, employs 15 childcare workers and has a 24-month waiting list for new spaces. For employees who take maternity leave, Georgian provides a generous top-up to 93% of salary for the first 52 weeks of their leave. Other family-friendly benefits include: flexible start and finish hours; shortened work week (fewer hours); compressed work week (same hours, fewer days); telecommuting and working from home; reduced summer hours.

***Vacation & Time Off*** — ***Rating: A***

Georgian's vacation and time off are rated as **above-average**. New employees receive 3 weeks of vacation allowance after their first year, which increases to 4 weeks after 10 years of service. The maximum vacation allowance is 6 weeks for long-serving employees. Employees at Georgian also receive 5 paid personal days off each year, in addition to their regular vacation allowance. (Faculty employees receive 9 weeks of vacation.) Each year, Georgian also provides employees with a paid holiday shutdown from Christmas to New Year's. Employees at the College can also apply for unpaid leaves of absence.

Employees can also take advantage of a number of sabbatical options, including professional development leaves, temporary work leaves and self-funded leaves.

***Employee Communications*** — ***Rating: A***

Georgian's internal communications program is rated as **above-average**. To keep employees informed about new developments, Georgian publishes an in-house newsletter (called *College Capsule*). The College also has an intranet site, which keeps employees informed about news and human resource policies that affect their work. To solicit feedback from employees, the College operates an email suggestion box. An employee satisfaction survey is conducted every 48 months. An outside consultant compiles the survey results for Georgian's management team.

***Performance Management*** — ***Rating: A***

Georgian's performance management program is rated as **above-average**. The College operates a formal performance management program. Once a year, employees and managers meet for review sessions. (Managers receive training in how to conduct effective reviews.) The review program encourages ongoing feedback between employees and managers regarding performance, training and development. The program also solicits feedback from employees about their managers and student feedback about the faculty.

### *Training & Skills Development* — *Rating: A*

Georgian's training and skills development program is rated as **above-average**. The College assists employees' career development with: reimbursement for professional association dues; career planning; in-house training; mentoring; reduced tuition for Georgian College courses (which can be taken during working hours); faculty laptop computers; software training.

Georgian recently established a mentoring program for new teachers. Through this program, the College offers a reduced workload and special ongoing orientation courses to teachers in their first year on the job.

### *Community Involvement* — *Rating: A*

Georgian's community involvement program is rated as **above-average**. A very good member of the community, Georgian actively supports a variety of charitable initiatives. Last year, employees contributed to the United Way, the MS Society, the Canadian Cancer Socety and the Canadian National Institute for the Blind.

As a public institution, Georgian also offers part-time courses to area residents interested in upgrading their skills or education. Area residents can also use some services at the College's career centre and at its learning disability centre. The College also provides sports facilities (such as baseball diamonds) to the City of Barrie and space for childcare centres in Barrie and Orillia.

**GREAT-WEST LIFE ASSURANCE COMPANY, THE**
**60 Osborne Street North**
**Winnipeg, MB R3C 1V3**

**Tel. 204-946-7693**
**Fax 204-946-4116**
**careers@gwl.ca**
**http://www.gwl.ca**

**INDUSTRY: LIFE INSURANCE COMPANIES**

***Highlights:***

- Work for an employer with an exceptional benefits plan that's used as a model for plans adopted by other employers.
- Invite friends and family for a healthy lunch at this employer's cafeteria, which was recognized by the Heart & Stroke Foundation for its appetizing "health smart" menus.
- Work at an employer that's serious about creating a friendly and positive work atmosphere — their social committee has been doing it right since 1909.

## *Employer Background*

The Great-West Life Assurance Company offers individuals, businesses and organizations a range of life and disability insurance, retirement savings, investment and employee benefits plans. Established in 1891, the company provides insurance and other financial services to more than nine million people across Canada.

Great-West also owns London, Ontario-based London Life. The two companies have integrated corporate and business functions, but maintain separate sales forces and distinct brands of financial services. The merger brought together London Life's strong individual life insurance business with Great-West's reputation as a leading group benefits insurer.

Great-West continues to grow and consolidate its position as one of Canada's leading insurance companies. Last year, the company completed its acquisition of Toronto-based Canada Life Financial Corporation. The combined company now has annual revenues of over $10 billion.

Great-West is a subsidiary of Montréal-based Power Corporation of Canada, a major financial services holding company.

**Workforce at a Glance:** Number of full-time employees: **4,000**. At this location: **2,300**. New jobs created in Canada in past year: **100**. Percentage of employees who are women: **76**. Of managers: **25**. Percentage of employees who are visible minorities: **15**. Of managers: **5**. Resumes received by their human resources staff in past year: **10,056**. Average employee age: **37**.

### *Physical Workplace* *Rating: A+*

Great-West's physical workplace is rated as **exceptional**. Great-West's downtown head office is situated on beautifully landscaped grounds across from the historic Manitoba Legislature. The company operates its own greenhouse and maintains over 2,000 plants and trees throughout the building. Inside, the head office houses a large collection of Canadian art.

**Physical Workplace at a Glance:** Their **onsite fitness facility** features: treadmills; stationary bikes; weights; instructor-led classes; indoor walking corridor; shower facilities; lockers; medical room with onsite nurse. Their **employee lounge and rest areas** feature: comfortable couches; sleep room. For **food and refreshment**, Great-West offers: outdoor eating area. The company has an onsite cafeteria that features: subsidized meals (a turkey sandwich costs $3.00); healthy menu items; special diet menus; an open invitation to family and friends. Nearby **amenities** include: variety of restaurants; major shopping mall; The Forks marketplace; local shops and services; park/wilderness area (The River Walk and Memorial Park); recreation centre (YMCA and YWCA). For **commuters**, Great-West offers: free onsite car parking; secure bicycle parking; nearby public transit; nearby water taxi. Other **work area amenities** include: open-concept workstations; wireless connectivity throughout office; ergonomic workstation design.

### *Work Atmosphere & Social* *Rating: A*

Great-West's work atmosphere is rated as **above-average**. Employees at Great-West enjoy business casual dress daily and can listen to radio or music while they are working. There is also a company-subsidized social committee, called the '*Great-West Life Staff Club*', which has operated since 1909.

The club plans events for employees and retirees throughout the year and even employs a full-time social coordinator, who helps organize numerous activities. Events include social nights, summer sports days, winter ski trips, a Festive Feast before the Christmas break, and a Christmas party for employees' children. Employees also participate in hockey, softball, curling and golf leagues.

### *Health, Financial & Family Benefits* *Rating: A+*

Great-West's health benefits plan is managed by the company itself and is rated as **exceptional**. Their health benefits plan is flexible, meaning that employees can tailor individual plans to their personal circumstances. Full-time and part-time employees who work more than 15 hours per week are covered by the plan. There is no waiting period before new employees are eligible for coverage.

**Health Benefits at a Glance:** Great-West's health plan includes the following coverage: dental; orthodontics; eyecare; prescription drug; extended health benefits; nutrition planning; massage therapy; physiotherapy; alternative therapies; personal and family counselling; employee assistance plan (EAP) for substance abuse/mental health.

The company's salary and financial benefits are rated as **exceptional**. To keep pay-levels competitive, Great-West participates in outside salary surveys every 12 months. Individual salaries are reviewed every 12 months. The company operates a traditional pension plan. Great-West also offers a RSP eligible share purchase plan. Employees can contribute up to 5% of their salary, with the company contributing 50¢ for every dollar that employees contribute.

> **Financial Benefits at a Glance:** Great-West provides an extensive set of financial benefits, including: subsidized auto insurance; subsidized home insurance; subsidized tenant and condominium insurance; life and disability insurance; discounted mortgage rates.

Great-West's family-friendly benefits are rated as **average**. Employees with pre-school children have access to a daycare facility located nearby. The company's flexible benefits plan also has a maternity supplement provision. Other family-friendly benefits include: flexible start and finish hours; shortened work week (fewer hours); telecommuting and working from home.

The company also has a full-time family services coordinator at the company's onsite medical centre who organizes seminars on a wide range of issues (from parenting to elder care) and provides referrals for employees in need of community services.

## *Vacation & Time Off* — *Rating: B+*

Great-West's vacation and time off are rated as **average**. New employees receive 2 weeks of vacation allowance after their first year, which increases to 3 weeks after 2 years of service. The maximum vacation allowance is 5 weeks for long-serving employees. As part of the company's flexible benefits plan, employees have the opportunity to "buy" vacation days (or trade them for additional income). Employees at the company can also apply for unpaid leaves of absence.

## *Employee Communications* — *Rating: B+*

Great-West's internal communications program is rated as **average**. To keep employees informed about new developments, Great-West publishes an in-house newsletter (called *Outlook/Horizon*), which is bilingual. The company also has a well-developed intranet site (called *Cybrary*), which keeps employees informed about news and human resource policies that affect their work. Great-West operates a unique confidential email question box (called *TAP*) for all employees. In addition, the company publishes a variety of corporate and divisional newsletters.

## *Performance Management* — *Rating: A*

Great-West's performance management program is rated as **above-average**. The company operates a formal performance management program. Once a year, employees and managers meet for review sessions. (Managers receive training in how to conduct effective reviews.) As part of the review process, employees can request reviews throughout the year and are encouraged to respond in writing to their evaluations.

Outstanding performance is rewarded with salary increases, bonuses and various non-monetary awards (such as gift certificates for dinner at local restaurants). In addition, managers receive bonuses for achieving departmental goals and objectives.

***Training & Skills Development*** ***Rating: A***

Great-West's training and skills development program is rated as **above-average**. The company provides tuition subsidies for courses related to an employee's current position (100% of tuition). Commendably, Great-West also offers subsidies for courses not related to an employee's current job (100% of tuition). The company assists employees' career development with: reimbursement for professional association dues; online training; training resource library; in-house training. The company's in-house training program covers a variety of subjects, including time management, leadership training, writing skills and project management.

***Community Involvement*** ***Rating: A+***

Great-West's community involvement program is rated as **exceptional**. An outstanding corporate citizen, Great-West actively supports a variety of local and national charitable initiatives. Employees take part in the selection of charitable groups assisted by the company. Last year, the company contributed to approximately 100 charitable groups.

Great-West is a founding member of the national "*Imagine*" program operated by the Canadian Centre for Philanthropy, and contributes 1% of its pre-tax earnings to charities and non-profit organizations. Through its charitable donations program, Great-West sponsors a variety of community organizations. In recent years, the company has funded long-term and innovative projects involving health and wellness, education, arts and culture, federated appeals (such as the United Way) and various civic initiatives. In addition, Great-West actively encourages volunteerism within the company through regional programs for branch employees.

# Halsall

ENGINEERS·CONSULTANTS

**HALSALL ASSOCIATES LIMITED**
**2300 Yonge Street**
**PO Box 2385**
**Toronto, ON M4P 1E4**

**Tel. 416-487-5256**
**Fax 416-487-9766**
**careers@halsall.com**
**http://www.halsall.com**

**INDUSTRY: ENGINEERING, ARCHITECTURAL & SURVEYING FIRMS**

*Highlights:*

- Work for a growing employer that's proving eco-friendly construction (from using reclaimed concrete to building "green" roofs in urban centres) is also good business.
- Meet your mentor on the first day of work, then get together every four months to discuss your progress at the firm and career development.
- Walk the talk: get transit subsidies (or assistance finding carpool mates) at an employer that's serious about the environmental impact of its operations.

*Employer Background*

Halsall Associates Limited is a consulting engineering firm that provides building restoration and design services. Founded in 1956, the firm provides building restoration services to building owners, as well as new building design services to architects, developers and contractors.

For existing structures, Halsall offers complete restoration services, from preliminary evaluations to managing repair programs. For new buildings, Halsall provides structural design and building envelope engineering services, including cost-benefit analysis and preparing construction documents. The firm has designed major projects across Canada and around the world, from hospitals to soccer stadiums.

On all its projects, Halsall incorporates sustainable design elements into each of its projects. The firm feels strongly that its buildings are legacies for future generations (not liabilities) and is changing how buildings are designed.

Halsall's enlightened philosophy percolates through employee ranks. In its industry, the firm's record of success provides an excellent example of how to minimize negative environmental impacts without significantly changing (and maybe even improving) the way business is done.

Halsall has five offices across Ontario and affiliations with firms in Vancouver, Washington, DC and Trinidad.

**Workforce at a Glance:** Number of full-time employees: **145**. At this location: **113**. New jobs created in Canada in past year: **7**. Percentage of employees who are women: **28**. Of managers: **15**. Percentage of employees who are visible minorities: **18**. Of managers: **6**. Resumes received by their human resources staff in past year: **1,100**. Average employee age: **38**. Person you should get to know first: **Hilda will bring treats or flowers to your desk, just because**. Car the president drives: **prefers to walk or bicycle to work**.

## *Physical Workplace* — *Rating: A*

Halsall's physical workplace is rated as **above-average**. Only steps from Toronto's trendy Yonge and Eglinton intersection, Halsall's head office is housed in a modern office tower. Workstations are arranged according to employees' training needs, as well as their current projects. To ensure employee work areas receive plenty of natural light (and the best views), senior managers are located in the center of the office, while employees are located around the perimeter.

**Physical Workplace at a Glance:** Their **employee lounge and rest areas** feature: comfortable couches; television; meditation or religious observance room. For **food and refreshment**, Halsall offers: free coffee and tea; free soft drinks; kitchen area; lunch room. Nearby **amenities** include: variety of restaurants; local shops and services; fitness facility; outdoor skating rink; major shopping mall; recreation centre (North Toronto Memorial). For **commuters**, Halsall offers: transit subsidies; nearby public transit; free onsite car parking; auto-share program. Other **work area amenities** include: open-concept workstations; ergonomic workstation design; access to natural light for all employees; wireless connectivity throughout office; plant life that is tended professionally.

## *Work Atmosphere & Social* — *Rating: A*

Halsall's work atmosphere is rated as **above-average**. Employees at Halsall enjoy business casual dress daily and can listen to radio or music while they are working. There is also a firm-subsidized social committee, called the '*SosHal*', which has operated since 1990.

The employee-run committee organizes numerous events, including holiday celebrations, summer barbeques, monthly outings (including curling and hockey), birthday parties, and subsidized ski and golf days. The company recognizes employee milestones at an annual banquet and hosts spontaneous celebrations for project successes. Halsall also sponsors two employee hockey teams (the appropriately named "*Hammers*" and "*Bulldogs*") and recently formed an employee rowing team.

## *Health, Financial & Family Benefits* — *Rating: A*

Halsall's health benefits plan is managed by Canada Life and is rated as **average**. New employees must wait 90 days before they can enroll in the plan.

**Health Benefits at a Glance:** Halsall's health plan includes the following coverage: dental (80% of eligible costs, with no annual maximum); prescription drug; extended health benefits; physiotherapy; massage therapy; personal and family counselling; employee assistance plan (EAP) for substance abuse/mental health.

The firm's salary and financial benefits are rated as **exceptional**. To keep pay-levels competitive, Halsall participates in outside salary surveys every 12 months. Individual salaries are reviewed every 6 months. The firm offers a group RSP that allows employees to contribute up to 5% of their salary, with matching employer contributions. Halsall also provides a generous pension plan with increasing company contributions based on years of service (from 50% to 250% of employee contributions).

> **Financial Benefits at a Glance:** Halsall provides an extensive set of financial benefits, including: life and disability insurance; share purchase plan; profit-sharing plan; referral bonuses for some employees (from $1,000 to $5,000); year-end bonuses (from $1,000 to $30,000 for non-executives).

Halsall's family-friendly benefits are rated as **average**. Employees with preschool children have access to a daycare facility located nearby. Other family-friendly benefits include: flexible start and finish hours; shortened work week (fewer hours); compressed work week (same hours, fewer days); telecommuting and working from home.

### *Vacation & Time Off* — *Rating: B+*

Halsall's vacation and time off are rated as **average**. New employees receive 2 weeks of vacation allowance after their first year, which increases to 3 weeks after 5 years of service. The maximum vacation allowance is 4 weeks for long-serving employees. Employees at Halsall also receive 2 paid personal days off each year, in addition to their regular vacation allowance. Each year, Halsall also provides employees with a paid holiday shutdown from Christmas to New Year's. Employees at the firm can also apply for unpaid leaves of absence. (Recently, one employee took a two-month leave to work for Doctors Without Borders. Another took a leave to extend a vacation to attend a friend's wedding in Australia.)

### *Employee Communications* — *Rating: A*

Halsall's internal communications program is rated as **above-average**. To keep employees informed about new developments, Halsall publishes an in-house newsletter (called *The Halsall News*). The firm also has an intranet site, which keeps employees informed about news and human resource policies that affect their work. To solicit feedback from employees, the firm operates a traditional suggestion box program and an email suggestion box. An in-house employee satisfaction survey is conducted by having employees complete an online questionnaire every 6 months.

### *Performance Management* — *Rating: A+*

Halsall's performance management program is rated as **exceptional**. All employees take part in a well-developed mentoring program. Employees are assigned a mentor on their first day at work. Every four months (or as often as desired), employees and mentors meet to discuss training options and to develop a personal mission statement and career strategy.

Employees are responsible for managing their own plans — and mentors receive training to ensure they provide appropriate support. Employees also provide confidential feedback on their mentor's performance through the in-house survey.

Feedback from mentors forms the basis for performance bonuses and salary increases. Exceptional work at Halsall is also recognized through a unique peer recognition program that lets employees nominate their co-workers for non-monetary awards.

***Training & Skills Development*** ***Rating: A***

Halsall's training and skills development program is rated as **above-average**. The firm provides tuition subsidies for courses related to an employee's current position (100% of tuition). The firm assists employees' career development with: reimbursement for professional association dues; travel to industry-sponsored training sessions; a knowledge sharing program between offices; career planning; in-house training.

***Community Involvement*** ***Rating: A+***

Halsall's community involvement program is rated as **exceptional**. An outstanding corporate citizen, Halsall actively supports a variety of local, national and international charitable initiatives. Employees take part in the selection of charitable groups assisted by the firm. Employees at Halsall receive paid time off to volunteer at local charities.

In the past, employees have provided support to the Canadian Cancer Society, the annual Terry Fox Run, the ALS Society of Canada, Big Brothers, Rose Cherry's Hospice (for children living with cancer) and the United Way. Through Foster Parents Plan, the firm also sponsors a child in Malawi, Africa — employees organize bake sales and raffles to raise money. In addition, Halsall employees and their families volunteer their time on Earth Day to clean up local beaches.

In support of youth education, Halsall sponsors two unique engineering competitions. These include a watercraft design competition for grade 7 and 8 students and an annual concrete toboggan and canoe competition for university engineering students.

**HALTON REGION CONSERVATION AUTHORITY**
**2596 Britannia Road West**
**RR 2**
**Milton, ON L9T 2X6**

**Tel. 905-336-1158**
**Fax 905-336-7014**
**admin@hrca.on.ca**
**http://www.conservationhalton.on.ca**

**INDUSTRY: GOVERNMENT, ENVIRONMENTAL REGULATION**

***Highlights:***

- Work for a growing non-profit employer that's taking an active role in preserving the natural habitat near Canada's fastest-growing urban area.
- Get free access to this employer's park system, which includes trails for skiing, snowboarding and mountain biking — and the world-famous Bruce Trail.
- Get three weeks of paid vacation allowance after your second year at this non-profit employer, plus one paid personal day off each year.

## *Employer Background*

Halton Region Conservation Authority is a community-based environmental protection agency. The Authority (which also operates under the name "Conservation Halton") is responsible for protecting local environmental ecosystems throughout a watershed that extends along the western border of Mississauga northward from Lake Ontario.

Founded in 1963, Conservation Halton is funded through a partnership between the Ontario Ministry of Natural Resources and 9 municipalities within its watershed area. The Authority's watershed area covers nearly 1,000 square kilometers and includes sections of the Niagara Escarpment, significant wetlands, numerous creeks, 36 kilometres of Lake Ontario shoreline and one of the largest remaining forest tracts in Southern Ontario.

Conservation Halton's 339 full- and part-time employees provide a range of services and programs, including: water control and flood warning; natural environment protection and stewardship; environmental planning; tree planting and forest management; and education and recreation programs through its parks system.

Located at the edge of the Greater Toronto Area, the Authority faces the familiar challenge of balancing environmental protection with rapid population growth. These pressures have made it necessary to develop creative solutions at the Authority, which has become a major employer for people interested in preserving natural habitats.

**Workforce at a Glance:** Number of full-time employees: **73**. New jobs created in Canada in past year: **11**. Percentage of employees who are women: **42**. Of managers: **33**. Percentage of employees who are visible minorities: **10**. Resumes received by their human resources staff in past year: **500**. Average employee age: **38**. Years longest-serving employee has worked there: **35**. Person you should get to know first: **Margaret in reception is famous for her baking and knows where everyone is working at all times**. Car the president drives: **1998 Jeep**. Where it's parked in the lot: **with everyone else**.

## *Physical Workplace* — *Rating: A*

Conservation Halton's physical workplace is rated as **above-average**. When choosing its new office space, Conservation Halton made an inspired decision to locate it in an unused school. Situated in a rural setting, the "recycled" building was renovated with employee feedback, ensuring that an environmental theme was part of the final design.

**Physical Workplace at a Glance:** For **food and refreshment**, Conservation Halton offers: free coffee and tea; barbeque. Nearby **amenities** include: golf course; park/wilderness area (Lowville Park). For **commuters**, Conservation Halton offers: free onsite car parking. Other **work area amenities** include: open-concept workstations; windows that open; shower facilities.

## *Work Atmosphere & Social* — *Rating: A*

Conservation Halton's work atmosphere is rated as **above-average**. Employees at Conservation Halton enjoy casual dress daily and can listen to radio or music while they are working. There is also an Authority-subsidized social committee, called the '*Fun Committee*'.

The committee organizes a variety of social events throughout the year, including a pot-luck Christmas lunch, an evening Christmas party, a summer picnic, fundraising barbeque lunches and an annual staff recognition dinner. Employees also receive free access to the Authority's park system, which includes skiing and snowboarding, mountain biking trails, swimming and hiking along the beautiful Bruce Trail. (Non-employees must pay for day-parking at most of these locations, as well as a ski pass at the small ski hill operated by the Authority.)

## *Health, Financial & Family Benefits* — *Rating: B+*

Conservation Halton's health benefits plan is managed by Maritime Life and is rated as **average**. New employees must wait 180 days before they can enroll in the plan.

**Health Benefits at a Glance:** Conservation Halton's health plan includes the following coverage: dental (100% of eligible costs, to $1,250 each year); eyecare (to $200 every 2 years); extended health benefits; prescription drug; massage therapy; physiotherapy; alternative therapies; personal and family counselling; employee assistance plan (EAP) for substance abuse/mental health.

The Authority's salary and financial benefits are rated as **average**. To keep pay-levels competitive, Conservation Halton participates in outside salary surveys. Individual salaries are reviewed every 12 months. The Authority operates a traditional pension plan. **Financial Benefits at a Glance:** Conservation Halton provides a variety of financial benefits, including: life and disability insurance.

Conservation Halton's family-friendly benefits are rated as **average**. Family-friendly benefits include: flexible start and finish hours; shortened work week (fewer hours); compressed work week (same hours, fewer days); telecommuting and working from home; reduced summer hours; job-sharing.

### *Vacation & Time Off* — *Rating: A*

Conservation Halton's vacation and time off are rated as **above-average**. New employees receive 2.2 weeks of vacation allowance after their first year, which increases to 3 weeks after 2 years of service. The maximum vacation allowance is 7 weeks for long-serving employees. Employees at Conservation Halton also receive 1 paid personal day off each year, in addition to their regular vacation allowance. Employees at the Authority can also apply for unpaid leaves of absence.

### *Employee Communications* — *Rating: B+*

Conservation Halton's internal communications program is rated as **average**. An in-house employee satisfaction survey is conducted by mail every 24 months. Employees return their completed surveys to the human resources department. The results are tabulated and shared with all employees.

### *Performance Management* — *Rating: A*

Conservation Halton's performance management program is rated as **above-average**. The Authority operates a formal performance management program. Once a year, employees and managers meet for review sessions. (Managers receive training in how to conduct effective reviews.) In addition, employees provide confidential feedback on their manager's performance through a separate manager review process.

To recognize exceptional performance, employees can nominate their co-workers for a series of peer recognition awards — including the unique "*Turkey-Vulture Award*", which recognizes humourous achievements and exceptional efforts. Winners can choose cash awards or up to two days off with pay.

### *Training & Skills Development* — *Rating: B+*

Conservation Halton's training and skills development program is rated as **average**. The Authority assists employees' career development with: reimbursement for professional association dues; in-house training.

### *Community Involvement* — *Rating: B+*

Conservation Halton's community involvement program is rated as **average**. A good member of the community, Conservation Halton actively supports a variety of charitable initiatives. Every year, the Authority provides free parking and skiing passes to numerous organizations throughout the region. These include local schools, hospitals and charitable organizations such as the MS Society, the Canadian National Institute for the Blind, the Canadian Diabetes Association and the Huntington Society of Canada, to name only a few.

**HAMILTON POLICE SERVICE**
**155 King William Street**
**PO Box 1060, LCD 1**
**Hamilton, ON L8N 4C1**

**Tel. 905-546-4925**
**Fax 905-540-5354**
**http://www.hamiltonpolice.on.ca**

**INDUSTRY: POLICE & LAW ENFORCEMENT**

***Highlights:***

- Work for an employer that cares about your quality of life so much so that they have a special Family Issues Committee that is responsible for improving your work-life balance.
- Expand your career horizons with an employer that encourages you to experience a variety of jobs with the service.

## *Employer Background*

The Hamilton Police Service provides law enforcement services in the city of Hamilton. Established in 1847, the Service is responsible for an area that covers 1,138 square kilometres and is home to nearly 500,000 residents.

The Service works closely with individuals and community organizations to fulfill its mandate. For over a decade, the Service has participated in a unique community-based planning process that develops a new "business plan" once every three years. This process enables individual citizens, local organizations and Service employees to provide feedback and help establish policing priorities.

The Hamilton Police Service's community-based policing model has led to the development of several nationally recognized (and widely adopted) programs. These programs include a victim services centre, a child abuse branch, a robbery management taskforce (BEAR), a seniors support program, a family resource and domestic violence initiative, as well as training and career development programs for police employees.

In a region where other police departments struggle to fill vacancies, the Hamilton Police Service boasts one of Ontario's lowest employee turnover rates and is expanding to serve the needs of its growing community. The Service employs 714 police officers and 275 civilian employees.

> **Workforce at a Glance:** Number of full-time employees: **989**. New jobs created in Canada in past year: **16**. Percentage of employees who are women: **37**. Of managers: **13**. Resumes received by their human resources staff in past year: **1,727**. Average employee age: **40**.

## *Physical Workplace* — *Rating: A+*

Hamilton Police Service's physical workplace is rated as **exceptional**. There are four police stations and eight community policing centres throughout the city. A new station is being built to replace two of the older stations — the new facility is connected to a library and recreation centre for employees to use. At each of its main stations, employees also have access to fully equipped exercise rooms that offer personalized workout programs. Police personnel also provide input into the design and purchase of new police vehicles and equipment. The Service's headquarters are located in downtown Hamilton, within easy walking distance to the city's courthouse.

**Physical Workplace at a Glance:** Their **onsite fitness facility** features: free memberships; treadmills; stationary bikes; stairmasters; rowing machines; weights; basketball court; fitness evaluation and training program; music; sauna; shower facilities. Their **employee lounge and rest areas** feature: comfortable couches; television; pool table; sleep room; Internet kiosk. For **food and refreshment**, Hamilton Police Service offers: outdoor eating area; barbeque; kitchen area and vending machines. Nearby **amenities** include: variety of restaurants (in the popular Hess Village); major shopping mall; Hamilton Art Gallery; park/wilderness area (Hamilton Waterfront Trails); recreation centre (YMCA and YWCA). For **commuters**, Hamilton Police Service offers: free onsite car parking; transit subsidies; nearby public transit; secure bicycle parking. Other **work area amenities** include: open-concept workstations; ergonomic workstation design; access to natural light for all employees; plant life that is tended professionally; onsite bank machine.

## *Work Atmosphere & Social* — *Rating: A*

Hamilton Police Service's work atmosphere is rated as **above-average**. Employees at Hamilton Police Service enjoy business casual dress daily and can listen to radio or music while they are working. There is also a Service-subsidized social committee, called the '*Social and Retirement Committee*', which has operated since 1978.

Each year, the Service hosts several social events, including a children's Christmas party, a Christmas Eve reception with carolling, a volunteer awards banquet and a police retirement dinner. Hamilton Police Service employees also participate in a variety of athletic activities, such as hockey, dragon boat races, women's football, and the annual "Cops and Cats" basketball tour with players from the Hamilton Tiger Cats football team.

## *Health, Financial & Family Benefits* — *Rating: A*

Hamilton Police Service's health benefits plan is managed by Liberty Health and is rated as **above-average**. There is no waiting period before new employees are eligible for coverage.

**Health Benefits at a Glance:** Hamilton Police Service's health plan includes the following coverage: dental (100% of eligible costs, with no annual maximum); orthodontics (80% of eligible costs with a lifetime maximum of $2,000); eyecare (to $250 every 2 years); prescription drug; extended health benefits; nutrition planning; physiotherapy; massage therapy; personal and family counselling; employee assistance plan (EAP) for substance abuse/mental health.

The Service's salary and financial benefits are rated as **average**. To keep paylevels competitive, Hamilton Police Service participates in outside salary surveys every 12 months. Individual salaries are reviewed every 12 months. The Service operates a traditional pension plan. **Financial Benefits at a Glance:** Hamilton Police Service provides a variety of financial benefits, including: life and disability insurance.

Hamilton Police Service's family-friendly benefits are rated as **exceptional**. For employees who take maternity leave, Hamilton Police Service provides a generous top-up to 75% of salary for the first 25 weeks of their leave. For employees with young children there is a daycare centre nearby (and an onsite facility at the new Mountain Station). The Service also operates a unique Family Issues Committee that develops programs to help employees balance their work and personal lives. Other family-friendly benefits include: flexible start and finish hours; shortened work week (fewer hours); compressed work week (same hours, fewer days); job sharing.

***Vacation & Time Off*** **Rating: B+**

Hamilton Police Service's vacation and time off are rated as **average**. New employees receive 2 weeks of vacation allowance after their first year, which increases to 3 weeks after 3 years of service. The maximum vacation allowance is 9 weeks for long-serving employees. Employees at the Service can also apply for unpaid leaves of absence.

***Employee Communications*** **Rating: A**

Hamilton Police Service's internal communications program is rated as **above-average**. To keep employees informed about new developments, Hamilton Police Service publishes an in-house newsletter (called *Police Informer*). The Service also has an intranet site, which keeps employees informed about news and human resource policies that affect their work. To solicit feedback from employees, the Service operates an email suggestion box. An employee satisfaction survey is conducted every 36 months. An outside consultant compiles the survey results for Hamilton Police Service's management team.

The Service also solicits employee feedback through its unique business plan development process, which is conducted in public every three years.

***Performance Management*** **Rating: A**

Hamilton Police Service's performance management program is rated as **above-average**. The Service operates a formal performance management program. Once a year, employees and managers meet for review sessions. In addition to the annual reviews, employees receive mid-year progress reviews and ongoing feedback from their supervisors. To ensure the process is constructive, all supervisors receive training in conducting effective reviews. Employees can also provide feedback on their review through a formalized appeal process.

Exceptional employee performance is recognized through "Member of the Month" and "Member of the Year" awards, community service awards and safety awards. The Service also celebrates length of service anniversaries, employee promotions and retirements.

***Training & Skills Development*** **Rating: A+**

Hamilton Police Service's training and skills development program is rated as **exceptional**. The Service provides tuition subsidies for courses related to an employee's current position (100% of tuition). Commendably, Hamilton Police Service also offers subsidies for courses not related to an employee's current job (50% of tuition). The Service assists employees' career development with: reimbursement for professional association dues; mentoring; in-house training. Employees can take advantage of a wide variety of in-house training courses, including firearms training, computer operations, stress management and front-line investigation techniques.

The Service also operates an extensive career development program. Developed jointly with the Hamilton Police Association (the union that represents police officers), the career development program provides the necessary training to ensure employees can experience a variety of jobs with the Service over their careers.

### *Community Involvement* *Rating: A+*

Hamilton Police Service's community involvement program is rated as **exceptional**. An outstanding member of the community, Hamilton Police Service actively supports a variety of local and national charitable initiatives. Employees take part in the selection of charitable groups assisted by the Service. Employees at Hamilton Police Service receive paid time off to volunteer at local charities. Last year, the Service also contributed to approximately 100 charitable groups.

For their part, members of the Service also volunteer time, raise money, organize events and serve as board members for numerous charities. These charities include the United Way, Kids Help Phone, the Children's Aid Society, Big Brothers and Big Sisters, the Children's Wish Foundation, McMaster University Children's Hospital, the Canadian Cancer Society and Project Concern (an initiative of the Service that supports 25 local charities).

HEWLETT-PACKARD (CANADA) CO.
5150 Spectrum Way
Mississauga, ON L4W 5G1

Tel. 905-206-4725
Fax 905-206-4122
staffingteam.canada@hp.com
http://www.hp.ca

INDUSTRY: COMPUTER HARDWARE MANUFACTURERS

*Highlights:*

- Take a break with your family at this employer's lakeside lodge in Ontario's cottage country (one of five company-owned retreats around the world) at no charge.
- Stay trim at this employer's health facility with fitness assessments, aerobics classes and even a massage service — as well as healthy meals in their cafeteria.
- Get great employee discounts on the latest computer equipment, from laptops to flat-screen monitors.

## *Employer Background*

Hewlett-Packard (Canada) Co. makes a wide range of computer products, including printers, personal computers and imaging devices. Although known mainly for its printers, the company manufactures a wide range of personal computers, servers and digital imaging devices. In addition, Hewlett-Packard has built a significant business providing supplies (such as toner cartridges) and consulting services to purchasers of its equipment.

Hewlett-Packard Canada is a subsidiary of California-based Hewlett-Packard Company. Established in 1939, the publicly-traded parent company completed the largest acquisition in its history last year — the purchase of Texas-based Compaq Computer Corporation. With combined revenues of over $81.7 billion, the merged company has operations in 160 countries.

The merger has led to significant growth at Hewlett-Packard's Canadian operations. The company now has over 50 locations across the country, in addition to its Mississauga head office.

**Workforce at a Glance:** Number of full-time employees: **3,996**. At this location: **936**. Worldwide: **140,000**. New jobs created in Canada in past year: **2,571**. Percentage of employees who are women: **26**. Of managers: **23**. Percentage of employees who are visible minorities: **13**. Of managers: **17**. Resumes received by their human resources staff in past year: **1,183**. Average employee age: **36**.

## *Physical Workplace* — *Rating: A+*

Hewlett-Packard's physical workplace is rated as **exceptional**. Hewlett-Packard Canada's head office is situated on 18 acres of land adjacent to an environmentally protected ravine. When constructing the head office, Hewlett-Packard planted more than 26,000 trees and shrubs to enhance the surrounding woodlands. Inside the head office, there is an impressive six-storey glass atrium and common areas are decorated with original art from young Canadian and Aboriginal artists.

**Physical Workplace at a Glance:** Their **onsite fitness facility** features: subsidized memberships; treadmills; stationary bikes; stairmasters; rowing machines; weights; instructor-led aerobics; pilates; fitness assessments; massage services; shower facilities. For **food and refreshment**, Hewlett-Packard offers: free coffee and tea; outdoor eating area; barbeque. The company has an onsite cafeteria that features: subsidized meals (a turkey sandwich costs $3.00); special diet menus; heart-smart meals. Nearby **amenities** include: variety of restaurants; major shopping mall; recreation and entertainment options; park/wilderness area. For **commuters**, Hewlett-Packard offers: free onsite car parking; secure bicycle parking; nearby public transit. Other **work area amenities** include: open-concept workstations; ergonomic workstation design; plant life that is tended professionally; music in lounge areas.

## *Work Atmosphere & Social* — *Rating: B+*

Hewlett-Packard's work atmosphere is rated as **average**. Employees at Hewlett-Packard enjoy business casual dress daily. The company organizes a variety of social events for employees and their families throughout the year. These events include a Christmas party for employees' children, summer family picnics and seasonal activities, such as apple picking and hayride afternoons.

## *Health, Financial & Family Benefits* — *Rating: A*

Hewlett-Packard's health benefits plan is rated as **above-average**. Their health benefits plan is flexible, meaning that employees can tailor individual plans to their personal circumstances.

**Health Benefits at a Glance:** Hewlett-Packard's health plan includes the following coverage: dental (80% of eligible costs, to $2,500 each year); orthodontics (50% of eligible costs with a lifetime maximum of $2,500); eyecare (to $250 every 2 years); prescription drug; extended health benefits; nutrition planning; massage therapy; physiotherapy; personal and family counselling; employee assistance plan (EAP) for substance abuse/mental health.

The company's salary and financial benefits are rated as **above-average**. To keep pay-levels competitive, Hewlett-Packard participates in outside salary surveys every 12 months. Individual salaries are reviewed every 12 months. The company operates a traditional pension plan where Hewlett-Packard makes a contribution equal to 6% of each employee's salary to their plan each year. The company also offers matching group RSP contributions.

**Financial Benefits at a Glance:** Hewlett-Packard provides a variety of financial benefits, including: life and disability insurance; share purchase plan; profit-sharing plan; discounted company products; discounted supplier products (including GM cars and American Express credit cards); subsidized auto insurance; subsidized home insurance; signing bonuses for some employees.

Hewlett-Packard's family-friendly benefits are rated as **above-average**. For employees who take maternity leave, Hewlett-Packard provides a generous top-up to 100% of salary for the first 17 weeks of their leave. Employees can also access helpful online resources (such as LifeWorks and Financial Educator) that address a variety of work-life balance, financial and legal issues. Other family-friendly benefits include: flexible start and finish hours; shortened work week (fewer hours); compressed work week (same hours, fewer days); telecommuting and working from home.

### *Vacation & Time Off* — *Rating: A*

Hewlett-Packard's vacation and time off are rated as **above-average**. New employees receive 3 weeks of vacation allowance after their first year, which increases to 4 weeks after 10 years of service. The maximum vacation allowance is 6 weeks for long-serving employees. Employees at the company can also apply for unpaid leaves of absence.

One of Hewlett-Packard's most interesting benefits is perhaps its beautiful lakeside cabin near Kingston, Ontario. Available for employees and their families to use at no charge, the retreat is one of six company-owned recreational facilities worldwide — other locations include Pennsylvania, Colorado, California, Germany and Japan.

### *Employee Communications* — *Rating: B+*

Hewlett-Packard's internal communications program is rated as **average**. The company has an intranet site, which keeps employees informed about news and human resource policies that affect their work. An in-house employee satisfaction survey — called "*Voice of the Workforce*" — is conducted every 12 months.

### *Performance Management* — *Rating: A+*

Hewlett-Packard's performance management program is rated as **exceptional**. The company operates a comprehensive performance management program. Once a year, employees and managers meet for review sessions. Hewlett-Packard uses a 360-degree feedback process to gather additional performance-related information from co-workers, supervisors and employees.

At the meetings, past performance is reviewed and employee development plans are established for the upcoming year. All managers receive training in how to conduct effective reviews and are encouraged to provide year-round feedback. Employees can also provide constructive feedback on their managers' performance directly to the human resources department.

The company recognizes exceptional employee performance with free dinners, sporting event passes, theatre tickets and gift certificates. Hewlett-Packard also honours service milestones and accomplishments with special luncheons and share option awards. In some departments, outstanding work is recognized with free trips to exotic destinations, such as Hawaii and the Caribbean.

### *Training & Skills Development* — *Rating: B+*

Hewlett-Packard's training and skills development program is rated as **average**. The company provides tuition subsidies for courses related to an employee's current position (100% of tuition). The company assists employees' career development with: career planning; mentoring; online training; in-house training; self-training resources (online, books and CD-ROMs).

***Community Involvement*** ***Rating: A+***

Hewlett-Packard's community involvement program is rated as **exceptional**. An outstanding corporate citizen, Hewlett-Packard actively supports a variety of local and national charitable initiatives. Every year, employees support Junior Achievement and local United Way campaigns across Canada. Employees at Hewlett-Packard receive paid time off to volunteer at local charities.

Hewlett-Packard provides substantial support to educational initiatives across the country. The company matches employee donations to universities and colleges. Employees can also purchase Hewlett-Packard equipment at a significant discount for donation to their favourite school or non-profit organization.

The company also operates an interesting employment initiative for Aboriginal Canadians and is one of four corporations supporting the "Taking Pulse" project in association with the National Aboriginal Achievement Foundation. This project aims to bring Aboriginal leaders, government officials and corporate executives together to address employment issues faced by Aboriginal Canadians.

**HUSKY ENERGY INC.**
**707 - 8th Avenue SW**
**PO Box 6525, Station D**
**Calgary, AB T2P 3G7**

**Tel. 403-298-6111**
**Fax 403-298-6799**
**http://www.huskyenergy.ca**

**INDUSTRY: OIL & GAS EXTRACTION**

*Highlights:*

- Maximize your free time with three weeks of paid vacation for new employees, plus an amazing 10 paid personal days off each year.
- Educate your kids easier with one of 50 scholarships (to $1,500 each) offered to employees' children each year.
- Advance your career at an employer that's been recognized for its industry leading workplace diversity and equity initiatives.

### *Employer Background*

Husky Energy Inc. is an integrated Canadian petroleum company involved in all facets of the industry, from exploration to retail marketing. Oil and gas insiders refer to these areas as "upstream", "midstream" and "downstream" business segments.

Husky's upstream segment includes the exploration, development and production of crude oil and natural gas (and related resources) in Western Canada, off Canada's East Coast, and in the South China Sea. The company's midstream segment includes upgrading operations, pipelines, oil and gas marketing and new energy infrastructure projects. Husky's downstream segment includes refined products, and its familiar chain of Husky and Mohawk service stations.

Established in 1938, the company is one of Canada's largest integrated oil and gas producers with annual revenues of over $6.3 billion. With new production from its East Coast and South China Sea operations, and new facilities under construction in Western Canada, Husky continues to expand and create new jobs for Canadians.

**Workforce at a Glance:** Number of full-time employees: **2,803**. At this location: **1,231**. Worldwide: **2,811**. New jobs created in Canada in past year: **252**. Percentage of employees who are women: **29**. Of managers: **9**. Resumes received by their human resources staff in past year: **13,000**. Average employee age: **41**.

### *Physical Workplace* — *Rating: B+*

Husky's physical workplace is rated as **average**. Located in downtown Calgary, Husky's head office tower offers plenty of natural light, great mountain views and modern furniture in employee work areas.

**Physical Workplace at a Glance:** For **food and refreshment**, Husky offers: free coffee and tea; Timothy's coffee shop downstairs. The company has an onsite cafeteria that features: subsidized meals (a turkey sandwich costs $3.75); healthy menu items. Nearby **amenities** include: variety of restaurants; fitness facility (with subsidized memberships); Calgary's downtown covered walkway system, which leads to a variety of shops and services; park/wilderness area (Centennial Park). For **commuters**, Husky offers: nearby public transit. Other **work area amenities** include: ergonomic workstation design.

## *Work Atmosphere & Social* — *Rating: B+*

Husky's work atmosphere is rated as **average**. Employees at Husky enjoy business casual dress daily and can listen to radio or music while they are working. There is also a company-subsidized social committee, which has operated since 1960.

Throughout the year, the company hosts a variety of celebrations, including a service awards celebration to recognize employee milestones and a children's Christmas party with entertainment, refreshments and gifts for employees' children.

## *Health, Financial & Family Benefits* — *Rating: A*

Husky's health benefits plan is managed by Great-West Life and is rated as **above-average**. Their health benefits plan is flexible, meaning that employees can tailor individual plans to their personal circumstances. There is no waiting period before new employees are eligible for coverage.

**Health Benefits at a Glance:** Husky's health plan includes the following coverage: dental (to $4,000 each year); orthodontics (with a lifetime maximum of $3,000); eyecare (to $270 every 2 years); prescription drug; extended health benefits; physiotherapy; massage therapy; alternative therapies; personal and family counselling; employee assistance plan (EAP) for substance abuse/mental health.

The company's salary and financial benefits are rated as **above-average**. To keep pay-levels competitive, Husky participates in outside salary surveys every 12 months. Individual salaries are reviewed every 12 months. The company offers a group RSP that allows employees to contribute up to 9% of their salary, with matching employer contributions. The company also operates a traditional pension plan.

**Financial Benefits at a Glance:** Husky provides a variety of financial benefits, including: life and disability insurance; discounted company products (employees receive a 5% discount on gas purchases); year-end bonuses (from $3,500).

Husky's family-friendly benefits are rated as **above-average**. For employees who take maternity leave, Husky provides a top-up to 95% of salary for the first 6 weeks of their leave. Other family-friendly benefits include: flexible start and finish hours.

The company also awards at least 50 academic scholarships (to $1,500 each) to employees' children attending university, technical school or community college.

### *Vacation & Time Off* — *Rating: A+*

Husky's vacation and time off are rated as **exceptional**. New employees receive 3 weeks of vacation allowance after their first year, which increases to 4 weeks after 10 years of service. The maximum vacation allowance is 5 weeks for long-serving employees. Employees at Husky also receive 10 paid personal days off each year, in addition to their regular vacation allowance. Employees at the company can also apply for unpaid leaves of absence. (An employee recently took a one month leave to extend a vacation in Australia.)

### *Employee Communications* — *Rating: B+*

Husky's internal communications program is rated as **average**. To keep employees informed about new developments, Husky publishes an in-house newsletter (called *The Weekly Bulletin*). The company also has an intranet site, which keeps employees informed about news and human resource policies that affect their work. To solicit feedback from employees, the company operates an email suggestion box. An in-house employee satisfaction survey is conducted every 18 months.

### *Performance Management* — *Rating: A*

Husky's performance management program is rated as **above-average**. The company operates a comprehensive performance management program. Once a year, employees and managers meet for review sessions. (Managers receive training in how to conduct effective reviews.)

The company also uses an online 360-degree feedback process to gather feedback about each manager's performance. Survey responses are anonymous and form the basis for future manager training. Husky also holds confidential exit interviews to capture valuable information from departing employees.

### *Training & Skills Development* — *Rating: A*

Husky's training and skills development program is rated as **above-average**. The company provides tuition subsidies for courses related to an employee's current position (100% of tuition to $600). Commendably, Husky also offers subsidies for courses not related to an employee's current job (100% of tuition). The company assists employees' career development with: reimbursement for professional association dues; mentoring; in-house training.

### *Community Involvement* — *Rating: A+*

Husky's community involvement program is rated as **exceptional**. An outstanding corporate citizen, Husky actively supports a variety of local and national charitable initiatives. Employees take part in the selection of charitable groups assisted by the company. Last year, the company also contributed to approximately 300 charitable groups, including: the Special Olympics, the Canadian Association of Disabled Skiers, a local Aboriginal women's shelter, and the Western Canada High School Partnership, to name a few.

Husky has received special recognition for its workforce diversity initiatives, which are related to its charitable efforts and are unique in the oil industry. In particular, the company has been recognized by the Government of Canada for its efforts to make its workplace more accommodating for women, Aboriginal Canadians and people with disabilities. The company's "Bridging" program, for example, helps women and Aboriginal Canadians prepare for non-traditional careers, while their "Job Shadow" program improves the career advancement of visible minorities.

**IANYWHERE SOLUTIONS, INC.**
**415 Phillip Street**
**Waterloo, ON N2L 3X2**

**Tel. 519-886-3700**
**Fax 519-747-4971**
**waterlooresumes@sybase.com**
**http://www.sybase.com/ianywhere**

**INDUSTRY: SOFTWARE COMPANIES**

*Highlights:*

- Work for an employer with an enlightened vacation plan that offers three weeks of paid vacation allowance in your first year, and four weeks after only two years.
- Slide into a full-time job after working here as a co-op student — more than 95% of this employer's engineers are former work-term students.
- Get up to $6,000 each year for professional development, plus a flex-hours program that lets you take courses during work days.

## *Employer Background*

iAnywhere Solutions, Inc. develops advanced mobile and wireless access software. The company's industry-leading software enables large organizations to provide wireless access to their office networks. iAnywhere's software works with laptops and hand-held computing devices, pagers and intelligent appliances.

iAnywhere's Canadian roots date back to 1980, when three University of Waterloo graduates founded Watcom Corporation and developed one of the first mobile database-access products. In 1995, Watcom was purchased by California-based Sybase, Inc., which serves customers in over 60 countries. The company's Waterloo location is a major research and development centre.

Today, over 10,000 organizations (representing 7 million individual users) in the financial services, healthcare, government, utilities, transportation and retail sectors rely on the company's software for mobile email, sales force automation, field service, customer relationship management and related applications.

> **Workforce at a Glance:** Number of full-time employees: **205**. Worldwide: **365**. New jobs created in Canada in past year: **7**. Percentage of employees who are women: **26**. Of managers: **25**. Percentage of employees who are visible minorities: **20**. Of managers: **11**. Resumes received by their human resources staff in past year: **8,000**. Average employee age: **31**. Years longest-serving employee has worked there: **22**.

## *Physical Workplace* — *Rating: A*

iAnywhere's physical workplace is rated as **above-average**. The company's Waterloo office is also home to Sybase's Canadian division and is located in the heart of Canada's technology triangle.

**Physical Workplace at a Glance:** Their **employee lounge and rest areas** feature: comfortable couches; foosball. For **food and refreshment**, iAnywhere offers: free coffee and tea; free soft drinks; outdoor eating area; barbeque. The company has an onsite cafeteria that features: subsidized meals (a turkey sandwich costs $3.00); healthy menu items. Nearby **amenities** include: variety of restaurants; major shopping mall; fitness facility; park/wilderness area (Laurel Creek Conservation Area); recreation centre (Waterloo Recreation Complex). For **commuters**, iAnywhere offers: free onsite car parking; nearby public transit; secure bicycle parking. Other **work area amenities** include: open-concept workstations; ergonomic workstation design; wireless connectivity throughout office; plant life that is tended professionally; windows that open.

### *Work Atmosphere & Social* — *Rating: A*

iAnywhere's work atmosphere is rated as **above-average**. With a relaxed dress code, employees are free to wear "whatever makes them comfortable".

A volunteer committee organizes social events for employees throughout the year, including box seats for professional hockey and basketball games in Toronto, evening boat cruises, dinners at a local racetrack, summer barbeques, golf tournaments, family picnics, a Christmas party (with a separate children's party) and monthly birthday celebrations.

iAnywhere also sponsors employee baseball and hockey teams. (The company helped establish Waterloo's popular high-technology hockey league).

### *Health, Financial & Family Benefits* — *Rating: B+*

iAnywhere's health benefits plan is managed by Clarica Life and is rated as **above-average**. There is no waiting period before new employees are eligible for coverage.

**Health Benefits at a Glance:** iAnywhere's health plan includes the following coverage: dental (100% of eligible costs, to $2,000 each year); orthodontics (50% of eligible costs with a lifetime maximum of $2,000); eyecare (to $200 every 2 years); extended health benefits; prescription drug; physiotherapy; massage therapy; alternative therapies; personal and family counselling; employee assistance plan (EAP) for substance abuse/mental health.

The company's salary and financial benefits are rated as **average**. To keep pay-levels competitive, iAnywhere participates in outside salary surveys every 12 months. Individual salaries are reviewed every 12 months. The company offers a group RSP.

**Financial Benefits at a Glance:** iAnywhere provides a variety of financial benefits, including: life and disability insurance; referral bonuses for some employees (from $1,000 to $4,000).

iAnywhere's family-friendly benefits are rated as **average**. Employees with pre-school children have access to a daycare facility located nearby. Other family-friendly benefits include: flexible start and finish hours; shortened work week (fewer hours); telecommuting and working from home.

### *Vacation & Time Off* — *Rating: A*

iAnywhere's vacation and time off are rated as **above-average**. New employees receive 3 weeks of vacation allowance after their first year, which increases to

4 weeks after 2 years of service. The maximum vacation allowance is 4 weeks for long-serving employees. Employees at iAnywhere also receive 2 paid personal days off each year, in addition to their regular vacation allowance. Employees at the company can also apply for unpaid leaves of absence.

### *Employee Communications* — *Rating: A*

iAnywhere's internal communications program is rated as **above-average**. The company has an intranet site (called *Syberspase*), which keeps employees informed about news and human resource policies that affect their work. To solicit feedback from employees, the company operates an email suggestion box. An employee satisfaction survey is conducted every 12 months. An outside consultant compiles the survey results for iAnywhere's management team.

### *Performance Management* — *Rating: A*

iAnywhere's performance management program is rated as **above-average**. The company operates a well-designed performance management program. Once a year, employees and managers meet for review sessions. (Managers receive training in how to conduct effective reviews.) As part of the review process, employees complete self-assessments. The entire review process is coordinated through the company's intranet site, which allows employees and managers to view past results and add comments using an online form.

### *Training & Skills Development* — *Rating: A*

iAnywhere's training and skills development program is rated as **above-average**. The company provides tuition subsidies for courses related to an employee's current position (100% of tuition to $6,000). The company assists employees' career development with: reimbursement for professional association dues; career planning; mentoring; in-house training. In addition, employees can use their flexible work options to attend class during the work day.

### *Community Involvement* — *Rating: A*

iAnywhere's community involvement program is rated as **above-average**. A very good corporate citizen, iAnywhere actively supports a variety of local and national charitable initiatives. Employees take part in the selection of charitable groups assisted by the company. Employees at iAnywhere receive paid time off to volunteer at local charities. Last year, the company contributed to approximately 11 charitable groups, including: the Waterloo Food Bank, the Children's Wish Foundation, and the University of Waterloo's summer science camp.

iAnywhere is also a major supporter of co-operative education. Every four months, the company's Waterloo office welcomes new co-op students — more than 1,400 have completed placements at the company since 1980. Co-op students are a significant source of new talent for the company.

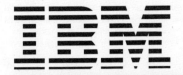

**IBM CANADA LTD.**
**3600 Steeles Avenue East**
**Markham, ON L3R 9Z7**

**Tel. 905-316-5000**
**http://www.ibm.ca**

**INDUSTRY: COMPUTER HARDWARE MANUFACTURERS**

*Highlights:*

- Get three weeks of vacation allowance after your first year, in addition to four paid personal days off each year.
- Work in a state-of-the-art software development lab with a mandate to develop world-class applications for customers around the world.
- Make a difference by joining 80 co-workers in the woods building a new camp for children with cancer.
- Leave your kids in good hands at the company's modern daycare facility, which is staffed by 25 childcare workers.

## *Employer Background*

IBM Canada Ltd. is one of Canada's largest providers of computing products and services. In addition to manufacturing computer hardware (from laptops and servers to supercomputers), the company is a major software developer, providing large-scale information technology consulting services to major clients across Canada.

IBM Canada is a subsidiary of Armonk, New York-based International Business Machines Corporation. Established in 1911, the publicly-traded parent company has annual revenues of $81 billion and operates in 160 countries. Last year, the company acquired PricewaterhouseCoopers Consulting, making its IT consulting practice one of the largest in the world.

IBM began operations in Canada in 1917. Since this time, the company has maintained an impressive record of growth. Last year, the company secured major new technology contracts with Sun Life Financial, National Bank and Aldo Shoes.

IBM's Canadian head office in Markham is responsible for overall company management, as well as marketing and support services. Other major facilities include a semiconductor manufacturing plant in Bromont, Québec, and software development laboratories in Markham and Ottawa.

**Workforce at a Glance:** Number of full-time employees: **19,373**. At this location: **3,799**. Worldwide: **315,889**. New jobs created in Canada in past year: **1,034**. Percentage of employees who are women: **33**. Of managers: **29**. Percentage of employees who are visible minorities: **17**. Of managers: **10**. Average employee age: **41**.

## *Physical Workplace* — *Rating: A+*

IBM's physical workplace is rated as **exceptional**. Situated on a 25-acre campus, IBM Canada's head office features six large atriums (almost six stories high) that flood the building with natural light. The modern building features bright conference rooms, a library, an employee education centre and a unique mobility centre for telecommuters (an impressive 25% of head office employees work offsite). The mobility centre offers concierge services and includes meeting rooms, comfortable lounge seating and workstations for mobile employees.

Within a few minutes' drive of its Canadian head office is IBM's showcase software development lab, which is also the third-largest research facility in Canada. This state-of-the-art building houses the company's onsite fitness and daycare centres, which are available to all IBM employees.

**Physical Workplace at a Glance:** Their **onsite fitness facility** features: free memberships; treadmills; stationary bikes; stairmasters; weights; elliptical trainers; instructor led classes; shower facilities. For **food and refreshment**, IBM offers: outdoor eating area; onsite Swiss Chalet, Pizza Pizza and Starbucks. The company has an onsite cafeteria that features: subsidized meals (turkey sandwich with carrots, celery and pretzels costs $3.51); special diet menus; healthy menu items; prepared take-out meals. Nearby **amenities** include: variety of restaurants; major shopping mall; indoor golfing facility; outside walking trails; park/wilderness area (Bishop's Cross and German Mills); recreation centre (Milliken Mills). For **commuters**, IBM offers: nearby public transit; convenient highway access; free onsite car parking; secure bicycle parking. Other **work area amenities** include: access to natural light for all employees; ergonomic workstation design; open-concept workstations; employee credit union with ATM; Government of Ontario service kiosk.

## *Work Atmosphere & Social* — *Rating: B+*

IBM's work atmosphere is rated as **average**. Employees at IBM enjoy business casual dress daily and can listen to radio or music while they are working. There is also a company-subsidized social committee, called the '*IBM Club*'.

The IBM Club organizes a variety of social events throughout the year, including subsidized evenings at the theatre and professional sporting events. In addition, the club coordinates an incredible range of sporting activities for employees, including hockey, badminton, basketball, golf, karate, rock climbing, ultimate frisbee and lawn bowling.

The company also celebrates significant business achievements and employee milestones. Employees with 25 years' experience join the company's prestigious "Quarter Century Club", which is celebrated with a $1,500 bonus and a special luncheon for their invited guests.

## *Health, Financial & Family Benefits* — *Rating: A*

IBM's health benefits plan is rated as **above-average**. Their health benefits plan is flexible, meaning that employees can tailor individual plans to their personal circumstances. There is no waiting period before new employees are eligible for coverage.

**Health Benefits at a Glance:** IBM's health plan includes the following coverage: dental (80% of eligible costs, with no annual maximum); orthodontics (80% of eligible costs with a lifetime maximum of $2,400); eyecare (to $200 every 2 years); prescription drug; extended health benefits; nutrition planning; physiotherapy; massage therapy; alternative therapies; personal and family counselling; orthopaedics; podiatry; speech therapy; Weight Watchers and first-aid training at work.

The company's salary and financial benefits are rated as **above-average**. The company operates a traditional pension plan where IBM makes a contribution equal to 3% of each employee's salary to their plan each year. (The contribution rate increases to 6% for long-serving employees.)

**Financial Benefits at a Glance:** IBM provides a variety of financial benefits, including: share purchase plan; life and disability insurance; discounted home computers; group auto and home insurance; signing bonuses for some employees; referral bonuses for some employees (from $2,000 to $5,000); year-end bonuses.

IBM's family-friendly benefits are rated as **exceptional**. Employees with preschool children have access to a daycare facility located onsite. The daycare facility has 132 spaces and employs 25 childcare workers. For employees who take maternity leave, IBM provides a top-up to 95% of salary for the first 6 weeks of their leave. The company also provides an adoption benefit of up to $1,500 per child. Other family-friendly benefits include: flexible start and finish hours; shortened work week (fewer hours); compressed work week (same hours, fewer days); telecommuting and working from home; reduced summer hours.

### *Vacation & Time Off* — *Rating: A*

IBM's vacation and time off are rated as **above-average**. New employees receive 3 weeks of vacation allowance after their first year, which increases to 4 weeks after 10 years of service. The maximum vacation allowance is 5 weeks for employees who spend 20 years with the company. Employees at IBM also receive 4 paid personal days off each year, in addition to their regular vacation allowance. Employees at the company can also apply for unpaid leaves of absence. (Recently, some employees have taken unpaid leaves to further their education, to extend their vacation, and to begin a transition to retirement.)

### *Employee Communications* — *Rating: B+*

IBM's internal communications program is rated as **average**. The company has a vast intranet site, which keeps employees informed about news and human resource policies that affect their work. To solicit feedback from employees, the company operates an email suggestion box. An in-house employee satisfaction survey is conducted every 2 months.

Administered by the parent company, this anonymous web-based survey polls randomly selected employees around the world. In Canada, the survey is translated into both official languages and results are posted on the intranet site.

### *Performance Management* — *Rating: B+*

IBM's performance management program is rated as **average**. Once a year, employees and managers meet for review sessions. (Managers receive training in how to conduct effective reviews.) IBM recognizes exceptional performance with pay increases, bonuses, and through a variety of awards. Prizes range from departmental awards to corporate contests that offer paid trips (for employees and guests) to exotic resorts around the world.

### *Training & Skills Development* — *Rating: A*

IBM's training and skills development program is rated as **above-average**. The company provides tuition subsidies for courses related to an employee's current position. Commendably, IBM also offers subsidies for courses not related to an employee's current job. The company assists employees' career development with: online training; in-house training; mentoring; career planning. As part of their annual review, employees also complete a individual development plan to identify future training needs.

### *Community Involvement* — *Rating: A+*

IBM's community involvement program is rated as **exceptional**. An outstanding corporate citizen, IBM actively supports a variety of local and national charitable initiatives. Employees take part in the selection of charitable groups assisted by the company. Employees at IBM receive paid time off to volunteer at local charities. Last year, the company also contributed a total of $2,800,000 (roughly $145 for each employee) to approximately 250 charitable groups.

IBM employees and retirees also operate their own "Employee Charitable Fund" to provide financial support to charitable organizations across the country — last year's campaign raised over $2.9 million!

In another unique initiative last year, 80 employee volunteers spent two days helping to construct a new building at a nearby summer camp ("Camp Trillium") for children living with cancer.

IBM also operates a matching program for contributions by employees and retirees to colleges, universities, hospitals, nursing homes, cultural and environmental organizations.

**IKEA CANADA**
**4065 Plains Road East**
**Burlington, ON L7T 4K1**

**Tel. 905-637-9440**
**Fax 905-637-2053**
**http://www.ikea.ca**

**INDUSTRY: HOME FURNISHINGS STORES**

*Highlights:*

- Build a career with an employer that dominates its industry worldwide — and offers employees great in-house job postings in (and relevant cultural information on) dozens of countries around the world.
- Enjoy the culture at a retail employer that explicitly tells employees that "life is more important than work" and offers a range of flexible work programs to help them balance work-life commitments.
- Work for a socially responsible employer that builds environmental concerns into every aspect of its business, proving that what's good for the environment really is good for business.

## *Employer Background*

IKEA Canada is a popular home furnishings retailer that operates stores across the country. IKEA Canada is part of Sweden-based Inter IKEA Systems BV, which developed the internationally recognized blue-and-yellow IKEA stores.

Founded in 1943 (by Ingvar Kamprad, who still works as an advisor for the company), IKEA is the world's most successful international home furnishings retailer, operating over 175 stores in 31 countries. In addition to its retail operations, the parent company has manufacturing plants in 11 countries, purchasing offices worldwide and distribution centres in 14 countries.

IKEA opened its first Canadian store in 1976 (also the first in North America) in Richmond, British Columbia. Today, IKEA Canada has 11 stores in Ontario, Québec, Alberta and British Columbia, employing over 3,350 full- and part-time people. Last year, the company opened two new stores in Montréal and Toronto.

**Workforce at a Glance:** Number of full-time employees: **1,469**. At this location: **75**. Worldwide: **70,000**. New jobs created in Canada in past year: **171**. Percentage of employees who are women: **55**. Of managers: **40**. Percentage of employees who are visible minorities: **45**. Of managers: **24**. Resumes received by their human resources staff in past year: **88,000**. Average employee age: **38**.

## *Physical Workplace* — *Rating: A*

IKEA Canada's physical workplace is rated as **above-average**. The company's head office is located above its Burlington store, which allows employees to remain close to the retail environment. As its head office expanded, IKEA has surveyed employees on everything from store location to the design of individual work areas — an easier task given IKEA's huge selection of office furnishings.

**Physical Workplace at a Glance:** Their **employee lounge and rest areas** feature: comfortable couches (of course); music; television; meditation or religious observance room; shower facilities; Internet kiosks. For **food and refreshment**, IKEA Canada offers: free coffee and tea; outdoor eating area; barbeque. The company has an onsite cafeteria that features: subsidized meals (a sandwich costs $3.50); healthy menu items. Nearby **amenities** include: variety of restaurants; major shopping mall; fitness facility; local shops and services; park/wilderness area (Royal Botanical Gardens); recreation centre (YMCA). For **commuters**, IKEA Canada offers: free onsite car parking; convenient highway access; nearby public transit. Other **work area amenities** include: open-concept workstations; ergonomic workstation design; access to natural light for all employees.

## *Work Atmosphere & Social* — *Rating: A*

IKEA Canada's work atmosphere is rated as **above-average**. Employees at IKEA Canada enjoy casual dress daily and can listen to radio or music while they are working.

Each year, employees from across the company enjoy a variety of social events, including summer barbeques, a holiday children's party (that includes breakfast with Santa) and a separate party for employees and their guests. As part of the holiday celebrations, local artists are commissioned to design artwork that reflect IKEA's culture. These unique gift items are presented to employees across the country.

## *Health, Financial & Family Benefits* — *Rating: A*

IKEA Canada's health benefits plan is managed by Great-West Life and is rated as **above-average**. Full-time and part-time employees who work more than 20 hours per week are covered by the plan. New employees must wait 90 days before they can enroll in the plan.

**Health Benefits at a Glance:** IKEA Canada's health plan includes the following coverage: dental (100% of eligible costs, to $1,500 each year); orthodontics (50% of eligible costs with a lifetime maximum of $1,000); extended health benefits; prescription drug; nutrition planning; physiotherapy; alternative therapies.

The company's salary and financial benefits are rated as **above-average**. To keep pay-levels competitive, IKEA Canada participates in outside salary surveys every 12 months. Individual salaries are reviewed every 12 months. The company offers a group RSP that allows employees to contribute up to 3% of their salary, with matching employer contributions.

Perhaps the most extraordinary financial bonus in this book is IKEA's worldwide "*Big Thank You Event*", which was held in 1999. Remarkably, this enlightened retailer turned over its gross sales for a single day to all its employees around the world. In Canada, the amazing event resulted in bonuses of over $2,200 for each employee!

**Financial Benefits at a Glance:** IKEA Canada provides a variety of financial benefits, including: life and disability insurance; discounted home computers; discounted company products; year-end bonuses.

IKEA Canada's family-friendly benefits are rated as **above-average**. Employees with pre-school children have access to a subsidized daycare facility located onsite. The daycare facility employs 6 childcare workers. For employees who take maternity leave, IKEA Canada provides a top-up to 100% of salary for the first week of their leave. Other family-friendly benefits include: telecommuting and working from home; compressed work week (same hours, fewer days); shortened work week (fewer hours); job sharing; flexible start and finish hours.

In addition, IKEA's emphasis on "adapting work to employees' lives" is truly a rarity in the retail industry. Exceptionally, the company tells its employees that "life is more important than work" and openly promotes flexible work arrangements. As part of this initiative, all IKEA managers receive training in how to implement these arrangements for their employees.

### *Vacation & Time Off* — *Rating: B+*

IKEA Canada's vacation and time off are rated as **average**. New employees receive 2 weeks of vacation allowance after their first year, which increases to 3 weeks after 3 years of service. The maximum vacation allowance is 5 weeks for long-serving employees. Employees at the company can also apply for unpaid leaves of absence.

### *Employee Communications* — *Rating: A*

IKEA Canada's internal communications program is rated as **above-average**. To keep employees informed about new developments, IKEA Canada publishes an in-house newsletter. The company also has an intranet site, which keeps employees informed about news and human resource policies that affect their work. To solicit feedback from employees, the company operates a traditional suggestion box program. An employee satisfaction survey — called "*Voice*" — is conducted worldwide every 12 months. An outside consultant compiles the survey results for IKEA Canada's management team.

### *Performance Management* — *Rating: A*

IKEA Canada's performance management program is rated as **above-average**. The company operates a well-designed performance management program. (Managers receive training in how to conduct effective reviews.) Salaried employees receive annual reviews and hourly-paid employees recieve performance reviews every 6 months. All employees can provide confidential feedback through the annual survey and via a telephone line IKEA provides directly to its Country Manager.

### *Training & Skills Development* — *Rating: A*

IKEA Canada's training and skills development program is rated as **above-average**. The company provides tuition subsidies for courses related to an employee's current position (75% of tuition). The company assists employees' career development with: reimbursement for professional association dues; mentoring; in-house training. IKEA Canada's in-house training program includes a range of courses, from retail training to management programs.

IKEA Canada employees also have the opportunity to expand their career horizons by working at company locations around the world. The company's intranet site includes job postings from divisions around the world, as well as cultural information for those interested in working abroad. The parent company also operates the IKEA Business College in Holland, which develops training programs for IKEA locations around the world.

***Community Involvement*** ***Rating: A+***

IKEA Canada's community involvement program is rated as **exceptional**. An outstanding corporate citizen, IKEA Canada actively supports a variety of charitable initiatives. Employees take part in the selection of charitable groups assisted by the company. Employees at IKEA Canada receive paid time off to volunteer at local charities.

Employees across Canada support numerous local organizations, such as school breakfast programs and tree-planting campaigns across the country. IKEA Canada is also a strong supporter of the Tree Canada Foundation.

Worldwide, IKEA takes environmental considerations into account in all its operations, particularly when it comes to using natural resources such as wood and paper. From retailing to manufacturing, the company's well-developed environmental philosophy weaves throughout IKEA's culture. This focus is based on the belief that environmentally sound business practices (such as reducing the amount of packaging they use) are also good for business. Given the company's unmatched success, they may have settled this issue once and for all.

IKEA also supports UNICEF programs to develop community awareness and education programs in the countries where its products are manufactured. The company has a strict code of conduct (based on the UN Convention on the Rights of the Child) to ensure that none of its suppliers (or their subcontractors) use child labour in manufacturing its products.

ims HEALTH

**IMS HEALTH CANADA LTD.**
**6100, route Transcanadienne**
**Pointe-Claire, QC H9R 1B9**

**Tel. 514-428-6000**
**Fax 514-428-6100**
**career@ca.imshealth.com**
**http://www.imshealthcanada.com**

**INDUSTRY: RESEARCH & TESTING FIRMS**

*Highlights:*

- Get recognized by your co-workers for a job well done — and receive gift certificates and cash awards from this employer.
- Work for a progressive employer that requested extensive employee feedback prior to deciding on the location and design of its new head office.
- Take advantage of a health benefits plan that includes a wellness subsidy and a program to help smokers kick the habit.

## *Employer Background*

IMS Health Canada Ltd. supplies healthcare information to public- and private-sector clients in the healthcare industry. IMS Health Canada Ltd. provides data on pharmaceutical trends, prescription drugs and diagnostic and treatment patterns. The company gathers this information from hospitals, pharmacies, pharmaceutical manufacturers, wholesalers and physicians.

The pharmaceutical industry uses IMS' data to determine the market share of various pharmaceuticals. The company's proprietary information is also used for research and planning purposes by physicians, medical researchers, public health boards and patient advocacy groups across the country.

Founded in 1960, IMS Health Canada is a subsidiary of Connecticut-based IMS Health Inc. The publicly-traded parent company employs more than 10,000 people in over 100 countries. In Canada, IMS has offices in Pointe-Claire and Mississauga.

**Workforce at a Glance:** Number of full-time employees: **304**. At this location: **214**. Worldwide: **10,242**. New jobs created in Canada in past year: **11**. Percentage of employees who are women: **62**. Of managers: **53**. Percentage of employees who are visible minorities: **9**. Of managers: **6**. Resumes received by their human resources staff in past year: **5,000**. Weeks of vacation their HR manager took last year: **4**. Years longest-serving employee has worked there: **25**. Person you should get to know first: **Della in Administration always knows what's going on and where to find everything**.

## *Physical Workplace* — *Rating: A*

IMS Health's physical workplace is rated as **above-average**. Most IMS employees (called *IMSians*) work at the company's head office in the Montréal suburb of Pointe-Claire, which is also one of the country's leading pharmaceutical centres. The company will be moving to a new head office next year. Employees have been consulted extensively on the new building's location and design.

**Physical Workplace at a Glance:** For **food and refreshment**, IMS Health offers: free snacks; free coffee and tea. The company has an onsite cafeteria that features: healthy menu items. Nearby **amenities** include: variety of restaurants; fitness facility; major shopping mall; recreation centre (YMCA). For **commuters**, IMS Health offers: free onsite car parking; convenient highway access; transit subsidies; secure bicycle parking. Other **work area amenities** include: ergonomic workstation design; traditional offices; plant life that is tended professionally.

### *Work Atmosphere & Social* — *Rating: A*

IMS Health's work atmosphere is rated as **above-average**. Employees at IMS Health enjoy business casual dress daily. There is also a company-subsidized social committee.

IMS organizes social events for employees throughout the year, including a Christmas party (with live music) and a holiday gift exchange. The employee social committee also organizes a variety of events, including a Halloween parade, weekend ski trips and sports events. The company also subsidizes an employee soccer team.

### *Health, Financial & Family Benefits* — *Rating: A*

IMS Health's health benefits plan is managed by Manulife Financial and is rated as **above-average**. Full-time and part-time employees who work more than 28 hours per week are covered by the plan.

**Health Benefits at a Glance:** IMS Health's health plan includes the following coverage: dental (100% of eligible costs, to $2,500 each year); orthodontics (50% of eligible costs with a lifetime maximum of $2,000); eyecare (to $200 every 2 years); prescription drug; extended health benefits; nutrition planning; physiotherapy; massage therapy; alternative therapies; personal and family counselling; employee assistance plan (EAP) for substance abuse/mental health; wellness subsidy (to $200); smoking cessation (to $200).

The company's salary and financial benefits are rated as **above-average**. To keep pay-levels competitive, IMS Health participates in outside salary surveys every 12 months. Individual salaries are reviewed every 12 months. The company operates a traditional pension plan where IMS Health makes a contribution equal to 7% of each employee's salary to their plan each year.

**Financial Benefits at a Glance:** IMS Health provides a variety of financial benefits, including: life and disability insurance; share purchase plan; discounted car leases; signing bonuses for some employees; referral bonuses for some employees (from $2,000 to $4,000); year-end bonuses (to $12,000 for non-executives).

IMS Health's family-friendly benefits are rated as **average**. Family-friendly benefits include: flexible start and finish hours; shortened work week (fewer hours); compressed work week (same hours, fewer days); reduced summer hours; telecommuting and working from home.

### *Vacation & Time Off* — *Rating: B+*

IMS Health's vacation and time off are rated as **average**. New employees receive 2 weeks of vacation allowance after their first year, which increases to 3 weeks after 2 years of service. The maximum vacation allowance is 5 weeks for long-serving employees. Employees at IMS Health also receive 2 paid personal days off each year, in addition to their regular vacation allowance. Employees at the company can also apply for unpaid leaves of absence. (Recently, one employee took a full year off to pursue studies in Europe.)

***Employee Communications*** ***Rating: A***

IMS Health's internal communications program is rated as **above-average**. To keep employees informed about new developments, IMS Health publishes an in-house newsletter (called *IMSpulse*), which is bilingual. The company also has an intranet site, which keeps employees informed about news and human resource policies that affect their work. To solicit feedback from employees, the company operates a traditional suggestion box program. An in-house employee satisfaction survey is conducted every 12 months.

***Performance Management*** ***Rating: A***

IMS Health's performance management program is rated as **above-average**. The company operates a comprehensive performance management program. Every 6 months, employees and managers meet for review sessions. (Managers receive training in how to conduct effective reviews.) Employees can also provide confidential feedback on their manager's performance directly to the human resources department.

IMS operates a unique rewards program that allows employees to nominate co-workers for excellent work. Under the program, winners receive gift certificates and cash awards (to $350). Winners are considered for the annual President's Award (to $1,500) in recognition of outstanding performance.

***Training & Skills Development*** ***Rating: B+***

IMS Health's training and skills development program is rated as **average**. The company provides tuition subsidies for courses related to an employee's current position (100% of tuition). The company assists employees' career development with: career planning; in-house training. In addition, all managers at the company participate in a leadership development program offered through a special partnership with McGill University.

***Community Involvement*** ***Rating: A***

IMS Health's community involvement program is rated as **above-average**. A very good corporate citizen, IMS Health actively supports a variety of local and national charitable initiatives. Employees take part in the selection of charitable groups assisted by the company. Last year, the company contributed to approximately 11 charitable groups, including: the Heart & Stroke Foundation, World Vision (employees sponsor a child), Big Brothers and Big Sisters, the Logifem Women's Shelter, Make-A-Wish Foundation and Héma-Québec.

During the Christmas season, a group of enthusiastic IMS employees (dressed as Santa and his elves) visit local hospitals and deliver toys and holiday cheer to sick children.

**INDUSTRIAL ACCIDENT PREVENTION ASSOCIATION**
**207 Queens Quay West**
**Suite 550**
**Toronto, ON M5J 2Y3**

**Tel. 416-506-8888**
**Fax 416-506-9092**
**http://www.iapa.on.ca**

**INDUSTRY: OTHER MEMBERSHIP ORGANIZATIONS**

***Highlights:***

- Make a difference in your community at an employer that offers three paid days off each year to volunteer with your favourite charity.
- Get excellent maternity leave benefits (93% for 17 weeks), which is something of a rarity in the not-for-profit sector.
- Work from home for an employer that believes in telecommuting — and will set you up with a fully-equipped home office to get you started.

## *Employer Background*

The Industrial Accident Prevention Association is a non-profit association dedicated to creating safe, healthy and productive workplaces in Ontario. Established in 1917, the IAPA works closely with its member organizations to reduce injury and improve health and safety in Ontario workplaces.

The Association represents over 45,000 Ontario employers and 1.5 million employees, making it the largest provincial workplace health and safety organization in Canada.

The IAPA has four main functions: developing training products and services to prevent workplace injury and sickness; consulting with members on how to improve their safety records; increasing community awareness of health and safety issues; and building partnerships with third parties for improved workplace safety.

In addition to the Toronto head office, the Association has 12 regional offices across Ontario.

**Workforce at a Glance:** Number of full-time employees: **216**. At this location: **82**. New jobs created in Canada in past year: **10**. Percentage of employees who are women: **59**. Of managers: **35**. Percentage of employees who are visible minorities: **33**. Of managers: **1**. Resumes received by their human resources staff in past year: **438**. Average employee age: **47**.

## *Physical Workplace* — *Rating: A*

IAPA's physical workplace is rated as **above-average**. IAPA's Toronto head office is located in the city's landmark Queen's Quay Terminal Warehouse on the waterfront. The renovated industrial building includes a combination of office, retail and residential space and is located in one of the city's most popular tourist destinations.

**Physical Workplace at a Glance:** Nearby **amenities** include: variety of restaurants; major shopping mall; fitness facility; numerous entertainment options; summer wading pool and winter skating rink. For **commuters**, IAPA offers: nearby public transit; convenient highway access; cycling trails along lakeshore. Other **work area amenities** include: open-concept workstations; ergonomic workstation design; access to natural light for all employees; plant life that is tended professionally; kitchen area.

### *Work Atmosphere & Social* — *Rating: B+*

IAPA's work atmosphere is rated as **average**. Employees at IAPA enjoy business casual dress daily and can listen to radio or music while they are working. The Association has an on-site concierge service. Throughout the year, employees enjoy pizza lunches, socials for new employees, a Christmas lunch, a family skate and an annual hockey day event.

### *Health, Financial & Family Benefits* — *Rating: A*

IAPA's health benefits plan is managed by Green Shield and is rated as **above-average**.

**Health Benefits at a Glance:** IAPA's health plan includes the following coverage: dental (100% of eligible costs, to $2,000 each year); orthodontics (50% of eligible costs with a lifetime maximum of $2,000); eyecare (to $200 every 2 years); prescription drug; extended health benefits; nutrition planning; physiotherapy; massage therapy; personal and family counselling; employee assistance plan (EAP) for substance abuse/mental health.

The Association's salary and financial benefits are rated as **average**. To keep pay-levels competitive, IAPA participates in outside salary surveys every 12 months. Individual salaries are reviewed every 12 months. The Association offers a group RSP. **Financial Benefits at a Glance:** IAPA provides a variety of financial benefits, including: life and disability insurance; discounted home computers (to $1,000).

IAPA's family-friendly benefits are rated as **above-average**. Employees with pre-school children have access to a daycare facility located nearby. For employees who take maternity leave, IAPA provides a generous top-up to 93% of salary for the first 17 weeks of their leave. Other family-friendly benefits include: flexible start and finish hours; shortened work week (fewer hours); reduced summer hours; telecommuting and working from home. Employees who work from home offices are equipped with cellular phones, laptops and ergonomic furniture.

### *Vacation & Time Off* — *Rating: A*

IAPA's vacation and time off are rated as **above-average**. New employees receive 3 weeks of vacation allowance after their first year, which increases to 4 weeks after 10 years of service. The maximum vacation allowance is 6 weeks for long-serving employees. Employees at the Association can also apply for unpaid leaves of absence.

### *Employee Communications* — *Rating: A*

IAPA's internal communications program is rated as **above-average**. To keep employees informed about new developments, IAPA publishes an in-house newsletter (called *Inside Track*). The Association also has an intranet site, which keeps employees informed about news and human resource policies that affect their work. An employee satisfaction survey is conducted every 24 months. An outside consultant compiles the survey results for IAPA's management team. IAPA has an interesting employee committee (called the *Elected Peers*) that meets quarterly to address staff concerns and reports directly to the president. The Association also has a retiree group that meets quarterly to discuss their particular concerns.

### *Performance Management* — *Rating: A*

IAPA's performance management program is rated as **above-average**. The Association operates a comprehensive performance management program. Once a year, employees and managers meet for review sessions. (Managers receive training in how to conduct effective reviews.) Employees and managers also meet for informal quarterly feedback sessions.

The review process forms the basis for salary increases. Employees can also nominate their colleagues for annual performance awards through a unique peer recognition program.

### *Training & Skills Development* — *Rating: B+*

IAPA's training and skills development program is rated as **average**. The Association provides tuition subsidies for courses related to an employee's current position. The Association assists employees' career development with: reimbursement for professional association dues; career planning; in-house training.

### *Community Involvement* — *Rating: A*

IAPA's community involvement program is rated as **above-average**. A very good member of the community, IAPA actively supports a variety of local and national charitable initiatives. Employees at IAPA receive paid time off to volunteer at local charities.

Employees volunteer and contribute to a variety of charities every year, including the United Way, the CNIB Crocus Campaign, the Muscular Dystrophy Society, CHUM City Christmas Wish, the Toronto food bank and a local women's shelter. Last year, employee teams also participated in the Heart and Stroke Foundation's Ride for Heart, and the Breast Cancer Society's Breast Cancer Walk.

IAPA also lends its expertise to several unique charitable causes. The Association has developed a young worker's awareness program and participates in the Safe and Sober Driving Coalition.

**INTUIT CANADA LIMITED**
**7008 Roper Road**
**Edmonton, AB T6B 3H2**

**Tel. 780-466-9996**
**Fax 780-440-5973**
**http://www.intuit.com/canada**

**INDUSTRY: SOFTWARE COMPANIES**

*Highlights:*

- Work in a showcase head office — which could double as a resort — that offers employees everything from billiards to seven outdoor patios.
- Sleep on the job in one of three nap rooms furnished with comfortable beds and alarm clocks.
- Workout with your spouse using a free membership to this employer's 24-hour onsite fitness facility, which offers everything from a gymnasium to complimentary shampoo.
- Invest in your future by taking part in this employer's share purchase plan, which lets employees buy shares at a 15% discount.

## *Employer Background*

Intuit Canada Limited is a leading developer of personal finance, small business accounting and tax return software. Most Canadians are familiar with Intuit's award-winning software, including Quicken, QuickBooks and QuickTax. The company's software and online products have helped millions of Canadians survive tax season with their sanity intact.

Intuit Canada's history dates back to 1992, when two University of Alberta graduates developed a software package ("WinTax") to help Canadians complete their annual tax returns. The company's early software has since become the country's leading tax preparation application and is now marketed under the name QuickTax.

In 1993, the company became part of Silicon Valley-based Intuit Incorporated, a publicly-traded corporation with annual revenues of over $1 billion. In addition to developing software and online products for Canada (in English and French), Intuit Canada develops software applications for the United Kingdom. Through its Calgary-based subsidiary, Intuit GreenPoint, the company also develops professional tax and financial planning software.

In addition to its Edmonton head office, Intuit operates offices in Calgary, Toronto and Montréal.

**Workforce at a Glance:** Number of full-time employees: **467**. At this location: **401**. Worldwide: **6,948**. New jobs created in Canada in past year: **167**. Percentage of employees who are women: **44**. Of managers: **21**. Percentage of employees who are visible minorities: **8**. Of managers: **8**. Resumes received by their human resources staff in past year: **8,990**. Average employee age: **32**.

### *Physical Workplace* *Rating: A+*

Intuit's physical workplace is rated as **exceptional**. Intuit's 90,000-square-foot head office in Edmonton has been praised for its unique design and employee amenities. Located near the city's popular Whyte Avenue shopping area, the head office overlooks a scenic ravine with natural parkland that features hundreds of kilometres of running and biking trails.

In designing the new office, Intuit used employee feedback to ensure the building would help attract the best computer industry talent. Inside, there are open spaces with colourful curving walls and floor-to-ceiling windows. In a unique touch, the new office is decorated with art on loan from the Edmonton Art Gallery. In addition to a 24-hour fitness facility, there is a multi-purpose gymnasium that can be converted for basketball, volleyball, badminton, floor hockey and employee gatherings.

**Physical Workplace at a Glance:** Their **onsite fitness facility** features: free memberships for employees (and spouses); treadmills; stationary bikes; rowing machines; weights; instructor-led classes; personal trainer; massage therapist (weekly); shower facilities; free towel service; hair dryers. Their **employee lounge and rest areas** feature: comfortable couches; fireplace; television; pool table; foosball; table tennis; outdoor horseshoe pitch; sleep room. For **food and refreshment**, Intuit offers: free coffee and tea; barbeque; outdoor eating area; café with patio. The company has an onsite cafeteria that features: subsidized meals (a turkey sandwich costs $3.00); healthy menu items. Nearby **amenities** include: variety of restaurants; major shopping mall; park/wilderness area (Millcreek Ravine); recreation centre (Millwoods Recreation Centre and Golf Course). For **commuters**, Intuit offers: free onsite car parking; convenient highway access; secure bicycle parking; nearby public transit. Other **work area amenities** include: open-concept workstations; ergonomic workstation design; windows that open; access to natural light for all employees; plant life that is tended professionally.

### *Work Atmosphere & Social* *Rating: A*

Intuit's work atmosphere is rated as **above-average**. Employees at Intuit enjoy business casual dress daily and can listen to radio or music while they are working. There is also a company-subsidized social committee.

The social committee organizes a variety of family-oriented events throughout the year, including sleigh rides, family barbeques and an annual children's carnival. During the summer and fall, employee teams host their own summer barbeques with themes, contests and prizes. To end the week, employees often gather on one of the head office's seven outdoor patios for Friday "beverage-bashes".

Intuit employees also participate in the annual "Edmonton and Area Corporate Challenge", which includes a full week of recreational and sporting competitions. Last year's event involved over 160 local employers and 17,000 participants — Intuit placed second in its division.

### *Health, Financial & Family Benefits* *Rating: A+*

Intuit's health benefits plan is managed by Canada Life and is rated as **exceptional**. Full-time and part-time employees who work more than 20 hours per week are covered by the plan. There is no waiting period before new employees are eligible for coverage.

**Health Benefits at a Glance:** Intuit's health plan includes the following coverage: dental (100% of eligible costs, to $1,500 each year); orthodontics (50% of eligible costs with a lifetime maximum of $1,500); eyecare (to $250 every 2 years); prescription drug; extended health benefits; physiotherapy; massage therapy; alternative therapies; personal and family counselling; employee assistance plan (EAP) for substance abuse/mental health.

The company's salary and financial benefits are rated as **exceptional**. Individual salaries are reviewed every 12 months. The company offers a group RSP that allows employees to contribute up to a maximum of $3,500 per year, with matching employer contributions.

**Financial Benefits at a Glance:** Intuit provides an extensive set of financial benefits, including: share purchase plan; profit-sharing plan; subsidized auto insurance; subsidized home insurance; free software; discounted home computers; discounted home Internet access; life and disability insurance; signing bonuses for some employees; referral bonuses for some employees (from $500 to $5,000); year-end bonuses (from $2,800 to $60,000 for non-executives).

Intuit's family-friendly benefits are rated as **above-average**. For employees who take maternity leave, Intuit provides a top-up to 100% of salary for the first 6 weeks of their leave. Other family-friendly benefits include: flexible start and finish hours; shortened work week (fewer hours); compressed work week (same hours, fewer days); reduced summer hours; telecommuting and working from home.

### *Vacation & Time Off* — *Rating: B+*

Intuit's vacation and time off are rated as **average**. New employees receive 2 weeks of vacation allowance after their first year, which increases to 3 weeks after 2 years of service. Employees at Intuit also receive 1 paid personal day off each year, in addition to their regular vacation allowance. Employees at the company can also apply for unpaid leaves of absence. (Leaves of absence range from one month to one year in length.)

### *Employee Communications* — *Rating: A+*

Intuit's internal communications program is rated as **exceptional**. To keep employees informed about new developments, Intuit publishes an in-house newsletter. The company also has an intranet site (called *Intuit.Intranet*), which keeps employees informed about news and human resource policies that affect their work. To solicit feedback from employees, the company operates a traditional suggestion box program. An employee satisfaction survey — called "*Great Place to Work*" — is conducted by email every 12 months. An outside consultant compiles the survey results for Intuit's management team.

### *Performance Management* — *Rating: A*

Intuit's performance management program is rated as **above-average**. The company operates a thorough performance management program. Once a year, employees and managers meet for review sessions. (Managers receive training in how to conduct effective reviews.) Intuit uses a 360-degree feedback process to gather additional performance-related information from co-workers, supervisors and employees. Manager are also encouraged to provide ongoing feedback to employees throughout the year.

Exceptional employee performance is recognized with gift certificates for everything from movie nights to small appliances to weekend getaways. The company also awards special gifts in celebration of individual employee milestones.

### *Training & Skills Development* — *Rating: A*

Intuit's training and skills development program is rated as **above-average**. The company provides tuition subsidies for courses related to an employee's current position (100% of tuition). The company assists employees' career development with: reimbursement for professional association dues; in-house training; online training.

### *Community Involvement* — *Rating: A*

Intuit's community involvement program is rated as **above-average**. A very good corporate citizen, Intuit actively supports a variety of local and national charitable initiatives. Employees take part in the selection of charitable groups assisted by the company. Last year, the company also contributed to approximately 10 charitable groups, including: the Canadian Breast Cancer Foundation, Heart and Stroke Foundation, Canadian Blood Services, Canadian Cancer Society and local emergency shelters.

The company operates a formal program (called *"We Care & Give Back"*) that matches employee donations to charities. As part of this program, Intuit hosts a major fundraising party every year in support of a different charity.

**KPMG LLP**
**Commerce Court West, Suite 3300**
**PO Box 31, Station Commerce Court**
**Toronto, ON M5L 1B2**

**Tel. 416-777-8500**
**Fax 416-777-8416**
**http://www.kpmg.ca**

**INDUSTRY: ACCOUNTING, AUDITING & BOOKKEEPING FIRMS**

*Highlights:*

- Get three weeks of paid vacation allowance after your first year — and seven paid personal days off each year.
- Get cash awards and great gifts for excellent performance, all on the recommendation of your co-workers.
- Spend time working down under on a unique inter-company exchange program with this employer's Australian and New Zealand affiliates.
- Live long and prosper with a unique fitness participation subsidy that puts up to $700 back in your pocket if you belong to a gym or health club.

## *Employer Background*

KPMG LLP is a leading accounting and professional services firm, providing auditing, tax and financial advisory services to businesses across Canada.

With roots in Canada dating back to 1840, KPMG is well-known as one the nation's leading accounting firms. The company provides audit, taxation, corporate finance, corporate recovery and transaction services to business customers across Canada. KPMG is the country's leading auditor in terms of market share. The company posted impressive profit growth on revenues of $721 million last year — the second best year in its history.

KPMG is the Canadian member of Switzerland-based KPMG International, which has operations in over 150 countries. In Canada, KPMG has 34 offices across the country.

**Workforce at a Glance:** Number of full-time employees: **4,100**. At this location: **1,443**. Worldwide: **100,000**. Percentage of employees who are women: **61**. Of managers: **46**. Percentage of employees who are visible minorities: **21**. Of managers: **15**. Resumes received by their human resources staff in past year: **25,500**. Weeks of vacation their HR manager took last year: **5**. Average employee age: **36**. Years longest-serving employee has worked there: **40**.

## *Physical Workplace* — *Rating: A*

KPMG's physical workplace is rated as **above-average**. Situated in the heart of Toronto's financial district, KPMG's head office is connected to Toronto's underground walking network. The downtown location is near major attractions, including live theatre and music, arts festivals and professional sporting events.

Inside, employee offices are generally larger than executive offices and the company reserves the best spaces (such as corner offices) for meeting rooms, so everyone can have access to natural light and great views.

**Physical Workplace at a Glance:** Their **employee lounge and rest areas** feature: television; great views of Lake Ontario and the surrounding city. For **food and refreshment**, KPMG offers: free snacks; free coffee and tea; free soft drinks; all-weather access to hundreds of restaurants and cafés. Nearby **amenities** include: major shopping mall; fitness facility; park/wilderness area (Melinda Park). For **commuters**, KPMG offers: nearby public transit; secure bicycle parking. Other **work area amenities** include: open-concept workstations; access to natural light for all employees; ergonomic workstation design; plant life that is tended professionally; illness recovery room.

## *Work Atmosphere & Social* — *Rating: A*

KPMG's work atmosphere is rated as **above-average**. Employees at KPMG enjoy business casual dress daily and can listen to radio or music while they are working.

Across the firm, each office organizes a variety of fun social events for employees, including year-end holiday parties, children's Christmas parties, onsite massage days, employee service milestone celebrations and company-paid parties to celebrate the end of tax season. Many offices also sponsor employee sports teams, including volleyball, softball, rowing and dragon-boat racing.

## *Health, Financial & Family Benefits* — *Rating: A+*

KPMG's health benefits plan is rated as **exceptional**. Their health benefits plan is flexible, meaning that employees can tailor individual plans to their personal circumstances. The health plan includes a special fitness subsidy (currently about $700 per employee) that can be used for health club dues or towards an employee's favorite sporting activity.

**Health Benefits at a Glance:** KPMG's health plan includes the following coverage: dental (100% of eligible costs, with no annual maximum); orthodontics (50% of eligible costs); eyecare (to $200 every 2 years); prescription drug; extended health benefits; nutrition planning; physiotherapy; massage therapy; personal and family counselling; employee assistance plan (EAP) for substance abuse/mental health; fitness subsidy ($700 per employee).

The firm's salary and financial benefits are rated as **exceptional**. To keep paylevels competitive, KPMG participates in outside salary surveys every 12 months. Individual salaries are reviewed every 12 months. The firm operates a traditional pension plan where KPMG makes a contribution equal to 7% of each employee's salary to their plan each year.

KPMG also operates a unique bonus program for all employees, in addition to partnership distributions. Last year, over 3,700 employees received bonuses, averaging $3,898 each. New campus recruits at KPMG receive a new pair of Adidas running shoes (to celebrate their "fit" with the company) as well as a laptop computer. Summer students who are asked to return to the firm receive a $2,000 education allowance.

**Financial Benefits at a Glance:** KPMG provides an extensive set of financial benefits, including: life and disability insurance; discounted car leases; discounted home Internet access; cellular phone discounts; travel insurance; signing bonuses for some employees; referral bonuses for some employees (from $1,000 to $2,500).

KPMG's family-friendly benefits are rated as **above-average**. Employees with pre-school children have access to a daycare facility located onsite. For employees who take maternity leave, KPMG provides a top-up to 100% of salary for the first 8 weeks of their leave. The firm also provides an adoption benefit of up to $5,000 per child. Other family-friendly benefits include: flexible start and finish hours; shortened work week (fewer hours); compressed work week (same hours, fewer days); telecommuting and working from home; reduced summer hours.

## *Vacation & Time Off* — *Rating: A+*

KPMG's vacation and time off are rated as **exceptional**. New employees receive 3 weeks of vacation allowance after their first year, which increases to 4 weeks after 5 years of service. The maximum vacation allowance is 5 weeks for long-serving employees. Employees at KPMG also receive 7 paid personal days off each year, in addition to their regular vacation allowance. Employees at the firm can also apply for unpaid leaves of absence.

KPMG's leave program is available to all employees. Leaves can extend from six weeks to six months (or longer) and can be used for travel, education or simply spending more time with family.

## *Employee Communications* — *Rating: A*

KPMG's internal communications program is rated as **above-average**. To keep employees informed about new developments, KPMG publishes an in-house newsletter (called *Common Thread*). The firm also has an intranet site, which keeps employees informed about news and human resource policies that affect their work. An employee satisfaction survey is conducted every 12 months. An outside consultant compiles the survey results for KPMG's management team.

KPMG also distributes timely information through a weekly electronic newsletter (called *InfoTrack*), corporate voicemail announcements and local and departmental newsletters.

## *Performance Management* — *Rating: A+*

KPMG's performance management program is rated as **exceptional**. The firm operates a thorough performance management program. Every 6 months, employees and managers meet for review sessions. (Managers receive training in how to conduct effective reviews.) KPMG uses a 360-degree feedback process to gather additional performance-related information from co-workers, supervisors and employees. (Managers, partners and executives also participate in the process.)

Because many of its employees work at client locations in the field, KPMG has developed a unique web-based program (called *Dialogue*) that allows employees to complete self-evaluations online and communicate directly with managers at any time from any location.

To recognize excellent performance, KPMG operates an outstanding program (called *Encore*) that enables employees to nominate colleagues for a variety of awards. These range from small gifts to significant cash awards ($500 to $5,000) — the company presented 2,650 awards totaling $856,000 last year. KPMG also offers informal awards, such as sports tickets, dinners and spa visits.

### *Training & Skills Development* — *Rating: A+*

KPMG's training and skills development program is rated as **exceptional**. The firm provides tuition subsidies for courses related to an employee's current position (100% of tuition). Commendably, KPMG also offers subsidies for courses not related to an employee's current job (75% of tuition). KPMG offers bonuses to employees who successfully complete certain professional accreditation programs and courses. The firm assists employees' career development with: in-house training; online training; mentoring; reimbursement for professional association dues. Across Canada, KPMG allocates over $15 million annually — more than $3,500 per employee — for education and training initiatives each year.

Employees studying for their final exams to become a Chartered Accountant receive mentoring from senior employees and take short leaves of absence (two to three months) to help prepare.

Through its international partnership, KPMG offers its employees access to world-class educational resources, including a unique online business mentoring program from Harvard University and an extensive worldwide intranet resource. KPMG's intranet site highlights employment opportunities around the world. The Canadian partnership operates a formal exchange program with its affiliates in Australia and New Zealand.

### *Community Involvement* — *Rating: A*

KPMG's community involvement program is rated as **above-average**. A very good corporate citizen, KPMG actively supports a variety of local and national charitable initiatives. Employees take part in the selection of charitable groups assisted by the firm. Last year, the firm also contributed to approximately 84 charitable groups, including: Big Brothers & Big Sisters, the United Way, the Heart & Stroke Foundation, Kids with Cancer, Juvenile Diabetes, and numerous community organizations.

KPMG operates its own foundation that donates funds to universities, hospitals, research organizations, women's support groups, arts organizations, and children's charities across the country. KPMG also awards four annual scholarships of $2,000 to Aboriginal students pursuing post-secondary studies.

LET RIGHT PREVAIL

The Law Society of Upper Canada | Barreau du Haut-Canada

**LAW SOCIETY OF UPPER CANADA, THE**
**130 Queen Street West**
**Osgoode Hall**
**Toronto, ON M5H 2N6**

**Tel. 416-947-3300**
**Fax 416-947-3448**
**hr@lsuc.on.ca**
**http://www.lsuc.on.ca**

**INDUSTRY: PROFESSIONAL MEMBERSHIP ORGANIZATIONS**

*Highlights:*

- Work in a Toronto landmark that is a six-acre downtown oasis with gardens and buildings dating from 1832 — and includes a four-star restaurant for employees.
- Develop yourself with an extensive range of in-house training courses plus a vast array of courses offered by this employer for its members.
- Get exceptional maternity benefits at this employer, including a 93% top-up payment for the first 17 weeks of your leave.

## *Employer Background*

The Law Society of Upper Canada is the self-governing body for the legal profession in Ontario. Established in 1797, the Law Society is the largest provincial governing organization for lawyers in Canada.

The Law Society's primary responsibility is to regulate the legal profession. In serving this mandate, the Society offers a variety of services to the public, including a lawyer referral service (which matches lawyers with clients' needs), online directories and a statutory compensation fund that assists clients who experience losses as a result of negligent or dishonest lawyers. Through Ontario's legal aid system, the Society also provides financial support for individuals who cannot afford legal representation.

The Law Society also operates a large continuing education branch, providing training for new lawyers (through the Bar Admission Course) and a vast array of refresher courses for experienced ones.

**Workforce at a Glance:** Number of full-time employees: **360**. At this location: **343**. New jobs created in Canada in past year: **5**. Percentage of employees who are women: **66**. Of managers: **60**. Resumes received by their human resources staff in past year: **2,000**. Weeks of vacation their HR manager took last year: **5**. Average employee age: **39**. Years longest-serving employee has worked there: **33**.

## *Physical Workplace* — *Rating: A+*

The Law Society's physical workplace is rated as **exceptional**. The Society's offices are located at Osgoode Hall, situated on a 6-acre garden oasis in the middle of downtown Toronto. The landmark building was constructed in 1832 and features a spectacular library and perhaps the most impressive employee dining hall in the country. (It's also the only workplace in this book rumoured to have ghosts wandering its halls.) Since its construction, Osgoode Hall has seen 10 major additions, the last completed in 1991.

**Physical Workplace at a Glance:** For **food and refreshment**, The Law Society offers: an affordable 4-star restaurant with an executive chef; kitchen areas; free coffee and tea. Nearby **amenities** include: major shopping mall; variety of restaurants; winter skating at Toronto's Nathan Phillip's Square; fitness facility (with subsidized memberships); park/wilderness area (its own professionally landscaped gardens). For **commuters**, The Law Society offers: nearby public transit; secure bicycle parking. Other **work area amenities** include: open-concept workstations; ergonomic workstation design; windows that open; plant life that is tended professionally; library with comfortable seating; fireplace; Canada's largest private law library.

## *Work Atmosphere & Social* — *Rating: A*

The Law Society's work atmosphere is rated as **above-average**. Employees at The Law Society enjoy business casual dress daily. There is also a Society-subsidized social committee, called the '*Spirit*', which has operated since 1996.

Each year, employees enjoy a summer barbeque and volleyball tournament, an employee Christmas party (with a separate party for employees' children) and a mid-winter social. The Law Society also sponsors an employee baseball team that competes in a local league.

## *Health, Financial & Family Benefits* — *Rating: A*

The Law Society's health benefits plan is managed by Sun Life and is rated as **above-average**. Full-time and part-time employees who work more than 20 hours per week are covered by the plan. New employees must wait 90 days before they can enroll in the plan.

**Health Benefits at a Glance:** The Law Society's health plan includes the following coverage: dental (80% of eligible costs, to $1,500 each year); orthodontics (50% of eligible costs); eyecare (to $200 every 4 years); extended health benefits; prescription drug; nutrition planning; massage therapy; physiotherapy; alternative therapies; wellness program; personal and family counselling; employee assistance plan (EAP) for substance abuse/mental health.

The Society's salary and financial benefits are rated as **above-average**. To keep pay-levels competitive, The Law Society participates in outside salary surveys every 12 months. Individual salaries are reviewed every 12 months. The Society operates a traditional pension plan where The Law Society makes a contribution equal to 6% of each employee's salary to their plan each year. **Financial Benefits at a Glance:** The Law Society provides a variety of financial benefits, including: life and disability insurance; discounted home computers; a group RRSP.

The Law Society's family-friendly benefits are rated as **above-average**. Employees with pre-school children have access to a daycare facility located nearby. For employees who take maternity leave, The Law Society provides a generous top-up to 93% of salary for the first 17 weeks of their leave. Other family-friendly benefits include: compressed work week (same hours, fewer days); flexible start and finish hours.

### *Vacation & Time Off* — *Rating: A*

The Law Society's vacation and time off are rated as **above-average**. New employees receive 3 weeks vacation allowance after their first year, which increases to 4 weeks after 5 years of service. The maximum vacation allowance is 5 weeks for long-serving employees. Employees at The Law Society also receive 3 paid personal days off each year, in addition to their regular vacation allowance. Employees at the Society can also apply for unpaid leaves of absence.

### *Employee Communications* — *Rating: A*

The Law Society's internal communications program is rated as **above-average**. To keep employees informed about new developments, The Law Society publishes an in-house newsletter (called *Ontario Lawyers Gazette*), which is a bilingual publication distributed to employees and members of the Society. The Society also has an intranet site, which keeps employees informed about news and human resource policies that affect their work. An employee satisfaction survey is conducted by having employees complete an online questionnaire every 24 months. An outside consultant compiles the survey results for The Law Society's management team.

### *Performance Management* — *Rating: A*

The Law Society's performance management program is rated as **above-average**. The Society operates a well-designed performance management program. Once a year, employees and managers meet for review sessions. (Managers receive training in how to conduct effective reviews.) Along with ongoing feedback, employees complete a self-assessment prior to the annual review. At the reviews, employees and managers discuss past performance and set goals for the upcoming year.

### *Training & Skills Development* — *Rating: A+*

The Law Society's training and skills development program is rated as **exceptional**. The Society provides tuition subsidies for courses related to an employee's current position (100% of tuition). Commendably, The Law Society also offers subsidies for courses not related to an employee's current job (50% of tuition). The Society assists employees' career development with: reimbursement for professional association dues; in-house training.

The Society's in-house training program includes a variety of courses, including computer training sessions, French language courses and classes on a wide range of subjects (from project management to workplace human rights issues). Employees at the Law Society can also attend some of the vast array of professional development programs developed by the Society for its members.

### *Community Involvement* — *Rating: A*

The Law Society's community involvement program is rated as **above-average**. A very good member of the community, The Law Society actively supports a variety of local charitable initiatives. Employees take part in the selection of charitable groups assisted by the Society. Last year, the Society contributed to approximately 7 charitable groups, including: the Canadian Cancer Society, the Parkinson Society of Canada, the Breast Cancer Foundation, the Daily Bread Foodbank and the Salvation Army.

**MACDONALD, DETTWILER AND ASSOCIATES LTD.**
**13800 Commerce Parkway**
**Richmond, BC V6V 2J3**

**Tel. 604-278-3411**
**Fax 604-278-2281**
**hrinfo@mda.ca**
**http://www.mda.ca**

**INDUSTRY: ENGINEERING, ARCHITECTURAL & SURVEYING FIRMS**

*Highlights:*

- Take charge of your career development with an individual training budget that every employee receives.
- Enjoy a lunch that's out of this world with the space shuttle crew who delivered this company's product to the International Space Station.
- Breathe deeply at a yoga class (led by the General Manager) at this company's onsite fitness facility.
- Tee-off with your co-workers with an after-work game of golf at a course just across the street.

## *Employer Background*

MacDonald, Dettwiler and Associates Ltd. / MDA develops information systems for aerospace and land registration applications. The company operates through two main business groups: Information and Robotic Systems; and Information Products.

The Information and Robotic Systems group, which accounts for nearly three-quarters of the company's revenues, provides sophisticated information systems for defence and aerospace applications. Canadarm2, which MDA designed for the International Space Station, is a spectacular example of this group's work.

The company's Information Products group supplies information management systems to local governments and real estate clients that need up-to-date information on property transactions and descriptions, including aerial and digital satellite mapping. This high-growth business offers tremendous potential as governments around the world update their property registration systems to allow customer access over the Internet and improve the quality of the data collected.

Founded in 1969, MDA has never laid off an engineer since its founding. The publicly-traded company has annual revenues over $570 million.

**Workforce at a Glance:** Number of full-time employees: **1,471**. At this location: **811**. Worldwide: **2,216**. Percentage of employees who are women: **31**. Of managers: **19**. Percentage of employees who are visible minorities: **23**. Of managers: **11**. Resumes received by their human resources staff in past year: **5,435**. Weeks of vacation their HR manager took last year: **4**. Average employee age: **39**. Years longest-serving employee has worked there: **30**. Person you should get to know first: **Dianne, she is MDA's "mother hen" and will take care of you from day one**. Car the president drives: **2001 Subaru Outback**. Where it's parked in the lot: **with everyone else**.

***Physical Workplace*** ***Rating: A+***

MDA's physical workplace is rated as **exceptional**. The company's Richmond head office is located next to a golf course (where many employees play) and only a short drive to Vancouver International Airport. In a gesture that speaks volumes about the company, the president's office is the same size as other employees' offices.

**Physical Workplace at a Glance:** Their **onsite fitness facility** features: subsidized memberships; treadmills; stationary bikes; stairmasters; weights; instructor-led classes (including pilates, kick-boxing and dance); shower facilities. Their **employee lounge and rest areas** feature: comfortable couches; sleep room; television; foosball; table tennis; dart board. For **food and refreshment**, MDA offers: free coffee and tea; kitchen areas; outdoor eating area; barbeque; vending machines. The company has an onsite cafeteria that features: subsidized meals (a turkey sandwich costs $3.75); healthy menu items; special diet menus. Nearby **amenities** include: variety of restaurants; major shopping mall; park/wilderness area (Richmond Nature Park); recreation centre (Cambie Community Centre). For **commuters**, MDA offers: free onsite car parking; convenient highway access; nearby public transit; secure bicycle parking. Other **work area amenities** include: open-concept workstations; ergonomic workstation design; access to natural light for all employees; plant life that is tended professionally.

***Work Atmosphere & Social*** ***Rating: A***

MDA's work atmosphere is rated as **above-average**. Employees at MDA enjoy business casual dress daily and can listen to radio or music while they are working. There is also a company-subsidized social committee, which has operated since 1979.

Throughout the year, employees enjoy a variety of activities, including golfing, kayaking, river rafting and skiing. MDA also sponsors employee sports teams, including hockey, curling, baseball, volleyball and a dragonboat racing team. In addition to a summer picnic and a Christmas party for employees, the company hosts special events for employees' children, including a Christmas party and spring break field trips to the zoo and Vancouver's Science World.

In addition, MDA's quarterly meetings are followed by wine and cheese receptions. Last year, employees were treated to a barbeque lunch with Canadian astronaut Chris Hatfield and the space shuttle crew who delivered Canadarm2 to the International Space Station!

***Health, Financial & Family Benefits*** ***Rating: A***

MDA's health benefits plan is managed by Sun Life and is rated as **above-average**. There is no waiting period before new employees are eligible for coverage.

**Health Benefits at a Glance:** MDA's health plan includes the following coverage: dental (80% of eligible costs, with no annual maximum); orthodontics (60% of eligible costs with a lifetime maximum of $3,000); eyecare (to $300 every 2 years); extended health benefits; prescription drug; physiotherapy; massage therapy; alternative therapies; personal and family counselling; employee assistance plan (EAP) for substance abuse/mental health; wellness plan.

The company's salary and financial benefits are rated as **exceptional**. To keep pay-levels competitive, MDA participates in outside salary surveys every 6 months.

Individual salaries are reviewed every 6 months. The company offers a group RSP that allows employees to contribute up to 5% of their salary, with matching employer contributions.

> **Financial Benefits at a Glance:** MDA provides an extensive set of financial benefits, including: life and disability insurance; discounted car leases; subsidized auto insurance; subsidized home insurance; discounted home computers; discounted home Internet access; share purchase plan; signing bonuses for some employees; referral bonuses for some employees (from $1,000 to $1,500); year-end bonuses (from $1,000 to $10,000 for non-executives).

MDA's family-friendly benefits are rated as **average**. Employees with pre-school children have access to a daycare facility located nearby. Other family-friendly benefits include: flexible start and finish hours; shortened work week (fewer hours); compressed work week (same hours, fewer days); telecommuting and working from home; reduced summer hours; job-sharing.

### *Vacation & Time Off* — *Rating: A*

MDA's vacation and time off are rated as **above-average**. New employees receive 3 weeks of vacation allowance after their first year, which increases to 4 weeks after 7 years of service. The maximum vacation allowance is 4 weeks for long-serving employees. Employees at the company can also apply for unpaid leaves of absence.

### *Employee Communications* — *Rating: A*

MDA's internal communications program is rated as **above-average**. To keep employees informed about new developments, MDA publishes an in-house newsletter. The company also has a detailed intranet site (called *Infoshare*), which keeps employees informed about news and human resource policies that affect their work. An employee satisfaction survey is conducted by having employees complete an online questionnaire every 12 months. An outside consultant compiles the survey results for MDA's management team. In addition, MDA's human resources department conducts an in-house survey every 36 months.

### *Performance Management* — *Rating: A+*

MDA's performance management program is rated as **exceptional**. The company operates a comprehensive performance management program. Once a year, employees and managers meet for review sessions. (Managers receive training in how to conduct effective reviews.) MDA uses a 360-degree feedback process to gather additional performance-related information from co-workers, supervisors and employees. Employees can also provide confidential feedback on their manager's performance through the 360-degree process.

In addition to the annual review, managers provide ongoing feedback throughout the year and recognize excellent work through a personalized awards program. Employees can even recognize co-workers through a special peer awards program.

*Training & Skills Development* *Rating: A+*

MDA's training and skills development program is rated as **exceptional**. The company assists employees' career development with: career planning; mentoring; in-house training. The company's in-house training program (called *MDA University*) offers a variety of programs for all employees, from administration to engineering. Employees' family members can enroll in weekend computer classes.

MDA also has an interesting program to manage external employee training. Each year, all permanent employees receive "professional development dollars," which vary according to each employee's salary range. The dollars (which are actual paper notes with pictures of the company's founders), can be used however an employee wishes — for publications, professional memberships, computer software, internet access, business conferences or for courses at outside institutions. Employees can even pool their dollars to bring in guest speakers or arrange specialized training. This program is unique in that it treats training dollars like a healthcare spending account or contributions to a pension plan. The message to employees is that training is a valuable asset and should be managed by each employee carefully.

*Community Involvement* *Rating: A*

MDA's community involvement program is rated as **above-average**. A very good corporate citizen, MDA actively supports a variety of local and national charitable initiatives. Employees take part in the selection of charitable groups assisted by the company. Employees at MDA receive paid time off to volunteer at local charities. Last year, the company contributed to approximately 110 charitable groups, including: the United Way, the Canadian Cancer Society, the Heart and Stroke Foundation, the Vancouver Children's Hospital, and the Covenant House clothing drive, to name a few.

MARITIME TRAVEL INC.
2000 Barrington Street
Suite 202
Halifax, NS B3J 3K1

Tel. 902-420-1554
Fax 902-420-0447
http://www.maritimetravel.ca

# Maritime Travel

We Know Travel Best.

**INDUSTRY: TRAVEL AGENCY & TOUR OPERATORS**

***Highlights:***

- Build your career at a growing employer in the travel industry that's rapidly building a national business with lots of room for career growth.
- Develop yourself at an employer that encourages continuous learning through tuition subsidies and cash bonuses for employees who complete professional accreditation programs.
- Get free trips and vacations for excellent performance on the job — it's part of this employer's business.

***Employer Background***

Maritime Travel Inc. provides travel agency services to individuals and businesses across Canada. The company services its customers through a network of 85 retail branches and its centralized reservation system. Maritime Travel also provides unique software that enables customers to manage their own reservations over the Internet.

In addition to reservations, Maritime Travel offers a variety of travel-related services to individuals and businesses. These include business travel management, conference organizing, air charters, foreign exchange services and ground handling services for cruise ship companies, such as Holland America and Princess Cruises.

Established in 1949, the company is Atlantic Canada's largest travel agency. The company's recent acquisition of the Hudson's Bay Company's travel division (The Bay Travel) has led to significant growth and an increased presence in markets across the country. Impressively, the privately-held company posted sales of $132 million last year.

**Workforce at a Glance:** Number of full-time employees: **336**. At this location: **34**. New jobs created in Canada in past year: **41**. Percentage of employees who are women: **97**. Of managers: **98**. Percentage of employees who are visible minorities: **2**. Of managers: **2**. Resumes received by their human resources staff in past year: **134**. Weeks of vacation their HR manager took last year: **3**. Average employee age: **38**. Years longest-serving employee has worked there: **28**. Person you should get to know first: **Joyce in reception pretty much knows everything about everybody**.

*Physical Workplace* *Rating: A*

Maritime Travel's physical workplace is rated as **above-average**. Located in a modern office building in downtown Halifax, the company's head office offers great views of Halifax Harbour. The building is close to the waterfront boardwalk as well as the Halifax-Dartmouth ferry. Inside, administrative employees work in a traditional office environment, while call-centre personnel work in an open-concept setting with a relaxed travel theme. Across the country, retail employees work at travel centres in major shopping malls and at outlets within major retailers (such as Atlantic Superstore, Wal-Mart and The Bay).

**Physical Workplace at a Glance:** For **food and refreshment**, Maritime Travel offers: kitchen area; outdoor eating area. Nearby **amenities** include: variety of restaurants; major shopping mall; fitness facility; park/wilderness area (Halifax Public Gardens). For **commuters**, Maritime Travel offers: nearby public transit; secure bicycle parking. Other **work area amenities** include: open-concept workstations; ergonomic workstation design; traditional offices; access to natural light for all employees; plant life that is tended professionally.

*Work Atmosphere & Social* *Rating: B+*

Maritime Travel's work atmosphere is rated as **average**. Employees at Maritime Travel enjoy business casual dress daily and can listen to radio or music while they are working. Every year, department and branch managers receive a budget (about $120 per employee) for celebrations and social activities. Across the company, employees enjoy potluck Christmas dinners, evenings at the theatre, Friday treats and year-end celebrations. In addition, Maritime Travel hosts regular dinners for employees and managers at the CEO's Halifax home.

*Health, Financial & Family Benefits* *Rating: B+*

Maritime Travel's health benefits plan is managed by Maritime Life and is rated as **average**. New employees must wait 90 days before they can enroll in the plan.

**Health Benefits at a Glance:** Maritime Travel's health plan includes the following coverage: dental (100% of eligible costs, to $1,000 each year); eyecare (to $100 every 2 years); extended health benefits; prescription drug; nutrition planning; massage therapy; physiotherapy; alternative therapies; personal and family counselling; employee assistance plan (EAP) for substance abuse/mental health.

The company's salary and financial benefits are rated as **above-average**. To keep pay-levels competitive, Maritime Travel participates in outside salary surveys every 24 months. Individual salaries are reviewed every 12 months. The company operates a traditional pension plan.

**Financial Benefits at a Glance:** Maritime Travel provides a variety of financial benefits, including: life and disability insurance; discounted home computers; discounted company products; share purchase plan; profit-sharing plan; signing bonuses for some employees; referral bonuses for some employees (from $250 to $1,100).

Maritime Travel's family-friendly benefits are rated as **average**. Family-friendly benefits include: reduced summer hours; telecommuting and working from home; compressed work week (same hours, fewer days); shortened work week (fewer hours); flexible start and finish hours.

### *Vacation & Time Off* — *Rating: B+*

Maritime Travel's vacation and time off are rated as **average**. New employees receive 2 weeks of vacation allowance after their first year, which increases to 3 weeks after 2 years of service. Employees at the company can also apply for unpaid leaves of absence. (Recently, one employee took time off during the summer for university studies.)

### *Employee Communications* — *Rating: B+*

Maritime Travel's internal communications program is rated as **average**. To keep employees informed about new developments, Maritime Travel publishes an in-house newsletter (called *TravelBound*). The company also has an intranet site (called *TravelBot*), which keeps employees informed about news and human resource policies that affect their work. To solicit feedback from employees, the company operates an email suggestion box.

### *Performance Management* — *Rating: A*

Maritime Travel's performance management program is rated as **above-average**. The company operates a formal performance management program. Once a year, employees and managers meet for review sessions. (Managers receive training in how to conduct effective reviews.) At the reviews, employees and managers discuss past performance and establish professional development plans for the upcoming year. As part of the review process, employees can provide feedback on their manager's performance. (Managers also participate in a similar review process.) Maritime Travel recognizes exceptional performance with several awards, including free trips and a profit-sharing plan.

### *Training & Skills Development* — *Rating: A+*

Maritime Travel's training and skills development program is rated as **exceptional**. The company provides tuition subsidies for courses related to an employee's current position (100% of tuition). Commendably, Maritime Travel also offers subsidies for courses not related to an employee's current job. Maritime Travel offers bonuses to employees who successfully complete certain professional accreditation programs and courses. The company assists employees' career development with: reimbursement for professional association dues; mentoring; career planning; in-house training.

### *Community Involvement* — *Rating: B+*

Maritime Travel's community involvement program is rated as **average**. A good corporate citizen, Maritime Travel actively supports a variety of local charitable initiatives. Employees take part in the selection of charitable groups assisted by the company.

Last year, the company supported the United Way, the Queen Elizabeth II Health Sciences Centre and the Abilities Foundation of Nova Scotia. In response to its recent expansion across Canada, the company has established an employee charitable committee to plan future donations to national organizations.

Matrikon
Solutions for Industrial Agility

**MATRIKON INC.**
**10405 Jasper Avenue**
**Suite 1800**
**Edmonton, AB T5J 3N4**

**Tel. 780-448-1010**
**Fax 780-448-9191**
**careers@matrikon.com**
**http://www.matrikon.com**

**INDUSTRY: INFORMATION TECHNOLOGY CONSULTING FIRMS**

*Highlights:*

- Build your career at a growing software employer that had record revenues last year and offers career opportunities around the world.
- Take part in a performance review that focuses less on technical skills and more on dedication, loyalty, commitment and personal qualities — a rarity in the high-tech field.
- Enjoy a relaxed work environment, including casual dress and a fully equipped employee lounge and games room.

## *Employer Background*

Matrikon Inc. develops plant optimization software and provides related consulting services to industrial customers around the world. Founded in 1988, the company's software products include web-based reporting and remote site monitoring software; diagnostic and industrial communications software; and planning and scheduling software. Matrikon's software collects operating data and identifies problems, helping customers streamline their plant operations. Impressively, Matrikon serves some of the world's largest companies in the oil and gas, chemical processing, utilities, forestry, mining, cement, and food processing industries.

The publicly-traded company has offices across Canada and in the United States, Bahrain, Qatar and Australia. Approximately 80% of Matrikon's revenues come from international sales, which provides employees with opportunities to work around the world.

Last year, Matrikon acquired an Australian software firm and expanded its Middle East offices to better serve its growing international customer base. Matrikon generated over $37 million in revenues last year — its 14th consecutive year of record revenues.

**Workforce at a Glance:** Number of full-time employees: **339**. At this location: **251**. Worldwide: **436**. New jobs created in Canada in past year: **55**. Percentage of employees who are women: **20**. Of managers: **22**. Percentage of employees who are visible minorities: **37**. Of managers: **35**. Resumes received by their human resources staff in past year: **6,000**. Average employee age: **32**. Person you should get to know first: **Val in reception knows how to handle every situation**. Car the president drives: **BMW X5 2002**. Where it's parked in the lot: **with everyone else**.

### *Physical Workplace* — *Rating: A*

Matrikon's physical workplace is rated as **above-average**. Located in downtown Edmonton, Matrikon's head office occupies the top three floors of a modern office tower providing great views of downtown Edmonton and the river valley below. The building is connected to the city's enclosed walkway system, which provides all-weather access to downtown restaurants, shops and services.

**Physical Workplace at a Glance:** Their **employee lounge and rest areas** feature: comfortable couches; 2 foosball tables; board games; dart board; putting green; meditation or religious observance room. For **food and refreshment**, Matrikon offers: free coffee and tea. Nearby **amenities** include: variety of restaurants; fitness facility (with subsidized memberships); local shops and services; park/wilderness area (Edmonton River Valley); recreation centre (Kinsmen Centre). For **commuters**, Matrikon offers: nearby public transit; secure bicycle parking; riverside cycling trails. Other **work area amenities** include: open-concept workstations; wireless connectivity throughout office; plant life that is tended professionally.

### *Work Atmosphere & Social* — *Rating: A*

Matrikon's work atmosphere is rated as **above-average**. Employees at Matrikon enjoy casual dress daily and can listen to radio or music while they are working. There is also a company-subsidized social committee, which has operated since 1997.

Throughout the year, Matrikon organizes a variety of special events. These include an annual employee appreciation dinner and dance, a Halloween pumpkin-carving contest, a Christmas party, a Valentine's Day celebration, a summer solstice pancake breakfast, an annual family barbeque and a unique video game tournament.

The company also organizes team-building events throughout the year, including pub nights, paintball challenges, soccer, golf games and bathtub races during Edmonton's popular Klondike Days festival. Matrikon always keeps its freezer stocked with frozen cakes to celebrate individual employee accomplishments and significant milestones.

### *Health, Financial & Family Benefits* — *Rating: A*

Matrikon's health benefits plan is managed by Blue Cross and is rated as **average**. New employees must wait 90 days before they can enroll in the plan.

**Health Benefits at a Glance:** Matrikon's health plan includes the following coverage: dental (80% of eligible costs, to $1,500 each year); eyecare (to $200 every 2 years); prescription drug; extended health benefits; nutrition planning; massage therapy; physiotherapy; alternative therapies; personal and family counselling; fitness subsidies.

The company's salary and financial benefits are rated as **exceptional**. To keep pay-levels competitive, Matrikon participates in outside salary surveys every 12 months. Individual salaries are reviewed every 12 months. The company offers a group RSP that allows employees to contribute up to 5% of their salary, with matching employer contributions. Prior to becoming a public company recently, Matrikon presented each employee with a gift of 1,000 shares for each year of service.

**Financial Benefits at a Glance:** Matrikon provides an extensive set of financial benefits, including: share purchase plan; life and disability insurance; discounted home computers; discounted products and services from local businesses; signing bonuses for some employees; referral bonuses for some employees (from $250 to $1,000).

Matrikon's family-friendly benefits are rated as **average**. Employees with preschool children have access to a daycare facility located nearby. Other family-friendly benefits include: flexible start and finish hours; compressed work week (same hours, fewer days); telecommuting and working from home.

***Vacation & Time Off*** — ***Rating: A***

Matrikon's vacation and time off are rated as **above-average**. New employees receive 3 weeks of vacation allowance after their first year, which increases to 4 weeks after 10 years of service. The maximum vacation allowance is 4 weeks for long-serving employees. Employees at the company can also apply for unpaid leaves of absence. (Recently, one employee took a 3 month leave to travel through Europe and another took 6 weeks to complete an MBA.)

***Employee Communications*** — ***Rating: A***

Matrikon's internal communications program is rated as **above-average**. To keep employees informed about new developments, Matrikon publishes an in-house newsletter. The company also has an intranet site (called *Konnect*), which keeps employees informed about news and human resource policies that affect their work. To solicit feedback from employees, the company operates an email suggestion box. An in-house employee satisfaction survey is conducted by having employees complete an online questionnaire every 12 months.

***Performance Management*** — ***Rating: A+***

Matrikon's performance management program is rated as **exceptional**. The company operates a well-designed performance management program. Once a year, employees and managers meet for review sessions. (Managers receive training in how to conduct effective reviews.) Employees can provide confidential feedback on their manager's performance directly to the human resources department.

Matrikon's hiring and review programs were adapted recently to place more emphasis on "human" factors such as dedication, loyalty, commitment and teamwork skills. Although more difficult to measure, these qualities are important in determining overall employee performance and satisfaction.

***Training & Skills Development*** — ***Rating: B+***

Matrikon's training and skills development program is rated as **average**. The company provides tuition subsidies for courses related to an employee's current position (100% of tuition). The company assists employees' career development with: reimbursement for professional association dues; in-house training; career planning; mentoring.

*Community Involvement* ***Rating: A***

Matrikon's community involvement program is rated as **above-average**. A very good corporate citizen, Matrikon actively supports a variety of charitable initiatives. Employees take part in the selection of charitable groups assisted by the company. Employees at Matrikon receive paid time off to volunteer at local charities. Last year, the company contributed to approximately 8 charitable groups, including: the United Way, the Alzheimer's Society, the Aga Khan Foundation Partnership Walk (to raise money for social programs in Africa and Asia) and a local youth shelter.

In addition, employees regularly take the lead in supporting their favourite charities. Last year, one employee collected toys and delivered them to an orphanage in Mexico while on vacation. Another employee challenged her co-workers to raise money for local residents who were left homeless after an apartment fire.

**MEI INC.**
**9001, boulevard l'Acadie**
**7é étage**
**Montréal, QC H4N 3H5**

**Tel. 514-384-6411**
**Fax 514-384-6410**
**resume@meicpg.com**
**http://www.meicpg.com**

**INDUSTRY: SOFTWARE COMPANIES**

*Highlights:*

- Build your career at this growing software company that has prospered through the recent high-tech meltdown by offering sophisticated technology to some of the world's largest consumer product companies.
- Work for an enlightened employer that offers an unpaid leave of absence program that's actually used — one employee here took a four-month leave to build a log cabin and another took a full year off to pursue a music career.
- Excel in your career at this smaller employer that annually awards its best-performing employee an all-expense-paid vacation or up to $2,500 in cash — your choice.

## *Employer Background*

MEI Inc. develops sales force automation software for retail applications and consumer products companies. Founded in 1983, the company's software allows consumer products marketers to gauge the effectiveness of their marketing efforts in the field instantly. At the store level, sales representatives use MEI's web-based software to generate instant reports for management on product placement, availability and contract compliance.

The company's multilingual software is used around the world by major consumer products companies, including Procter & Gamble, Nestle, Kraft, SC Johnson and Molson Breweries. MEI has also developed strategic partnerships with hardware manufacturers around the world.

In addition to its Montréal head office, MEI has international offices in the United States, France and the United Kingdom.

**Workforce at a Glance:** Number of full-time employees: **68**. Worldwide: **81**. New jobs created in Canada in past year: **2**. Percentage of employees who are women: **34**. Of managers: **6**. Percentage of employees who are visible minorities: **19**. Of managers: **2**. Resumes received by their human resources staff in past year: **350**. Weeks of vacation their HR manager took last year: **3**. Average employee age: **35**. Years longest-serving employee has worked there: **20**. Person you should get to know first: **Therese in reception knows everyone and is the "life of the party" at company events**. Car the president drives: **BMW**. Where it's parked in the lot: **reserved spot**.

### *Physical Workplace* — *Rating: A*

MEI's physical workplace is rated as **above-average**. In addition to an onsite fitness facility, the 10-storey building features a rooftop jogging track. Inside, the office is decorated using relaxing colours, with most employees working in open-concept areas. (Most managers work in traditional offices.)

**Physical Workplace at a Glance:** Their **onsite fitness facility** features: subsidized memberships; treadmills; stationary bikes; stairmasters; rowing machines; weights; instructor-led classes; shower facilities. Their **employee lounge and rest areas** feature: comfortable couches; music; board games. For **food and refreshment**, MEI offers: subsidized coffee and tea (with proceeds going to the social committee); kitchen area; outdoor eating area; small restaurant on main floor. Nearby **amenities** include: variety of restaurants; major shopping mall; park/wilderness area (Mont Royal). For **commuters**, MEI offers: free onsite car parking; nearby public transit; secure bicycle parking. Other **work area amenities** include: open-concept workstations; access to natural light for all employees; ergonomic workstation design.

### *Work Atmosphere & Social* — *Rating: A*

MEI's work atmosphere is rated as **above-average**. Employees at MEI enjoy casual dress daily and can listen to radio or music while they are working. There is also a company-subsidized social committee, which has operated since 1993.

The social committee organizes numerous events throughout the year, a summer family day (with overnight camping) at a nearby lake, an employee Christmas party and an annual awards celebration. MEI also has a pick-up hockey team that plays just for fun.

### *Health, Financial & Family Benefits* — *Rating: A*

MEI's health benefits plan is rated as **above-average**. MEI pays 65% of the premiums associated with the plan, with employees paying the remaining 35%. There is no waiting period before new employees are eligible for coverage.

**Health Benefits at a Glance:** MEI's health plan includes the following coverage: dental; eyecare; extended health benefits; prescription drug; massage therapy; physiotherapy; alternative therapies; personal and family counselling; employee assistance plan (EAP) for substance abuse/mental health.

The company's salary and financial benefits are rated as **above-average**. To keep pay-levels competitive, MEI participates in outside salary surveys every 24 months. Individual salaries are reviewed every 12 months. The company offers a group RSP that allows employees to contribute up to 10% of their salary to a maximum of $5,000 per year, with matching employer contributions at the rate of 50¢ for each employee dollar contributed.

**Financial Benefits at a Glance:** MEI provides a variety of financial benefits, including: life and disability insurance; share purchase plan; referral bonuses for some employees (to $3,000).

MEI's family-friendly benefits are rated as **average**. Family-friendly benefits include: personal time off as needed; telecommuting and working from home; flexible start and finish hours.

*Vacation & Time Off* *Rating: A*

MEI's vacation and time off are rated as **above-average**. New employees receive 2.3 weeks of vacation allowance after their first year, which increases to 3 weeks after 2 years of service. The maximum vacation allowance is 5 weeks for long-serving employees. Employees at the company can also apply for unpaid leaves of absence. (Recent examples include one employee who took a 4 month leave to build a log cabin, and another who took a full year off to pursue a career in music.)

*Employee Communications* *Rating: B+*

MEI's internal communications program is rated as **average**. An in-house employee satisfaction survey is conducted by having employees complete questionnaires every 24 months. The company also posts a weekly news bulletin for all employees.

*Performance Management* *Rating: A+*

MEI's performance management program is rated as exceptional. The company operates a well-designed performance management program. Every 6 months, employees and managers meet for review sessions. (Managers receive training in how to conduct effective reviews.) The reviews focus on career development and planning and form the basis for salary increases and bonuses. MEI recognizes exceptional performance with restaurant dinners, cash bonuses and a chance to win the annual President's Award — winners can choose an all-expense-paid vacation or a cash bonus (to $2,500).

*Training & Skills Development* *Rating: A*

MEI's training and skills development program is rated as **above-average**. The company provides tuition subsidies for courses related to an employee's current position (100% of tuition to $700). The company assists employees' career development with: reimbursement for professional association dues; mentoring; in-house training; paid industry seminars.

*Community Involvement* *Rating: A*

MEI's community involvement program is rated as **above-average**. A very good corporate citizen, MEI actively supports a variety of charitable initiatives. Employees take part in the selection of charitable groups assisted by the company. Employees at MEI receive paid time off to volunteer at local charities.

Many employees volunteer their time with community organizations, including coaching minor league sports, teaching literacy and raising money for charitable groups such as the Canadian Cancer Society, the Heart and Stroke Foundation and Doctors Without Borders.

As a group, MEI employees support Montreal's Welcome Home Mission, which helps children and young adults living in poverty, the homeless and individuals with drug addictions.

MERCK FROSST

MERCK FROSST
CP 1005
Pointe-Claire, QC H9R 4P8

Tel. 514-428-7920
Fax 514-428-4940
hr_montreal@merck.com
http://www.merckfrosst.com

**INDUSTRY: PHARMACEUTICAL & DRUG MANUFACTURERS**

*Highlights:*

- Get an excellent maternity top-up payment (100% of salary for 18 weeks) plus two onsite daycare facilities.
- Get five paid days off when your spouse has a baby.
- Work for an employer that actively encourages alternative work arrangements (such as working from home) by clearly explaining the process needed to approve such arrangements.

## *Employer Background*

Merck Frosst (a subsidiary of Merck & Co., Inc.) is one of Canada's leading research-based pharmaceutical companies, developing medicines for human health. The company develops medicines that are sold around the world and has received awards for many of its innovative products.

In addition to being one of Canada's largest pharmaceutical companies, Merck Frosst is one of the top five research and development organizations in the country. The company recently committed $1 million to the establishment of a research chair at Vancouver's Arthritis Research Centre of Canada.

Merck Frosst's roots in Canada date back to 1899, when Charles E. Frosst & Co. was established in Montréal. In 1965, the company became part of New Jersey-based Merck & Co., Incorporated.

**Workforce at a Glance:** Number of full-time employees: **1,902**. At this location: **1,407**. Worldwide: **77,300**. New jobs created in Canada in past year: **39**. Percentage of employees who are women: **50**. Of managers: **39**. Percentage of employees who are visible minorities: **8**. Of managers: **7**. Resumes received by their human resources staff in past year: **20,575**. Average employee age: **40**.

## *Physical Workplace* — *Rating:* A+

Merck Frosst's physical workplace is rated as **exceptional**. Located on the West Island of Montréal, Merck Frosst's head office is a campus of interconnected buildings covering over one million square feet.

Last year, the company moved into its new head office in Montréal — a six year construction project valued at over $250 million. The modern building is one of the only facilities in Canada that combines office space, state-of-the-art research labs, manufacturing and packaging operations. The head office is also home to Canada's largest private research library and biomedical research facility. To conserve energy, the new building uses innovative technology, such as motion sensitive lighting and recovered energy from its manufacturing operations to heat the building.

**Physical Workplace at a Glance:** Their **employee lounge and rest areas** feature: comfortable couches; television; outdoor softball and soccer field. The company has an onsite cafeteria that features: subsidized meals (a turkey sandwich costs $1.47); healthy menu items; special diet menus; outdoor patio; prepared meals to take home; vendor who delivers fresh produce; healthy choice vending machine. Nearby **amenities** include: variety of restaurants; major shopping mall; fitness facility (with subsidized memberships); park/wilderness area (Cap Saint-Jacques Regional Park); recreation centre. For **commuters**, Merck Frosst offers: nearby public transit; free onsite car parking; secure bicycle parking; easy highway access. Other **work area amenities** include: wireless connectivity throughout office; plant life that is tended professionally; access to natural light for all employees; ergonomic workstation design; open-concept workstations; individual temperature control for workstations; onsite banking (ATM); onsite dry cleaning.

## *Work Atmosphere & Social* — *Rating: A*

Merck Frosst's work atmosphere is rated as **above-average**. Employees at Merck Frosst enjoy business casual dress daily. There is also a company-subsidized social committee.

The company organizes several social events every year, including a banquet recognizing long serving employees, a Christmas party for employees' children, a holiday lunch served by senior management, an Italian-themed lunch, a summer Olympiad (held during working hours), and an open house for friends and family. The company also sponsors employee hockey, softball and soccer teams that compete in local leagues.

## *Health, Financial & Family Benefits* — *Rating: A*

Merck Frosst's health benefits plan is rated as **above-average**. Their health benefits plan is flexible, meaning that employees can tailor individual plans to their personal circumstances. Merck Frosst's health plan also covers employees in their retirement.

**Health Benefits at a Glance:** Merck Frosst's health plan includes the following coverage: dental; eyecare (to $150 every 2 years); extended health benefits; prescription drug; employee assistance plan (EAP) for substance abuse/mental health; health information newsletter; healthclub subsidies ($300 per year).

The company's salary and financial benefits are rated as **above-average**. To keep pay-levels competitive, Merck Frosst participates in outside salary surveys every 12 months. Individual salaries are reviewed every 12 months. The annual review process forms the basis for salary increases.

**Financial Benefits at a Glance:** Merck Frosst provides a variety of financial benefits, including: life and disability insurance; subsidized auto insurance; performance bonuses (to 2 months salary); share purchase plan; year-end bonuses.

Merck Frosst's family-friendly benefits are rated as **exceptional**. For employees who take maternity leave, Merck Frosst provides a generous top-up to 100% of salary for the first 18 weeks of their leave. Incredibly, Merck Frosst has two onsite daycare centres with a total of 140 spaces. In addition, the daycare facilities operate unique summer and holiday camps for school children between the ages of 5 and 12. Other family-friendly benefits include: flexible start and finish hours; shortened work week (fewer hours); compressed work week (same hours, fewer days); telecommuting and working from home; reduced summer hours; job-sharing; ability to move to part-time status.

In addition, employees whose spouses have given birth receive a paid leave of 5 days so they can spend time with their new family. For employees who have a company car (e.g. sales representatives), Merck Frosst allows them to keep their car during their leave, to a maximum of 70 weeks.

### *Vacation & Time Off* — *Rating: A*

Merck Frosst's vacation and time off are rated as **above-average**. New employees receive 3 weeks of vacation allowance after their first year, which increases to 4 weeks after 8 years of service. The maximum vacation allowance is 6 weeks for employees who spend 25 years with the company.

Merck Frosst encourages its employees to take advantage of a variety of alternative work arrangements (such as shortened work weeks, compressed work weeks and working from home) with a 12-page booklet that clearly sets out the process involved in approving such arrangements.

### *Employee Communications* — *Rating: A*

Merck Frosst's internal communications program is rated as **above-average**. To keep employees informed about new developments, Merck Frosst publishes an in-house newsletter (called *The Capsule*), which is bilingual. The company also has a bilingual intranet site, which keeps employees informed about news and human resource policies that affect their work.

To gain valuable employee feedback, Merck Frosst operates a unique employee advisory council that aims to improve company programs. These employees work with management and attend regular review meetings. The company also conducts regular surveys of employee teams to identify workgroup problems and develop solutions. The company also uses traditional bulletin board postings and email announcements to communicate with all employees.

### *Performance Management* — *Rating: A*

Merck Frosst's performance management program is rated as **above-average**. Merck Frosst has a well-developed performance management program that begins with a comprehensive orientation for all new employees. Afterwards, employees move to a review process that sets leadership and performance goals each year. The process involves ongoing reviews with managers and is an important tool for feedback and coaching.

For managers, Merck Frosst has a leadership development program that provides them with timely feedback on their performance from peers, staff and customers. Managers also receive individual counselling to improve their performance.

For all employees (including managers), performance excellence is recognized through a number of cash and non-cash awards that range in value from $100 to two months' salary.

*Training & Skills Development* *Rating: A*

Merck Frosst's training and skills development program is rated as **above-average**. The company provides tuition subsidies for courses related to an employee's current position. The company assists employees' career development with: in-house training; mentoring; career planning.

Merck Frosst encourages employees to upgrade their skills continually and work with their managers to create individual career development plans. A special mentoring program pairs new employees with senior staff for one full year.

In addition, Merck Frosst invests nearly $1.5 million each year to encourage Canadian students to pursue careers in science. In a unique program ("Exploring Minds"), Merck Frosst provides students with hands-on experience in scientific work — and encourages parents to support their children's interest in science. The company awards scholarships to children of employees who are pursuing higher education.

*Community Involvement* *Rating: A*

Merck Frosst's community involvement program is rated as **above-average**. A very good corporate citizen, Merck Frosst actively supports a variety of local and national charitable initiatives. Employees take part in the selection of charitable groups assisted by the company.

Merck Frosst has an entirely employee-run donations program that raised over $302,000 last year (including matching company donations) and donated funds to over 40 organizations, including the West Island Community Share, the United Way, Hôpital du Suroît and the Lakeshore General Hospital, to name a few.

**MERIDIAN TECHNOLOGIES INC.**
**155 High Street East**
**Strathroy, ON N7G 1H4**

**Tel. 519-245-4040**
**Fax 519-245-4620**
**inquiries@meridian-mag.com**
**http://www.meridian-mag.com**

**INDUSTRY: AUTO PART MANUFACTURERS**

*Highlights:*

- Develop yourself at an employer that takes training so seriously that its state-of-the-art training centre is also used by customers.
- Build your career at an employer that's leading the way toward lighter, more fuel-efficient cars — creating more jobs and opportunities for employees in the process.
- Work abroad thanks to this employer's international operations, which include a plant in Italy that frequently hosts Canadian employees for two-week training sessions.

*Employer Background*

Meridian Technologies Inc. manufactures lightweight magnesium components for the automotive industry. Founded in 1981, the company's unique technology allows auto manufacturers to replace heavy steel components with lightweight magnesium ones.

Meridian's modern manufacturing facility in Strathroy, Ontario, produces full- and half-instrument panels, steering components, housings, brackets and transfer cases. Recently, the company completed construction of a second state-of-the-art plant in Strathroy. This plant joins Meridian's new Global Technology Centre, which provides magnesium-related research and development services to automotive manufacturers around the world.

Meridian's products are interesting because they help automobile manufactures to build lighter, more fuel-efficient vehicles. Recently, General Motors used Meridian's technology to replace a steel instrument support panel weighing 10 kilograms with a magnesium one weighing half this amount. Ford also recently announced that it plans to increase the magnesium content in its cars from 2 kilograms to 100 kilograms.

Along with its Strathroy facilities, Meridian operates plants in Michigan and Italy. The company is jointly owned by Italy-based Teksid S.p.A. and Norway-based Norsk Hydro Produksjon.

**Workforce at a Glance:** Number of full-time employees: **540**. At this location: **449**. Worldwide: **1,500**. New jobs created in Canada in past year: **61**. Percentage of employees who are women: **15**. Of managers: **20**. Percentage of employees who are visible minorities: **6**. Resumes received by their human resources staff in past year: **4,000**. Weeks of vacation their HR manager took last year: **3**. Average employee age: **34**.

## *Physical Workplace* *Rating: B+*

Meridian's physical workplace is rated as **average**. Meridian's Strathroy manufacturing facilities have a fast-paced atmosphere because of frequent production changes and just-in-time delivery commitments. Employees at the nearby Global Technology Centre use the latest computer technology to design new lightweight metal components and create prototypes for auto manufacturers. Manufacturing employees at both Strathroy plants use leading-edge die-casting technology to transform molten magnesium into lightweight auto components.

**Physical Workplace at a Glance:** Their **employee lounge and rest areas** feature: television. Nearby **amenities** include: variety of restaurants; major shopping mall; fitness facility; park/wilderness area (Strathroy Park). For **commuters**, Meridian offers: free onsite car parking; nearby public transit. Other **work area amenities** include: ergonomic workstation design; open-concept workstations; open manufacturing work areas.

## *Work Atmosphere & Social* *Rating: A*

Meridian's work atmosphere is rated as **above-average**. Employees at Meridian enjoy casual dress daily and can listen to radio or music while they are working. There is also a company-subsidized social committee, called the '*MPD Social Club*', which has operated since 1981.

Each year, the committee organizes regular draws for sporting event tickets and fun activities, such as the annual employee golf tournament. The company also hosts an employee Christmas party (with a separate party for employees' children) and recognizes employee achievements and continued service milestones with special events, such as pizza lunches, restaurant dinners and a unique summer pig-roast.

Meridian also subsidizes employee hockey and baseball teams and sponsors the sports teams of employees' children.

## *Health, Financial & Family Benefits* *Rating: A*

Meridian's health benefits plan is managed by Maritime Life and is rated as **above-average**.

**Health Benefits at a Glance:** Meridian's health plan includes the following coverage: dental (100% of eligible costs, with no annual maximum); orthodontics (50% of eligible costs with a lifetime maximum of $2,000); eyecare (to $400 every year); extended health benefits; prescription drug; massage therapy; physiotherapy; alternative therapies; personal and family counselling; employee assistance plan (EAP) for substance abuse/mental health.

The company's salary and financial benefits are rated as **above-average**. To keep pay-levels competitive, Meridian participates in outside salary surveys every 12 months. Individual salaries are reviewed every 12 months. The company offers a group RSP that allows employees to contribute up to 4% of their salary, with matching employer contributions.

**Financial Benefits at a Glance:** Meridian provides a variety of financial benefits, including: life and disability insurance; discounted home computers; profit-sharing plan; year-end bonuses (to $1,500 for non-executives).

Meridian's family-friendly benefits are rated as **average**. Family-friendly benefits include: flexible start and finish hours.

### *Vacation & Time Off* — *Rating: B+*

Meridian's vacation and time off are rated as **average**. New employees receive 2 weeks of vacation allowance after their first year, which increases to 3 weeks after 5 years of service. The maximum vacation allowance is 5 weeks for long-serving employees. Each year, Meridian also provides employees with a paid holiday shutdown in the summer and from Christmas to New Year's. Employees at the company can also apply for unpaid leaves of absence.

### *Employee Communications* — *Rating: A*

Meridian's internal communications program is rated as **above-average**. To keep employees informed about new developments, Meridian publishes an in-house newsletter (called *The Mag Scene*). The company also has an intranet site, which keeps employees informed about news and human resource policies that affect their work. An employee satisfaction survey is conducted every 36 months. An outside consultant compiles the survey results for Meridian's management team. Employees also serve on company committees that address employee grievances, health and safety issues and other policy matters.

### *Performance Management* — *Rating: B+*

Meridian's performance management program is rated as **average**. The company operates a formal performance management program. Once a year, employees and managers meet for review sessions. (Managers receive training in how to conduct effective reviews.) At the reviews, employees and managers work together to establish future training needs. Meridian recognizes exceptional performance with company insignia merchandise and share options.

### *Training & Skills Development* — *Rating: A+*

Meridian's training and skills development program is rated as **exceptional**. The company provides tuition subsidies for courses related to an employee's current position (100% of tuition). Commendably, Meridian also offers subsidies for courses not related to an employee's current job (100% of tuition). Meridian offers bonuses to employees who successfully complete certain professional accreditation programs and courses. The company assists employees' career development with: reimbursement for professional association dues; mentoring; flexible apprenticeship training; in-house training.

Employees at the Strathroy plant also play a significant role in identifying and developing training programs for Meridian's international locations. (The company's state-of-the-art training centre is even used to train automotive employees who work for Meridian's customers.) Meridian employees also have the opportunity to work at the company's other locations, including two-week training sessions at the company's plant in Italy.

Meridian's progressive attitude towards training can also be seen in its partnership with the Strathroy campus of Fanshawe College. The College designs tailor-made technical courses for the company's employees.

*Community Involvement* *Rating: A*

Meridian's community involvement program is rated as **above-average**. A very good corporate citizen, Meridian actively supports a variety of local charitable initiatives. Employees take part in the selection of charitable groups assisted by the company. Last year, the company contributed to approximately 40 charitable groups.

The company directs donations towards charities focused on children, healthy workplaces, social issues and cultural events. The company recently donated funds for renovations at a local hospital and is a major contibutor to the local United Way campaign.

MISSISSAUGA

**MISSISSAUGA, CITY OF**
**300 City Centre Drive**
**5th Floor**
**Mississauga, ON L5B 3C1**

**Tel. 905-896-5000**
**Fax 905-615-4185**
**hr.info@mississauga.ca**
**http://www.mississauga.ca**

**INDUSTRY: GOVERNMENT, GENERAL**

*Highlights:*

- Work in an architectural landmark that offers everything from ice skating in the winter to an outdoor Japanese garden in the summer.
- Spend more time with your family thanks to a 35-hour work week, onsite daycare and a variety of flexible work options.

## *Employer Background*

The City of Mississauga provides municipal government services to residents and businesses in Canada's sixth-largest city.

Incorporated in 1974, the City of Mississauga manages one of Canada's fastest-growing urban areas. Last year, the municipality issued over $1.5 billion in building permits, placing it among the largest in Canada. This was the sixth consecutive year that city building permits topped the billion-dollar level.

Located in Canada's most populous region, Mississauga's near-continuous growth is the result of low municipal taxes, ample land for development, competitive commercial leasing rates, excellent highway connections, great amenities and a proactive local government.

With a growing population of over 600,000 residents, Mississsauga has also seen steady employment growth in its municipal government. Over 6,000 full- and part-time employees work in various departments overseeing community services, administration, planning, transportation and public works.

The City also operates several community organizations and major facilities such as the Mississauga Heritage Foundation, the Art Gallery of Mississauga, the Living Arts Centre and the Hershey Centre sports complex.

**Workforce at a Glance:** Number of full-time employees: **3,581**. New jobs created in Canada in past year: **250**. Percentage of employees who are women: **47**. Of managers: **34**. Resumes received by their human resources staff in past year: **13,800**. Weeks of vacation their HR manager took last year: **5**. Average employee age: **37**. Years longest-serving employee has worked there: **43**.

## *Physical Workplace* — *Rating: A+*

The City of Mississauga's physical workplace is rated as **exceptional**. The City's main offices are located at the landmark Mississauga Civic Centre. Completed in 1987, the Centre is a multi-purpose facility for government and community use. The building has received Canada's highest award for architecture — the Governor General's Award from the Royal Architectural Institute of Canada. Along with its landmark status, the Centre has also become a popular location for movie and television filming.

**Physical Workplace at a Glance:** Their **onsite fitness facility** features: subsidized memberships; treadmills; stationary bikes; stairmasters; rowing machines; weights; a squash league; instructor-led classes; sauna; shower facilities. For **food and refreshment**, The City of Mississauga offers: outdoor eating area; barbeque; free coffee and tea. The City has an onsite cafeteria that features: healthy menu items. Nearby **amenities** include: variety of restaurants; major shopping mall; library; theatre; park/wilderness area (Kariya Park); recreation centre (YMCA). For **commuters**, The City of Mississauga offers: nearby public transit; free onsite car parking; convenient highway access; secure bicycle parking. Other **work area amenities** include: open-concept workstations; access to natural light for all employees; ergonomic workstation design; wireless connectivity throughout office; plant life that is tended professionally; onsite gift shop; art gallery; indoor conservatory; outdoor Japanese garden; winter ice rink; and even a wedding chapel.

## *Work Atmosphere & Social* — *Rating: B+*

The City of Mississauga's work atmosphere is rated as **average**. Employees at The City of Mississauga enjoy business casual dress daily and can listen to radio or music while they are working.

Throughout the year, individual departments host special recognition dinners and barbeques, as well as holiday celebrations. Every year, the City hosts a unique family transit day as well as a special awards dinner for long-serving employees.

## *Health, Financial & Family Benefits* — *Rating: B+*

The City of Mississauga's health benefits plan is managed by Sun Life and is rated as **average**. New employees must wait 60 days before they can enroll in the plan.

**Health Benefits at a Glance:** The City of Mississauga's health plan includes the following coverage: dental (to $2,000 each year); orthodontics (50% of eligible costs with a lifetime maximum of $4,000); eyecare (to $300 every 2 years); prescription drug; extended health benefits; massage therapy; physiotherapy; alternative therapies; personal and family counselling; employee assistance plan (EAP) for substance abuse/mental health; annual health fair; monthly wellness campaign.

The City's salary and financial benefits are rated as **average**. To keep pay-levels competitive, The City of Mississauga participates in outside salary surveys every 12 months. Individual salaries are reviewed every 12 months. The City operates a traditional pension plan. (The City matches employee contributions up to 2.1% of their yearly pensionable earnings.) **Financial Benefits at a Glance:** The City of Mississauga provides a variety of financial benefits, including: life and disability insurance.

The City of Mississauga's family-friendly benefits are rated as **above-average**. Employees with pre-school children have access to a daycare facility located onsite. The daycare facility has 46 spaces and employs 6 childcare workers. (The daycare facility is operated by Sheridan College's early childhood education program.) Other family-friendly benefits include: flexible start and finish hours; shortened work week (fewer hours); compressed work week (same hours, fewer days); telecommuting and working from home; job sharing.

***Vacation & Time Off*** — ***Rating: B+***

The City of Mississauga's vacation and time off are rated as **average**. New employees receive 2 weeks of vacation allowance after their first year, which increases to 3 weeks after 3 years of service. The maximum vacation allowance is 6 weeks for long-serving employees. Employees at the City can also apply for unpaid leaves of absence.

***Employee Communications*** — ***Rating: A***

The City of Mississauga's internal communications program is rated as **above-average**. To keep employees informed about new developments, The City of Mississauga publishes an in-house newsletter (called *Network*). The City also has an intranet site, which keeps employees informed about news and human resource policies that affect their work. An in-house employee satisfaction survey is conducted by having employees complete questionnaires every 24 months.

***Performance Management*** — ***Rating: A***

The City of Mississauga's performance management program is rated as **above-average**. The City operates a formal performance management program. Once a year, employees and managers meet for review sessions. (Managers receive training in how to conduct effective reviews.) At the reviews, employees and managers develop a performance plan for the upcoming year, which forms the basis for future training, bonuses and salary increases.

***Training & Skills Development*** — ***Rating: B+***

The City of Mississauga's training and skills development program is rated as **average**. The City provides tuition subsidies for courses related to an employee's current position (100% of tuition). The City assists employees' career development with: reimbursement for professional association dues; career planning; in-house training; safety training.

***Community Involvement*** — ***Rating: A***

The City of Mississauga's community involvement program is rated as **above-average**. A very good member of the community, The City of Mississauga actively supports a variety of local charitable initiatives. Employees at The City of Mississauga receive paid time off to volunteer at local charities. Last year, the City also contributed to approximately 18 charitable groups.

In addition to supporting the local United Way campaign, the City has developed a variety of programs with volunteer organizations in Mississauga. A good example is the Jerry Love Children's Fund, which provides children with recreational activities throughout the city.

**MITRA INC.**
**455 Phillip Street**
**Waterloo, ON N2L 3X2**

**Tel. 519-746-2900**
**Fax 519-746-3745**
**careers@mitra.com**
**http://www.mitra.com**

**INDUSTRY: MEDICAL EQUIPMENT & SUPPLIES MANUFACTURERS**

*Highlights:*

- Work in a quiet environment at an employer that's installed a unique electronic noise suppression system to reduce distractions.
- Build your career at a Canadian innovator that offers international career growth through its Belgian parent and an outstanding training program that rewards professional development.
- Get three weeks of paid vacation allowance in your first year, which rises to four weeks after only four years on the job.

*Employer Background*

Mitra Inc. develops advanced imaging and information management technology for healthcare providers. Founded in 1991, the company's software and systems let hospitals capture and display medical images digitally, allowing specialists to access medical images and data from different parts of a hospital or from locations around the world.

Mitra's revolutionary imaging technology is used by healthcare equipment manufacturers worldwide and is changing the way medicine is practiced. The company's software has rapidly become the industry standard for medical imaging and information management, with thousands of hospitals in over 35 countries relying on Mitra's technology.

Mitra is now a subsidiary of Belgium-based Agfa-Gaevert N.V. Established in 1867, publicly-traded Agfa has worked closely with Mitra since its founding. The parent company is a leading manufacturer of photographic and electronic imaging products, with over 30,000 employees and operations in 20 countries.

**Workforce at a Glance:** Number of full-time employees: **323**. Worldwide: **395**. New jobs created in Canada in past year: **20**. Percentage of employees who are women: **35**. Of managers: **27**. Percentage of employees who are visible minorities: **16**. Of managers: **12**. Resumes received by their human resources staff in past year: **8,218**. Weeks of vacation their HR manager took last year: **3**. Average employee age: **32**. Years longest-serving employee has worked there: **10**. Person you should get to know first: **Julie in Human Resources knows all there is to know about working and socializing at the company.**

### *Physical Workplace* — *Rating: A*

Mitra's physical workplace is rated as **above-average**. Situated in the heart of Canada's technology triangle, Mitra's modern head office features lots of natural light, abundant plant life, two large aquariums and a unique electronic noise suppression system to reduce distractions.

**Physical Workplace at a Glance:** Their **onsite fitness facility** features: free memberships; treadmills; stationary bikes; stairmasters; rowing machines; weights; instructor-led classes (also known as "*Darryl's House of Pain*"); shower facilities. Their **employee lounge and rest areas** feature: comfortable couches; music; table tennis; board games; meditation or religious observance room. For **food and refreshment**, Mitra offers: free snacks; free coffee and tea; free herbal teas and hot cider; outdoor eating area; barbeque; lunch room; kitchen area; a well-travelled path to the Tim Hortons across the street. Nearby **amenities** include: variety of restaurants; local shops and services; University of Waterloo; Wilfrid Laurier University; park/wilderness area (Laurel Creek Conservation Area); recreation centre (Waterloo Recreation Centre and RIM Park). For **commuters**, Mitra offers: free onsite car parking; nearby public transit; secure bicycle parking. Other **work area amenities** include: open-concept workstations; ergonomic workstation design; wireless connectivity throughout office; technology library; access to natural light for all employees; plant life that is tended professionally.

### *Work Atmosphere & Social* — *Rating: A*

Mitra's work atmosphere is rated as **above-average**. Employees at Mitra enjoy business casual dress daily and can listen to radio or music while they are working. There is also a company-subsidized social committee.

Employees organize a variety of social events every year, including a family day at an amusement park (Canada's Wonderland), as well as sporting activities such as golfing, volleyball, floor hockey, tobogganing, skiing, snowboarding, dragonboat racing and indoor soccer. The company also provides financial support for employee soccer, volleyball and two baseball teams (the "*Sharks*" and "*Stingrays*") as well as an annual golf tournament.

Mitra also hosts a summer family picnic, an employee Christmas party (with gifts and free taxi rides) and a separate party for employees' children.

### *Health, Financial & Family Benefits* — *Rating: A*

Mitra's health benefits plan is managed by Clarica Life and is rated as **above-average**. New employees must wait 90 days before they can enroll in the plan.

**Health Benefits at a Glance:** Mitra's health plan includes the following coverage: dental (80% of eligible costs, to $1,500 each year); orthodontics (50% of eligible costs with a lifetime maximum of $1,500); eyecare (to $150 every 2 years); extended health benefits; prescription drug; nutrition planning; physiotherapy; massage therapy; alternative therapies; personal and family counselling; employee assistance plan (EAP) for substance abuse/mental health; wellness program (including blood pressure and cholesterol clinics).

The company's salary and financial benefits are rated as **above-average**. To keep pay-levels competitive, Mitra participates in outside salary surveys every 6 months. Individual salaries are reviewed every 6 months. The company offers a group RSP that allows employees to contribute up to 8% of their salary, with matching employer contributions.

> **Financial Benefits at a Glance:** Mitra provides a variety of financial benefits, including: life and disability insurance; subsidized auto insurance; subsidized home insurance; low-interest home loans; discounted home computers; profit-sharing plan; referral bonuses for some employees (to $1,000).

Mitra's family-friendly benefits are rated as **average**. Employees with pre-school children have access to a daycare facility located nearby. Other family-friendly benefits include: flexible start and finish hours; telecommuting and working from home.

### *Vacation & Time Off* — *Rating: A*

Mitra's vacation and time off are rated as **above-average**. New employees receive 3 weeks of vacation allowance after their first year, which increases to 4 weeks after 4 years of service. The maximum vacation allowance is 4 weeks for long-serving employees. Employees at Mitra also receive 5 paid personal days off each year, in addition to their regular vacation allowance. Employees at the company can also apply for unpaid leaves of absence. (Recently, one employee took several one week leaves to complete an MBA degree.)

### *Employee Communications* — *Rating: A*

Mitra's internal communications program is rated as **above-average**. The company has a useful intranet site (called *Livelink*), which keeps employees informed about news and human resource policies that affect their work. To solicit feedback from employees, the company operates an email suggestion box. The company's intranet site has a unique feature that also allows employees to "introduce" themselves to co-workers through a personal homepage and even buy or sell items through the employee classifieds. Mitra's parent company also publishes a corporate newsletter (called *Know*) for all Agfa employees across Canada.

### *Performance Management* — *Rating: A*

Mitra's performance management program is rated as **above-average**. The company operates a thorough performance management program. Once a year, employees and managers meet for review sessions. (Managers receive training in how to conduct effective reviews.) As part of the review process, employees and managers may also meet for mid-year reviews. In addition, employees have the opportunity to provide confidential feedback on their manager's performance through the company's intranet.

### *Training & Skills Development* — *Rating: A+*

Mitra's training and skills development program is rated as **exceptional**. The company provides tuition subsidies for courses related to an employee's current position (100% of tuition). Commendably, Mitra also offers subsidies for courses not related to an employee's current job (100% of tuition). Mitra offers bonuses to employees who successfully complete certain professional accreditation programs and courses. The company assists employees' career development with: reimbursement for professional association dues; mentoring; in-house training; online training; in-house resource library; regular guest speakers.

***Community Involvement*** ***Rating: A***

Mitra's community involvement program is rated as **above-average**. A very good corporate citizen, Mitra actively supports a variety of local and national charitable initiatives. Employees take part in the selection of charitable groups assisted by the company. Last year, the company contributed to approximately 27 charitable groups.

Last year, the company contributed to the United Way, Canadian Blood Services, the Heart and Stroke Foundation, Kitchener-Waterloo Volunteer Day, and Tim Hortons Camp Day. In addition, Mitra makes a significant donation in support of local healthcare and education initiatives every year.

**MONTGOMERY SISAM ASSOCIATES INC.**
**35 Britain Street**
**Toronto, ON M5A 1R7**

MontgomerySisam

**Tel. 416-364-8079**
**Fax 416-364-7723**
**eapplebaum@montgomerysisam.com**
**http://www.montgomerysisam.com**

**INDUSTRY: ENGINEERING, ARCHITECTURAL & SURVEYING FIRMS**

*Highlights:*

- Pack your bags for a company-wide pilgrimage to a different architectural site across North America every year.
- Develop your design talents quickly at a firm where junior designers meet with the senior architects who serve as their mentors every four months.
- Work fewer hours when business is slow — so your co-workers can keep their jobs — at a firm that takes care of all its employees in a cyclical industry.

## *Employer Background*

Montgomery Sisam Associates Inc. is a mid-sized architectural firm. The growing architectural firm works on a wide range of projects, from renovations to large building projects. The firm focuses on healthcare, education and urban infrastructure projects.

Many of the firm's completed projects can be found in Toronto, including the showpiece Humber River Pedestrian Bridge on Toronto's lakeshore and the new Bloorview MacMillan Children's Centre. The firm is currently working on several interesting local projects, including: the redevelopment of the former Queen Street Mental Health Centre site; a new convent for the Sisters of St. John Divine; and a new private school, Greenwood College School.

In addition to industry recognition for its innovative designs, Montgomery Sisam has experienced steady growth since its inception in 1987.

> **Workforce at a Glance:** Number of full-time employees: **50**. New jobs created in Canada in past year: **5**. Percentage of employees who are women: **32**. Of managers: **21**. Percentage of employees who are visible minorities: **22**. Of managers: **7**. Resumes received by their human resources staff in past year: **500**. Weeks of vacation their HR manager took last year: **3**. Average employee age: **35**. Years longest-serving employee has worked there: **10**. Car the president drives: **Subaru Forester**. Where it's parked in the lot: **with everyone else**.

## *Physical Workplace* — *Rating: A*

Montgomery Sisam's physical workplace is rated as **above-average**. The firm is located in a renovated historic building in Toronto's expanding east downtown area. In addition to indoor bike storage, there are shower facilities available for those who cycle to work, which includes about one-quarter of the firm's employees.

The interior workspace was custom-designed by Montgomery Sisam architects. The thoughtful design promotes flexibility and features lots of natural light for each workstation. Junior employees, associates and senior staff are often seated side-by-side organized by project.

**Physical Workplace at a Glance:** Their **employee lounge and rest areas** feature: music; architectural reading library. For **food and refreshment**, Montgomery Sisam offers: free snacks (including Timbits, bagels and cream cheese); free coffee and tea; free soft drinks; kitchen areas. Nearby **amenities** include: variety of restaurants; local shops and services; fitness facility; park/wilderness area (St. James Park). For **commuters**, Montgomery Sisam offers: nearby public transit; secure bicycle parking. Other **work area amenities** include: open-concept workstations; windows that open; plant life that is tended professionally.

## *Work Atmosphere & Social* — *Rating: A*

Montgomery Sisam's work atmosphere is rated as **above-average**. Employees at Montgomery Sisam enjoy business casual dress daily and can listen to radio or music while they are working. There is also a firm-subsidized social committee, called the '*Office Culture*'.

Every Friday afternoon, employees gather over beer and snacks for informal discussions about projects and upcoming events. During the year, employees make regular visits to local construction sites and celebrate project accomplishments with evening dinners and pub nights. The firm also hosts an offsite Christmas party for its employees.

In a unique initiative, Montgomery Sisam takes its employees to a significant North American architectural site every year. Last year, employees visited the restored areas of Old Montréal to delight in its storied architecture.

## *Health, Financial & Family Benefits* — *Rating: B+*

Montgomery Sisam's health benefits plan is rated as **above-average**. Montgomery Sisam pays 100% of the premiums associated with the plan. New employees must wait 90 days before they can enroll in the plan.

**Health Benefits at a Glance:** Montgomery Sisam's health plan includes the following coverage: dental; eyecare (to $250 every 2 years); prescription drug; extended health benefits; nutrition planning; massage therapy; physiotherapy; personal and family counselling.

The firm's salary and financial benefits are rated as **average**. To keep paylevels competitive, Montgomery Sisam participates in outside salary surveys every 12 months. Individual salaries are reviewed every 12 months. Given the project-based nature of architectural work, the firm has an enlightened policy of rotating employees from project to project to ensure continual employment. In the case of poor economic times, the firm also has a unique reduced attendance policy to help share the workload and provide all employees with steady employment.

**Financial Benefits at a Glance:** Montgomery Sisam provides a variety of financial benefits, including: life and disability insurance; year-end bonuses (from $10,000 to $40,000 for non-executives).

Montgomery Sisam's family-friendly benefits are rated as **average**. Employees can begin their maternity leave up to 17 weeks before their baby is due. (Of course, employees can work up to their due date if they wish.) Other family-friendly benefits include: compressed work week (same hours, fewer days); reduced summer hours.

### *Vacation & Time Off* — *Rating: B+*

Montgomery Sisam's vacation and time off are rated as **average**. New employees receive 2 weeks of vacation allowance after their first year, which increases to 3 weeks after 4 years of service. Employees at the firm can also apply for unpaid leaves of absence.

### *Employee Communications* — *Rating: B+*

Montgomery Sisam's internal communications program is rated as **average**. To keep employees informed about new developments, Montgomery Sisam publishes an in-house newsletter. An in-house employee satisfaction survey is conducted every 24 months.

The firm also has an intranet site, which provides employees with a variety of technical and project information, as well as links to external resources.

### *Performance Management* — *Rating: A*

Montgomery Sisam's performance management program is rated as **above-average**. The firm operates a formal performance management program. Once a year, employees and managers meet for review sessions. (Managers receive training in how to conduct effective reviews.)

Prior to the review meetings, employees complete self-evaluations. Reviews address past performance, establish future career objectives and form the basis for salary increases. To ensure the process is constructive, employees are also invited to provide confidential feedback on their manager's performance.

Exceptional work is recognized through annual bonuses and individual performance bonuses. In addition, employee teams are treated to restaurant dinners after significant accomplishments and project completions. The firm also awards Blue Jays baseball tickets in recognition of excellent work.

### *Training & Skills Development* — *Rating: A+*

Montgomery Sisam's training and skills development program is rated as **exceptional**. The firm provides tuition subsidies for courses related to an employee's current position (100% of tuition). The firm assists employees' career development with: reimbursement for professional association dues; in-house training.

Montgomery Sisam is also well known for mentoring its junior staff. Through this program, employees and mentors meet every four months over lunch for open discussions about their jobs and workplace concerns. The firm's frequent lunch-hour training sessions cover a range of topics, from innovations in sustainable design to flooring materials for healthcare facilities.

*Community Involvement* *Rating: A*

Montgomery Sisam's community involvement program is rated as **above-average**. A very good corporate citizen, Montgomery Sisam actively supports a variety of local charitable initiatives. The firm shows how a small employer can make a difference in its community. Last year, the firm also contributed to approximately 29 charitable groups, including: the Salvation Army, Trinity Village Care Centre, Providence Centre, and the Japanese Canadian Community Centre.

In a unique initiative, Montgomery Sisam provides employees with time off to volunteer at a local home for senior citizens. Employee use this time to visit residents and help with dinner.

In addition, Montgomery Sisam sponsors guest speakers at the Ontario Hospital Association's annual conference, and co-sponsors an annual lecture series at the University of Toronto's Faculty of Architecture, Landscape and Design.

Our Service is Non Stop

**MSM GROUP OF TRANSPORTATION COMPANIES**
**124 Commercial Road**
**Bolton, ON L7E 1K4**

**Tel. 905-951-6800**
**Fax 905-951-1534**
**http://www.shipmsm.com**

**INDUSTRY: TRUCKING & GROUND COURIER SERVICES**

*Highlights:*

- Work for a thoughtful employer in the trucking industry that operates a special program where its drivers mail postcards from across North America to a local school so students can learn more about geography.
- Excel in your job at this employer and get rewarded with salary increases, additional holidays, use of a Muskoka cottage and free trips to California.
- Celebrate your 10th anniversary at this employer and get $10,000 paid into your retirement savings plan.

## *Employer Background*

MSM Group of Transportation Companies provides freight transportation and related support services. The company's satellite-tracked fleet and comprehensive distribution system moves goods quickly between Canada and the United States.

Founded in 1989, MSM's main business ("MSM Transportation") provides less-than-truckload (LTL) shipping between Canada and the United States. The Group's other businesses include: MSM Canadian Transport (direct shipping between California and Canada); MSM Dedicated (contract shipping); Tandem Trailer and Storage (truck trailer rentals); MSM & Associates (transportation consulting and training services); and MSM Cartage and Distribution (local expedited services).

When establishing its new business divisions, MSM follows an enlightened strategy of recruiting employees from within the company to head these new ventures. By recognizing the capabilities of its employees (and offering equity positions), MSM has created a winning strategy that fuels its growth and encourages creativity and hard work among its employees.

In addition to its head office and main warehouse in Bolton (northwest of Toronto), the company maintains a shipping facility in Los Angeles, California.

**Workforce at a Glance:** Number of full-time employees: **80**. Worldwide: **108**. New jobs created in Canada in past year: **6**. Percentage of employees who are women: **37**. Of managers: **14**. Percentage of employees who are visible minorities: **6**. Of managers: **14**. Resumes received by their human resources staff in past year: **140**. Weeks of vacation their HR manager took last year: **4**. Average employee age: **37**. Years longest-serving employee has worked there: **11**. Car the president drives: **2001 Lincoln Navigator**. Where it's parked in the lot: **reserved spot**.

## *Physical Workplace* — *Rating: A*

MSM's physical workplace is rated as **above-average**. Located in the town of Bolton, MSM employees work in one of the Greater Toronto Area's most beautiful areas. The growing community is situated among the rolling Caledon hills near several established conservation areas that offer great recreational opportunities. MSM is one of the town's largest employers, operating from a 27,000 square foot head office and shipping facility.

**Physical Workplace at a Glance:** Their **employee lounge and rest areas** feature: comfortable couches; television. Nearby **amenities** include: variety of restaurants; fitness facility; park/wilderness area (Bruce Trail); recreation centre (Caledon Centre for Recreation & Wellness). For **commuters**, MSM offers: free onsite car parking; convenient highway access. Other **work area amenities** include: open-concept workstations; individual temperature control for workstations; shower facilities.

## *Work Atmosphere & Social* — *Rating: A*

MSM's work atmosphere is rated as **above-average**. Employees at MSM enjoy casual dress daily and can listen to radio or music while they are working. Employees enjoy a variety of social events every year, including a summer picnic, a popular charitable golf tournament, Halloween and Easter celebrations, an employee Christmas party, go-kart racing, evenings at the horse races and box seats at the Air Canada Centre. MSM also sponsors an employee baseball team (called the *MSM Road Sharks*) that competes in a local league.

## *Health, Financial & Family Benefits* — *Rating: A*

MSM's health benefits plan is rated as **above-average**. MSM pays 100% of the premiums associated with the plan.

**Health Benefits at a Glance:** MSM's health plan includes the following coverage: dental; orthodontics; eyecare (to $200 every 2 years); extended health benefits; prescription drug; nutrition planning; massage therapy; physiotherapy; alternative therapies; personal and family counselling; employee assistance plan (EAP) for substance abuse/mental health.

The company's salary and financial benefits are rated as **above-average**. To keep pay-levels competitive, MSM participates in outside salary surveys every 24 months. Individual salaries are reviewed every 12 months. The company offers a group RSP. (Employees celebrating their 10th anniversary with the company receive a lump-sum contribution of $10,000 to their RSP.)

**Financial Benefits at a Glance:** MSM provides a variety of financial benefits, including: life and disability insurance; discounted home Internet access; personal loans (no interest); perfomance bonues; profit-sharing plan; referral bonuses for some employees (to $500); year-end bonuses.

MSM's family-friendly benefits are rated as **average**. Family-friendly benefits include: reduced summer hours; telecommuting and working from home; compressed work week (same hours, fewer days); shortened work week (fewer hours); flexible start and finish hours.

### *Vacation & Time Off* — *Rating: B+*

MSM's vacation and time off are rated as **average**. New employees receive 2 weeks of vacation allowance after their first year, which increases to 3 weeks after 5 years of service. The maximum vacation allowance is 6 weeks for long-serving employees. Employees at the company can also apply for unpaid leaves of absence.

### *Employee Communications* — *Rating: A*

MSM's internal communications program is rated as **above-average**. To keep employees informed about new developments, MSM publishes an in-house newsletter (called *Sharktales*), which is published monthly. To solicit feedback from employees, the company operates an email suggestion box. An in-house employee satisfaction survey is conducted periodically.

Twice a year, the company also hosts unique overnight "boot-camp" retreats at the owners' cottages in Ontario's Muskoka region. The camps are attended by all employees and involve a day of team-building exercises — followed by a home-cooked dinner that everyone helps prepare.

### *Performance Management* — *Rating: A*

MSM's performance management program is rated as **above-average**. The company operates a well-designed performance management program. Every month, employees and managers meet for review sessions. (Managers receive training in how to conduct effective reviews.) Employees also have the opportunity to provide confidential feedback on their manager's performance through the company's in-house survey.

MSM recognizes exceptional performance with salary increases, performance bonuses, tickets to sports events (the company also owns a local Junior A hockey team), additional holidays, free trips to California and use of the owners' cottages.

### *Training & Skills Development* — *Rating: A+*

MSM's training and skills development program is rated as **exceptional**. The company provides tuition subsidies for courses related to an employee's current position (100% of tuition). Commendably, MSM also offers subsidies for courses not related to an employee's current job (100% of tuition). The company assists employees' career development with: reimbursement for professional association dues; quarterly lunch hour training sessions; driver safety and performance program. In addition, the company provides full coverage for employees taking an Executive MBA (to $60,000).

### *Community Involvement* — *Rating: A+*

MSM's community involvement program is rated as **exceptional**. An outstanding corporate citizen, MSM actively supports a variety of local charitable initiatives. Employees take part in the selection of charitable groups assisted by the company. Employees at MSM receive paid time off to volunteer at local charities.

Every August, MSM hosts a popular golf tournament and sports memorabilia auction to raise money for local charities, including the Princess Margaret Hospital Cancer Research Foundation and the Stephanie Gaetz Keepsafe Foundation (a children's safety program). The one-day event is organized by MSM employees and includes participants from other trucking firms. The event is one of the largest charitable initiatives in the trucking industry and has raised over $500,000 in the past five years — including over $128,000 last year alone.

The company also supports several local initiatives throughout the year, including the Caledon Santa Claus Parade (the company supplies trucks), Rose of Sharon Christmas for Young Mothers (supports single mothers at Christmas) and the Caledon Community Centre. MSM also supports a local skateboard and rollerblade park, as well as sponsoring children's soccer, hockey and softball teams.

Most notably, the company operates an interesting educational program with local school children called "*Pen Pals and Trucker Buddies*". Drivers travelling across North America send post cards from cities along the way, allowing students to trace their journey on a map. At the end of the year, drivers visit the school to answer questions about the places they've been (and give the kids an opportunity to check-out the truck). This wonderful program provides an excellent example of how employers can "give back" to the community in an interesting way that involves employees and builds on their unique skills.

MURRAY

CHEVROLET · Oldsmobile · HUMMER

**MURRAY AUTO GROUP, THE**
**1700 Waverley Street**
**Winnipeg, MB R3T 5V7**

**Tel. 204-261-6200**
**Fax 204-261-1641**
**http://www.murraychevrolet.ca**

**INDUSTRY: AUTOMOBILE DEALERS**

*Highlights:*

- Build your career at the industry consolidator in Canada's auto dealership business — and a growing employer that offers excellent advancement and job opportunities.
- Get a great employee discount on a new General Motors car as well as discounted parts and service down the road.
- Give back to your community at this employer, which offers matching donations and paid time off to employees who volunteer on community projects.

## *Employer Background*

The Murray Auto Group operates automotive dealerships across Western Canada. Established in 1926, the family-owned company has been in the car business for three generations and operates 14 General Motor dealerships. Over the past 15 years the company has expanded steadily from its first location in Winnipeg and now operates dealerships in all four western provinces.

At each of its locations, the Murray Group uses the same formula that has worked for over 70 years – by treating customers and employees with respect and fairness. The company's exceptional growth has led to excellent career opportunities for its employees. With a strong focus on employee training and a policy of promoting from within, many of the company's key managers are long-time employees.

In the rapidly consolidating automotive dealership industry, the Murray Group stands apart as an excellent — and stable place — to build a career. (As experience in the United States shows, it is almost always better to work for an industry consolidator than smaller independent dealerships, which are often purchased.)

**Workforce at a Glance:** Number of full-time employees: **750**. At this location: **155**. New jobs created in Canada in past year: **160**. Percentage of employees who are women: **20**. Of managers: **20**. Percentage of employees who are visible minorities: **2**. Of managers: **2**. Resumes received by their human resources staff in past year: **1,000**. Average employee age: **35**. Years longest-serving employee has worked there: **51**. Car the president drives: **GM vehicle (of course!)**. Where it's parked in the lot: **with everyone else**.

## *Physical Workplace* — *Rating: B+*

Murray Group's physical workplace is rated as **average**. Across the company, employees work in a variety of settings within each dealership, including sales, parts, service and bodyshop repair. In Winnipeg, employees at the company were invited to provide feedback on the design of their new workspace.

**Physical Workplace at a Glance:** Their **employee lounge and rest areas** feature: music; foosball. For **food and refreshment**, Murray Group offers: outdoor eating area; barbeque. The company has an onsite cafeteria that features: subsidized meals (breakfast and lunch); subsidized coffee fund ($4.00 per month). Nearby **amenities** include: variety of restaurants; major shopping mall; fitness facility (with subsidized memberships); golf course; park/wilderness area (St. Vital Park); recreation centre (Max Bell Centre). For **commuters**, Murray Group offers: free onsite car parking; nearby public transit. Other **work area amenities** include: open-concept workstations; ergonomic workstation design; shower facilities.

### *Work Atmosphere & Social* — *Rating: A*

Murray Group's work atmosphere is rated as **above-average**. Employees at Murray Group enjoy casual dress on Fridays and can listen to radio or music while they are working. There is also a company-subsidized social committee.

The committee organizes a variety of social activities every year, including a Christmas party (with a separate event for employees' children), an annual pig-roast, a summer barbeque, pancake breakfasts, golfing, go-kart racing, billiard nights, hockey, baseball and curling.

### *Health, Financial & Family Benefits* — *Rating: B+*

Murray Group's health benefits plan is rated as **average**. **Health Benefits at a Glance:** Murray Group's health plan includes the following coverage: dental; orthodontics; eyecare; prescription drug; extended health benefits; massage therapy; physiotherapy; alternative therapies; personal and family counselling.

The company's salary and financial benefits are rated as **above-average**. To keep pay-levels competitive, Murray Group participates in outside salary surveys every 12 months. Individual salaries are reviewed every 12 months. The company operates a traditional pension plan where Murray Group makes a contribution equal to 3.5% of each employee's salary to their plan each year. Each dealership also offers a group RSP.

**Financial Benefits at a Glance:** Murray Group provides a variety of financial benefits, including: life and disability insurance; discounted car leases; discounted company products (auto purchases, parts and service); discounted home computers; referral bonuses for some employees (to $100).

Murray Group's family-friendly benefits are rated as **average**. Employees with pre-school children have access to a daycare facility located nearby.

### *Vacation & Time Off* — *Rating: B+*

Murray Group's vacation and time off are rated as **average**. New employees receive 2 weeks of vacation allowance after their first year, which increases to 3 weeks after 5 years of service. The maximum vacation allowance is 3 weeks for long-serving employees.

***Employee Communications*** ***Rating: B+***

Murray Group's internal communications program is rated as **average**. To keep employees informed about new developments, Murray Group publishes an in-house newsletter. Every year, employees at each dealership meet privately with senior managers for open discussions about all aspects of their employment.

***Performance Management*** ***Rating: B+***

Murray Group's performance management program is rated as **average**. The company operates a formal performance management program. Once a year, employees and managers meet for review sessions. (Managers receive training in how to conduct effective reviews.) At the reviews, employees identify training needs and establish performance objectives for the upcoming year.

***Training & Skills Development*** ***Rating: A***

Murray Group's training and skills development program is rated as **above-average**. The company provides tuition subsidies for courses related to an employee's current position (100% of tuition). Commendably, Murray Group also offers subsidies for courses not related to an employee's current job (100% of tuition). The company assists employees' career development with: reimbursement for professional association dues; career planning; in-house training; industry training seminars.

***Community Involvement*** ***Rating: A***

Murray Group's community involvement program is rated as **above-average**. A very good corporate citizen, Murray Group actively supports a variety of local and national charitable initiatives. Employees take part in the selection of charitable groups assisted by the company. Employees at Murray Group receive paid time off to volunteer at local charities.

Last year, the company contributed to the United Way, the Canadian Cancer Society, the Alzheimer's Society of Canada, the Heart and Stroke Foundation, the Children's Wish Foundation, the Canadian Diabetes Association, Winnipeg Harvest (a food bank) and the Winnipeg Children's Hospital. The company also operates a program that matches employee donations to charitable groups.

**NATURE'S PATH FOODS INC.**
**9100 Van Horne Way**
**Richmond, BC V6X 1W3**

**Tel. 604-248-8777**
**Fax 604-248-8765**
**resumes@naturespath.com**
**http://www.naturespath.com**

**INDUSTRY: FOOD & BEVERAGE MANUFACTURERS**

*Highlights:*

- Break the junk food habit — and build a great career — at an employer that's become an international success story in the movement towards healthier living.
- Get a free healthy breakfast each morning at this employer, along with a company-sponsored wellness program and onsite fitness facility.
- Save the whales (and other endangered species) while you work — this employer donates a portion of the sales of one of its major product lines to the World Wildlife Fund.

## *Employer Background*

Nature's Path Foods Inc. is a leading manufacturer of organic and natural breakfast foods. Founded in 1985, the company manufactures healthy cereals, breads, waffles and bars, with most being certified organic and made from whole grains.

The company's products are sold under the Nature's Path, EnviroKidz and LifeStream brands. Nature's Path supplies supermarkets and health food stores across North America, the United Kingdom, Australia and New Zealand.

The company's success mirrors the trend towards healthier eating and lifestyles. From one plant in 1989, Nature's Path now has additional manufacturing facilities in nearby Delta, British Columbia and Blaine, Washington. To meet increasing demand for its products, 65,000 square feet of manufacturing space is currently being added to the Blaine facility.

**Workforce at a Glance:** Number of full-time employees: **100**. At this location: **36**. Worldwide: **175**. New jobs created in Canada in past year: **10**. Percentage of employees who are women: **46**. Of managers: **4**. Percentage of employees who are visible minorities: **57**. Of managers: **3**. Resumes received by their human resources staff in past year: **300**. Weeks of vacation their HR manager took last year: **2**. Average employee age: **41**. Years longest-serving employee has worked there: **16**. Car the president drives: **2000 BMW**. Where it's parked in the lot: **reserved spot in front**.

## *Physical Workplace* — *Rating: A*

Nature's Path's physical workplace is rated as **above-average**. Located in the Vancouver suburb of Richmond, the head office is located in the company's original manufacturing building. (The company sought employee feedback when renovating the new workspace.) The location offers great mountain views as well as easy access to highways and Vancouver International Airport.

**Physical Workplace at a Glance:** Their **onsite fitness facility** features: free memberships; treadmills; stationary bikes; stairmasters; weights; fitness program; shower facilities; first-aid room. For **food and refreshment**, Nature's Path offers: free snacks (including breakfast cereal); free coffee and tea. Nearby **amenities** include: variety of restaurants; major shopping mall; park/wilderness area (Richmond Nature Park); recreation centre (Cambie Community Centre). For **commuters**, Nature's Path offers: free onsite car parking; convenient highway access; nearby public transit; secure bicycle parking. Other **work area amenities** include: open-concept workstations; access to natural light for all employees; ergonomic workstation design; wireless connectivity throughout office; windows that open.

### *Work Atmosphere & Social* — *Rating: A*

Nature's Path's work atmosphere is rated as **above-average**. Employees at Nature's Path enjoy business casual dress daily and can listen to radio or music while they are working. There is also a company-subsidized social committee, called the '*TEAM*'.

Every year, employees celebrate Christmas, Dawali (the Hindu Festival of Lights) and Earth Day. The company also hosts a summer fun day and a service awards celebration to recognize exceptional employee performance. Nature's Path also sponsors an employee sports team.

### *Health, Financial & Family Benefits* — *Rating: B+*

Nature's Path's health benefits plan is managed by National Life and is rated as **average**. New employees must wait 90 days before they can enroll in the plan.

**Health Benefits at a Glance:** Nature's Path's health plan includes the following coverage: dental (80% of eligible costs, to $1,500 each year); orthodontics (50% of eligible costs with a lifetime maximum of $1,500); eyecare (to $200 every 2 years); extended health benefits; prescription drug; nutrition planning; massage therapy; physiotherapy; alternative therapies; personal and family counselling; employee assistance plan (EAP) for substance abuse/mental health.

The company's salary and financial benefits are rated as **above-average**. To keep pay-levels competitive, Nature's Path participates in outside salary surveys every 12 months. Individual salaries are reviewed every 12 months. The company offers a group RSP that allows employees to contribute up to 3% of their salary, with matching employer contributions.

**Financial Benefits at a Glance:** Nature's Path provides a variety of financial benefits, including: life and disability insurance; share purchase plan; signing bonuses for some employees; referral bonuses for some employees (to $300); year-end bonuses (from $50 to $12,500 for non-executives).

Nature's Path's family-friendly benefits are rated as **average**. Employees with pre-school children have access to a daycare facility located nearby. Other family-friendly benefits include: free family coverage on health plan; flexible start and finish hours; compressed work week (same hours, fewer days); telecommuting and working from home.

### *Vacation & Time Off* — *Rating: B+*

Nature's Path's vacation and time off are rated as **average**. New employees receive 2 weeks of vacation allowance after their first year, which increases to 3 weeks after 4 years of service. The maximum vacation allowance is 5 weeks for long-serving employees. Employees at the company can also apply for unpaid leaves of absence.

### *Employee Communications* — *Rating: B+*

Nature's Path's internal communications program is rated as **average**. To keep employees informed about new developments, Nature's Path publishes an in-house newsletter. An employee satisfaction survey is conducted every 24 months. An outside consultant compiles the survey results for Nature's Path's management team.

### *Performance Management* — *Rating: A*

Nature's Path's performance management program is rated as **above-average**. The company operates a formal performance management program. Once a year, employees and managers meet for review sessions. (Managers receive training in how to conduct effective reviews.) Nature's Path uses a 360-degree feedback process to gather additional performance-related information from co-workers, supervisors and employees. As part of the review process, training objectives are set and quarterly reviews are held to highlight progress.

### *Training & Skills Development* — *Rating: A*

Nature's Path's training and skills development program is rated as **above-average**. The company provides tuition subsidies for courses related to an employee's current position (100% of tuition). The company assists employees' career development with: reimbursement for professional association dues; in-house training. The company's in-house training program includes communication skills, coaching and leadership training courses.

### *Community Involvement* — *Rating: A*

Nature's Path's community involvement program is rated as **above-average**. A very good corporate citizen, Nature's Path actively supports a variety of local and national charitable initiatives. Last year, the company contributed to approximately 27 charitable groups.

In a unique initiative, Nature's Path also donates 1% of all sales from its EnviroKidz product line to the World Wildlife Fund, which helps preserve endangered species around the world.

NEILL AND GUNTER LIMITED
845 Prospect Street
PO Box 713
Fredericton, NB E3B 5B4

Tel. 506-452-7000
Fax 506-452-0112
ngl@ngl.ca
http://www.neillandgunter.com

INDUSTRY: ENGINEERING, ARCHITECTURAL & SURVEYING FIRMS

*Highlights:*

- Build your career at a growing engineering firm based in the Maritimes that works on significant projects across North America.
- Perform well on the job — and get to use this employer's chalet in Maine at no cost.
- Develop yourself at an employer that offers extensive training opportunities and tuition subsidies for continuing education.

## *Employer Background*

Neill and Gunter Limited is a leading design and consulting engineering firm. Founded in 1964, Neill and Gunter serves a broad range of private- and public-sector clients across North America and around the world.

The firm provides multi-disciplinary consulting engineering, project management and construction services. Neill and Gunter has expertise in a range of areas, including: industrial facilities and processes; renewable energy resources; forest products; petroleum and natural gas; power generation and utilities; computer-based control systems; mining and mineral processing systems; transportation design; urban industrial planning; food and beverage processing; and environmental services.

Last year, the firm received several environmental engineering contracts from the Canadian Clean Power Coalition, an association of major coal-fired electricity producers. Neill and Gunter will take a leading role in developing new technologies to reduce the coal producers' harmful emissions.

Over the past few years, the Frederiction-based firm has experienced significant growth, creating new job opportunities throughout its network of offices. In addition to its head office, the firm has three offices in Canada (Dartmouth, Sydney and Vancouver) and four in the USA (Maine, Maryland, Tennessee and Florida).

**Workforce at a Glance:** Number of full-time employees: **337**. At this location: **180**. Worldwide: **475**. New jobs created in Canada in past year: **58**. Percentage of employees who are women: **20**. Of managers: **5**. Resumes received by their human resources staff in past year: **600**. Weeks of vacation their HR manager took last year: **4**. Average employee age: **47**. Years longest-serving employee has worked there: **35**.

### *Physical Workplace* *Rating: B+*

Neill and Gunter's physical workplace is rated as **average**. The suburban head office is located in a modern four-storey building that's near the Fredericton airport.

**Physical Workplace at a Glance:** For **food and refreshment**, Neill and Gunter offers: free coffee and tea; daily catering service. Nearby **amenities** include: variety of restaurants; major shopping mall; fitness facility; park/wilderness area (O'Dell Park). For **commuters**, Neill and Gunter offers: free onsite car parking; nearby public transit. Other **work area amenities** include: open-concept workstations; ergonomic workstation design; plant life that is tended professionally.

### *Work Atmosphere & Social* *Rating: A*

Neill and Gunter's work atmosphere is rated as **above-average**. Employees at Neill and Gunter enjoy business casual dress daily and can listen to radio or music while they are working. Each year, employees enjoy a summer golf tournament and a Christmas dinner dance. The company also sponsors an employee hockey team (called the *T-Squares*).

### *Health, Financial & Family Benefits* *Rating: B+*

Neill and Gunter's health benefits plan is managed by Blue Cross and is rated as **average**.

**Health Benefits at a Glance:** Neill and Gunter's health plan includes the following coverage: dental (100% of eligible costs, with no annual maximum); orthodontics (50% of eligible costs with a lifetime maximum of $2,000); eyecare (to $200 every 2 years); extended health benefits; prescription drug; massage therapy; physiotherapy; personal and family counselling.

The company's salary and financial benefits are rated as **above-average**. To keep pay-levels competitive, Neill and Gunter participates in outside salary surveys every 12 months. Individual salaries are reviewed every 12 months. The company operates a traditional pension plan. **Financial Benefits at a Glance:** Neill and Gunter provides a variety of financial benefits, including: life and disability insurance; profit-sharing plan.

Neill and Gunter's family-friendly benefits are rated as **average**. Family-friendly benefits include: flexible start and finish hours; shortened work week (fewer hours); job-sharing.

### *Vacation & Time Off* *Rating: B+*

Neill and Gunter's vacation and time off are rated as **average**. New employees receive 2 weeks of vacation allowance after their first year, which increases to 3 weeks after 5 years of service. The maximum vacation allowance is 4 weeks for long-serving employees.

### *Employee Communications* *Rating: B+*

Neill and Gunter's internal communications program is rated as **average**. To keep employees informed about new developments, Neill and Gunter publishes an in-house newsletter (called *Design Notes*). An employee satisfaction survey is conducted every 18 months. An outside consultant compiles the survey results for Neill and Gunter's management team. In addition, individual departments periodically survey their employees to obtain feedback on workplace-related issues.

### *Performance Management* — *Rating: A*

Neill and Gunter's performance management program is rated as **above-average**. The company operates a formal performance management program. Once a year, employees and managers meet for review sessions. (Managers receive training in how to conduct effective reviews.) Neill and Gunter uses a 360-degree feedback process to gather additional performance-related information from co-workers, supervisors and employees. The review process forms the basis for individual salary increases. Neill and Gunter also recognizes exceptional performance by providing employees with free use of the company's chalet in Maine.

### *Training & Skills Development* — *Rating: A*

Neill and Gunter's training and skills development program is rated as **above-average**. The company provides tuition subsidies for courses related to an employee's current position (100% of tuition). Commendably, Neill and Gunter also offers subsidies for courses not related to an employee's current job (50% of tuition). The company assists employees' career development with: reimbursement for professional association dues; in-house training.

### *Community Involvement* — *Rating: B+*

Neill and Gunter's community involvement program is rated as **average**. A good corporate citizen, Neill and Gunter actively supports a variety of local and national charitable initiatives. Employees at Neill and Gunter receive paid time off to volunteer at local charities.

Last year, the company supported a variety of charities, including the United Way, the Canadian Cancer Society, World Vision and the Association for Community Living. Employees also held a chili cook-off and bake sale to raise money for local families in need during the Christmas season.

OMERS
1 University Avenue
Suite 1000
Toronto, ON M5J 2P1

Tel. 416-369-2400
Fax 416-363-6723
careers@omers.com
http://www.omers.com

# OMERS

**INDUSTRY: PENSION & RETIREMENT BENEFIT FUNDS**

*Highlights:*

- Earn generous performance bonuses (over $4.7 million distributed last year) and be automatically enrolled in one of Canada's best-managed pension plans.
- Take advantage of excellent funding for continuing employee education — this employer spent over $1.3 million on training and development last year.
- Work 45 minutes extra each day and take off every second Friday.

## *Employer Background*

OMERS (formerly called the Ontario Municipal Employees Retirement System) is one of Canada's largest pension plans.

Founded in 1962 by the Ontario government as a pension fund for local government employees, OMERS has grown into a multi-employer plan that serves over 327,000 contributors and pensioners throughout the province. The fund has assets of over $30 billion.

OMERS' financial success has been achieved through a prudent investment strategy that focuses on long-term results and cost management. The fund has a record of achieving outstanding returns and exceeding forecasted performance levels. OMERS' financial strength has also made it a stable employer.

**Workforce at a Glance:** Number of full-time employees: **352**. Percentage of employees who are women: **61**. Of managers: **52**. Resumes received by their human resources staff in past year: **2,500**. Weeks of vacation their HR manager took last year: **4**. Average employee age: **39**. Years longest-serving employee has worked there: **34**. Person you should get to know first: **Raj and Pamela in Human Resources are fountains of information**.

## *Physical Workplace* — *Rating: B+*

OMERS' physical workplace is rated as **average**. OMERS' offices are located on nine floors of a modern building in Toronto's financial district. The downtown location is within walking distance to an incredible variety of restaurants, shops and entertainment venues, including outdoor concerts and skating. In a unique touch, over 200 original paintings by Ontario artists adorn the office walls. (An employee committee and an outside curator manage the art collection.)

**Physical Workplace at a Glance:** Their **employee lounge and rest areas** feature: meditation or religious observance room; comfortable couches. For **food and refreshment**, OMERS offers: free coffee and tea; kitchen areas; onsite Second Cup coffee shop. Nearby **amenities** include: variety of restaurants; major shopping mall; theatre district; fitness facility (with subsidized memberships). For **commuters**, OMERS offers: nearby public transit; bicycle racks; shower facilities. Other **work area amenities** include: ergonomic workstation design; plant life that is tended professionally.

### *Work Atmosphere & Social* — *Rating: A*

OMERS' work atmosphere is rated as **above-average**. Employees at OMERS enjoy business casual dress daily and can listen to radio or music while they are working. There is also a company-subsidized social committee.

Throughout the year, employees enjoy a variety of social events, including a winter luncheon for all employees at the luxurious Royal York Hotel, a summer day of fun at Toronto Centre Island (or Canada's Wonderland), and parties to celebrate project completions and the release of OMERS' annual report. In addition, all employees contribute to a unique gift fund that is used to celebrate important milestones (e.g. marriages, new babies) in the lives of all employees.

### *Health, Financial & Family Benefits* — *Rating: A*

OMERS' health benefits plan is managed by Sun Life and is rated as **above-average**. Full-time and part-time employees who work more than 20 hours per week are covered by the plan.

**Health Benefits at a Glance:** OMERS' health plan includes the following coverage: dental (100% of eligible costs, to $2,000 each year); orthodontics (50% of eligible costs with a lifetime maximum of $2,000); eyecare (to $200 every 2 years); prescription drug; extended health benefits; massage therapy; physiotherapy; alternative therapies; personal and family counselling; employee assistance plan (EAP) for substance abuse/mental health; Weight Watchers at Work.

The company's salary and financial benefits are rated as **above-average**. To keep pay-levels competitive, OMERS participates in outside salary surveys every 6 months. Individual salaries are reviewed every 12 months. Employees are automatically enrolled in an OMERS-managed pension plan, with matching company contributions.

**Financial Benefits at a Glance:** OMERS provides a variety of financial benefits, including: life and disability insurance; subsidized auto insurance; subsidized home insurance; discounted home computers; year-end bonuses (from $1,400 to $85,000 for non-executives).

OMERS' family-friendly benefits are rated as **above-average**. Employees with pre-school children have access to a daycare facility located nearby. For employees who take maternity leave, OMERS provides generous top-up to 93% of salary for the first 17 weeks of their leave. Other family-friendly benefits include: flexible start and finish hours; compressed work week (same hours, fewer days).

### *Vacation & Time Off* — *Rating: A*

OMERS' vacation and time off are rated as **above-average**. New employees receive 3 weeks of vacation allowance after their first year, which increases to 4 weeks after 10 years of service. The maximum vacation allowance is 5 weeks for long-serving employees. Employees at OMERS also receive 3 paid personal days off each year, in addition to their regular vacation allowance. Employees at the company can also apply for unpaid leaves of absence.

OMERS recently introduced a earned days off program. The popular program allows employees to work an extra 45 minutes each day and enjoy a long weekend every second week.

### *Employee Communications* — *Rating: A*

OMERS' internal communications program is rated as **above-average**. The company has an intranet site (called *Ozone*), which keeps employees informed about news and human resource policies that affect their work. An employee satisfaction survey is conducted by having employees complete an online questionnaire every 12 months. An outside consultant compiles the survey results for OMERS' management team.

### *Performance Management* — *Rating: A*

OMERS' performance management program is rated as **above-average**. The company operates a well-designed performance management program. Once a year, employees and managers meet for review sessions. (Managers receive training in how to conduct effective reviews.) OMERS uses a 360-degree feedback process to gather additional performance-related information from co-workers, supervisors and employees. Managers are encouraged to provide on-going feedback throughout the year. OMERS' new performance management program also ensures that employees have direct input into identifying their training needs.

OMERS operates a formal recognition program (called *Bravo*) to recognize excellent employee performance. Employees receive a variety of monthly awards, including restaurant dinners and home computer equipment.

### *Training & Skills Development* — *Rating: A+*

OMERS' training and skills development program is rated as **exceptional**. The company provides tuition subsidies for courses related to an employee's current position (100% of tuition). Commendably, OMERS also offers subsidies for courses not related to an employee's current job (100% of tuition). The company assists employees' career development with: reimbursement for professional association dues; mentoring; in-house training. (OMERS spent over $1.3 million in support of employee education last year.)

### *Community Involvement* — *Rating: B+*

OMERS' community involvement program is rated as **average**. A good corporate citizen, OMERS actively supports a variety of local and national charitable initiatives. Last year, OMERS' employees supported the Salvation Army Christmas Elves Program (employees collected 270 toys), The Terry Fox Run (eight employees participated and raised over $3,000), and the annual United Way campaign (employees donated over $74,000).

PARKLANE HOMES
www.parklane.com

**PARK LANE HOMES LTD.**
95 Schooner Street
Coquitlam, BC V3K 7A8

Tel. 604-516-0600
Fax 604-516-0677
http://www.parklane.com

**INDUSTRY: BUILDING CONTRACTORS**

*Highlights:*

- Get a 4% employee discount off the price of a new home from this employer that's also a home builder — a significant saving on a big ticket item.
- Work for a small employer that offers "big employer" benefits, including a complete health benefits plan, generous maternity top-up and flexible work options.
- Give back to your community with an exceptional corporate citizen that provides employees with five paid days off each year to volunteer with local charities.

## *Employer Background*

Park Lane Homes Ltd. is one of the largest and most recognized residential builders in British Columbia.

Founded in 1981, the award-winning builder is involved in all aspects of residential development, from acquiring vacant properties to developing entire planned communities.

Park Lane is a rare independent firm. Over the past several years, when other small builders disappeared or merged with larger competitors, the privately-held company survived British Columbia's construction slowdown, emerging with significant land holdings and new developments under construction. With revenues of $52 million last year, the company expects its revenues to more than double over the next year.

**Workforce at a Glance:** Number of full-time employees: **42**. New jobs created in Canada in past year: **3**. Percentage of employees who are women: **29**. Of managers: **33**. Percentage of employees who are visible minorities: **4**. Resumes received by their human resources staff in past year: **962**. Weeks of vacation their HR manager took last year: **4**. Average employee age: **39**. Years longest-serving employee has worked there: **22**. Person you should get to know first: **Gina in Payroll will fit you with your new company jacket**. Car the president drives: **2000 BMW 328 (but prefers a '90 Miata)**. Where it's parked in the lot: **with everyone else**.

## *Physical Workplace* — *Rating: A*

Park Lane's physical workplace is rated as **above-average**. The modern 4 storey head office was designed and built by the company. The suburban location was chosen because it's within easy commuting distance for most employees. An employee committee provided feedback on the building's design prior to construction.

**Physical Workplace at a Glance:** Their **employee lounge and rest areas** feature: comfortable couches; music; television; sleep room; a world map with employee trips flagged; basketball hoops. For **food and refreshment**, Park Lane offers: free snacks (including fresh fruit, cookies, crackers and trail mix); free coffee and tea; free soft drinks; outdoor eating area. Nearby **amenities** include: variety of restaurants; major shopping mall; fitness facility; casino; park/wilderness area (MacBee Park); recreation centre (Planet Ice). For **commuters**, Park Lane offers: free onsite car parking; convenient highway access; nearby public transit. Other **work area amenities** include: open-concept workstations; wireless connectivity throughout office; access to natural light for all employees; and great mountain views.

### *Work Atmosphere & Social* — *Rating: A*

Park Lane's work atmosphere is rated as **above-average**. Employees at Park Lane enjoy business casual dress daily and can listen to radio or music while they are working. There is also a company-subsidized social committee, which has operated since 1986.

The social club organizes a variety of events throughout the year, including potluck lunches, themed pub nights, a unique maze challenge in a local cornfield and tickets to Vancouver Canucks hockey games. The company also sponsors an employee slow-pitch team that competes in a local league.

Each year, Park Lane hosts a Christmas party for employees and their guests, a separate holiday party for employees' children at a fun location, an employee golf tournament, a summer boat cruise and an all-inclusive retreat in the fall — last year, employees and their guests enjoyed 3 nights at Victoria's luxurious Hotel Grand Pacific.

### *Health, Financial & Family Benefits* — *Rating: A*

Park Lane's health benefits plan is managed by Manulife Financial and is rated as **above-average**. Park Lane's health plan also covers employees in their retirement.

**Health Benefits at a Glance:** Park Lane's health plan includes the following coverage: dental (100% of eligible costs, to $2,000 each year); orthodontics (50% of eligible costs with a lifetime maximum of $2,000); eyecare (to $200 every 2 years); extended health benefits; prescription drug; massage therapy; physiotherapy; alternative therapies; personal and family counselling.

The company's salary and financial benefits are rated as **exceptional**. To keep pay-levels competitive, Park Lane participates in outside salary surveys every 12 months. Individual salaries are reviewed every 12 months. The company offers a group RSP that allows employees to contribute up to 3% of their salary, with matching employer contributions.

One of the most unique financial benefits in this book is the 4% discount employees receive on the purchase of a Park Lane home. In addition to the significant savings for employees, this is an excellent example of a creative inhouse benefit that's good for everyone.

**Financial Benefits at a Glance:** Park Lane provides an extensive set of financial benefits, including: discounted company products; life and disability insurance; discounted home computers; profit-sharing plan; signing bonuses for some employees.

Park Lane's family-friendly benefits are rated as **above-average**. Employees with pre-school children have access to a daycare facility located nearby. For employees who take maternity leave, Park Lane provides a generous top-up to 80% of salary for the first 27 weeks of their leave. Other family-friendly benefits include: job-sharing; flexible start and finish hours; shortened work week (fewer hours); telecommuting and working from home.

*Vacation & Time Off* — *Rating: B+*

Park Lane's vacation and time off are rated as **average**. New employees receive 2 weeks of vacation allowance after their first year, which increases to 3 weeks after 2 years of service. The maximum vacation allowance is 4 weeks for long-serving employees. Employees at the company can also apply for unpaid leaves of absence.

*Employee Communications* — *Rating: A*

Park Lane's internal communications program is rated as **above-average**. To keep employees informed about new developments, Park Lane publishes an in-house newsletter (called *In-House*). To solicit feedback from employees, the company operates a traditional suggestion box program and an email suggestion box. An employee satisfaction survey is conducted every 24 months. An outside consultant compiles the survey results for Park Lane's management team.

*Performance Management* — *Rating: A*

Park Lane's performance management program is rated as **above-average**. The company operates a well-designed performance management program. Once a year, employees and managers meet for review sessions. (Managers receive training in how to conduct effective reviews.)

Employees complete self-assessments prior to meeting their managers. At the annual reviews, employees and managers compare assessments and work together to establish performance goals for the upcoming year. Employees also have the opportunity to provide confidential feedback on their manager's performance.

*Training & Skills Development* — *Rating: A*

Park Lane's training and skills development program is rated as **above-average**. The company provides tuition subsidies for courses related to an employee's current position (100% of tuition). Commendably, Park Lane also offers subsidies for courses not related to an employee's current job (100% of tuition). The company assists employees' career development with: reimbursement for professional association dues; mentoring; in-house training.

*Community Involvement* — *Rating: A+*

Park Lane's community involvement program is rated as **exceptional**. An outstanding corporate citizen, Park Lane actively supports a variety of charitable initiatives. Employees take part in the selection of charitable groups assisted by the company. Employees at Park Lane receive paid time off (5 days each year) to volunteer at local charities. Last year, the company contributed to approximately 36 charitable groups, including: libraries, hospitals, schools, cultural centres and environmental groups in the communities in which it operates.

In the past, Park Lane has made major financial donations to the Eagle Ridge Hospital, Evergreen Cultural Centre, British Columbia Children's Hospital and the YMCA. The company also organizes a variety of community events every year, such as the construction of new playgrounds.

**PATHEON INC.**
**7070 Mississauga Road**
**Suite 350**
**Mississauga, ON L5N 7J8**

**Tel. 905-821-4001**
**Fax 905-812-2129**
**hr@patheon.com**
**http://www.patheon.com**

**INDUSTRY: PHARMACEUTICAL & DRUG MANUFACTURERS**

*Highlights:*

- Work for a growing employer with an impressive record of expansion — last year, this company added over 450 new employees.
- Take advantage of a unique mentoring program that improves language skills in employees whose first language is not English.
- Keep fit at a new onsite fitness facility, with nearby walking trails and a baseball diamond.
- Enjoy a paid holiday shutdown each year between Christmas and New Year's, in addition to your annual paid vacation allowance.

*Employer Background*

Patheon Inc. provides drug development and outsourced contract manufacturing services for brand-name pharmaceutical companies. Founded in 1974, the company makes (and packages) consumer pharmaceutical products for more than 100 customers, including 15 of the world's 20 largest pharmaceutical companies.

As a publicly-traded company, Patheon uses its financial resources to purchase under-used drug manufacturing plants from larger pharmaceutical companies. Then Patheon finds additional contract manufacturing business for the plant so that it can operate at a more efficient level. (This strategy is similar to what Magna has done in the automotive industry.)

Patheon's strategy is working well. Last year, the company had record revenues of over $418 million from plants in Canada, the United Kingdom, France, Italy and the United States. The company recently purchased a manufacturing facility in Cincinnati, Ohio, from France-based Aventis S.A. As part of the acquisition, Patheon also signed a long-term agreement to supply products back to Aventis.

In addition to its Mississauga head office, Patheon has Canadian facilities in Whitby, Toronto, Burlington and Fort Erie.

**Workforce at a Glance:** Number of full-time employees: **1,825**. At this location: **560**. Worldwide: **3,619**. New jobs created in Canada in past year: **456**. Percentage of employees who are women: **40**. Of managers: **3**. Percentage of employees who are visible minorities: **20**. Of managers: **2**. Resumes received by their human resources staff in past year: **7,540**. Weeks of vacation their HR manager took last year: **3**. Average employee age: **44**. Years longest-serving employee has worked there: **29**.

*Physical Workplace* *Rating: A*

Patheon's physical workplace is rated as **above-average**. To accommodate its growth, Patheon recently moved its head office to a modern office tower across the street from its manufacturing and development facility. Head office employees still have easy access to Patheon's campus setting, which offers excellent opportunities for a lunch-hour jog or a relaxing walk.

**Physical Workplace at a Glance:** Their **onsite fitness facility** features: subsidized memberships; treadmills; stationary bikes; stairmasters; rowing machines; weights; instructor-led classes (including pilates, yoga and aerobics); outdoor baseball diamond and walking trails; shower facilities. For **food and refreshment**, Patheon offers: free coffee and tea; outdoor eating area. The company has an onsite cafeteria that features: subsidized meals (a turkey sandwich costs $3.25); healthy menu items. Nearby **amenities** include: variety of restaurants; major shopping mall; park/wilderness area (Streetsville Memorial Park); recreation centre (Meadowvale Community Centre). For **commuters**, Patheon offers: free onsite car parking; convenient highway access; nearby public transit; secure bicycle parking. Other **work area amenities** include: open-concept workstations; modern laboratories; clean manufacturing facilities; ergonomic workstation design; plant life that is tended professionally.

*Work Atmosphere & Social* *Rating: A*

Patheon's work atmosphere is rated as **above-average**. Employees at Patheon enjoy casual dress on Fridays and can listen to radio or music while they are working. There is also a company-subsidized social committee, which has operated since 1993.

Employees enjoy social events throughout the year, including a summer picnic and boat cruise, golfing, baseball and hockey tournaments, a Christmas party (with separate event for employees' children), lunches to celebrate company successes and evening socials. The company also sponsors an employee baseball team (called the *Patheon Pylons*) that competes in a local league.

*Health, Financial & Family Benefits* *Rating: A*

Patheon's health benefits plan is managed by Great-West Life and is rated as **above-average**. There is no waiting period before new employees are eligible for coverage. Patheon's health plan also covers employees in their retirement.

**Health Benefits at a Glance:** Patheon's health plan includes the following coverage: dental (100% of eligible costs, with no annual maximum); orthodontics (50% of eligible costs with a lifetime maximum of $2,000); eyecare (to $100 every 2 years); extended health benefits; prescription drug; nutrition planning; massage therapy; physiotherapy; alternative therapies; personal and family counselling; employee assistance plan (EAP) for substance abuse/mental health; wellness plan.

The company's salary and financial benefits are rated as **above-average**. To keep pay-levels competitive, Patheon participates in outside salary surveys every 12 months. Individual salaries are reviewed every 12 months. The company operates a traditional pension plan.

**Financial Benefits at a Glance:** Patheon provides a variety of financial benefits, including: life and disability insurance; discounted company products; share purchase plan; signing bonuses for some employees; referral bonuses for some employees (to $1,000); year-end bonuses (from $113 to $43,350 for non-executives).

Patheon's family-friendly benefits are rated as **average**. Employees with pre-school children have access to a daycare facility located nearby. Other family-friendly benefits include: flexible start and finish hours; compressed work week (same hours, fewer days).

*Vacation & Time Off* *Rating: B+*

Patheon's vacation and time off are rated as **average**. New employees receive 2 weeks of vacation allowance after their first year, which increases to 3 weeks after 5 years of service. The maximum vacation allowance is 5 weeks for long-serving employees. Each year, Patheon also provides employees with a paid holiday shutdown from Christmas to New Year's.

*Employee Communications* *Rating: B+*

Patheon's internal communications program is rated as **average**. To keep employees informed about new developments, Patheon publishes an in-house newsletter (called *Compass*). An in-house employee satisfaction survey is conducted periodically.

*Performance Management* *Rating: A*

Patheon's performance management program is rated as **above-average**. The company operates a thorough performance management program. Once a year, employees and managers meet for review sessions. (Managers receive training in how to conduct effective reviews.) At the reviews, employees and managers review past performance and set goals for the upcoming year.

*Training & Skills Development* *Rating: A*

Patheon's training and skills development program is rated as **above-average**. The company provides tuition subsidies for courses related to an employee's current position (100% of tuition). Commendably, Patheon also offers subsidies for courses not related to an employee's current job (100% of tuition). The company assists employees' career development with: reimbursement for professional association dues; career planning; in-house training; mentoring. Patheon also offers a unique mentoring program for employees wishing to improve their English language skills.

*Community Involvement* *Rating: B+*

Patheon's community involvement program is rated as **average**. A good corporate citizen, Patheon actively supports a variety of local and national charitable initiatives. Employees take part in the selection of charitable groups assisted by the company.

Last year the company supported the the United Way, local firefighter and police services and the Canadian Cancer Society. The company also sponsors sports teams for employees' children.

**PCL CONSTRUCTION GROUP INC.**
**5410 - 99th Street**
**Edmonton, AB T6E 3P4**

**Tel. 780-435-9711**
**Fax 780-436-2247**
**info@pcl.com**
**http://www.pcl.com**

**INDUSTRY: BUILDING CONTRACTORS**

*Highlights:*

- Work for an innovative construction company that has a policy of moving staff from job to job to ensure steady employment.
- Invest in your future with a highly-regarded company that's 100% employee-owned.
- Grow your career at an employer with an active "promote from within" strategy — all senior managers are long-time employees.
- Face-off against your co-workers at a hockey tournament like no other — employee teams from across North America compete every year for the prized "*Schmauch Cup.*"

## *Employer Background*

PCL Constructors Inc. is one of North America's largest general contractors. Established in 1906, PCL operates a family of companies, each specializing in a different sector and geographic region. PCL is one of the most financially stable general contractors in North America, with annual revenues of over $3 billion.

Over the years, PCL has built virtually every kind of construction project, including offices and apartment buildings, retail stores, hotels, education and healthcare facilities, casinos, sports and leisure complexes, bridges, roads, airports and high-tech facilities. Some of the company's better-known projects include BCE Place (Toronto), the Pan Pacific Hotel (Vancouver), the Air Canada Centre (Toronto), Alex Fraser Bridge (Vancouver), Staples Center (Los Angeles), Denver International Airport and sections of the massive Hibernia offshore drilling platform.

Although known for larger projects, PCL works mostly on smaller construction jobs: 65% of its projects are valued at less than $1 million. Each working day, PCL bids on an average of five construction projects across North America.

The company's nearly 1,600 employees comprise one of the most experienced construction workforces in North America. (PCL also employs over 3,900 contract professionals and tradespeople.)

**Workforce at a Glance:** Number of full-time employees: **961**. At this location: **391**. Worldwide: 1,590. New jobs created in Canada in past year: **32**. Percentage of employees who are women: **24**. Of managers: **3**. Resumes received by their human resources staff in past year: **4,000**. Average employee age: **40**.

## *Physical Workplace* — *Rating: B+*

PCL's physical workplace is rated as **average**. In addition to its Edmonton head office, PCL maintains regional and project offices across North America. At project sites, offices are generally in portable buildings (it comes with the territory). Regardless of a project's location, PCL takes extraordinary measures to provide safe and healthy work environments. Not only does PCL employ full-time safety professionals who enforce the company's strict safety policy, but it also awards cash bonuses for strong safety performance. (PCL's accident rate is less than one-fourth the industry average in North America.) The company's suburban Edmonton head office is a one-storey buiding that the company built in 1968.

**Physical Workplace at a Glance:** For **food and refreshment**, PCL offers: free snacks; outdoor eating area. Nearby **amenities** include: variety of restaurants; major shopping mall; fitness facility. For **commuters**, PCL offers: convenient highway access; free onsite car parking; nearby public transit; secure bicycle parking. Other **work area amenities** include: lounge area; classroom; meeting areas; plant life that is tended professionally.

## *Work Atmosphere & Social* — *Rating: A*

PCL's work atmosphere is rated as **above-average**. Employees at PCL enjoy business casual dress daily. There is also a company-subsidized social committee.

Employees enjoy a variety of social events throughout the year, including a Christmas dinner and dance, a special Christmas party for employees' children, a curling bonspiel, summer barbeques, a golf tournament and Edmonton Oilers hockey games. PCL recognizes significant employee milestones and birthdays with lunch or coffee-and-cake celebrations.

PCL also sponsors employee baseball and hockey teams that compete in local leagues across North America. In a unique initiative, the company hosts an annual hockey tournament. Employee teams from across the company gather in Manitoba (or North Dakota) to compete for the coveted Schmauch Cup, which is named after the two employees who started the competition.

## *Health, Financial & Family Benefits* — *Rating: A*

PCL's health benefits plan is rated as **above-average**. The plan includes a healthcare spending account, which lets employees select levels of coverage. (The company has provided a healthcare spending account since 1988, making it one of Canada's first employers to offer the benefit.) PCL recently created an Employee Wellness Committee to promote and support healthy lifestyles.

**Health Benefits at a Glance:** PCL's health plan includes the following coverage: dental; orthodontics; extended health benefits; prescription drug; physiotherapy; massage therapy; alternative therapies; personal and family counselling; employee assistance plan (EAP) for substance abuse/mental health.

The company's salary and financial benefits are rated as **exceptional**. To keep pay-levels competitive, PCL participates in outside salary surveys every 24 months. Individual salaries are reviewed every 12 months. The company operates a traditional pension plan where PCL makes a contribution equal to 5% of each employee's salary to their plan each year. The plan lets employees specify their contribution levels and investment options.

PCL is wholly-owned by current employees and, each year, qualifying employees are invited to purchase shares in the company. Employees can purchase 100 shares annually with an interest-free company loan, which is repaid through payroll deductions. Over the years, employees have enjoyed significant returns on their shares from annual dividends and higher share prices.

> **Financial Benefits at a Glance:** PCL provides an extensive set of financial benefits, including: life and disability insurance; share purchase plan; year-end bonuses.

PCL's family-friendly benefits are rated as **average**. Employees with pre-school children have access to a daycare facility located nearby. Other family-friendly benefits include: flexible start and finish hours.

### *Vacation & Time Off* — *Rating: A*

PCL's vacation and time off are rated as **above-average**. New employees receive 3 weeks of vacation allowance after their first year, which increases to 4 weeks after 10 years of service. The maximum vacation allowance is 4 weeks for long-serving employees. Employees at the company can also apply for unpaid leaves of absence. (Recently, one engineering employee took a year off to volunteer in a developing country.)

### *Employee Communications* — *Rating: A*

PCL's internal communications program is rated as **above-average**. To keep employees informed about new developments, PCL publishes an in-house newsletter (called *Hard Hat*). The company also has an intranet site, which keeps employees informed about news and human resource policies that affect their work. An in-house employee satisfaction survey is conducted by having employees complete questionnaires every 36 months. The company also distributes regular news bulletins, a client newsletter ("*Horizons*") and several division-specific newsletters. Twice yearly, senior executives hold "fireside chats" to update employees on financial results and projections. Once a year, these meetings include a video highlighting PCL construction projects across North America.

### *Performance Management* — *Rating: B+*

PCL's performance management program is rated as **average**. The company operates a thorough performance management program. Once a year, employees and managers meet for review sessions. (Managers receive training in how to conduct effective reviews.) As part of the review process, employees receive regular feedback from their managers. PCL recognizes exceptional performance with a variety of non-monetary awards.

### *Training & Skills Development* — *Rating: A+*

PCL's training and skills development program is rated as **exceptional**. The company provides tuition subsidies for courses related to an employee's current position (100% of tuition). The company assists employees' career development with: reimbursement for professional association dues; mentoring; in-house training; online training.

PCL's well-developed in-house training department (the "*PCL College of Construction*") offers a wide range of management and technical programs at the company's head office and online. In addition, the company recently introduced new career development guides for all major occupational groups. The guides provide career path information and direct employees to specific educational resources.

In an industry where work often lasts only as long as a project, PCL strives to offer continuous employment for its employees. Experienced personnel are regularly transferred to fill ongoing needs at other projects, creating promotional opportunities for remaining employees. Advancement opportunities at PCL are good because the company follows a strict "promote from within" policy — PCL's senior management team are all long-time employees.

***Community Involvement*** ***Rating: A***

PCL's community involvement program is rated as **above-average**. A very good corporate citizen, PCL actively supports a variety of local, national and international charitable initiatives. Employees take part in the selection of charitable groups assisted by the company.

The company is a strong supporter of local United Way campaigns across North America and matches employee contributions to the charity (last year, the company contributed over $724,000).

PCL takes an active role in its industry and the communities where it operates. The company matches employee contributions to educational institutions and supports charitable projects across Canada and the United States, with each PCL location choosing donations on a case-by-case basis.

Pfizer

*Life is our life's work*

**PFIZER CANADA INC.**
**17300, route Transcanadienne**
**Kirkland, QC H9J 2M5**

**Tel. 514-695-0500**
**Fax 514-426-7085**
**hrh@pfizer.com**
**http://www.pfizer.ca**

**INDUSTRY: PHARMACEUTICAL & DRUG MANUFACTURERS**

*Highlights:*

- Get three weeks of paid vacation allowance in your first year — or more if you have experience elsewhere — with an employer that takes work experience into account in setting your vacation entitlement.
- Stay healthy through an onsite fitness centre (with instructor-led yoga and circuit training), extended health benefits and discounts on Pfizer's over-the-counter health products.
- Get exceptional family-friendly benefits at an employer that offers onsite daycare and generous maternity top-up (100% for salary for 18 weeks).

## *Employer Background*

Pfizer Canada Inc. is one of Canada's largest manufacturers of brand-name pharmaceuticals. Founded in 1953, the research-based healthcare company develops, manufactures and markets drugs for the treatment of a wide range of illnesses and conditions.

Pfizer Canada's product portfolio includes five of the world's 20 top-selling medicines (including such well-known drugs as Viagra and Lipitor). In addition to prescription drugs, Pfizer Canada markets consumer healthcare products (including brands such as Listerine and Rolaids), confectionery, personal care products and veterinary medicines.

Pfizer Canada is a subsidiary of New York-based Pfizer Incorporated. Established in 1849, Pfizer Incorporated is one the world's largest pharmaceutical companies. Last year, the company acquired New Jersey-based Pharmacia Corporation and, together, the merged company posted revenues of over $32 billion.

In Canada, Pfizer operates facilities in Montréal, Toronto, Mississauga and Arnprior, Ontario.

**Workforce at a Glance:** Number of full-time employees: **1,066**. At this location: **453**. Worldwide: **36,543**. New jobs created in Canada in past year: **22**. Percentage of employees who are women: **60**. Of managers: **58**. Percentage of employees who are visible minorities: **7**. Of managers: **6**. Resumes received by their human resources staff in past year: **30,000**. Weeks of vacation their HR manager took last year: **4**. Average employee age: **37**. Years longest-serving employee has worked there: **36**. Car the president drives: **2002 Cadillac**. Where it's parked in the lot: **with everyone else**.

### *Physical Workplace* — *Rating: A+*

Pfizer Canada's physical workplace is rated as **exceptional**. Located in the Montréal suburb of Kirkland, Pfizer Canada's head office was recently renovated. The new interior incorporates "feng shui" design principles to create an open and innovative office environment. New work areas receive more natural light and offer greater privacy for employees. During the renovation planning, employees were asked to choose the design and colour of their personal work areas.

**Physical Workplace at a Glance:** Their **onsite fitness facility** features: free memberships; treadmills; stationary bikes; stairmasters; weights; shower facilities; instructor-led classes; outdoor soccer field. For **food and refreshment**, Pfizer Canada offers: outdoor eating area; barbeque. The company has an onsite cafeteria that features: subsidized meals (a turkey sandwich costs $1.75); special diet menus; take-home dinners (a great idea). Nearby **amenities** include: variety of restaurants; major shopping mall; park/wilderness area (Morgan Arboretum); recreation centre (West Island YMCA). For **commuters**, Pfizer Canada offers: nearby public transit; free onsite car parking; secure bicycle parking; convenient highway access; valet service. Other **work area amenities** include: ergonomic workstation design; access to natural light for all employees; plant life that is tended professionally; onsite ATM, pharmacy and dry cleaner.

### *Work Atmosphere & Social* — *Rating: B+*

Pfizer Canada's work atmosphere is rated as **average**. Employees at Pfizer Canada enjoy business casual dress daily.

Pfizer Canada holds a variety of social events every year, including summer barbeques, Christmas parties, ski weekends and and golf tournaments. The company also organizes special awards dinners for long-serving employees. Pfizer also sponsors employee soccer, softball and hockey teams that compete in local leagues.

### *Health, Financial & Family Benefits* — *Rating: A+*

Pfizer Canada's health benefits plan is managed by Clarica Life and is rated as **above-average**. Their health benefits plan is flexible, meaning that employees can tailor individual plans to their personal circumstances.

**Health Benefits at a Glance:** Pfizer Canada's health plan includes the following coverage: dental (100% of eligible costs, to $1,250 each year); orthodontics (50% of eligible costs with a lifetime maximum of $2,500); eyecare (to $200 every 2 years); prescription drug; extended health benefits; nutrition planning; physiotherapy; massage therapy; alternative therapies; personal and family counselling; employee assistance plan (EAP) for substance abuse/mental health.

The company's salary and financial benefits are rated as **exceptional**. To keep pay-levels competitive, Pfizer Canada participates in outside salary surveys every 12 months. Individual salaries are reviewed every 12 months. The company offers a group RSP that allows employees to contribute up to 4% of their salary, with matching employer contributions. Pfizer Canada also operates a traditional pension plan.

**Financial Benefits at a Glance:** Pfizer Canada provides an extensive set of financial benefits, including: life and disability insurance; discounted company products; share purchase plan; signing bonuses for some employees; referral bonuses for some employees (from $750 to $1,500); year-end bonuses (from $1,000 to $56,860 for non-executives).

Pfizer Canada's family-friendly benefits are rated as **exceptional**. Employees with pre-school children have access to a subsidized daycare facility located onsite. The daycare facility has 62 spaces, employs 20 childcare workers and has a 12-month waiting list for new spaces. For employees who take maternity leave, Pfizer Canada provides a generous top-up to 100% of salary for the first 18 weeks of their leave. Other family-friendly benefits include: reduced summer hours.

***Vacation & Time Off*** — ***Rating: A***

Pfizer Canada's vacation and time off are rated as **above-average**. New employees receive 3 weeks of vacation allowance after their first year, which increases to 4 weeks after 10 years of service. The maximum vacation allowance is 6 weeks for long-serving employees. Employees at Pfizer Canada also receive 2 paid personal days off each year, in addition to their regular vacation allowance. The company recently changed its vacation policy to take previous work experience into consideration when establishing vacation entitlement for new employees. Employees at the company can also apply for unpaid leaves of absence.

***Employee Communications*** — ***Rating: A***

Pfizer Canada's internal communications program is rated as **above-average**. To keep employees informed about new developments, Pfizer Canada publishes an in-house newsletter (called *Pfizerama*). The company also has an intranet site, which keeps employees informed about news and human resource policies that affect their work. To solicit feedback from employees, the company operates an email suggestion box. An employee satisfaction survey is conducted every 12 months. An outside consultant compiles the survey results for Pfizer Canada's management team.

***Performance Management*** — ***Rating: A+***

Pfizer Canada's performance management program is rated as **exceptional**. The company operates a well-designed performance management program. Once a year, employees and managers meet for review sessions. (Managers receive training in how to conduct effective reviews.) Pfizer Canada uses a 360-degree feedback process to gather additional performance-related information from co-workers, supervisors and employees. Employees also receive coaching and feedback from their managers throughout the year. At the annual reviews, employees and managers discuss past performance and prepare written plans for future objectives.

***Training & Skills Development*** — ***Rating: A***

Pfizer Canada's training and skills development program is rated as **above-average**. The company provides tuition subsidies for courses related to an employee's current position (100% of tuition). Pfizer Canada offers bonuses to employees who successfully complete certain professional accreditation programs and courses. The company assists employees' career development with: in-house training. Pfizer Canada also provides company-paid language training programs for employees (and their families) who are interested in learning English or French.

***Community Involvement*** ***Rating: A+***

Pfizer Canada's community involvement program is rated as **exceptional**. An outstanding corporate citizen, Pfizer Canada actively supports a variety of charitable initiatives. A member of the Canadian Centre for Philanthropy's "*Imagine*" program, Pfizer Canada donates over 1% of its pre-tax profits to charity each year. In the past year, the company donated over $9 million, making it one of the nation's top corporate donors. Last year, the company contributed to approximately 600 charitable groups, including: the Alzheimer Society of Canada, the Canadian Paralympic Committee and the Active Living Alliance for Canadians with a Disability, to name a few.

Pfizer Canada also supports numerous local organizations in the communities where it operates. The company matches employee charitable contributions (to $5,000) through a generous donations program. The company also closely with local doctors to provide medicines to Canadian families in need. Through MAP International of Canada, the company also donates significant quantities of medicine for humanitarian causes around the world.

**POWER MEASUREMENT LTD.**
**2195 Keating Cross Road**
**Saanichton, BC V8M 2A5**

**Tel. 250-652-7100**
**Fax 250-544-3053**
**careers@pwrm.com**
**http://www.pwrm.com**

**INDUSTRY: MEASUREMENT & CONTROL EQUIPMENT MANUFACTURERS**

*Highlights:*

- Work for a growing high-tech employer on Vancouver Island with customers in over 80 countries and offices in the United States, Europe and Asia.
- Arrive for work each day at a custom-built headquarters that's only minutes away from beautiful beaches, lakeside jogging paths and coastal hiking trails.

## *Employer Background*

Power Measurement Ltd. manufactures advanced power meters and develops energy control software for electricity utilities and consumers worldwide. Founded in 1983, the company's products enable power producers and users to locate problem areas easily, measure usage and monitor fluctuating prices in the energy marketplace.

For commercial electricity, Power Measurement's technology provides real-time data that highlights usage patterns, identifies technical problems and determines where electricity is being wasted.

For electrical utilities, Power Measurement's control systems and software provide convenient monitoring services, identifying distribution problems and managing complex billing arrangements.

Power Measurement's technology is already in use at thousands of installations worldwide. Recently, the company completed new installations at the Channel Tunnel rail link between the United Kingdom and France, NASA's Ames Research Center in California and power utilities in India, Singapore and Switzerland.

In addition to Canada, Power Measurement has offices in the United States, Europe, Asia and Australia, as well as a sales and distribution network that serves customers in 80 countries.

**Workforce at a Glance:** Number of full-time employees: **250**. Worldwide: **300**. New jobs created in Canada in past year: **25**. Percentage of employees who are women: **30**. Of managers: **20**. Percentage of employees who are visible minorities: **15**. Of managers: **5**. Resumes received by their human resources staff in past year: **1,200**. Weeks of vacation their HR manager took last year: **1**. Average employee age: **34**. Years longest-serving employee has worked there: **15**. Person you should get to know first: **Jane in Reception can answer all questions**. Car the president drives: **1991 Lexus LS 400**. Where it's parked in the lot: **with everyone else**.

***Physical Workplace*** ***Rating: B+***

Power Measurement's physical workplace is rated as **average**. Located in the Victoria suburb of Saanichton, Power Measurement's custom-built head office is only a short drive from downtown Victoria, the city's international airport and the beautiful seaside community of Sidney. Numerous skylights and oversized windows provide plenty of natural light and great views. Employees can also take advantage of nearby beaches, hiking trails and hilltop views.

**Physical Workplace at a Glance:** For **food and refreshment**, Power Measurement offers: free coffee and tea; outdoor eating area; barbeque. Nearby **amenities** include: variety of restaurants; major shopping mall; fitness facility; park/wilderness area (Island View Beach). For **commuters**, Power Measurement offers: free onsite car parking; nearby public transit; bicycle trail (Galloping Goose Trail); shower facilities. Other **work area amenities** include: open-concept workstations; ergonomic workstation design; spacious manufacturing facility; plant life that is tended professionally.

***Work Atmosphere & Social*** ***Rating: A+***

Power Measurement's work atmosphere is rated as **exceptional**. Employees at Power Measurement enjoy business casual dress daily and can listen to radio or music while they are working. There is also a company-subsidized social committee, called the '*The Fungineers*', which has operated since 2001.

Throughout the year, Power Measurement organizes a variety of excellent social activities, including golf and curling tournaments, weekly lunches, summer barbeques (with managers doing the cooking), and pizza and beer celebrations for new product launches. Every Christmas, the company throws an employee party that begins with a touring eggnog cart in the afternoon and ends with dinner and dancing at a nearby venue. A separate Christmas party is held for employees' children.

Employees also maintain an activity page on the company's intranet site to help organize a variety of recreational activities, including floor hockey, mountain biking, tennis, skiing, softball, volleyball, squash, sailing and rowing.

***Health, Financial & Family Benefits*** ***Rating: B+***

Power Measurement's health benefits plan is managed by Green Shield and is rated as **above-average**. Power Measurement pays 100% of the premiums associated with the plan.

**Health Benefits at a Glance:** Power Measurement's health plan includes the following coverage: dental (100% of eligible costs, with no annual maximum); eyecare (to $250 every 2 years); prescription drug; nutrition planning; massage therapy; physiotherapy; personal and family counselling; employee assistance plan (EAP) for substance abuse/mental health; extended health benefits (optional).

The company's salary and financial benefits are rated as **average**. To keep pay-levels competitive, Power Measurement participates in outside salary surveys every 12 months. Individual salaries are reviewed every 12 months.

**Financial Benefits at a Glance:** Power Measurement provides a variety of financial benefits, including: life and disability insurance; share purchase plan; signing bonuses for some employees.

Power Measurement's family-friendly benefits are rated as **average**. Other family-friendly benefits include: flexible start and finish hours; compressed work week (same hours, fewer days); telecommuting and working from home.

***Vacation & Time Off*** ***Rating: B+***

Power Measurement's vacation and time off are rated as **average**. New employees receive 2 weeks of vacation allowance after their first year, which increases to 3 weeks after 5 years of service. The maximum vacation allowance is 4 weeks for long-serving employees.

***Employee Communications*** ***Rating: B+***

Power Measurement's internal communications program is rated as **average**. The company has an intranet site, which keeps employees informed about news and human resource policies that affect their work. To solicit feedback from employees, the company operates an email suggestion box. An in-house employee satisfaction survey is conducted periodically.

***Performance Management*** ***Rating: A***

Power Measurement's performance management program is rated as **above-average**. The company operates a formal performance management program. Once a year, employees and managers meet for review sessions. (Managers receive training in how to conduct effective reviews.) Power Measurement uses a 360-degree feedback process to gather additional performance-related information from co-workers, supervisors and employees. Employees can provide confidential feedback on their manager's performance through the feedback process.

***Training & Skills Development*** ***Rating: B+***

Power Measurement's training and skills development program is rated as **average**. The company provides tuition subsidies for courses related to an employee's current position (50% of tuition). The company assists employees' career development with: reimbursement for professional association dues; mentoring; in-house training.

***Community Involvement*** ***Rating: A***

Power Measurement's community involvement program is rated as **above-average**. A very good corporate citizen, Power Measurement actively supports a variety of charitable initiatives. Employees take part in the selection of charitable groups assisted by the company. Last year, the company contributed to approximately 10 charitable groups, including: the Vancouver Island 24 Hour Relay for the Kids, the Victoria Corporate Games (which supports local youth organizations), the Victoria City Police Rock Solid Youth Assistance Program (the company donates computers), and the British Columbia Children's Hospital.

To raise money for the annual United Way campaign, employees host barbeques, bake sales and a popular indoor golf tournament. Inspired by their beautiful surroundings, employees also manage an in-house program to recycle batteries, telephone books and other items.

P&G

**PROCTER & GAMBLE INC.**
**4711 Yonge Street**
**Toronto, ON  M3N 2K8**

**Tel. 416-730-4168**
**Fax 416-730-4771**
**http://www.pg.com/canada**

**INDUSTRY: CLEANING SUPPLIES & TOILETRIES MANUFACTURERS**

*Highlights:*

- Work for an employer where performance matters more than job titles — this employer's president works in an office that's the same size as an entry-level employee's!
- Balance your life better at a family-friendly employer that offers generous maternity leave, flexible work options and a special women's workshop series that addresses work-life issues affecting female employees.
- Get three weeks of paid vacation allowance in your first year — plus four paid personal days off each year.

## *Employer Background*

Procter & Gamble Inc. is a leading manufacturer and marketer of a wide range of consumer products. The company is a subsidiary of the Cincinnati, Ohio-based Procter Gamble Company. Established in 1837, the parent company markets over 300 consumer products, including such household names as Tide, Pampers, Crest, Pringles and Folgers, to name a few. The company has manufacturing, distribution and marketing operations in over 75 countries, serving billions of customers around the world each year.

Procter & Gamble Canada was established in 1915 as the company's first international operation. Today, the company has annual sales over $2 billion and locations in Toronto, Brockville, Belleville, Hamilton, Cambridge, Halifax, Montréal and Calgary.

**Workforce at a Glance:** Number of full-time employees: **1,999**. At this location: **850**. Percentage of employees who are women: **41**. Of managers: **52**. Percentage of employees who are visible minorities: **8**. Of managers: **13**. Resumes received by their human resources staff in past year: **5,000**. Weeks of vacation their HR manager took last year: **3**. Years longest-serving employee has worked there: **40**. Person you should get to know first: **Art in the cafeteria serves great food and always with a smile**. Car the president drives: **2002 Land Rover**. Where it's parked in the lot: **with everyone else**.

## *Physical Workplace* — *Rating: A*

Procter & Gamble Canada's physical workplace is rated as **above-average**. Located in Toronto's bustling "northern" downtown at Yonge & Sheppard, the company's head office building is located above a subway stop and offers convenient highway access for commuters. Inside, the office was recently redesigned using bright colours and a more relaxed decor. In a gesture that speaks volumes, the president's office in the redesigned headquarters is the same size as an entry-level employee's.

**Physical Workplace at a Glance:** Their **onsite fitness facility** features: subsidized memberships; treadmills; stationary bikes; stairmasters; rowing machines; weights; instructor-led classes; shower facilities. Their **employee lounge and rest areas** feature: comfortable couches; television; magazines. For **food and refreshment**, Procter & Gamble Canada offers: free coffee and tea; outdoor eating area; barbeque. The company has an onsite cafeteria that features: subsidized meals (a turkey sandwich costs $2.50); healthy menu items; special diet menus. Nearby **amenities** include: variety of restaurants; major shopping mall. For **commuters**, Procter & Gamble Canada offers: nearby public transit; subsidized car parking; secure bicycle parking. Other **work area amenities** include: open-concept workstations; ergonomic workstation design; access to natural light for all employees; plant life that is tended professionally.

## *Work Atmosphere & Social* — *Rating: A*

Procter & Gamble Canada's work atmosphere is rated as **above-average**. Employees at Procter & Gamble Canada enjoy business casual dress daily. Each year, employees enjoy a variety of social events, including a summer celebration, an annual holiday party at a Toronto hotel (with over 1,000 employees, retirees and guests) and a separate Christmas party for employees' children. The company also hosts unique events to celebrate the diversity of its workforce — including cultural fairs with food, traditional costumes, guest speakers and informative displays. Across the company, P&G Canada subsidizes employee teams in several sports, including dragonboat racing, hockey, curling, squash and golfing.

## *Health, Financial & Family Benefits* — *Rating: A*

Procter & Gamble Canada's health benefits plan is managed by Clarica Life and is rated as **exceptional**. Their health benefits plan is flexible, meaning that employees can tailor individual plans to their personal circumstances. Full-time and part-time employees are covered by the plan. There is no waiting period before new employees are eligible for coverage.

**Health Benefits at a Glance:** Procter & Gamble Canada's health plan includes the following coverage: dental (100% of eligible costs, to $3,000 each year); orthodontics (60% of eligible costs); eyecare (to $275 every 2 years); extended health benefits; prescription drug; massage therapy; physiotherapy; alternative therapies; employee assistance plan (EAP) for substance abuse/mental health.

The company's salary and financial benefits are rated as **above-average**. To keep pay-levels competitive, Procter & Gamble Canada participates in outside salary surveys every 12 months. Individual salaries are reviewed every 12 months. The company operates a traditional pension plan.

**Financial Benefits at a Glance:** Procter & Gamble Canada provides a variety of financial benefits, including: life and disability insurance; share purchase plan; signing bonuses for some employees.

Procter & Gamble Canada's family-friendly benefits are rated as **above-average**. For employees who take maternity leave, Procter & Gamble Canada provides a top-up to 95% of salary for the first 15 weeks of their leave. Other family-friendly benefits include: flexible start and finish hours; shortened work week (fewer hours); compressed work week (same hours, fewer days); telecom-muting and working from home.

***Vacation & Time Off*** — ***Rating: A***

Procter & Gamble Canada's vacation and time off are rated as **above-average**. New employees receive 3 weeks of vacation allowance after their first year, which increases to 4 weeks after 10 years of service. The maximum vacation allowance is 5 weeks for long-serving employees. Employees at Procter & Gamble Canada also receive 4 paid personal days off each year, in addition to their regular vacation allowance. Employees at the company can also apply for unpaid leaves of absence. (One employee recently took a 3 month leave to write music.)

***Employee Communications*** — ***Rating: A***

Procter & Gamble Canada's internal communications program is rated as **above-average**. The company has an intranet site, which keeps employees informed about news and human resource policies that affect their work. An employee satisfaction survey is conducted by having employees complete an online questionnaire every 12 months. An outside consultant compiles the survey results for Procter & Gamble Canada's management team.

***Performance Management*** — ***Rating: A***

Procter & Gamble Canada's performance management program is rated as **above-average**. The company operates a thorough performance management program. Once a year, employees and managers meet for review sessions. (Managers receive training in how to conduct effective reviews.) Employees and managers work to create a long-term career development plan. As part of the review process, employees also have the opportunity to evaluate their manager.

***Training & Skills Development*** — ***Rating: A***

Procter & Gamble Canada's training and skills development program is rated as **above-average**. The company provides tuition subsidies for courses related to an employee's current position (100% of tuition to $2,500). Commendably, Procter & Gamble Canada also offers subsidies for courses not related to an employee's current job. The company assists employees' career development with: career planning; mentoring; in-house training; online training.

Through its online training program, Procter & Gamble offers over 600 courses on a wide variety of subjects. The company also operates a unique "Women Supporting Women" workshop to address the challenges that female employees face in balancing their personal and working lives.

***Community Involvement*** — ***Rating: A+***

Procter & Gamble Canada's community involvement program is rated as **exceptional**. An outstanding corporate citizen, Procter & Gamble Canada actively supports a variety of local and national charitable initiatives. Employees at Procter & Gamble Canada receive paid time off (3 days each year) to volunteer at local charities. Last year, the company contributed to approximately 300 charitable groups.

As part of the company's fundraising activities for the United Way, employees hold special "*Survivor*" competitions to remove company executives from the tribe and even a "*United Way Idol*" singing contest to showcase employees' vocal talents.

Qunara

**QUNARA INC.**
**136 Market Avenue**
**8th Floor**
**Winnipeg, MB R3B 0P4**

**Tel. 204-925-0050**
**Fax 204-925-0069**
**hrwest@qunara.com**
**http://www.qunara.com**

**INDUSTRY: INFORMATION TECHNOLOGY CONSULTING FIRMS**

*Highlights:*

- Build your career at an IT consulting firm that offers the stability of a solid parent company, together with "blue chip" clients and a reputation for large-scale and profitable consulting assignments.
- Work in Winnipeg's historic Exchange district in a renovated warehouse that's at the center of the city's growing high-tech community.
- Take advantage of generous maternity leave top-up payments (93% of salary for 17 weeks), good vacation allowance and a training program that grooms you for advancement within the company.

## *Employer Background*

Qunara Inc. is an information technology consulting firm. Founded in 1982 (as the Exocom Group Inc.), Qunara has evolved from a developer of small personal computer applications to a high-growth IT consulting firm, specializing in e-business applications. The company is a subsidiary of Winnipeg-based Manitoba Telecom Services.

Qunara serves an expanding list of customers in a range of industries, including telecommunications, transportation, energy, government, banking and insurance. Some of the company's better-known clients include: Sprint Canada, NBTel, Nova Scotia Power, the Ontario Provincial Police and the Government of Canada. Last year, Qunara was awarded a $13-million contract from the Government of Ontario to develop security software for a new e-health service.

The company serves its customers from offices in Winnipeg, Calgary, Ottawa, Mississauga, Moncton and Halifax. Most employees work at the Ottawa and Winnipeg offices.

**Workforce at a Glance:** Number of full-time employees: **213**. Percentage of employees who are women: **29**. Of managers: **2**. Percentage of employees who are visible minorities: **37**. Of managers: **2**. Average employee age: **36**.

## *Physical Workplace* — *Rating: A*

Qunara's physical workplace is rated as **above-average**. The company's Winnipeg office is located in the city's historic Exchange district, in the heart of Winnipeg's growing high-tech community. Quanara occupies three floors of a renovated warehouse, which features exposed brick walls and large wood beams mixed with contemporary furniture and colourful curving walls. (For many years, the building was occupied by a wholesale business that stocked everything from machine parts to bananas.)

**Physical Workplace at a Glance:** Their **employee lounge and rest areas** feature: comfortable couches; quiet areas. For **food and refreshment**, Qunara offers: free coffee and tea; kitchen areas. Nearby **amenities** include: local shops and services; variety of restaurants; major shopping mall; park/wilderness area (The Forks and The River Walkway). For **commuters**, Qunara offers: nearby public transit; secure bicycle parking. Other **work area amenities** include: open-concept workstations; ergonomic workstation design.

## *Work Atmosphere & Social* — *Rating: A*

Qunara's work atmosphere is rated as **above-average**. Employees at Qunara enjoy business casual dress daily. Across the company, Qunara employees enjoy a variety of company-sponsored events, including golf games, baseball tournaments, summer barbeques, scavenger hunts, dragonboat races, skiing/skating parties and Christmas celebrations.

## *Health, Financial & Family Benefits* — *Rating: A*

Qunara's health benefits plan is managed by Great-West Life and is rated as **above-average**. Qunara pays 100% of the premiums associated with the plan. Full-time and part-time employees who work more than 15 hours per week are covered by the plan. New employees must wait 60 days before they can enroll in the plan.

**Health Benefits at a Glance:** Qunara's health plan includes the following coverage: dental (100% of eligible costs, to $1,250 each year); orthodontics (50% of eligible costs, to $1,000 each year); eyecare (to $100 every 2 years); extended health benefits; prescription drug; nutrition planning; massage therapy; physiotherapy; alternative therapies; personal and family counselling.

The company's salary and financial benefits are rated as **above-average**. To keep pay-levels competitive, Qunara participates in outside salary surveys. Individual salaries are reviewed every 12 months. The company offers a group RSP that allows employees to contribute up to 3% of their salary, with matching employer contributions.

**Financial Benefits at a Glance:** Qunara provides a variety of financial benefits, including: life and disability insurance; share purchase plan; year-end bonuses (to 5% of salary).

Qunara's family-friendly benefits are rated as **exceptional**. For employees who take maternity leave, Qunara provides a generous top-up to 93% of salary for the first 17 weeks of their leave. Other family-friendly benefits include: flexible start and finish hours.

## *Vacation & Time Off* — *Rating: A*

Qunara's vacation and time off are rated as **above-average**. New employees receive 3 weeks of vacation allowance after their first year, which increases to 4 weeks after 10 years of service. Employees at the company can also apply for unpaid leaves of absence.

*Employee Communications* *Rating: A*

Qunara's internal communications program is rated as **above-average**. To keep employees informed about new developments, Qunara publishes an in-house newsletter. The company also has an intranet site, which keeps employees informed about news and human resource policies that affect their work. To solicit feedback from employees, the company operates an email suggestion box. An in-house employee satisfaction survey is conducted periodically. Qunara also sends regular email announcements and hosts quarterly update meetings for all employees.

*Performance Management* *Rating: A*

Qunara's performance management program is rated as **above-average**. The company operates a comprehensive performance management program. Once a year, employees and managers meet for review sessions. (Managers receive training in how to conduct effective reviews.) To ensure that there are no surprises at the annual review, managers provide ongoing feedback to employees and host informal meetings throughout the year. The reviews also form the basis for salary increases.

Exceptional employee performance is recognized through a number of special awards, including weekend getaways at nearby resorts, electronic equipment, dinner and movie certificates, and vouchers for books and software.

*Training & Skills Development* *Rating: A*

Qunara's training and skills development program is rated as **above-average**. The company provides tuition subsidies for courses related to an employee's current position. The company assists employees' career development with: reimbursement for professional association dues; career planning; in-house training; mentoring.

Qunara has a policy of "promoting from within", which places special demands on the company's training and development program. Employees who improve their skills and education stand an excellent chance of advancing in this organization.

*Community Involvement* *Rating: A*

Qunara's community involvement program is rated as **above-average**. A very good corporate citizen, Qunara actively supports a variety of charitable initiatives. Qunara supports several national charities, including the Canadian National Institute for the Blind, the Canadian Cancer Society, the Heart and Stroke Foundation, Salvation Army and the United Way. The company also sponsors a variety of local initiatives in the communities where it operates.

recruitsoft

**RECRUITSOFT, INC.**
**330, rue St-Vallier est**
**Bureau 400**
**Québec, QC G1K 9C5**

**Tel. 418-524-5665**
**Fax 418-524-8899**
**hr-canada@recruitsoft.com**
**http://www.recruitsoft.com**

**INDUSTRY: INFORMATION TECHNOLOGY CONSULTING FIRMS**

*Highlights:*

- Work in beautiful Québec City for a growing high-tech employer that added 50 new positions in the past year.
- Travel to exotic locations for periodic department meetings (one such meeting was recently held at a resort in Cancun, Mexico).
- Develop yourself at an employer that provides each employee with over 100 hours of formal training every year, through tuition subsidies and company-paid courses.

## *Employer Background*

Recruitsoft, Inc. develops web-based employee recruitment and staffing management software for large employers.

For many large employers, the advent of online recruiting is a blessing and a burden. Through the Internet, employers easily attract thousands of applicants for a single position, but then must identify the best candidates from a vast pool of resumes. Recruitsoft's staffing management software automates this process, as well as the task of keeping track of existing employees' talents.

Founded in 1998, Recruitsoft serves many of the world's leading employers in a variety of industries. The company's clients include Bombardier, Bank of Montreal, Air Canada, Alliance Atlantis, Deloitte & Touche, Hewlett-Packard and Dow Chemical, to name a few. With over 100 clients in over 60 countries, Recruitsoft's revenues increased at an quarterly rate of 27% last year!

In addition to its Québec City head office, the company has offices in Montréal and Mississauga as well as locations in the United States, Europe and Asia.

**Workforce at a Glance:** Number of full-time employees: **250**. At this location: **231**. Worldwide: **353**. New jobs created in Canada in past year: **50**. Percentage of employees who are women: **27**. Of managers: **39**. Percentage of employees who are visible minorities: **1**. Average employee age: **33**.

## *Physical Workplace* — *Rating: A*

Recruitsoft's physical workplace is rated as **above-average**. Most of Recruitsoft's Canadian employees work at its recently renovated head office and primary research and development facility in historic Québec City. The landmark building previously housed the Le Soleil newspaper and is now home to several high-tech companies.

**Physical Workplace at a Glance:** Their **employee lounge and rest areas** feature: piano; pool table; board games. For **food and refreshment**, Recruitsoft offers: free snacks; free coffee and tea; free soft drinks; kitchen area. Nearby **amenities** include: variety of restaurants; major shopping mall; fitness facility; skiing at Mont Ste-Anne (a 30 minute drive); park/wilderness area (Parc St-Roch); recreation centre (Plains of Abraham). For **commuters**, Recruitsoft offers: transit subsidies; nearby public transit; secure bicycle parking; subsidized car parking. Other **work area amenities** include: open-concept workstations; large windows; plant life that is tended professionally.

## *Work Atmosphere & Social* — *Rating: A*

Recruitsoft's work atmosphere is rated as **above-average**. Employees at Recruitsoft enjoy business casual dress daily. The company has an onsite dry cleaning pick-up and delivery service.

Throughout the year, employees enjoy a variety of fun events, including a golf tournament, a Christmas party, a unique chocolate-themed event, a wine and cheese party, a pool tournament as well as Halloween and Valentine's Day celebrations. Employees also organize informal activities, such as extreme frisbee, go-cart racing, baseball and hockey. The company also sponsors an employee hockey team.

## *Health, Financial & Family Benefits* — *Rating: A*

Recruitsoft's health benefits plan is rated as **above-average**. Recruitsoft pays 100% of the premiums associated with the plan. There is no waiting period before new employees are eligible for coverage.

**Health Benefits at a Glance:** Recruitsoft's health plan includes the following coverage: dental (100% of eligible costs, to $750 each year); eyecare (to $200 every 2 years); extended health benefits; prescription drug; physiotherapy; massage therapy; alternative therapies; personal and family counselling; employee assistance plan (EAP) for substance abuse/mental health.

The company's salary and financial benefits are rated as **above-average**. To keep pay-levels competitive, Recruitsoft participates in outside salary surveys every 12 months. Individual salaries are reviewed every 12 months.

**Financial Benefits at a Glance:** Recruitsoft provides a variety of financial benefits, including: life and disability insurance; discounted home Internet access; subsidized home office hardware and supplies; performance bonuses; signing bonuses for some employees; referral bonuses for some employees (to $1,000).

Recruitsoft's family-friendly benefits are rated as **average**. Family-friendly benefits include: flexible start and finish hours; telecommuting and working from home.

## *Vacation & Time Off* — *Rating: A*

Recruitsoft's vacation and time off are rated as **above-average**. New employees receive 3 weeks of vacation allowance after their first year, which increases to 4 weeks after 5 years of service. The maximum vacation allowance is 5 weeks for long-serving employees. Employees at Recruitsoft also receive 3 paid personal days off each year, in addition to their regular vacation allowance. Employees at the company can also apply for unpaid leaves of absence. (Recently, one employee took a three-month leave of absence to complete a university degree)

***Employee Communications*** ***Rating: A***

Recruitsoft's internal communications program is rated as **above-average**. To keep employees informed about new developments, Recruitsoft publishes an in-house newsletter. An employee satisfaction survey is conducted by having employees complete an online questionnaire every 12 months. An outside consultant compiles the survey results for Recruitsoft's management team.

***Performance Management*** ***Rating: A***

Recruitsoft's performance management program is rated as **above-average**. The company operates a well-designed performance management program. Once a year, employees and managers meet for review sessions. (Managers receive training in how to conduct effective reviews.) Prior to each review, employees complete self-evaluations and managers collect feedback from those familiar with the employee's work. The reviews form the basis for salary increases.

***Training & Skills Development*** ***Rating: A+***

Recruitsoft's training and skills development program is rated as **exceptional**. The company provides tuition subsidies for courses related to an employee's current position (100% of tuition). The company assists employees' career development with: reimbursement for professional association dues; online training; in-house training.

The company's focus on training begins with a five-day orientation at its head office — all new employees are flown to Québec City to participate. New employees also receive job-specific training after their orientation.

Recruitsoft provides all employees with at least 100 hours of formal training every year. The company offers in-house and online courses on a variety of subjects, including technical training, customer service, project management and language training (French and English). Individual departments also plan unique overnight retreats for their employees every year — such as the operations meeting recently held in Cancún, Mexico.

***Community Involvement*** ***Rating: B+***

Recruitsoft's community involvement program is rated as **average**. A good corporate citizen, Recruitsoft actively supports a variety of charitable initiatives. The company invites employees to promote individual charities at work through fundraising or volunteering. Each Christmas, the company places baskets throughout the office to encourage employees to donate non-perishables to a local food bank. In addition, the company recently introduced automatic payroll donations in support of the United Way.

**ROGERS COMMUNICATIONS INC.**
**1 Mount Pleasant Road**
**5th Floor**
**Toronto, ON M4Y 2Y5**

**Tel. 416-935-7222**
**Fax 416-764-1855**
**careers@rmpublishing.com**
**http://www.rogers.com**

**INDUSTRY: OTHER COMMUNICATIONS SERVICES**

*Highlights:*

- Increase your visibility company-widc with this employer's unique skills database, which lets managers in other divisions know when you've completed new training or certification programs.
- Work in one of this book's best workplaces, which features Starbucks coffee stations, a healthy menu cafeteria, an onsite fitness centre and a rooftop patio with great views of the surrounding city.
- Get great employee discounts on company products, from cellphones and digital television services to Blue Jays baseball tickets.

## *Employer Background*

Rogers Communications Inc. is one of Canada's largest integrated communications companies, with significant cable television, entertainment, publishing and wireless businesses across the country. With a history dating back to 1927, Rogers Communications Inc. operates through three main divisions.

Rogers Cable Inc. is the country's largest cable television provider, providing digital cable, video-on-demand and high-speed Internet access to over 2.3 million households. This division also operates Canada's largest chain of video rental stores (Rogers Video), with over 260 locations across the country.

Rogers Media Inc. is one of Canada's largest media companies, publishing some of the country's most familiar consumer magazines (such as Maclean's and Chatelaine). This division also operates a network of television and radio stations, as well as several popular Internet sites.

Finally, Rogers Wireless Inc. (which operates under the Rogers AT&T banner) is one of the country's largest wireless communications providers, offering cellular, paging and wireless data services. This division serves over 3.5 million subscribers nationwide and has been a spectacular growth area for the company in recent years.

A dominant player in many of its markets, Rogers continues to grow. Last year, the company opened a state-of-the-art call centre in New Brunswick and acquired 13 radio stations in Ontario. The company generated over $4.3 billion in revenues last year.

**Workforce at a Glance:** Number of full-time employees: **13,054**. At this location: **7,620**. New jobs created in Canada in past year: **1,038**. Percentage of employees who are women: **49**. Of managers: **44**. Percentage of employees who are visible minorities: **16**. Of managers: **9**. Resumes received by their human resources staff in past year: **110,000**. Average employee age: **33**. Years longest-serving employee has worked there: **47**.

## *Physical Workplace* — *Rating: A+*

Rogers' physical workplace is rated as **exceptional**. Located in downtown Toronto, the company's head office (known as the "*Rogers Campus*") is a state-of-the-art facility that combines modern and classic architectural styles. Inside the head office, most management offices are located in the middle of the building to ensure staff have the best access to natural light. All new work areas are wheelchair-accessible and can be easily modified to accommodate the special needs of disabled employees.

**Physical Workplace at a Glance:** Their **onsite fitness facility** features: subsidized memberships; treadmills; stationary bikes; stairmasters; rowing machines; weights; instructor-led classes; shower facilities. Their **employee lounge and rest areas** feature: comfortable couches; television; meditation or religious observance room. For **food and refreshment**, Rogers offers: free coffee and tea; outdoor eating area; Starbucks coffee stations. The company has an onsite cafeteria that features: subsidized meals (a turkey sandwich costs $3.21); special diet menus; healthy menu items; onsite pizza shop. Nearby **amenities** include: variety of restaurants; major shopping mall; small parkette. For **commuters**, Rogers offers: nearby public transit. Other **work area amenities** include: open-concept workstations; ergonomic workstation design; access to natural light for all employees.

## *Work Atmosphere & Social* — *Rating: B+*

Rogers' work atmosphere is rated as **average**. Employees at Rogers enjoy business casual dress daily. Across the company, a variety of social events are held throughout the year to celebrate individual accomplishments and corporate achievements. These include traditional Christmas parties, product launch events and celebrations for employee milestones.

## *Health, Financial & Family Benefits* — *Rating: A*

Rogers' health benefits plan is managed by Liberty Health and is rated as **above-average**. Rogers pays 75% of the premiums associated with the plan, with employees paying the remaining 25%. Full-time and part-time employees who work more than 20 hours per week are covered by the plan.

**Health Benefits at a Glance:** Rogers' health plan includes the following coverage: dental (100% of eligible costs, with no annual maximum); orthodontics (50% of eligible costs with a lifetime maximum of $1,500); eyecare (to $200 every 2 years); prescription drug; extended health benefits; nutrition planning; massage therapy; physiotherapy; alternative therapies; personal and family counselling; employee assistance plan (EAP) for substance abuse/mental health.

The company's salary and financial benefits are rated as **exceptional**. To keep pay-levels competitive, Rogers participates in outside salary surveys every 6 months. Individual salaries are reviewed every 12 months. The company operates a traditional pension plan.

One of the best benefits of working at Rogers are the discounts that employees receive on company products and services, including cellular phones (with free airtime), discounts on high-speed Internet access, cable television service, movie rentals, magazine subscriptions and even tickets to the Toronto Blue Jays (the baseball team is owned by the company).

**Financial Benefits at a Glance:** Rogers provides an extensive set of financial benefits, including: life and disability insurance; subsidized auto insurance; discounted car leases; subsidized home insurance; share purchase plan; year-end bonuses.

Rogers' family-friendly benefits are rated as **above-average**. For employees who take maternity leave, Rogers provides a generous top-up to 100% of salary for the first 15 weeks of their leave. Other family-friendly benefits include: flexible start and finish hours; telecommuting and working from home.

### *Vacation & Time Off* — *Rating: B+*

Rogers' vacation and time off are rated as **average**. New employees receive 2 weeks of vacation allowance after their first year, which increases to 3 weeks after 3 years of service. The maximum vacation allowance is 6 weeks for long-serving employees. Employees at Rogers also receive 2 paid personal days off each year, in addition to their regular vacation allowance. Employees at the company can also apply for unpaid leaves of absence.

### *Employee Communications* — *Rating: A*

Rogers' internal communications program is rated as **above-average**. To keep employees informed about new developments, Rogers publishes an in-house newsletter (called *FYI*). The company also has an intranet site, which keeps employees informed about news and human resource policies that affect their work. To solicit feedback from employees, the company operates an email suggestion box. An employee satisfaction survey is conducted by having employees complete an online questionnaire every 12 months. An outside consultant compiles the survey results for Rogers' management team.

### *Performance Management* — *Rating: A*

Rogers' performance management program is rated as **above-average**. The company operates a comprehensive performance management program. Once a year, employees and managers meet for review sessions. (Managers receive training in how to conduct effective reviews.) Managers are encouraged to provide quarterly coaching sessions during the year.

Exceptional employee performance is recognized through a variety of awards, including baseball tickets, weekend getaways, dinner certificates, cash bonuses, TV sets and additional days off. Employees who go "above and beyond" the call of duty are presented with a new pair of cowboy boots — a reminder to all that Rogers has always been a rough-and-tumble upstart in its businesses.

### *Training & Skills Development* — *Rating: A+*

Rogers' training and skills development program is rated as **exceptional**. The company provides tuition subsidies for courses related to an employee's current position (100% of tuition). Commendably, Rogers also offers subsidies for courses not related to an employee's current job (75% of tuition). The company assists employees' career development with: reimbursement for professional association dues; career planning; mentoring; in-house training; online training.

One of Rogers' most interesting employee programs is its "Rogers Employee Database". This intranet program enables employees to make sure their managers — as well as other managers across the company — are familiar with their current education, licenses, certifications and language skills. This unique skills inventory allows Rogers employees with particular qualifications to be considered for new positions across all operating divisions.

***Community Involvement*** ***Rating: A+***

Rogers' community involvement program is rated as **exceptional**. An outstanding corporate citizen, Rogers actively supports a variety of local and national charitable initiatives.

Rogers supports numerous charitable organizations and initiatives with donations and an extraordinary level of employee involvement. The company supports the Kids Help Phone, the Hospital for Sick Children (Toronto), the B.C. Children's Hospital, Child Find, the Cross Cancer Institute (Edmonton), local United Way campaigns and the very popular "Jolly Trolley Caboose" program, which delivers movies to hospitalized children.

Each Halloween, Rogers Cable employees can be seen in their familiar red vans, patrolling neighbourhood streets (called the *Pumpkin Patrol*) to ensure the safety of local children. This well-regarded program has been operating for more than 17 years and provides an excellent example of how to involve employees actively in community work.

Another unique initiative is the company's "Help is Just a Call Away" program. In conjunction with the Ontario Provincial Police and the Victims Service Program, Rogers provides free cellular phones and pagers to people working with victims of domestic violence.

Rogers is a major sponsor of community events and initiatives across Canada, including the Nova Scotia International Tattoo, Ski-Québec, PEI's Diamond in the Rough women's golf tournament and the Rogers Writers' Trust fiction prize (worth $10,000). The company is a major contributor to several funds that provide loans to independent television and film producers. Rogers also supports the Media Awareness Network, a non-profit organization that aims to improve media literacy and Internet awareness for families and individuals.

**SAS INSTITUTE (CANADA) INC.**
**181 Bay Street**
**Suite 2220, BCE Place**
**Toronto, ON M5J 2T3**

**Tel. 416-363-4424**
**Fax 416-307-4562**
**hr@can.sas.com**
**http://www.sas.com/canada**

**INDUSTRY: SOFTWARE COMPANIES**

*Highlights:*

- Work at an employer that celebrates its employees' multicultural diversity by holding special food tasting days on ethnic holidays and providing explanatory emails.
- Stay in shape at an employer that provides a generous $900 annual fitness club subsidy to each employee.
- Get three weeks of paid vacation allowance to start — plus four paid days off each year to volunteer at a local charity.

## *Employer Background*

SAS Institute (Canada) Inc. develops data warehousing and specialized business decision support software. The company's software helps customers integrate data from across their organizations and create usable information ("intelligence") that assists in making more accurate and informed decisions.

SAS Canada is a subsidiary of North Carolina-based SAS Institute Incorporated. Founded in 1976, the parent company is the world's largest privately-held software company, with over $1.1 billion in annual revenues. SAS' software is in use at more than 33,000 customer sites in over 100 countries. The company primarily serves large customers in the automotive, financial, manufacturing, retail, telecommunications, education and government sectors.

SAS has operated in Canada since 1986. Despite the software sector's recent difficulties, the Canadian division increased its revenues by over 20% to over $57 million last year. In addition to its Toronto head office, the company has locations in Vancouver, Calgary, Ottawa, Montréal and Québec.

**Workforce at a Glance:** Number of full-time employees: **141**. At this location: **109**. Worldwide: **8,978**. Percentage of employees who are women: **47**. Of managers: **19**. Percentage of employees who are visible minorities: **26**. Of managers: **19**. Resumes received by their human resources staff in past year: **4,000**. Weeks of vacation their HR manager took last year: **4.5**. Average employee age: **37**. Years longest-serving employee has worked there: **16**.

## *Physical Workplace* — *Rating: A*

SAS Institute's physical workplace is rated as **above-average**. The head office is located in one of the city's landmark skyscrapers, offering great views of Lake

Ontario and the downtown area. The building's architecturally acclaimed atrium leads to the city's underground walking network, providing all-weather access to restaurants, shops and the subway system.

**Physical Workplace at a Glance:** Their **employee lounge and rest areas** feature: comfortable couches; pool table. For **food and refreshment**, SAS Institute offers: free snacks (including fresh fruit, soup, granola bars and pastries); free coffee and tea; free soft drinks. Nearby **amenities** include: variety of restaurants; major shopping mall; fitness facility (the company provides each employee with an annual $900 fitness club subsidy); Hockey Hall of Fame; Hummingbird Centre for the Arts; recreation centre (Harbourfront). Other **work area amenities** include: open-concept workstations; ergonomic workstation design; access to natural light for all employees; plant life that is tended professionally.

## *Work Atmosphere & Social* — *Rating: A+*

SAS Institute's work atmosphere is rated as **exceptional**. Employees at SAS Institute enjoy business casual dress daily and can listen to radio or music while they are working. There is also a company-subsidized social committee, which has operated since 1990.

The committee organizes a number of fun events every year, including a winter party for employees and their spouses, a Christmas party with gifts from Santa for employees' children, an evening boat cruise on Lake Ontario, a summer family day (held at the Toronto Zoo last year) and evening socials, including an evening performance by an employee band (called the "*SASations*") at a downtown club.

In a unique initiative, each SAS employee receives a $100 annual budget for socializing with other employees in their department. In the past, employees have pooled their money and enjoyed restaurant dinners, bowling nights and evenings at the theatre. In recognition of its cultural diversity, the company celebrates significant cultural and religious holidays throughout the year with food samples and informative emails explaining each event.

## *Health, Financial & Family Benefits* — *Rating: A*

SAS Institute's health benefits plan is managed by Canada Life and is rated as **above-average**. New employees must wait 30 days before they can enroll in the plan.

**Health Benefits at a Glance:** SAS Institute's health plan includes the following coverage: dental (100% of eligible costs, with no annual maximum); orthodontics (50% of eligible costs with a lifetime maximum of $2,500); eyecare (to $300 every 2 years); extended health benefits; prescription drug; massage therapy; physiotherapy; alternative therapies; personal and family counselling; employee assistance plan (EAP) for substance abuse/mental health.

The company's salary and financial benefits are rated as **above-average**. To keep pay-levels competitive, SAS Institute participates in outside salary surveys every 12 months. Individual salaries are reviewed every 12 months.

**Financial Benefits at a Glance:** SAS Institute provides a variety of financial benefits, including: life and disability insurance; subsidized auto insurance; subsidized home insurance; discounted home computers; signing bonuses for some employees; referral bonuses for some employees (from $2,000 to $6,000); year-end bonuses.

SAS Institute's family-friendly benefits are rated as **above-average**. Employees with pre-school children have access to a daycare facility located nearby. For employees who take maternity leave, SAS Institute provides a top-up to 100% of salary for the first 6 weeks of their leave. Other family-friendly benefits include: telecommuting and working from home; flexible start and finish hours.

***Vacation & Time Off*** **Rating: A**

SAS Institute's vacation and time off are rated as **above-average**. New employees receive 3 weeks of vacation allowance after their first year, which increases to 4 weeks after 5 years of service. The maximum vacation allowance is 4 weeks for long-serving employees. Employees at the company can also apply for unpaid leaves of absence.

***Employee Communications*** **Rating: A**

SAS Institute's internal communications program is rated as **above-average**. To keep employees informed about new developments, SAS Institute publishes an in-house newsletter (called *SAS com*), which is available online. The company also has an intranet site, which keeps employees informed about news and human resource policies that affect their work. An in-house employee satisfaction survey is conducted by email every 12 months. To ensure confidentiality, employees print their survey responses and return them in sealed envelopes.

***Performance Management*** **Rating: A+**

SAS Institute's performance management program is rated as **exceptional**. The company operates a thorough performance management program. Every 6 months, employees and managers meet for review sessions. (Managers receive training in how to conduct effective reviews.) SAS Institute uses a 360-degree feedback process to gather additional performance-related information from co-workers, supervisors and employees. As part of the review process, managers provide ongoing feedback and support throughout the year.

SAS Institute recognizes exceptional performance with cash awards (to $1,000), spa weekends, movie passes and restaurant dinners. In addition, the top-performing sales employee each quarter gets to use a leased Porsche for 3 months (to 5,000 km). At the end of the year, leading sales performers also receive fully-paid vacations — last year, they spent 5 days in the Virgin Islands at company expense!

***Training & Skills Development*** **Rating: A**

SAS Institute's training and skills development program is rated as **above-average**. The company provides tuition subsidies for courses related to an employee's current position (100% of tuition). The company assists employees' career development with: reimbursement for professional association dues; in-house training.

SAS operates internal training centres across Canada and the United States. In addition, all new sales employees complete an extensive training program at the company head office in Cary, North Carolina.

***Community Involvement*** ***Rating: A+***

SAS Institute's community involvement program is rated as **exceptional**. An outstanding corporate citizen, SAS Institute actively supports a variety of charitable initiatives. Employees take part in the selection of charitable groups assisted by the company. Employees at SAS Institute receive paid time off (4 days each year) to volunteer at local charities.

The company organizes a variety of fundraising events every year for the United Way. Employees also entered a team in a slo-pitch tournament last year to raise money for the Toronto Children's Breakfast Club. In addition, employees donated money to a variety of charities, including the Toronto Humane Society, the Multiple Sclerosis Society, the Breast Cancer Foundation and the Heart and Stroke Foundation, to name a few. SAS also matches employee donations to registered charities.

**SASKTEL**
**2121 Saskatchewan Drive**
**13th Floor**
**Regina, SK S4P 3Y2**

**Tel. 306-777-4117**
**Fax 306-777-3277**
**http://www.sasktel.com**

**INDUSTRY: TELEPHONE COMPANIES**

*Highlights:*

- Build your career at a telecom employer that is expanding (through an impressive overseas division and by investing in high-speed Internet access in many remote communities) and creating jobs when others in its industry are downsizing.
- Develop yourself at an employer that has moved most of its training programs online, ensuring that employees in all locations have access to the same quality of training materials.
- Work for a community leader that supports over 1,600 charitable organizations and where employees (and even retirees) donate over 70,000 volunteer hours each year for community projects.

## *Employer Background*

SaskTel is a large regulated utility that provides telephone and communications services to residential and business customers across Saskatchewan. Established in 1909, SaskTel is the province's main provider of communications services. The company provides local and long-distance telephone, wireless and high-speed Internet services to customers across Saskatchewan.

A Crown corporation, SaskTel is obliged to provide affordable service to all residents of Saskatchewan, including those living in rural areas. The company's high-speed Internet service is now available in every Saskatchewan community of 1,000 or more residents (over 74% of the population). The company's cellular telephone network serves over 270,000 wireless customers and is available to more than 90% of the population.

While many telecommunications providers have experienced difficult conditions in recent years, SaskTel has diversified its operations and avoided laying off employees. In addition to its core businesses at home, the company's successful international division (SaskTel International) has built and improved telephone systems in over 30 countries, from the United States to Tanzania. Over the past decade, this division has completed projects in East Africa worth more than $56 million. The division also helped to install communications systems in the Channel Tunnel linking England and France and, more recently, deployed 1,500 kilometres of fibre-optic cable under the South China Sea.

Last year, SaskTel had operating revenues of over $893 million, a 5% improvement over the previous year.

**Workforce at a Glance:** Number of full-time employees: **3,693**. New jobs created in Canada in past year: **116**. Percentage of employees who are women: **49**. Of managers: **36**. Percentage of employees who are visible minorities: **3**. Of managers: **3**. Resumes received by their human resources staff in past year: **15,446**. Average employee age: **41**.

## *Physical Workplace* — *Rating: A*

SaskTel's physical workplace is rated as **above-average**. Employees work in a variety of environments, including traditional offices, call centres and switching stations. Installation and repair personnel work at customer sites throughout the province. Employees at the international division experience a variety of work environments, depending on the country and project.

Located in downtown Regina, SaskTel's head office is within easy walking distance to restaurants and the city's Victoria Park, which comes alive in the summer with sun-seekers, live entertainment and a farmer's market.

**Physical Workplace at a Glance:** Their **onsite fitness facility** features: free memberships; treadmills; stationary bikes; stairmasters; rowing machines; weights; cross-trainer; shower facilities; medical department with staff nurse. The company has an onsite cafeteria that features: subsidized meals (a turkey sandwich costs $2.50); special diet menus; healthy menu items. Nearby **amenities** include: major shopping mall; variety of restaurants; art galleries; Globe Theatre. For **commuters**, SaskTel offers: subsidized car parking; nearby public transit; secure bicycle parking. Other **work area amenities** include: ergonomic workstation design; auditorium; conference rooms with great views.

## *Work Atmosphere & Social* — *Rating: B+*

SaskTel's work atmosphere is rated as **average**. Employees at SaskTel enjoy business casual dress daily. Throughout the year, SaskTel hosts numerous employee social events, including an annual banquet to celebrate long-serving employees. Individual departments often organize their own events to recognize excellent job performance. The company also sponsors employee curling and hockey teams, softball leagues and golf tournaments.

## *Health, Financial & Family Benefits* — *Rating: A*

SaskTel's health benefits plan is managed by Canada Life and is rated as **above-average**. Full-time and part-time employees are covered by the plan.

**Health Benefits at a Glance:** SaskTel's health plan includes the following coverage: dental; orthodontics; eyecare (to $250 every 2 years); extended health benefits; prescription drug; nutrition planning; massage therapy; physiotherapy; alternative therapies; personal and family counselling; employee assistance plan (EAP) for substance abuse/mental health; a wellness program that includes financial help for smoking cessation and weight loss programs.

The company's salary and financial benefits are rated as **exceptional**. To keep pay-levels competitive, SaskTel participates in outside salary surveys every 12 months. Individual salaries are reviewed every 12 months. The company operates a traditional pension plan where SaskTel makes a contribution equal to 6% of each employee's salary to their plan each year. The company also offers a group RSP.

**Financial Benefits at a Glance:** SaskTel provides an extensive set of financial benefits, including: life and disability insurance; discounted home Internet access; discounted company products (10% discount at company stores).

SaskTel's family-friendly benefits are rated as **above-average**. Employees with pre-school children have access to a daycare facility located nearby. For employees who take maternity leave, SaskTel provides a top-up to 95% of salary for the first 2 weeks of their leave. Other family-friendly benefits include: flexible start and finish hours; shortened work week (fewer hours); compressed work week (same hours, fewer days).

### *Vacation & Time Off* — *Rating: A*

SaskTel's vacation and time off are rated as **above-average**. New employees receive 3 weeks of vacation allowance after their first year, which increases to 4 weeks after 8 years of service. The maximum vacation allowance is 6 weeks for long-serving employees. Employees at the company can also apply for unpaid leaves of absence.

### *Employee Communications* — *Rating: A*

SaskTel's internal communications program is rated as **above-average**. To keep employees informed about new developments, SaskTel publishes an in-house newsletter (called *Ink*), which is available online. The company also has an intranet site (called *The Source*), which keeps employees informed about news and human resource policies that affect their work. To solicit feedback from employees, the company operates an email suggestion box. An in-house employee satisfaction survey is conducted by email every 12 months.

### *Performance Management* — *Rating: A+*

SaskTel's performance management program is rated as **exceptional**. The company operates a comprehensive performance management program. Once a year, employees and managers meet for review sessions. (Managers receive training in how to conduct effective reviews.) The annual reviews are a critical component of employee development — managers receive bonuses for meeting their review responsibilities.

As part of the review process, employees solicit feedback from their peers, evaluate their own performance and receive coaching from managers throughout the year. To complement this process, SaskTel has developed an intranet tool that guides employees through the self-assessment process so they can develop their own career action plans.

### *Training & Skills Development* — *Rating: A*

SaskTel's training and skills development program is rated as **above-average**. The company provides tuition subsidies for courses related to an employee's current position (100% of tuition). The company assists employees' career development with: reimbursement for professional association dues; career planning; in-house training; online training. For employees living outside Regina, the company's advanced online learning site provides equal access to essential training programs.

*Community Involvement* *Rating: A+*

SaskTel's community involvement program is rated as **exceptional**. An outstanding corporate citizen, SaskTel actively supports a variety of local and national charitable initiatives. Employees take part in the selection of charitable groups assisted by the company.

A member of the Canadian Centre for Philanthropy's "*Imagine*" program, SaskTel donates at least 1% of its annual pre-tax profits to an astounding number of community organizations. Last year, the company donated $1.8 million to over 1,600 charities in the fields of education, health, family and youth services. The company has a formal corporate sponsorship program that coordinates donations with an employee benevolent fund. In addition, current and retired employees donate over 70,000 volunteer hours each year (and almost $500,000 in cash donations last year) to community projects through the SaskTel Pioneers service club.

SaskTel provides major financial support to the SaskTel Dream Network (to support healthy parenting and prevent child abuse), the Saskatchewan Jazz Festival, the Saskatchewan Roughriders, the Kinsmen Big Valley Jamboree, Tourism Saskatchewan, the Regina Symphony Orchestra, Habitat for Humanity and the National Aboriginal Achievement Foundation.

SaskTel is also a major supporter of youth education. The company hired over 125 summer students last year and awarded 19 scholarships (to $3,000 each) to students from across the province.

A careful steward of the environment, SaskTel has an admirable program of environmental management in the communities where it operates. A good example can be seen in the company's decision to return northern radio tower sites back to their natural condition. The company also sponsors local recycling projects for telephone directories, batteries and household paint — employees collected over 14,760 gallons of paint last year.

**SEASPAN INTERNATIONAL LTD.**
**10 Pemberton Avenue**
**North Vancouver, BC V7P 2R1**

**Tel. 604-988-3111**
**Fax 604-984-1615**
**info@seaspan.com**
**http://www.washingtonmarinegroup.com**

**INDUSTRY: MARINE FREIGHT SERVICES**

*Highlights:*

- Build your career at a growing BC employer that's been building the province's economy for more than 100 years — and offers career opportunities around the world through its parent company.
- Keep in shape on the job at this employer — and at their massive new onsite fitness facility, which is free for employees to use and includes personal trainers.
- Work at a maritime employer that offers good health benefits and a pension plan that includes company contributions.

## *Employer Background*

Seaspan International Ltd. is one of Canada's largest and oldest marine transportation companies. Established in 1898, the company provides water transportation services, primarily for the forest products industry.

Seaspan transports logs, lumber, petroleum products, chemicals and pulp and paper products for mills along the West Coast. The company also transports limestone, aggregates, gypsum, steel components, railcars, prefabricated structures and general cargo. In addition, Seaspan provides ship docking and bunkering (fueling) services at Vancouver's main terminals. The company has 51 tug boats, over 200 barges and two self-propelled trainships, operating in waters from Alaska to Mexico.

Seaspan is a subsidiary of the Washington Marine Group, which consists of 15 separate companies that provide a range of marine services and equipment, from deep-sea transportation to ship building and repair. Washington Marine Group is in turn owned by Montana-based Washington Corporation. The parent company's other businesses include mining, construction, truck and rail transportation, communications, financial services and property management. The group has 48,000 employees in 38 countries.

**Workforce at a Glance:** Number of full-time employees: **1,652**. At this location: **664**. Worldwide: **1,664**. New jobs created in Canada in past year: **324**. Percentage of employees who are women: **6**. Of managers: **3**. Percentage of employees who are visible minorities: **6**. Resumes received by their human resources staff in past year: **1,482**. Average employee age: **45**. Car the president drives: **GMC Denali**. Where it's parked in the lot: **with everyone else**.

### *Physical Workplace* — *Rating: A*

Seaspan's physical workplace is rated as **above-average**. The recently renovated head office features great views of the surrounding mountains and harbour. (As part of the company's broader focus on employee health and safety, the renovations included the addition an impressive new fitness centre.)

**Physical Workplace at a Glance:** Their **onsite fitness facility** features: free memberships; treadmills; stationary bikes; stairmasters; rowing machines; weights; personal trainer; rehabilitation specialist; sauna; shower facilities. Their **employee lounge and rest areas** feature: comfortable couches; music; television; sleep room. For **food and refreshment**, Seaspan offers: free coffee and tea; outdoor eating area; barbeque. The company has an onsite cafeteria that features: subsidized meals (a turkey sandwich costs $4.00); healthy menu items; special diet menus. Nearby **amenities** include: variety of restaurants; major shopping mall; park/wilderness area (Mosquito Creek); recreation centre (Lonsdale Recreation Centre). For **commuters**, Seaspan offers: free onsite car parking; nearby public transit. Other **work area amenities** include: open-concept workstations; ergonomic workstation design; windows that open; a marine work environment that's straight from the movie "On the Waterfront".

### *Work Atmosphere & Social* — *Rating: B+*

Seaspan's work atmosphere is rated as **average**. Employees at Seaspan enjoy business casual dress daily and can listen to radio or music while they are working. The company hosts a number of social events for employees every year, including an employee Christmas party (with a separate event for employees' children), a summer golf tournament, and long service awards celebrations and retirement parties.

### *Health, Financial & Family Benefits* — *Rating: A*

Seaspan's health benefits plan is managed by Blue Cross and is rated as **above-average**. New employees must wait 30 days before they can enroll in the plan.

**Health Benefits at a Glance:** Seaspan's health plan includes the following coverage: dental (100% of eligible costs, with no annual maximum); orthodontics (60% of eligible costs with a lifetime maximum of $2,500); eyecare (to $250 every 2 years); extended health benefits; prescription drug; massage therapy; physiotherapy; alternative therapies; personal and family counselling; employee assistance plan (EAP) for substance abuse/mental health; wellness committee.

The company's salary and financial benefits are rated as **above-average**. To keep pay-levels competitive, Seaspan participates in outside salary surveys every 12 months. Individual salaries are reviewed every 12 months. The company operates a traditional pension plan where Seaspan makes a contribution equal to 5% of each employee's salary to their plan each year. **Financial Benefits at a Glance:** Seaspan provides a variety of financial benefits, including: discounted home Internet access; profit-sharing plan.

Seaspan's family-friendly benefits are rated as **average**. Employees with preschool children have access to a daycare facility located nearby. Other family-friendly benefits include: flexible start and finish hours; compressed work week (same hours, fewer days); telecommuting and working from home.

### *Vacation & Time Off* — *Rating: B+*

Seaspan's vacation and time off are rated as **average**. New employees receive 2 weeks of vacation allowance after their first year, which increases to 3 weeks after 2 years of service. The maximum vacation allowance is 6 weeks for long-serving employees. Employees at the company can also apply for unpaid leaves of absence.

### *Employee Communications* — *Rating: B+*

Seaspan's internal communications program is rated as **average**. To keep employees informed about new developments, Seaspan publishes an in-house newsletter (called *Wheelwash*). The company also has an intranet site, which keeps employees informed about news and human resource policies that affect their work.

### *Performance Management* — *Rating: B+*

Seaspan's performance management program is rated as **average**. The company operates a performance management program. Once a year, employees and managers meet for review sessions. Seaspan recognizes exceptional performance with company insignia merchandise and special barbeques.

### *Training & Skills Development* — *Rating: A*

Seaspan's training and skills development program is rated as **above-average**. The company provides tuition subsidies for courses related to an employee's current position (100% of tuition). Commendably, Seaspan also offers subsidies for courses not related to an employee's current job (50% of tuition). The company assists employees' career development with: reimbursement for professional association dues; in-house computer training.

### *Community Involvement* — *Rating: B+*

Seaspan's community involvement program is rated as **average**. A good corporate citizen, Seaspan actively supports a variety of local charitable initiatives. Employees take part in the selection of charitable groups assisted by the company. Employees at Seaspan receive paid time off to volunteer at local charities.

Last year the company supported the United Way, the British Columbia Children's Hospital Foundation, the Harvest Project (daily food donations), and local drives for food, clothing and gifts at Christmas and Easter. In a thoughtful initiative, the company also donates 25% of the revenues from its vending machines to a variety of local charities.

**SHELL CANADA LIMITED**
**400 - 4th Avenue SW**
**PO Box 100, Station M**
**Calgary, AB T2P 2H5**

**Tel. 403-691-3300**
**Fax 403-691-3350**
**questions.benefits@shell.ca**
**http://www.shell.ca**

**INDUSTRY: OIL & GAS EXTRACTION**

***Highlights:***

- Take part in an exceptional financial benefits plan that includes a host of attractive features, from generous pension contributions to a 5% discount on all your gas purchases.
- Build a career in the energy industry at an employer that's already looking beyond petroleum-based fuels at renewable sources of energy.
- Work for a community-spirited employer that ranks among the country's leading donors and incorporates environmental planning into its daily operations.

## *Employer Background*

Shell Canada Limited is one of the largest integrated petroleum companies in Canada. Established in 1911, Shell is one of the country's most profitable companies and operates through four main divisions.

The Resources division carries out exploration, production and marketing activities for crude oil, natural gas, natural gas liquids, sulphur and bitumen. The Oil Products division manufactures and sells refined petroleum products (familiar roadside Shell stations are part of this division). The Oil Sands division is active in Alberta's Athabasca region. Finally, the Corporate division is responsible for head office and administrative functions.

The company is a major partner in the Sable energy project off Nova Scotia and the Athabasca oil sands project, both of which generatie handsome returns for Shell. These projects represent two of the largest investments ever made in Canada's oil and gas industry and are a major part of Shell's strategy for future growth.

The company continues to invest heavily in its future — and the nation's energy prospects — with new natural gas exploration off Nova Scotia and in the Mackenzie Delta, Northwest Territories. Shell is also taking a leadership role in integrating environmental and business concerns through investments in the development of commercial wind power. Shell Canada is also the first major integrated oil and gas company in Canada to achieve ISO 14001 registration, the international standard for environmental management systems.

**Workforce at a Glance:** Number of full-time employees: **3,764**. At this location: **1,516**. New jobs created in Canada in past year: **95**. Percentage of employees who are women: **29**. Of managers: **22**. Percentage of employees who are visible minorities: **6**. Of managers: **3**. Average employee age: **43**.

### *Physical Workplace* *Rating: A*

Shell Canada's physical workplace is rated as **above-average**. The work environment at Shell varies with the company's diverse operations across the country. These operations include downtown office buildings, remote exploration sites and refineries. (Workplace safety is of primary importance at all work locations.) Shell also strives to accommodate the needs of employees with disabilities, adapting workstations, offices and equipment where necessary. Shell's head office in downtown Calgary is located in a modern office tower.

**Physical Workplace at a Glance:** Their **onsite fitness facility** features: subsidized memberships; treadmills; stationary bikes; stairmasters; rowing machines; weights; instructor led classes (pilates); personal trainer; indoor running track; shower facilities. For **food and refreshment**, Shell Canada offers: kitchen areas; free coffee and tea. Nearby **amenities** include: variety of restaurants; major shopping mall; local shops and services; park/wilderness area (Princess Island Park); recreation centre (YMCA). For **commuters**, Shell Canada offers: nearby public transit; secure bicycle parking. Other **work area amenities** include: open-concept workstations; ergonomic workstation design.

### *Work Atmosphere & Social* *Rating: A*

Shell Canada's work atmosphere is rated as **above-average**. Employees at Shell Canada enjoy business casual dress daily and can listen to radio or music while they are working. There is also a company-subsidized social committee, called the '*Chinook Club*', which has operated since 1953.

The social committee organizes a variety of recreational and social events for employees as well as discounts on tickets to special events. Across the company, Shell hosts a number of celebrations for employees, including awards banquets, dinners, lunches to celebrate group accomplishments, safety awards and Christmas parties.

With employees from a wide range of ethnic backgrounds, Shell is also an industry leader when it comes to workforce diversity. The company operates an extensive diversity awareness program across all its operating divisions.

### *Health, Financial & Family Benefits* *Rating: A*

Shell Canada's health benefits plan is managed by Clarica Life and is rated as **above-average**. Their health benefits plan is flexible, meaning that employees can tailor individual plans to their personal circumstances. Depending on the level of coverage selected, Shell Canada pays for 25% or 75% of the premiums associated with the plan, with employees paying the remainder. Full-time and part-time employees are covered by the plan. There is no waiting period before new employees are eligible for coverage.

The benefits plan also inclues a unique healthcare spending account (HCSA) to pay for expenses (such as acupuncturist's or chiropractor's fees) not covered under its regular benefit plan. At the beginning of each year, the company deposits $500 into each employee's HCSA, which can be used to pay nearly any health or medical expense incurred during the year.

**Health Benefits at a Glance:** Shell Canada's health plan includes the following coverage: dental (100% of eligible costs, with no annual maximum); orthodontics (60% of eligible costs with a lifetime maximum of $2,500); eyecare (to $200 every 2 years); extended health benefits; prescription drug; nutrition planning; massage therapy; physiotherapy; alternative therapies; personal and family counselling; employee assistance plan (EAP) for substance abuse/mental health.

The company's salary and financial benefits are rated as **exceptional**. To keep pay-levels competitive, Shell Canada participates in outside salary surveys every 12 months. Individual salaries are reviewed every 12 months. The company operates a traditional pension plan where Shell Canada makes a contribution equal to 4% of each employee's salary to their plan each year. Employees have the option of contributing up to 3% of their salary, which is then matched by an additional company contribution. Employees can choose from six investment funds in deciding where their pension funds are invested.

**Financial Benefits at a Glance:** Shell Canada provides an extensive set of financial benefits, including: life and disability insurance; discounted car leases; discounted company products (5% off gas purchases); discounted financial services through the Shell Credit Union; share purchase plan; year-end bonuses.

Shell Canada's family-friendly benefits are rated as **above-average**. Employees with pre-school children have access to a daycare facility located nearby. For employees who take maternity leave, Shell Canada provides a top-up to 100% of salary for the first 6 weeks of their leave. Other family-friendly benefits include: flexible start and finish hours; telecommuting and working from home; job sharing.

## *Vacation & Time Off* — *Rating: A*

Shell Canada's vacation and time off are rated as **above-average**. New employees receive 3 weeks of vacation allowance after their first year, which increases to 4 weeks after 10 years of service. The maximum vacation allowance is 6 weeks for long-serving employees. Employees at the company can also apply for unpaid leaves of absence. (Recently, one employee took a full year off to travel across Canada.)

## *Employee Communications* — *Rating: A+*

Shell Canada's internal communications program is rated as **exceptional**. To keep employees informed about new developments, Shell Canada publishes an in-house newsletter. The company also has an intranet site, which keeps employees informed about news and human resource policies that affect their work. An employee satisfaction survey is conducted every 12 months. An outside consultant compiles the survey results for Shell Canada's management team. Shell also publishes a variety of corporate publications and maintains an ombudsman office to ensure that workplace issues are resolved quickly and fairly.

## *Performance Management* — *Rating: A*

Shell Canada's performance management program is rated as **above-average**. The company operates a formal performance management program. Once a year, employees and managers meet for review sessions. (Managers receive training in how to conduct effective reviews.) Employees and managers are encouraged to meet informally throughout the year. Employees also have the opportunity to provide confidential feedback on their manager's performance through the annual employee survey.

The review results help to determine annual bonus payments, which are awarded to all regular employees. Employees can also nominate their co-workers (or deserving managers) for special recognition awards. These awards include restaurant dinners, special event tickets, chocolates and flowers, and even weekend getaways.

***Training & Skills Development*** ***Rating: A+***

Shell Canada's training and skills development program is rated as **exceptional**. The company provides tuition subsidies for courses related to an employee's current position (75% of tuition). Commendably, Shell Canada also offers subsidies for courses not related to an employee's current job (75% of tuition). The company assists employees' career development with: reimbursement for professional association dues; mentoring; career planning; in-house training.

Shell Canada also operates an interesting online career development service that is available on the company's intranet site. The service allows employees to view the qualifications and competencies required for other positions at the company. It then highlights the in-house training programs (or courses at outside institutions) needed to qualify for each position. Once employees have completed their training, the online program updates their individual profiles so they are considered for new career opportunities that arise.

***Community Involvement*** ***Rating: A+***

Shell Canada's community involvement program is rated as **exceptional**. An outstanding corporate citizen, Shell Canada actively supports a variety of local and national charitable initiatives. The company has a long history of contributing to charitable projects that make a difference in the communities where it operates. Designated as a caring company by the Canadian Centre for Philanthropy's "*Imagine*" program, Shell consistently ranks among the country's leading corporate donors. Employees at Shell Canada receive paid time off to volunteer at local charities.

The company's charitable program focuses on three areas: the environment, education and local community initiatives. Projects range from grassroots campaigns to high-profile environmental and educational initiatives. Shell has developed working partnerships with charitable organizations across the country, including the United Way, Red Cross, Nature Conservatory of Canada, National Aboriginal Achievement Foundation, Junior Achievement Foundation and numerous post-secondary institutions.

Shell has also endowed programs, such as the Shell Environmental Fund and the Community Service Fund, to let employees assist public service initiatives in their communities.

Sierra
New thinking.

**SIERRA SYSTEMS GROUP INC.**
**1177 West Hastings Street**
**Suite 2500**
**Vancouver, BC V6E 2K3**

**Tel. 604-688-1371**
**Fax 604-688-6482**
**vancouverrecruitment@sierrasystems.com**
**http://www.sierrasystems.com**

**INDUSTRY: INFORMATION TECHNOLOGY CONSULTING FIRMS**

*Highlights:*

- Get three weeks paid vacation allowance in your first year and flexible "personal days off" that let you take as much time off as you need — so long as your work gets done.
- Keep your West Coast zen intact with amazing free food — including smoked salmon, sushi, tapas, satay skewers — after this employer's monthly staff meeting.
- Exercise with your co-workers on sports and recreation teams — and get free company merchandise as a reward.
- Lose yourself in Vancouver's 1,000-acre Stanley Park, located just down the street from this employer.

## *Employer Background*

Sierra Systems Group Inc. provides information technology consulting services for customers in a wide range of industries. Founded in 1966, the Vancouver-based company serves businesses and governments across North America.

Sierra Systems specializes in the financial services, telecommunications, healthcare, justice, utilities and government sectors. The company works closely with many leading software companies, including Microsoft, Oracle, PeopleSoft and Sun Microsystems.

In addition to its Vancouver head office, Sierra has offices in Victoria, Calgary, Edmonton, Winnipeg, Toronto, Ottawa, Halifax and seven U.S. cities. Each branch has developed a specialized consulting practice to serve the unique needs of local clients.

The past few years have offered extraordinary career opportunities and growth at Sierra. Since becoming a publicly-traded company, Sierra has seen its annual revenues grow to over $129 million.

**Workforce at a Glance:** Number of full-time employees: **731**. At this location: **167**. Worldwide: **906**. New jobs created in Canada in past year: **85**. Percentage of employees who are women: **40**. Of managers: **22**. Percentage of employees who are visible minorities: **13**. Of managers: **5**. Resumes received by their human resources staff in past year: **2,100**. Weeks of vacation their HR manager took last year: **4**. Average employee age: **38**. Years longest-serving employee has worked there: **35**. Car the president drives: **2000 Audi A6**. Where it's parked in the lot: **with everyone else**.

### *Physical Workplace* — *Rating: A*

Sierra Systems' physical workplace is rated as **above-average**. The company's Vancouver head office occupies four floors of a modern office complex on the city's waterfront. With spectacular views of the harbour and coastal mountains, the head office is only a short walk from Vancouver's renowned Stanley Park.

> **Physical Workplace at a Glance:** Their **employee lounge and rest areas** feature: comfortable couches; great views (corner offices are reserved for meetings and relaxing). For **food and refreshment**, Sierra Systems offers: free snacks (including sushi, smoked salmon wine and beer at monthly meetings); free coffee and tea; outdoor eating area. Nearby **amenities** include: variety of restaurants; major shopping mall; fitness facility; local shops and services (on trendy Robson Street); park/wilderness area (Stanley Park). For **commuters**, Sierra Systems offers: nearby public transit; shoreline park with bicycle path; secure bicycle parking; shower facilities. Other **work area amenities** include: open-concept workstations; ergonomic workstation design; wireless connectivity throughout office; plant life that is tended professionally.

### *Work Atmosphere & Social* — *Rating: A*

Sierra Systems' work atmosphere is rated as **above-average**. Employees at Sierra Systems enjoy business casual dress daily and can listen to radio or music while they are working. There is also a company-subsidized social committee, which has operated since 1973.

The committee organizes a number of fun activities for employees, including beer and pizza nights, golf games, ultimate-frisbee tournaments, participation in Vancouver's "Grouse Grind" endurance race, dragonboat races and group outings to local sports events. The company encourages employees to participate in the various sporting activities by awarding Sierra clothing and merchandise to participants.

The company also sponsors a variety of events for employees during the year, including month-end meetings that are followed by informal social gatherings, a year-end Christmas dinner and dance (with a separate event for employees' children), summer barbeques and family picnics.

### *Health, Financial & Family Benefits* — *Rating: A*

Sierra Systems' health benefits plan is managed by Blue Cross and is rated as **above-average**. Full-time and part-time employees who work more than 22.5 hours per week are covered by the plan. New employees must wait 30 days before they can enroll in the plan.

> **Health Benefits at a Glance:** Sierra Systems' health plan includes the following coverage: dental (100% of eligible costs, with no annual maximum); orthodontics (50% of eligible costs with a lifetime maximum of $1,500); eyecare (to $250 every 2 years); extended health benefits; prescription drug; physiotherapy; massage therapy; alternative therapies; personal and family counselling; employee assistance plan (EAP) for substance abuse/mental health.

The company's salary and financial benefits are rated as **above-average**. To keep pay-levels competitive, Sierra Systems participates in outside salary surveys every 12 months. Individual salaries are reviewed every 12 months.

**Financial Benefits at a Glance:** Sierra Systems provides a variety of financial benefits, including: life and disability insurance; discounted car leases; discounted home computers; discounted home Internet access; share purchase plan; profit-sharing plan; referral bonuses for some employees (to $2,500); year-end bonuses.

Sierra Systems' family-friendly benefits are rated as **above-average**. Employees with pre-school children have access to a daycare facility located nearby. For employees who take maternity leave, Sierra Systems provides a top-up to 70% of salary for the first 6 weeks of their leave. Other family-friendly benefits include: flexible start and finish hours; shortened work week (fewer hours); compressed work week (same hours, fewer days); telecommuting and working from home.

### *Vacation & Time Off* — *Rating: A*

Sierra Systems' vacation and time off are rated as **above-average**. New employees receive 3 weeks of vacation allowance after their first year, which increases to 4 weeks after 5 years of service. The maximum vacation allowance is 5 weeks for long-serving employees. The company also has an enlightened personal days off program, which allows employees to take as many unpaid days off as they need, providing their work is complete. Employees at the company can also apply for unpaid leaves of absence. (Recently, one employee took a one-year leave of absence to trek around the world.)

### *Employee Communications* — *Rating: A+*

Sierra Systems' internal communications program is rated as **exceptional**. To keep employees informed about new developments, Sierra Systems publishes an in-house newsletter (called *Corporate Link*). The company also has a well-developed intranet site (called *Sierra Knowledge Net*), which keeps employees informed about news and human resource policies that affect their work. To solicit feedback from employees, the company operates an email suggestion box. An employee satisfaction survey is conducted every 36 months. An outside consultant compiles the survey results for Sierra Systems' management team. An extremely "flat" organization, Sierra has few managers and an open-door policy that extends all the way to the CEO. (It's not uncommon to see senior managers in the coffee room unloading the dishwasher.) The company president attends employee orientations to answer questions, share stories and have lunch with new employees. (Apart from senior managers, Sierra employees do not have titles.)

### *Performance Management* — *Rating: A*

Sierra Systems' performance management program is rated as **above-average**. The company operates a comprehensive performance management program. Once a year, employees and managers meet for review sessions. Sierra Systems uses a 360-degree feedback process to gather additional performance-related information from co-workers, supervisors and employees. The process allows employees to provide confidential feedback on their manager's performance. As part of the review process, employees participate in project reviews and ongoing feedback sessions. Sierra Systems recognizes exceptional performance with bonuses and non-monetary rewards, including restaurant dinners, spa certificates and ski weekends in Jasper.

### *Training & Skills Development* *Rating: A*

Sierra Systems' training and skills development program is rated as **above-average**. The company provides tuition subsidies for courses related to an employee's current position (100% of tuition). The company assists employees' career development with: reimbursement for professional association dues; career planning; mentoring; in-house training; online training. The company's online training program (called *Sierra Systems University*) includes a range of courses, from computer data modelling to people management skills.

### *Community Involvement* *Rating: A*

Sierra Systems' community involvement program is rated as **above-average**. A very good corporate citizen, Sierra Systems actively supports a variety of national charitable initiatives. Employees take part in the selection of charitable groups assisted by the company. Employees at Sierra Systems receive paid time off to volunteer at local charities. Last year, the company contributed to approximately 25 charitable groups, including: the United Way, AIDS Walk Canada, the Alzheimer's Foundation, the Audubon Society, the Canadian Cancer Society, the Canadian Breast Cancer Foundation, the Heart and Stroke Foundation, Junior Achievement, MS Mountain Bike Tour, Big Brothers and the United Way, to name a few.

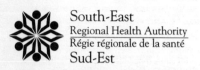

South-East
Regional Health Authority
Régie régionale de la santé
Sud-Est

**SOUTH-EAST REGIONAL HEALTH AUTHORITY**
**135 MacBeath Avenue**
**Moncton, NB E1C 6Z8**

**Tel. 506-857-5585**
**Fax 506-857-5590**
**hrapplications@serha.health.nb.ca**
**http://www.sehcc.org**

**INDUSTRY: HOSPITALS**

***Highlights:***

- Work for an enlightened Maritime employer that offers three weeks of paid vacation allowance for new employees, moving to four weeks after five years.
- Get excellent family-friendly benefits at this employer, including onsite daycare, generous maternity top-up (80% of salary for 17 weeks) and flexible work options.
- Develop yourself faster at an employer where managers are rated according to their ability to provide effective performance management reviews.

## *Employer Background*

South-East Regional Health Authority (SERHA) provides healthcare services to residents in southeastern New Brunswick. Established in 2002 as part of a major healthcare reorganization, SERHA manages one of 8 health regions in the province.

With roots dating back to 1895, Moncton-based SERHA operates 7 healthcare facilities. The Authority's 2,120 full- and part-time employees provide a complete range of healthcare services for patients who live in southeastern New Brunswick, Prince Edward Island and northwestern Nova Scotia.

SERHA is also an accredited teaching hospital, operating a family medicine residency program with Halifax's Dalhousie University. As a teaching hospital, SERHA has been responsible for many healthcare initiatives in the province, including the first MRI clinic as well as major investments in telehealth technology and information systems. Recently, the provincial government announced a $30 million investment for the development of new ambulatory care and laboratory facilities at SERHA.

**Workforce at a Glance:** Number of full-time employees: **1,495**. New jobs created in Canada in past year: **55**. Percentage of employees who are women: **83**. Of managers: **70**. Percentage of employees who are visible minorities: **1**. Of managers: **2**. Resumes received by their human resources staff in past year: **1,600**. Weeks of vacation their HR manager took last year: **6**. Average employee age: **42**. Years longest-serving employee has worked there: **39**. Car the president drives: **1999 Ford Explorer**. Where it's parked in the lot: **with everyone else**.

## *Physical Workplace* — *Rating: A*

SERHA's physical workplace is rated as **above-average**. The Authority's main location, The Moncton Hospital, has been continually developed since the first building was constructed in 1953. The latest addition was completed in 1989.

**Physical Workplace at a Glance:** Their **onsite fitness facility** features: subsidized memberships; treadmills; stationary bikes; stairmasters; weights; instructor-led classes; shower facilities. Their **employee lounge and rest areas** feature: comfortable couches; music; television; sleep room. For **food and refreshment**, SERHA offers: outdoor eating area; barbeque; kitchen areas; onsite Tim Hortons. The Authority has an onsite cafeteria that features: subsidized meals (a turkey sandwich costs $2.25); healthy menu items. Nearby **amenities** include: variety of restaurants; major shopping mall; fitness facility; golf course; park/wilderness area (Mapleton Park); recreation centre (at nearby University of Moncton). For **commuters**, SERHA offers: nearby public transit; subsidized car parking; secure bicycle parking. Other **work area amenities** include: ergonomic workstation design; open-concept workstations; windows that open; onsite ATM, hair salon and gift shop in the atrium; onsite library.

## *Work Atmosphere & Social* — *Rating: A*

SERHA's work atmosphere is rated as **above-average**. Employees at SERHA enjoy business casual dress daily and can listen to radio or music while they are working. There is also an Authority-subsidized social committee, which has operated since 1980.

Employees are treated to a variety of social events each year, including a Christmas dinner (served by managers), summer barbeques, an employee craft fair, awards celebrations for long-serving employees and an annual dinner for retiring employees.

## *Health, Financial & Family Benefits* — *Rating: B+*

SERHA's health benefits plan is rated as **average**. Full-time and part-time employees are covered by the plan.

**Health Benefits at a Glance:** SERHA's health plan includes the following coverage: dental; eyecare (to $140 every 2 years); extended health benefits; prescription drug; nutrition planning; massage therapy; physiotherapy; alternative therapies; personal and family counselling; employee assistance plan (EAP) for substance abuse/mental health.

The Authority's salary and financial benefits are rated as **average**. The Authority operates a traditional pension plan. **Financial Benefits at a Glance:** SERHA provides a variety of financial benefits, including: life and disability insurance; signing bonuses for some employees.

SERHA's family-friendly benefits are rated as **exceptional**. Employees with pre-school children have access to a subsidized daycare facility located onsite. The daycare facility has 75 spaces, employs 11 childcare workers and has a 12-month waiting list for new spaces. For employees who take maternity leave, SERHA provides a top-up to 80% of salary for the first 17 weeks of their leave. Other family-friendly benefits include: flexible start and finish hours; compressed work week (same hours, fewer days); telecommuting and working from home.

***Vacation & Time Off*** ***Rating: A***

SERHA's vacation and time off are rated as **above-average**. New employees receive 3 weeks of vacation allowance after their first year, which increases to 4 weeks after 5 years of service. The maximum vacation allowance is 6 weeks for long-serving employees. Employees can also take up to 3 paid personal days for educational purposes. Employees at the Authority can also apply for unpaid leaves of absence.

The Authority also operates an interesting deferred salary program, which allows employees to forego a portion of their salary in exchange for a paid sabbatical later. Sabatticals can extend to a year in length and offer excellent opportunities to travel abroad for work or pleasure.

***Employee Communications*** ***Rating: A***

SERHA's internal communications program is rated as **above-average**. To keep employees informed about new developments, SERHA publishes an in-house newsletter (called *Vital Signs*). The Authority also has an intranet site, which keeps employees informed about news and human resource policies that affect their work. To solicit feedback from employees, the Authority operates a traditional suggestion box program. An employee satisfaction survey is conducted every 24 months. An outside consultant compiles the survey results for SERHA's management team.

***Performance Management*** ***Rating: A***

SERHA's performance management program is rated as **above-average**. The Authority operates a well-designed performance management program. Once a year, employees and managers meet for review sessions. (Managers receive training in how to conduct effective reviews.) At the reviews, employees and managers work together to develop career and personal development plans with a focus on succession planning. Ongoing feedback is encouraged and employees have the opportunity to provide confidential feedback on their manager's performance. In their own reviews, managers are rated on their ability to effectively manage the review process.

***Training & Skills Development*** ***Rating: A+***

SERHA's training and skills development program is rated as **exceptional**. The Authority provides tuition subsidies for courses related to an employee's current position (100% of tuition). Commendably, SERHA also offers subsidies for courses not related to an employee's current job (50% of tuition). SERHA offers bonuses to employees who successfully complete certain professional accreditation programs and courses. The Authority assists employees' career development with: reimbursement for professional association dues; mentoring; career planning; in-house training. SERHA's extensive in-house training program offers a variety of courses, from computer software training to French language instruction.

***Community Involvement*** ***Rating: A***

SERHA's community involvement program is rated as **above-average**. A very good member of the community, SERHA actively supports a variety of charitable initiatives. Employees take part in the selection of charitable groups assisted by the Authority. Employees at SERHA receive paid time off to volunteer at local charities.

Beyond their role as care providers in the community, SERHA employees are active supporters and volunteers with numerous organizations, including the foundations for each of SERHA's hospitals, local United Way campaigns, the Alzheimer's Society and the Canadian Breast Cancer Foundation.

SPIELO MANUFACTURING INC.
328 Urquhart Avenue
Moncton, NB E1H 2R6

Tel. 506-859-7598
Fax 506-852-7640
jobs@spielo.com
http://www.spielo.com

INDUSTRY: OTHER MANUFACTURERS

*Highlights:*

- Build a career at a growing high-tech employer in the Maritimes that serves customers around the world and has been recognized for its stellar employment growth.
- Work in this employer's new state-of-the-art facility that offers everything from an onsite fitness facility to billiards and video games.
- Give back to your community by taking part in this employer's charitable program, which supports a variety of local charitable and artistic organizations.

## *Employer Background*

Spielo Manufacturing Inc. is a leading manufacturer of lottery and casino equipment. The company's products include video lottery terminals, central computers for gaming applications and high-tech slot machines. Founded in 1990, Spielo designs and manufactures this equipment for lottery operators and casinos across North America and Europe.

The Moncton-based company serves a fast growing market, which has led to rapid growth and more high-tech jobs in New Brunswick. (Spielo has been recognized by industry and the Government of Canada for its enviable record of creating employment.)

**Workforce at a Glance:** Number of full-time employees: **398**. At this location: **270**. Worldwide: **411**. New jobs created in Canada in past year: **127**. Percentage of employees who are women: **48**. Of managers: **14**. Resumes received by their human resources staff in past year: **5,000**. Average employee age: **32**.

## *Physical Workplace* — *Rating: A*

Spielo's physical workplace is rated as **above-average**. Located in a new industrial park, the company's modern head office and manufacturing facility is a 10 minute drive from the Moncton airport.

**Physical Workplace at a Glance:** Their **onsite fitness facility** features: free memberships; treadmills; stairmasters; weights; shower facilities. Their **employee lounge and rest areas** feature: comfortable couches; television; video games; pool table. For **food and refreshment**, Spielo offers: free coffee and tea; outdoor eating area. The company has an onsite cafeteria that features: healthy menu items. Nearby **amenities** include: variety of restaurants; major shopping mall; nearby walking and skiing trails. For **commuters**, Spielo offers: convenient highway access; free onsite car parking; nearby public transit. Other **work area amenities** include: open-concept workstations; ergonomic workstation design; static free flooring; plant life that is tended professionally.

## *Work Atmosphere & Social* — *Rating: B+*

Spielo's work atmosphere is rated as **average**. Employees at Spielo enjoy casual dress daily. On the last Thursday of every month, employees gather for complimentary treats such as donuts and cake. The company also hosts a summer family picnic and a Christmas party for employees every year. There is also a company-subsidized social committee.

## *Health, Financial & Family Benefits* — *Rating: B+*

Spielo's health benefits plan is managed by Blue Cross and is rated as **average**.

**Health Benefits at a Glance:** Spielo's health plan includes the following coverage: dental (80% of eligible costs, with no annual maximum); eyecare (to $125 every 2 years); extended health benefits; prescription drug; physiotherapy; massage therapy; alternative therapies; personal and family counselling; worldwide travel benefits.

The company's salary and financial benefits are rated as **average**. To keep pay-levels competitive, Spielo participates in outside salary surveys every 12 months. Individual salaries are reviewed every 12 months.

**Financial Benefits at a Glance:** Spielo provides a variety of financial benefits, including: life and disability insurance; profit-sharing plan; referral bonuses for some employees (to $500).

Spielo's family-friendly benefits are rated as **average**. Family-friendly benefits include: flexible start and finish hours; shortened work week (fewer hours).

## *Vacation & Time Off* — *Rating: B+*

Spielo's vacation and time off are rated as **average**. New employees receive 2 weeks of vacation allowance after their first year, which increases to 3 weeks after 4 years of service. The maximum vacation allowance is 5 weeks for long-serving employees. Employees at the company can also apply for unpaid leaves of absence.

## *Employee Communications* — *Rating: B+*

Spielo's internal communications program is rated as **average**. The company has an intranet site, which keeps employees informed about news and human resource policies that affect their work. Employees can also provide feedback and have questions answered through the intranet site.

## *Performance Management* — *Rating: B+*

Spielo's performance management program is rated as **average**. The company operates a formal performance management program. Every 6 months, employees and managers meet for review sessions.

***Training & Skills Development*** ***Rating: B+***

Spielo's training and skills development program is rated as **average**. The company provides tuition subsidies for courses related to an employee's current position. The company assists employees' career development with: reimbursement for professional association dues; in-house training.

***Community Involvement*** ***Rating: A***

Spielo's community involvement program is rated as **above-average**. A very good corporate citizen, Spielo actively supports a variety of local and national charitable initiatives. Employees take part in the selection of charitable groups assisted by the company.

During the Christmas season, the social committee organizes a variety of activities to raise money for families in need. Employees also manage the annual United Way campaign, which is the company's largest charitable initiative. Spielo also provided corporate donations to the Capital Theatre Foundation and several other local initiatives last year.

**STANDARD AERO LIMITED**
**33 Allen Dyne Road**
**Winnipeg, MB R3H 1A1**

**Tel. 204-775-9711**
**Fax 204-788-2333**
**human_resources@standardaero.ca**
**http://www.standardaero.ca**

**INDUSTRY: AIRCRAFT & AIRCRAFT PART MANUFACTURERS**

*Highlights:*

- Build a career at a stable Canadian company that's a world leader in the aerospace field, offering international career opportunities in cities around the world.
- Work for a benevolent employer where managers serve Christmas lunch each year and give a free turkey to every employee (over 1,400 last year).
- Have fun at an employer where the social commitee organizes an annual fishing derby, hockey teams, dragonboat races, baseball games and even curling matches.

## *Employer Background*

Standard Aero Limited provides gas turbine engine repair and overhaul services for the worldwide aerospace industry. The company services Pratt & Whitney Canada, Rolls-Royce, Honeywell and General Electric engines used in regional airlines, business and government fleets, military aircraft and a variety of industrial applications.

Established in 1938, Standard Aero is a subsidiary of Winnipeg-based Dunlop Standard Aerospace Group. As the world's largest independent engine repair company, Standard Aero serves customers in over 75 countries.

In addition to its head office and primary repair facility in Winnipeg, the company operates maintenance facilities in the United States, Mexico, Europe, Asia and Australia.

**Workforce at a Glance:** Number of full-time employees: **1,435**. At this location: **1,421**. Worldwide: **2,487**. New jobs created in Canada in past year: **17**. Percentage of employees who are women: **19**. Of managers: **13**. Percentage of employees who are visible minorities: **12**. Of managers: **4**. Resumes received by their human resources staff in past year: **6,000**. Average employee age: **38**. Years longest-serving employee has worked there: **42**.

## *Physical Workplace* — *Rating: A*

Standard Aero's physical workplace is rated as **above-average**. Located near Winnipeg International Airport, Standard Aero's head office complex consists of six separate buildings. Each building houses a specific business unit, with employees organized by function in each building. Technical personnel work in bright, immaculate shop areas and many administrative employees work in open offices within the shop areas.

**Physical Workplace at a Glance:** The company has an onsite cafeteria that features: subsidized meals (a turkey sandwich costs $1.75); healthy menu items; special diet menus. Nearby **amenities** include: variety of restaurants; major shopping mall; fitness facility; recreation centre. For **commuters**, Standard Aero offers: free onsite car parking; nearby public transit; secure bicycle parking. Other **work area amenities** include: windows that open; plant life that is tended professionally; employee lounge area with comfortable seating; onsite bank with ATM.

## *Work Atmosphere & Social* — *Rating: A+*

Standard Aero's work atmosphere is rated as **exceptional**. Employees at Standard Aero enjoy business casual dress daily and can listen to radio or music while they are working. There is also a company-subsidized social committee, called the '*Standard Aero Recreational Association / SARA*', which has operated since 1987.

The committee organizes a variety of social and sporting activities for employees, including an annual fishing derby, a walking and running club (employees collect rewards for distances covered over the year) as well as curling, baseball, hockey and dragon boat racing teams.

For Christmas, the company hosts a huge party with a formal four-course dinner and dancing for employees and their guests — over 2,100 people attended last year. The evening also includes generous door prizes — last year's prizes included a trip for two to anywhere in North America.

Prior to the holiday break, Standard Aero's executives serve a subsidized Christmas lunch in the company's cafeterias. In a unique gesture, the company distributes free Christmas turkeys to all employees (1,400 last year). The company also holds a huge Christmas party for employees' children (730 attended last year) and lets the kids decorate the company float in Winnipeg's Santa Claus parade.

Each summer, employees enjoy a family picnic at the city's leading water park. Employees and their children enjoy a full day of games and fun activities and a barbeque lunch — over 1,360 people attended last year.

## *Health, Financial & Family Benefits* — *Rating: B+*

Standard Aero's health benefits plan is managed by Blue Cross and is rated as **average**. New employees must wait 60 days before they can enroll in the plan.

**Health Benefits at a Glance:** Standard Aero's health plan includes the following coverage: dental (90% of eligible costs, to $1,000 each year); orthodontics (50% of eligible costs with a lifetime maximum of $2,000); eyecare; prescription drug; nutrition planning; physiotherapy; massage therapy; alternative therapies; personal and family counselling; employee assistance plan (EAP) for substance abuse/mental health.

The company's salary and financial benefits are rated as **above-average**. To keep pay-levels competitive, Standard Aero participates in outside salary surveys every 6 months. The company operates a traditional pension plan where

Standard Aero makes a contribution equal to 5% of each employee's salary to their plan each year.

> **Financial Benefits at a Glance:** Standard Aero provides a variety of financial benefits, including: life and disability insurance; discounted products and services from local companies (from jewelry to karate lessons); year-end bonuses (to $1,400 for non-executives).

Standard Aero's family-friendly benefits are rated as **average**. Employees with pre-school children have access to a daycare facility located nearby. Other family-friendly benefits include: flexible start and finish hours; shortened work week (fewer hours); compressed work week (same hours, fewer days).

***Vacation & Time Off*** ***Rating: B+***

Standard Aero's vacation and time off are rated as **average**. New employees receive 2 weeks of vacation allowance after their first year, which increases to 3 weeks after 3 years of service. The maximum vacation allowance is 4 weeks for long-serving employees. Employees at the company can also apply for unpaid leaves of absence.

***Employee Communications*** ***Rating: A+***

Standard Aero's internal communications program is rated as **exceptional**. To keep employees informed about new developments, Standard Aero publishes an in-house newsletter (called the *Standard Flyer*). The company also has an intranet site, which keeps employees informed about news and human resource policies that affect their work. To solicit feedback from employees, the company operates an email suggestion box program. For its retirees, the company publishes a special newsletter that addresses their concerns.

Standard Aero also hosts unique monthly meetings, called "*Beefs and Bouquets*". Each month, employees who celebrate birthdays that month join the president for a breakfast meeting, where problems are discussed and outstanding employee performance is recognized.

***Performance Management*** ***Rating: A***

Standard Aero's performance management program is rated as **above-average**. The company operates a formal performance management program. Once a year, employees and managers meet for review sessions. (Managers receive training in how to conduct effective reviews.) At the reviews, past performance is evaluated and future training and development plans are set. The annual reviews form the basis for salary increases.

***Training & Skills Development*** ***Rating: A***

Standard Aero's training and skills development program is rated as **above-average**. The company provides tuition subsidies for courses related to an employee's current position (100% of tuition). The company assists employees' career development with: reimbursement for professional association dues; mentoring; in-house training.

Standard Aero's in-house training program includes a variety of courses, from technical skills development to leadership training. The company also works closely with local technical schools to develop training programs for its employees (such as Red River College's gas turbine engine repair and overhaul program).

*Community Involvement* *Rating: A*

Standard Aero's community involvement program is rated as **above-average**. A very good corporate citizen, Standard Aero actively supports a variety of local and national charitable initiatives. Employees take part in the selection of charitable groups assisted by the company.

Last year, the company contributed to a number of charitable groups, including the United Way, the Children's Wish Foundation, Winnipeg Harvest and the Canadian Diabetes Association. Employees also volunteer (on company time) for the local Christmas Cheer Board, collecting non-perishable food items, clothing, toys and money for families in need.

Sun Life Financial

**SUN LIFE FINANCIAL SERVICES OF CANADA INC.**
**150 King Street West**
**Toronto, ON M5H 1J9**

**Tel. 416-408-7585**
**Fax 416-595-1587**
**http://www.sunlife.com**

**INDUSTRY: LIFE INSURANCE COMPANIES**

*Highlights:*

- Get three weeks paid vacation allowance in your first year — in addition to three paid personal days off each year to use as you wish.
- Get your tuition reimbursed by the company — even when you enroll in a course that's unrelated to your current position.
- Unclutter your life with a 20-minute telephone consultation with a company-paid "Life Coach", who helps correct work or personal issues affecting your life.
- Earn up to $2,500 in cash bonuses as a high-performing summer student.

## *Employer Background*

Sun Life Financial Services Company of Canada Inc. provides insurance and other financial services to customers across Canada and around the world.

Established in 1871, Sun Life Financial is one of the country's largest financial services companies. The publicly-traded company, which operates in Canada as the Sun Life Assurance Company, provides life insurance and a range of other financial services, including mutual funds, pension and savings plans, investment management services, group retirement plans and group health plans.

Last year, Sun Life acquired Waterloo, Ontario-based Clarica Life Insurance Company. The merger nearly doubled Sun Life's employee count in Canada and has made it one of Canada's largest insurance companies.

Sun Life has an extensive network of international offices, including the United States, the United Kingdom, Hong Kong, the Philippines, Japan, Indonesia, India and Bermuda. Last year, the company became the first foreign-owned life insurance company to operate in China through a partnership agreement with China Everbright Group.

In Canada, Sun Life serves over 7 million customers from offices in Vancouver, Edmonton, Waterloo, Toronto, Ottawa, Montréal and Moncton.

**Workforce at a Glance:** Number of full-time employees: **8,053**. Worldwide: **14,905**. Percentage of employees who are women: **73**. Of managers: **58**. Resumes received by their human resources staff in past year: **33,000**. Average employee age: **34**.

## *Physical Workplace* — *Rating: B+*

Sun Life's physical workplace is rated as **average**. The Toronto office operates as the company's international head office, while the Waterloo location is home to the company's Canadian operations.

In Toronto, Sun Life's office is located in a modern office tower in the downtown core. Employees have convenient access to public transit, as well as numerous restaurants, shops, services and entertainment options.

The Waterloo office is located in a funky 1970s-style renovated department store. Designed with employee feedback, the unique $42 million workplace offers outdoor barbeques, an on-site fitness centre, nearby walking trails and lots of free parking for commuters.

**Physical Workplace at a Glance:** Their **onsite fitness facility** features: subsidized memberships (Toronto and Waterloo). The company has an onsite cafeteria that features: subsidized meals (Waterloo). Nearby **amenities** include: park/wilderness area (Toronto's Harbourfront). For **commuters**, Sun Life offers: nearby public transit; transit subsidies (Waterloo and Ottawa); free onsite car parking (Waterloo); free shuttle bus for employees travelling between Toronto and Waterloo. Other **work area amenities** include: ergonomic workstation design; plant life that is tended professionally; open-concept workstations.

## *Work Atmosphere & Social* — *Rating: A*

Sun Life's work atmosphere is rated as **above-average**. Employees at Sun Life enjoy business casual dress daily and can listen to radio or music while they are working. The company has an on-site concierge service. (Concierge services are available in departments where employees have particularly heavy workloads.)

Employees across the company enjoy a variety of company-paid social events every year, including a Christmas party (with a separate children's party), and company-subsidized day at a local amusement park for employees and their families. The company sponsors employee teams in golf tournaments as well as local hockey, curling, softball, soccer and basketball leagues. Sun Life also celebrates company milestones, employee anniversaries and retirements throughout the year.

## *Health, Financial & Family Benefits* — *Rating: A*

Sun Life's health benefits plan is rated as **above-average**. Their health benefits plan is flexible, meaning that employees can tailor individual plans to their personal circumstances.

Employees can also book a free 20-minute telephone session with a "Life Coach", who can help sort out issues that are cluttering employees' work or personal lives. The Company's "Unclutter Your Life" initiative won a special award last year from an international coaching federation.

**Health Benefits at a Glance:** Sun Life's health plan includes the following coverage: dental (90% of eligible costs, with no annual maximum); orthodontics (50% of eligible costs with a lifetime maximum of $2,000); eyecare (to $150 every 2 years); prescription drug; extended health benefits; nutrition planning; massage therapy; physiotherapy; alternative therapies; personal and family counselling; employee assistance plan (EAP) for substance abuse/mental health; life coach and wellness consultant; blood pressure and flu shot clinics.

The company's salary and financial benefits are rated as **above-average**. To keep pay-levels competitive, Sun Life participates in outside salary surveys every 12 months. Individual salaries are reviewed every 12 months. The company operates a traditional pension plan where Sun Life makes a contribution equal to 1.5% of each employee's salary to their plan each year. (The company's pension plans are managed by Sun Life itself and its Clarica subsidiary.)

Sun Life also offers emergency loans (and grants) to employees facing financial hardship due to unforeseen personal circumstances.

**Financial Benefits at a Glance:** Sun Life provides a variety of financial benefits, including: life and disability insurance; share purchase plan; discounted home computers; cash bonuses for high-performing summer students (to $2,000); referral bonuses for some employees.

Sun Life's family-friendly benefits are rated as **above-average**. Employees with pre-school children have access to a daycare facility located nearby. For employees who take maternity leave, Sun Life provides a top-up to 100% of salary for the first 6 weeks of their leave. Other family-friendly benefits include: flexible start and finish hours; shortened work week (fewer hours); compressed work week (same hours, fewer days); telecommuting and working from home; reduced summer hours.

The company also has a fund that provides 80 scholarships to the children of employees ($2,000 each for up to 3 years) attending college or university.

### *Vacation & Time Off* — *Rating: A*

Sun Life's vacation and time off are rated as **above-average**. New employees receive 3 weeks of vacation allowance after their first year, which increases to 4 weeks after 10 years of service. The maximum vacation allowance is 5 weeks for long-serving employees. Employees at Sun Life also receive 3 paid personal days off each year, in addition to their regular vacation allowance. Employees at the company can also apply for unpaid leaves of absence.

### *Employee Communications* — *Rating: A*

Sun Life's internal communications program is rated as **above-average**. To keep employees informed about new developments, Sun Life publishes an in-house newsletter. The company also has a well-developed intranet site, which keeps employees informed about news and human resource policies that affect their work. To solicit feedback from employees, the company operates a traditional suggestion box program and an email suggestion box.

The company also hosts regular employee satisfaction surveys to gather additional employee feedback. Held at least every 12 months, the surveys address issues from business planning to individual career development.

### *Performance Management* — *Rating: B+*

Sun Life's performance management program is rated as **average**. The company operates a thorough performance management program. Every 6 months, employees and managers meet for review sessions. (Managers receive training in how to conduct effective reviews.) Employees also have the opportunity to provide confidential feedback on their manager's performance.

In addition to cash bonuses, Sun Life rewards excellent performance with dinner passes, theatre tickets and paid trips to conferences at resort locations. The company also has in-house reward programs to recognize individual and group accomplishments.

### *Training & Skills Development* — *Rating: A+*

Sun Life's training and skills development program is rated as **exceptional**. The company provides tuition subsidies for courses related to an employee's current position (100% of tuition). Commendably, Sun Life also offers subsidies for courses not related to an employee's current job (100% of tuition). Sun Life offers bonuses to employees who successfully complete certain professional accreditation programs and courses. The company assists employees' career development with: in-house training; online training; mentoring; career planning; reimbursement for professional association dues.

Sun Life also has training partnerships with leading academic institutions in Canada and the USA, enabling employees to attend prestigious graduate business programs (such as MBA degrees) at company expense. In addition, the company hosts "lunch and learn" sessions on a variety of interesting topics.

### *Community Involvement* — *Rating: A+*

Sun Life's community involvement program is rated as **exceptional**. An outstanding corporate citizen, Sun Life actively supports a variety of local and national charitable initiatives. Last year, the company also contributed to approximately 110 charitable groups, including: the United Way, Alzheimer Society of Canada, The Salvation Army, The New Brunswick Association for Community Living, Montréal Neurological Institute, Vancouver Community College, and The National Ballet of Canada, to name a few.

The company also encourages employee volunteerism. Employees who volunteer at least 50 hours annually receive a cheque for $750, which is donated to the charity of their choice.

Sun Life employees also operate community foundations across the country to raise money for local charities. Employees choose the organizations, organize events, volunteer and make contributions through payroll deductions.

SUNCOR ENERGY INC.
112 - 4th Avenue SW
PO Box 38
Calgary, AB T2P 2V5

Tel. 403-269-8100
Fax 403-269-6240
calgaryresumes@suncor.com
http://www.suncor.com

INDUSTRY: OIL & GAS EXTRACTION

*Highlights:*

- Get three weeks of paid vacation allowance in your first year at this employer — plus an astounding 17 paid personal days off each year!
- Build your career at a forward-thinking energy company that's a major investor in both oil sands technology and large-scale wind power generation projects.
- Invest in your children's future with an employer that awards an unlimited number of academic scholarships (to $1,800 each) each year to employees' children who attend college or university.

## *Employer Background*

Suncor Energy Inc. is a leading Canadian-based integrated energy company. Established in 1917 (as Sun Company Inc.), Suncor is one of the pioneering companies developing Alberta's vast oil sands. In 1967, the company opened the first commercially viable processing facility in the region. Today, the company produces more than 205,000 barrels of oil per day with plans to more than double production within the next decade.

In addition to its vast oil sands operations, Suncor is active in the exploration, development and marketing of natural gas. The company has also made significant investments in renewable energy, including an 11-megawatt wind power project in Saskatchewan (in partnership with Enbridge Inc.) and a planned 30-megawatt wind power project in southern Alberta that will provide enough energy for 13,000 homes.

Suncor also operates a major refinery in Sarnia, Ontario, and markets refined products to commercial and industrial customers across Ontario, Québec and the northeastern United States. The company also sells gasoline directly to consumers across Ontario through its familiar chain of Sunoco service stations. Recently, Suncor purchased a major refinery operation in Denver, Colorado, which includes distribution facilities and retail gas stations.

**Workforce at a Glance:** Number of full-time employees: **3,462**. Percentage of employees who are women: **19**. Of managers: **15**. Percentage of employees who are visible minorities: **7**. Of managers: **6**. Average employee age: **42**.

### *Physical Workplace* — *Rating: B+*

Suncor's physical workplace is rated as **average**. The downtown head office is located in a modern 28-storey building overlooking the Bow River. The building is connected to Calgary's enclosed walkway system, providing employees with all-weather access to local restaurants, stores and services.

> **Physical Workplace at a Glance:** For **food and refreshment**, Suncor offers: free coffee and tea; outdoor eating area. Nearby **amenities** include: popular Chinatown neighbourhood; local shops and services; variety of restaurants; park/wilderness area (Prince's Island Park). For **commuters**, Suncor offers: nearby public transit; secure bicycle parking; shower facilities and change rooms. Other **work area amenities** include: open-concept workstations; traditional offices; ergonomic workstation design; plant life that is tended professionally.

### *Work Atmosphere & Social* — *Rating: A*

Suncor's work atmosphere is rated as **above-average**. Employees at Suncor enjoy casual dress on Fridays and can listen to radio or music while they are working. There is also a company-subsidized social committee.

Each year, the company hosts an employee holiday party as well as a huge Christmas party for employees' children, which includes clowns, face-painting, fun activities and skating. Suncor also hosts a summer picnic, a family Calgary Stampede barbeque (which includes pony rides and live rodeo demonstrations), as well as employee golf, softball and hockey tournaments. The company also hosts lunches and special dinners to celebrate significant accomplishments and events.

### *Health, Financial & Family Benefits* — *Rating: B+*

Suncor's health benefits plan is rated as **average**. Full-time and part-time employees are covered by the plan.

> **Health Benefits at a Glance:** Suncor's health plan includes the following coverage: dental; orthodontics; extended health benefits; prescription drug; nutrition planning; massage therapy; physiotherapy; alternative therapies; personal and family counselling; employee assistance plan (EAP) for substance abuse/mental health.

The company's salary and financial benefits are rated as **average**. To keep pay-levels competitive, Suncor participates in outside salary surveys every 12 months. Individual salaries are reviewed every 12 months. The company operates a traditional pension plan. **Financial Benefits at a Glance:** Suncor provides a variety of financial benefits, including: life and disability insurance; share purchase plan; year-end bonuses.

Suncor's family-friendly benefits are rated as **above-average**. For employees who take maternity leave, Suncor provides a top-up to 100% of salary for the first 6 weeks of their leave. (Fort McMurray employees receive daycare subsidies, while Toronto employees have access to a subsidized onsite daycare facility.) Other family-friendly benefits include: flexible start and finish hours; telecommuting and working from home.

To help offset rising tuition costs, Suncor awards an unlimited number of academic scholarships (to $1,800 each) each year to employees' children for post-secondary studies. These scholarships are renewable for up to 4 years.

### *Vacation & Time Off* — *Rating: A+*

Suncor's vacation and time off are rated as **exceptional**. New employees receive 3 weeks of vacation allowance after their first year, which increases to 4 weeks after 10 years of service. The maximum vacation allowance is 6 weeks for long-serving employees. Employees at Suncor also receive 17 paid personal days off each year, in addition to their regular vacation allowance. Depending on an employee's location, these popular personal days are scheduled by the company (Fort McMurray), scheduled by the employee and the company (Calgary), or flexible for employees to schedule as needed (Ontario). Employees at the company can also apply for unpaid leaves of absence.

### *Employee Communications* — *Rating: A*

Suncor's internal communications program is rated as **above-average**. To keep employees informed about new developments, Suncor publishes an in-house newsletter (called *Spectrum*), which is available online to all employees. The company also has an intranet site (called *SunNet*), which keeps employees informed about news and human resource policies that affect their work. To solicit feedback from employees, the company operates an email suggestion box. An employee satisfaction survey is conducted by having employees complete an online questionnaire every 24 months. An outside consultant compiles the survey results for Suncor's management team.

### *Performance Management* — *Rating: A*

Suncor's performance management program is rated as **above-average**. The company operates a comprehensive performance management program. Once a year, employees and managers meet for review sessions. (Managers receive training in how to conduct effective reviews.) Employees and managers review past performance and set personal development goals for the upcoming year. Managers also provide ongoing coaching and host informal mid-year progress reviews. The review process forms the basis for annual bonuses and salary increases. Employees also have the opportunity to provide confidential feedback on their manager's performance.

### *Training & Skills Development* — *Rating: A*

Suncor's training and skills development program is rated as **above-average**. The company provides tuition subsidies for courses related to an employee's current position (100% of tuition). The company assists employees' career development with: reimbursement for professional association dues; career planning.

### *Community Involvement* — *Rating: A+*

Suncor's community involvement program is rated as **exceptional**. An outstanding corporate citizen, Suncor actively supports a variety of local and national charitable initiatives. A member of the Canadian Centre for Philanthropy's "*Imagine*" program, Suncor donates at least 1% of its pre-tax profits to charities through its own foundation. Last year, the company contributed to approximately 265 charitable groups.

Through its foundation, the company matches charitable donations by its employees and retirees. Suncor also operates a unique bereavement fund, which makes charitable donations on behalf of employees mourning the loss of a family member.

Suncor also supports a unique program in Calgary that connects employees with community organizations that need volunteers. Through this program, head office employees donated over 2,500 hours of volunteer time last year — a 25% increase over the previous year.

In another program, Sunoco retailers (as part of their franchise agreement with Suncor) agree to provide a minimum of 100 volunteer hours in their respective communities. Like several forward-thinking employers in this book, Sunoco has found a way to ensure that its employees and franchisees take an active role in their communities.

**TDL GROUP LTD., THE**
**874 Sinclair Road**
**Oakville, ON L6K 2Y1**

**Tel. 905-845-6511**
**Fax 905-845-0265**
**tdlgroup_hr@timhortons.com**
**http://www.timhortons.com**

Tim Hortons®

**INDUSTRY: RESTAURANTS & FOODSERVICE**

*Highlights:*

- Build your career at a growing employer that's taking its successful Canadian track record and expanding into the United States.
- Work for an employer that operates one of the most successful charitable programs in this book, a highly focused initiative that leverages the resources of employees, franchisees and customers to send over 9,000 underprivileged children to camp every summer.
- Develop yourself with an employer that provides exceptional training and continuous learning opportunities for its own employees — and the employees of its franchisees.

*Employer Background*

The TDL Group Ltd. operates Tim Hortons restaurants, which is Canada's largest casual food chain. Founded in 1964, the Tim Hortons restaurant chain has over 2,200 locations in Canada and now over 160 locations in the United States. Amazingly, Tim Hortons is larger than McDonald's in Canada and sells over two-thirds of the coffee and donuts sold in Canada. The company has annual revenues of $1.7 billion and continues to expand across Canada and the United States.

In 1995, Tim Hortons was purchased by Ohio-based Wendy's International, Inc. While the two companies continue to operate as separate entities, they have been successful in developing combination restaurants in Canada and the United States. Tim Hortons is now focusing on expansion into the U.S. market. (The new division is one of the brightest growth areas in the Wendy's group.)

Because its stores are franchised and locally owned, TDL's role is to provide operational and marketing support to franchisees. In addition to its Oakville head office, the company has regional offices in Langley (British Columbia), Calgary, Kingston, Montréal and Debert (Nova Scotia). TDL's U.S. head office is located in Columbus, Ohio.

**Workforce at a Glance:** Number of full-time employees: **1,012**. At this location: **715**. Worldwide: **1,096**. New jobs created in Canada in past year: **37**. Percentage of employees who are women: **33**. Of managers: **44**. Resumes received by their human resources staff in past year: **16,000**.

***Physical Workplace*** ***Rating: A***

TDL's physical workplace is rated as **above-average**. The company's Oakville head office features a recently redesigned lunch area and an outdoor patio complete with barbeques. In addition, the head office and the Calgary regional office have onsite fitness facilities. (Employees at other locations receive healthclub subsidies.)

> **Physical Workplace at a Glance:** Their **onsite fitness facility** features: subsidized memberships; treadmills; stationary bikes; stairmasters; weights; raquetball court; instructor-led classes; shower facilities. For **food and refreshment**, TDL offers: free coffee and tea; outdoor eating area; barbeque; kitchen area. Nearby **amenities** include: variety of restaurants; major shopping mall; park/wilderness area (Oakdale Park); recreation centre (Glen Abbey Recreation Centre). For **commuters**, TDL offers: nearby public transit; free onsite car parking. Other **work area amenities** include: open-concept workstations; ergonomic workstation design; access to natural light for all employees; sleep room.

***Work Atmosphere & Social*** ***Rating: B+***

TDL's work atmosphere is rated as **average**. Every year, the company hosts an employee Christmas party and a holiday skating party for employees' children. Last year the company also hosted a grand opening celebration for its new children's summer camp in Kentucky.

***Health, Financial & Family Benefits*** ***Rating: A***

TDL's health benefits plan is managed by Manulife Financial and is rated as **above-average**. TDL pays 100% of the premiums associated with the plan.

> **Health Benefits at a Glance:** TDL's health plan includes the following coverage: dental (90% of eligible costs, to $1,500 each year); orthodontics (50% of eligible costs with a lifetime maximum of $2,000); eyecare (to $250 every 2 years); extended health benefits; prescription drug; massage therapy; physiotherapy; personal and family counselling; employee assistance plan (EAP) for substance abuse/mental health.

The company's salary and financial benefits are rated as **above-average**. To keep pay-levels competitive, TDL participates in outside salary surveys every 12 months. Individual salaries are reviewed every 12 months. The company operates a traditional pension plan where TDL makes a contribution equal to 4% of each employee's salary to their plan each year.

> **Financial Benefits at a Glance:** TDL provides a variety of financial benefits, including: life and disability insurance; discounted company products; referral bonuses for some employees (from $200 to $1,000); year-end bonuses.

TDL's family-friendly benefits are rated as **above-average**. Employees with pre-school children have access to a daycare facility located nearby. For employees who take maternity leave, TDL provides a top-up to 70% of salary for the first 6 weeks of their leave. Other family-friendly benefits include: telecommuting and working from home; flexible start and finish hours.

*Vacation & Time Off* — *Rating: B+*

TDL's vacation and time off are rated as **average**. New employees receive 2 weeks of vacation allowance after their first year, which increases to 3 weeks after 3 years of service. The maximum vacation allowance is 5 weeks for long-serving employees.

*Employee Communications* — *Rating: A*

TDL's internal communications program is rated as **above-average**. To keep employees informed about new developments, TDL publishes an in-house newsletter (called *Coffee Talk*). TDL also publishes a corporate newsletter and a quarterly newsletter for franchisees. An employee advisory committee meets quarterly to address employee issues and highlight new initiatives. In addition, senior management attend regular meetings with employees at the corporate office, where they are free to raise issues of concern.

*Performance Management* — *Rating: A*

TDL's performance management program is rated as **above-average**. The company operates a comprehensive performance management program. Once a year, employees and managers meet for review sessions. (Managers receive training in how to conduct effective reviews.) At the reviews, employees and managers set performance goals for the upcoming year. Managers provide ongoing feedback throughout the year. Employees can provide confidential feedback on their manager's performance directly to the vice president of their department. TDL recognizes exceptional performance with salary increases, bonuses and share options.

*Training & Skills Development* — *Rating: A+*

TDL's training and skills development program is rated as **exceptional**. The company provides tuition subsidies for courses related to an employee's current position (90% of tuition). Commendably, TDL also offers subsidies for courses not related to an employee's current job (90% of tuition). The company assists employees' career development with: reimbursement for professional association dues; career planning; in-house training. TDL's in-house training program includes a variety of courses, from interviewing skills to employment law.

The company also operates a unique training centre that includes classrooms and a fully operational Tim Hortons store. New franchisees and many TDL staff take an intensive eight-week program that emphasizes food hygiene, employee relations, equipment maintenance and in-store security.

*Community Involvement* — *Rating: A+*

TDL's community involvement program is rated as **exceptional**. An outstanding corporate citizen, TDL actively supports a variety of charitable initiatives. Across Canada, the company supports community events, professional sports teams, the Canadian Cycling Association and children's "Timbit" sports teams

— over 100,000 children participate in hockey, soccer, curling, lacrosse, football and baseball leagues.

Canadians who have enjoyed the occasional coffee or donut at Tim Hortons will be familiar with the company's primary charitable focus, the Tim Horton Children's Foundation. Every summer, the Foundation sends more than 9,000 underprivileged children to camp. Franchisees work with schools, churches, local agencies and organizations to select deserving children from their communities. There are 6 summer camps, located in Alberta, Ontario (two camps), Québec, Nova Scotia and Kentucky. Many of the children attend camps in other regions so they can travel in a plane to other regions.

Funding for the summer camps is provided by TDL, franchisees, customers (who donate through the familiar counter coin boxes) and special fundraising events. These include the annual "Camp Day" event in which 100% of coffee sales from across the chain for one day are donated to the Foundation.

The company's focused charitable program provides two constructive lessons for other organizations interested in improving their community involvement. First, it is almost always better to focus charitable resources on a single, well-run program where your funds can have a significant impact. And second, never underestimate the leverage a company can use to motivate employees, suppliers, franchisees and customers to help with a cause.

**TELVENT CANADA LTD.**
**10333 Southport Road SW**
**Calgary, AB T2W 3X6**

**Tel. 403-253-8848**
**Fax 403-212-3459**
**careers.canada@telvent.abengoa.com**
**http://www.telventcanada.com**

# TELVENT

**INDUSTRY: MEASUREMENT & CONTROL EQUIPMENT MANUFACTURERS**

*Highlights:*

- Work at an employer with one of the most active social calendars in this book, with activities that include snowboarding, whitewater rafting, spelunking, wine tasting and gourmet cooking.
- Get extra time off to enjoy the precious Canadian summer with this employer's innovative "long weekend" policy — employees can take one Friday off in June and work half-days on Fridays in July and August.
- Work at the only employer in this book with its own brand of specialty beer, served to employees each Friday afternoon.

## *Employer Background*

Telvent Canada Ltd. (formerly Metso Automation SCADA Solutions Ltd.) manufactures automation control, information management and simulation systems for oil and gas, electric and water utility industries around the world.

The Calgary-based company is North America's leading supplier of process, information management and simulation systems for oil and gas, electric and water utility applications. In addition to customized software and networking tools, Telvent provides conventional data gathering and remote monitoring equipment to these industries.

Telvent's technology can be found in some of the world's largest heavy industry projects. The company has over 500 installations worldwide serving some of the world's largest energy companies, including TransCanda Pipelines, Alberta Energy Company, Chevron, Saudi Aramco, Edison Gas of Italy, Rio Light Brazil and Petrobas Brazil, to name a few.

Recently, Telvent became the information technology subsidiary of Madrid-based Abengoa Corporation. Established in 1941, the Spanish parent company has operations in 40 countries. In addition to its Calgary head office, Telvent has offices in Houston, Baltimore and Ankara, Turkey.

**Workforce at a Glance:** Number of full-time employees: **318**. Worldwide: **10,000**. New jobs created in Canada in past year: **3**. Percentage of employees who are women: **27**. Of managers: **20**. Percentage of employees who are visible minorities: **33**. Of managers: **25**. Resumes received by their human resources staff in past year: **1,800**. Average employee age: **37**. Years longest-serving employee has worked there: **24**. Person you should get to know first: **Debbie in reception will strive to pronounce your name correctly over the public address system**. Car the president drives: **2003 Hummer**. Where it's parked in the lot: **only one spot in the garage is big enough**.

### *Physical Workplace* — *Rating: A+*

Telvent's physical workplace is rated as **exceptional**. Located 20 kilometres south of downtown Calgary, the head office features large windows facing an indoor atrium, allowing pleasant views throughout the office. The cafeteria includes a patio that also serves as a meeting area and entertainment venue for employee gatherings.

**Physical Workplace at a Glance:** Their **onsite fitness facility** features: free memberships; treadmills; stationary bikes; stairmasters; rowing machines; weights; elliptical trainer; exercise balls; shower facilities. Their **employee lounge and rest areas** feature: music; pool table; foosball; board games. For **food and refreshment**, Telvent offers: their own specialty beer (brewed by Calgary's Big Rock Brewery); free soft drinks; free coffee and tea. The company has an onsite cafeteria that features: healthy menu items. Nearby **amenities** include: variety of restaurants; major shopping mall; park/wilderness area (Glenmore Reservoir Park); recreation centre (Calgary YMCA South). For **commuters**, Telvent offers: free onsite car parking; subsidized underground parking; convenient highway access. Other **work area amenities** include: private offices that open onto large staging areas for meetings; ergonomic workstation design; plant life that is tended professionally; fresh flowers delivered weekly.

### *Work Atmosphere & Social* — *Rating: A+*

Telvent's work atmosphere is rated as **exceptional**. Employees at Telvent enjoy casual dress daily and can listen to radio or music while they are working. There is also a company-subsidized social committee, which has operated since 1986.

The club organizes a variety of events throughout the year, including the popular Valentine "*Beatnik Bash*" (featuring a 10-piece employee jazz band and awards for the best beatnik poetry), excursions to Calgary hockey and football games, ski trips, theatre nights and even a "Survivor" contest. The club also sends cards and flowers to recognize events that are important in employees' lives, such as marriages and new babies.

In addition, the company hosts a summer picnic for employees' families, a Calgary Stampede luncheon, a Christmas party (with a separate party for employees' children) and ad hoc parties to celebrate new product launches, such as last year's event at the Calgary Science Centre.

Telvent subsidizes several employee sports activities, including hockey, soccer, curling, basketball, jogging and table tennis. The company also sponsors an employee team in Calgary's annual "*Corporate Challenge*" and hosts numerous team-building exercises each year, including snowboarding, whitewater rafting, spelunking, wine tasting, gourmet cooking and potluck lunches.

### *Health, Financial & Family Benefits* — *Rating: A+*

Telvent's health benefits plan is managed by Great-West Life and is rated as **exceptional**. Telvent pays 100% of the premiums associated with the plan. There is no waiting period before new employees are eligible for coverage.

**Health Benefits at a Glance:** Telvent's health plan includes the following coverage: dental (100% of eligible costs, to $1,500 each year); orthodontics (50% of eligible costs with a lifetime maximum of $2,000); eyecare (to $175 every 2 years); extended health benefits; prescription drug; massage therapy; physiotherapy; alternative therapies; personal and family counselling; employee assistance plan (EAP) for substance abuse/mental health.

The company's salary and financial benefits are rated as **exceptional**. To keep pay-levels competitive, Telvent participates in outside salary surveys every 12 months. Individual salaries are reviewed every 12 months. The company offers a group RSP that allows employees to contribute up to 4.25% of their salary, with matching employer contributions.

**Financial Benefits at a Glance:** Telvent provides an extensive set of financial benefits, including: life and disability insurance; discounts at local shops and restaurants; annual in-house computer auction; profit-sharing plan; signing bonuses for some employees; referral bonuses for some employees (from $250 to $1,000); year-end bonuses (from $150 to $17,000 for non-executives).

Telvent's family-friendly benefits are rated as **above-average**. For employees who take maternity leave, Telvent provides a top-up to 60% of salary for the first 6 weeks of their leave. Other family-friendly benefits include: flexible start and finish hours; shortened work week (fewer hours); compressed work week (same hours, fewer days); telecommuting and working from home.

### *Vacation & Time Off* — *Rating: A*

Telvent's vacation and time off are rated as **above-average**. New employees receive 3 weeks of vacation allowance after their first year, which increases to 4 weeks after 10 years of service. The maximum vacation allowance is 5 weeks for long-serving employees. Employees at the company can also apply for unpaid leaves of absence.

Telvent introduced two unique initiatives last year to provide employees with extra time off in the summer — employees now receive an extra long weekend in June and work half-days on Fridays in July and August.

### *Employee Communications* — *Rating: A+*

Telvent's internal communications program is rated as **exceptional**. To keep employees informed about new developments, Telvent publishes an in-house newsletter (called *The Scoop*), which even features restaurant reviews and employee classified ads. The company also has an intranet site, which keeps employees informed about news and human resource policies that affect their work. To solicit feedback from employees, the company operates a traditional suggestion box program and an email suggestion box. An employee satisfaction survey is conducted by having employees complete an online questionnaire every 12 months. An outside consultant compiles the survey results for Telvent's management team.

### *Performance Management* — *Rating: A*

Telvent's performance management program is rated as **above-average**. The company operates a comprehensive performance management program. Once a year, employees and managers meet for review sessions. (Managers receive training in how to conduct effective reviews.) At the reviews, employees and managers discuss past progress and work together to set training objectives for the upcoming year. Telvent recognizes exceptional performance with cash payments ($250 to $5,000), restaurant dinners, golf clubs, Palm Pilots, Calgary Stampeder football tickets, gift certificates and days at the spa.

*Training & Skills Development* *Rating: A+*

Telvent's training and skills development program is rated as **exceptional**. The company provides tuition subsidies for courses related to an employee's current position (100% of tuition). The company assists employees' career development with: reimbursement for professional association dues; career planning; mentoring; leadership development program; in-house training.

As part of its in-house training program, Telvent has academic partnerships with the University of Calgary and the Southern Alberta Institute of Technology (SAIT), which provide customized training programs to Telvent employees. The company also offers financial awards to employees who publish articles in technical and trade magazines.

*Community Involvement* *Rating: B+*

Telvent's community involvement program is rated as **average**. A good corporate citizen, Telvent actively supports a variety of local and national charitable initiatives. Employees take part in the selection of charitable groups assisted by the company.

Last year the company contributed to a variety of charitable initiatives, including the United Way, the Canadian Cancer Society, local food bank drives and the annual Take Our Kids to Work Day.

**TERANET INC.**
**1 Adelaide Street East**
**Suite 600**
**Toronto, ON M5C 2V9**

**Tel. 416-360-8863**
**Fax 416-360-1687**
**info@teranet.ca**
**http://www.teranet.ca**

# TERANET

**INDUSTRY: INFORMATION TECHNOLOGY CONSULTING FIRMS**

*Highlights:*

- Work for a stable high-tech employer in a growing industry — providing government services electronically, from land registration to parking ticket administration.
- Get three weeks of paid vacation allowance in your first year and extra time off on your 5th, 10th and 15th anniversaries with the company.
- Take advantage of a generous benefits package that includes cash referral bonuses (to $2,000).

## *Employer Background*

Teranet Inc. provides electronic land registration and related information systems for public-sector clients. Founded in 1991, Teranet was formed as a joint venture between the Government of Ontario and a consortium of private-sector companies headed by Teramira Holdings Inc. (Last year, Teramira purchased the Government of Ontario's share in the partnership.)

The company was originally formed to take on the huge task of creating an electronic land registration system for Ontario. The company successfully transformed an archaic 200 year-old paper filing system into an accessible and streamlined electronic information system.

The first of its kind in Canada, the new system enables individuals, lawyers and financial institutions to access land information quickly and remotely, instead of sifting through mountains of paper at local land registry offices. In addition to attracting widespread industry attention, Teranet's impressive accomplishment has led to the development of unique skills and expertise in managing large-scale information technology projects. The company has quickly evolved into a specialized information technology company serving the needs of government, business and professional organizations.

Some of Teranet's recent projects include: a web-based parking ticket payment system for municipalities developed with the Royal Bank of Canada; a web portal for the exchange of legal information, supplies and services with the Law Society of Upper Canada; and an online geographic information service for municipalities and utilities.

In addition to its Toronto head office, Teranet has offices in London and Chatham, Ontario.

**Workforce at a Glance:** Number of full-time employees: **861**. At this location: **310**. New jobs created in Canada in past year: **94**. Percentage of employees who are women: **58**. Of managers: **42**. Percentage of employees who are visible minorities: **37**. Of managers: **15**. Resumes received by their human resources staff in past year: **3,000**. Average employee age: **37**. Person you should get to know first: **Laura in Mapping Production supplies lots of treats for her co-workers.**

## *Physical Workplace* — *Rating: B+*

Teranet's physical workplace is rated as **average**. Their head office is located in a modern office tower in the heart of downtown Toronto. The building is connected to the city's underground walking network, which provides all-weather access to the subway and numerous entertainment attractions, including the theatre district and major sporting events.

**Physical Workplace at a Glance:** Their **employee lounge and rest areas** feature: sleep room; comfortable seating in the reception area. For **food and refreshment**, Teranet offers: free coffee and tea. Nearby **amenities** include: fitness facility (with subsidized memberships); variety of restaurants; major shopping mall; park/wilderness area (St. James Park). For **commuters**, Teranet offers: nearby public transit; secure bicycle parking. Other **work area amenities** include: open-concept workstations; ergonomic workstation design; access to natural light for all employees.

## *Work Atmosphere & Social* — *Rating: A*

Teranet's work atmosphere is rated as **above-average**. Employees at Teranet enjoy business casual dress daily and can listen to radio or music while they are working. There is also a company-subsidized social committee, called the '*Social Work Group*', which has operated since 1991.

The social committee organizes fun monthly events for employees and their families, including pub nights, miniature golf, indoor beach volleyball, bowling, go-kart racing, skating and hiking. Employees also enjoy a number of annual events, including a winter holiday celebration, a summer family picnic, and golf and baseball tournaments.

## *Health, Financial & Family Benefits* — *Rating: A*

Teranet's health benefits plan is managed by Desjardins Financial and is rated as **above-average**. There is no waiting period before new employees are eligible for coverage.

**Health Benefits at a Glance:** Teranet's health plan includes the following coverage: dental (100% of eligible costs, to $1,500 each year); orthodontics (50% of eligible costs with a lifetime maximum of $2,000); eyecare (to $300 every 2 years); extended health benefits; prescription drug; nutrition planning; massage therapy; physiotherapy; personal and family counselling; employee assistance plan (EAP) for substance abuse/mental health.

The company's salary and financial benefits are rated as **above-average**. The company operates a traditional pension plan where Teranet makes a contribution equal to 5% of each employee's salary to their plan each year.

**Financial Benefits at a Glance:** Teranet provides a variety of financial benefits, including: life and disability insurance; low-interest home loans; profit-sharing plan; referral bonuses for some employees (to $2,000).

Teranet's family-friendly benefits are rated as **above-average**. For employees who take maternity leave, Teranet provides a generous top-up to 93% of salary for the first 17 weeks of their leave. Other family-friendly benefits include: flexible start and finish hours; compressed work week (same hours, fewer days); telecommuting and working from home.

### *Vacation & Time Off* — *Rating: A*

Teranet's vacation and time off are rated as **above-average**. New employees receive 3 weeks of vacation allowance after their first year, which increases to 4 weeks after 10 years of service. The maximum vacation allowance is 6 weeks for long-serving employees. Employees at Teranet also receive 2 paid personal days off each year, in addition to their regular vacation allowance. In addition, employees celebrating five years on the job receive a bonus week of vacation. Employees celebrating ten years receive two extra weeks. Employees at the company can also apply for unpaid leaves of absence. (Recently, one employee took a six month leave to care for an elderly parent.)

### *Employee Communications* — *Rating: A*

Teranet's internal communications program is rated as **above-average**. The company has an intranet site, which keeps employees informed about news and human resource policies that affect their work. To solicit feedback from employees, the company operates a traditional suggestion box program. An in-house employee satisfaction survey is conducted every 6 months. The company's in-house surveys includes focus groups, simple question-and-answer emails and formal satisfaction surveys. A recent example includes an employee survey that sought feedback about the company's office location prior to its lease renewal. The results showed that employees wanted to remain in the downtown core.

### *Performance Management* — *Rating: A*

Teranet's performance management program is rated as **above-average**. The company operates a formal performance management program. Once a year, employees and managers meet for review sessions. (Managers receive training in how to conduct effective reviews.) Managers also have access to a custom-designed software application that helps them manage the process. At the reviews, past performance is reviewed and new training goals are set for the upcoming year.

### *Training & Skills Development* — *Rating: A*

Teranet's training and skills development program is rated as **above-average**. The company provides tuition subsidies for courses related to an employee's current position (100% of tuition). Commendably, Teranet also offers subsidies for courses not related to an employee's current job. The company assists employees' career development with: reimbursement for professional association dues; career planning; in-house training; online training. Teranet's popular online learning program includes over 80 professional development courses that employees can access anytime through the company's intranet.

***Community Involvement*** ***Rating: A***

Teranet's community involvement program is rated as **above-average**. A very good corporate citizen, Teranet actively supports a variety of local and national charitable initiatives. Employees take part in the selection of charitable groups assisted by the company. Employees at Teranet receive paid time off (2 days each year) to volunteer at local charities. Last year, the company contributed to approximately 20 charitable groups, including: the United Way, the Canadian Diabetes Association, Operation Christmas Child (toys for children in need worldwide), Operation Springboard, Reach for the Rainbow, the Raptors Foundation, the Justin Eves Foundation (for learning disabled youth) and Assumption University in Windsor.

**TORONTO TRANSIT COMMISSION**
**1900 Yonge Street**
**Toronto, ON M4S 1Z2**

**Tel. 416-393-4000**
**Fax 416-397-8307**
**jobs@ttc.ca**
**http://www.ttc.ca**

**INDUSTRY: LOCAL TRANSIT SYSTEMS**

*Highlights:*

- Build your career at a reinvigorated public-sector employer that's embarking on an ambitious 10 year expansion program supported by all levels of government.
- Work for the only employer in this book that gives you a free ride to work.
- Make a difference in your community with an employer that uses its unique position to help charities reach out to millions of people every year.

*Employer Background*

The Toronto Transit Commission operates Canada's largest public transit system, offering subway, bus and light rail transit transportation. Like the city it serves, the TTC is a 24-hour operation. Established in 1921, the system includes an underground subway system, buses, streetcars and the Wheel-Trans division for persons with disabilities.

The TTC is a critical component of Toronto's infrastructure and contributes to the economic well being of the entire region. Over the past decade, the TTC has moved aggressively to keep fares low, improve service and keep the system one of the safest in the world.

In the past few years, the TTC has embarked on a major program of expansion and modernization. The Commission recently opened the new Sheppard subway line, which connects the system to residential areas in the city's northeast. In partnership with all levels of government, the Commission recently released its growth strategy for the coming decade, which includes new subway construction and expanded streetcar and bus right-of-ways.

These investments will ensure that the TTC continues to attract more riders to the system — in addition to the over 400 million passengers carried every year — and create new jobs.

**Workforce at a Glance:** Number of full-time employees: **10,165**. New jobs created in Canada in past year: **212**. Percentage of employees who are women: **12**. Of managers: **13**. Percentage of employees who are visible minorities: **21**. Resumes received by their human resources staff in past year: **14,500**. Average employee age: **45**.

### *Physical Workplace* — *Rating: B+*

TTC's physical workplace is rated as **average**. The TTC's operational employees work in a range of environments, from subway cars to maintenance yards. In all cases, the focus on safety is paramount. (Over the past few years, the TTC has received safety awards from the American Public Transportation Association and the Canadian Urban Transportation Association.) The Commission's recent safety and expansion initiatives have resulted in a considerable increase in the size of its information technology and systems group. At the TTC's head office, employees work in a professional setting with traditional offices and modern workstations.

**Physical Workplace at a Glance:** Nearby **amenities** include: variety of restaurants; major shopping mall; fitness facility. For **commuters**, TTC offers: nearby public transit; free transit; secure bicycle parking; subsidized car parking.

### *Work Atmosphere & Social* — *Rating: A*

TTC's work atmosphere is rated as **above-average**. Employees at TTC enjoy business casual dress daily. There is also a Commission-subsidized social committee, called the '*TTC Recreation Council*'.

The social committee organizes a variety of sporting events throughout the year, including baseball, soccer and basketball team. The TTC also has its own all-star hockey team. The team competes against the NHL old-timers every year to raise money for charity — last year's game raised over $45,000 for the MS Society.

The TTC also hosts several employee recognition events every year, including a long-service reception, a safety dinner and dance, and a special reception to recognize employees for excellent performance.

### *Health, Financial & Family Benefits* — *Rating: A*

TTC's health benefits plan is managed by Great-West Life and is rated as **above-average**. There is no waiting period before new employees are eligible for coverage.

**Health Benefits at a Glance:** TTC's health plan includes the following coverage: dental (100% of eligible costs, with no annual maximum); orthodontics (50% of eligible costs); eyecare (to $250 every 2 years); prescription drug; extended health benefits; massage therapy; physiotherapy; personal and family counselling; employee assistance plan (EAP) for substance abuse/mental health.

The Commission's salary and financial benefits are rated as **average**. To keep pay-levels competitive, TTC participates in outside salary surveys every 12 months. Individual salaries are reviewed every 12 months. The Commission operates a traditional pension plan. **Financial Benefits at a Glance:** TTC provides a variety of financial benefits, including: life and disability insurance.

TTC's family-friendly benefits are rated as **above-average**. Employees with pre-school children have access to a daycare facility located nearby. For employees who take maternity leave, TTC provides a top-up to 75% of salary for the first 17 weeks of their leave.

### *Vacation & Time Off* — *Rating: B+*

TTC's vacation and time off are rated as **average**. New employees receive 2 weeks of vacation allowance after their first year, which increases to 3 weeks after 2 years of service. The maximum vacation allowance is 6 weeks for long-serving employees. Employees at TTC also receive 2 paid personal days off each year, in addition to their regular vacation allowance. Employees at the Commission can also apply for unpaid leaves of absence.

### *Employee Communications* — *Rating: A*

TTC's internal communications program is rated as **above-average**. To keep employees informed about new developments, TTC publishes an in-house newsletter (called *Coupler*), which is available online and mailed to employees and retirees.

### *Performance Management* — *Rating: B+*

TTC's performance management program is rated as **average**. The Commission operates a formal performance management program. Once a year, employees and managers meet for review sessions. (Managers receive training in how to conduct effective reviews.)

### *Training & Skills Development* — *Rating: A*

TTC's training and skills development program is rated as **above-average**. The Commission provides tuition subsidies for courses related to an employee's current position (100% of tuition). Commendably, TTC also offers subsidies for courses not related to an employee's current job (50% of tuition). The Commission assists employees' career development with: reimbursement for professional association dues; career planning; in-house training.

The TTC's extensive in-house training program offers a variety of courses, from conflict resolution to first-aid to computer training. The Commission also works closely with the Ministry of Education to provide community college courses at its training facilities.

### *Community Involvement* — *Rating: A*

TTC's community involvement program is rated as **above-average**. A very good member of the community, TTC actively supports a variety of local and national charitable initiatives.

With millions of riders passing through its system every year, the TTC uses its unique position to assist charities with fundraising through various subway events, such as the Canadian Cancer Society's Daffodil Campaign.

Many TTC employees also take leading roles in raising money for charitable organizations. Last year, employees participated in Toronto's annual United Way campaign, raising over $950,000 for the charity last year.

Trillium HEALTH CENTRE

**TRILLIUM HEALTH CENTRE**
**100 Queensway West**
**Mississauga, ON L5B 1B8**

**Tel. 905-848-7100**
**Fax 905-804-7901**
**careers@thc.on.ca**
**http://www.trilliumhealthcentre.org**

**INDUSTRY: HOSPITALS**

***Highlights:***

- Take advantage of excellent maternity benefits at this employer — an outstanding 85% top-up for the first 25 weeks of your leave!
- Get equal treatment as a part-time worker at this employer — full benefits (which can be traded for more pay) and guaranteed minimum hours are just two of the benefits part-time employees enjoy here.
- Take a leave from your current job at this employer to "try out" another in-house position (or even a job with another employer) — then return to your old job if the new one doesn't work out as planned.

## *Employer Background*

Trillium Health Centre is a major healthcare facility, serving one of Canada's fastest-growing regions. Through its two main hospitals (Mississauga Hospital and Queensway General), Trillium Health Centre has been serving the rapidly growing populations of Peel Region and western Toronto since 1956.

Formed in 1998, the Centre provides a comprehensive range of acute care and selected tertiary services. Trillium also operates chronic and continuing care facilities in partnership with Extendicare Canada Inc.

With over 3,740 full- and part-time employees, Trillium is one of the few hospitals to build new facilities in recent years, including an advanced cardiac centre and emergency department. Recently, health information centres were opened at both hospital sites, providing employees and patients with literature, videos, CD-ROMs and access to online services in the comfort of a library setting. Trillium also operates a care facility for sexual assault victims in partnership with Peel Regional Police and a regional stroke program.

In redeveloping its Queensway site, Trillium significantly expanded the hospital's outpatient department, which now includes a surgical centre, a women's breast centre, an eyecare centre and psychiatric day services. The $70-million project has been designed with staff and patients in mind. With lots of natural lighting, the new facility offers more space for employees and patients, large waiting areas and sleep-over rooms for guests.

**Workforce at a Glance:** Number of full-time employees: **2,028**. New jobs created in Canada in past year: **71**. Percentage of employees who are women: **87**. Of managers:

**83**. Resumes received by their human resources staff in past year: **38,250**. Average employee age: **41.5**. Years longest-serving employee has worked there: **42**.

## *Physical Workplace* *Rating: A*

Trillium's physical workplace is rated as **above-average**. The Mississauga site features a small grocery store with a pharmacy and a clinic offering esthetic and massage services. The Centre operates a shuttle service between its Queensway and Mississauga sites.

**Physical Workplace at a Glance:** Their **employee lounge and rest areas** feature: comfortable couches; music; meditation or religious observance room; sleep room; aquarium. For **food and refreshment**, Trillium offers: outdoor eating area; barbeque; Tim Hortons coffee shop. The Centre has an onsite cafeteria that features: subsidized meals (a turkey sandwich costs $3.29); healthy menu items. Nearby **amenities** include: variety of restaurants; major shopping mall; fitness facility; park/wilderness area (Port Credit). For **commuters**, Trillium offers: nearby public transit; convenient highway access. Other **work area amenities** include: traditional nursing stations; open-concept workstations; ergonomic workstation design; windows that open; bank machines.

## *Work Atmosphere & Social* *Rating: B+*

Trillium's work atmosphere is rated as **average**. Employees at Trillium enjoy business casual dress daily. Throughout the year, the Centre hosts a variety of social events for employees, including tea parties and dinners to acknowledge long-serving staff, employee Christmas parties, summer barbeques and special events to recognize significant accomplishments.

## *Health, Financial & Family Benefits* *Rating: A*

Trillium's health benefits plan is managed by Sun Life and is rated as **above-average**. Full-time and part-time employees are covered by the plan. New employees must wait 90 days before they can enroll in the plan. Trillium's health plan also covers employees in their retirement.

Trillium's benefits plan is available to both full- and part-time employees. It is unique in that part-timers can opt out and receive cash payments instead. Trillium also provides a commendable "guaranteed hours" program for part-time employees, providing them with a stable, predictable income.

**Health Benefits at a Glance:** Trillium's health plan includes the following coverage: dental; orthodontics (50% of eligible costs with a lifetime maximum of $1,000); eyecare (to $200 every 2 years); extended health benefits; prescription drug; massage therapy; physiotherapy; employee assistance plan (EAP) for substance abuse/mental health.

The Centre's salary and financial benefits are rated as **average**. To keep pay-levels competitive, Trillium participates in outside salary surveys every 6 months. Individual salaries are reviewed every 6 months. The Centre operates a traditional pension plan.

**Financial Benefits at a Glance:** Trillium provides a variety of financial benefits, including: life and disability insurance; referral bonuses for some employees (from $100 to $2,500).

Trillium's family-friendly benefits are rated as **above-average**. For employees who take maternity leave, Trillium provides a generous top-up to 84% of salary for the first 25 weeks of their leave. Other family-friendly benefits include: flexible start and finish hours.

***Vacation & Time Off*** **_Rating: B+_**

Trillium's vacation and time off are rated as **average**. New employees receive 2 weeks of vacation allowance after their first year, which increases to 3 weeks after 2 years of service. The maximum vacation allowance is 6 weeks for long-serving employees. Employees at Trillium also receive 2 paid personal days off each year, in addition to their regular vacation allowance. (These days give employees from various religious and ethnic backgrounds time off for their holidays.) Employees at the Centre can also apply for unpaid leaves of absence.

***Employee Communications*** **_Rating: A_**

Trillium's internal communications program is rated as **above-average**. To keep employees informed about new developments, Trillium publishes an in-house newsletter (called *Connecting*). The Centre also has an intranet site, which keeps employees informed about news and human resource policies that affect their work. An employee satisfaction survey is conducted every 24 months. An outside consultant compiles the survey results for Trillium's management team.

***Performance Management*** **_Rating: A_**

Trillium's performance management program is rated as **above-average**. The Centre operates a formal performance management program. Once a year, employees and managers meet for review sessions. (Managers receive training in how to conduct effective reviews.) At the meetings, managers and employees review past performance and set objectives for the upcoming year.

As part of Trillium's nursing staff review process, each hospital solicits additional feedback from senior managers and co-workers. Managers also receive similar reviews from their supervisors and peers.

***Training & Skills Development*** **_Rating: A_**

Trillium's training and skills development program is rated as **above-average**. The Centre provides tuition subsidies for courses related to an employee's current position. The Centre assists employees' career development with: in-house training.

For those pursuing full-time studies, Trillium offers paid leaves of absence for some educational programs (such as advanced nursing certifications) and bursaries (to $5,000) for employees completing health-related studies. Employees can also apply for unpaid leaves of absence to pursue other studies or "try out" new employment opportunities.

***Community Involvement*** **_Rating: A_**

Trillium's community involvement program is rated as **above-average**. A very good member of the community, Trillium actively supports a variety of charitable initiatives. The Centre supports healthcare-related organizations by making its facilities available each month for fundraising efforts. Trillium also hosts renowned speakers in the healthcare field to present community lectures on new developments in healthcare.

To help offset rising tuition costs, Trillium also provides 10 annual post-secondary scholarships ($1,000 each) to employees' children.

L'UNION CANADIENNE
COMPAGNIE D'ASSURANCES

**L'UNION CANADIENNE, COMPAGNIE D'ASSURANCES**
**2475, boulevard Laurier**
**Sillery, QC G1T 1C4**

**Tel. 418-651-3551**
**Fax 418-650-4713**
**http://www.unioncanadienne.com**

**INDUSTRY: LIFE INSURANCE COMPANIES**

*Highlights:*

- Work for an employer that's a leader in its field — in a city that leads the nation in "Old World" charm.
- Get automatic salary increases at this employer when you complete certain academic programs and professional accreditations.
- Become fluent in French and English at this employer and get a $1,200 bonus.

## *Employer Background*

L'Union Canadienne, Compagnie d'Assurances provides personal and commercial insurance products and services to customers throughout Québec. The company serves customers through a network of independent brokers across the province.

Established in 1943, L'Union Canadienne is a subsidiary of Guelph, Ontario-based The Co-operators Group Limited. The parent company is one of Canada's largest general insurance companies, with over $4.9 billion in assets under management. The Québec-based subsidiary had revenues of over $206 million last year.

**Workforce at a Glance:** Number of full-time employees: **321**. New jobs created in Canada in past year: **24**. Percentage of employees who are women: **74**. Of managers: **59**. Percentage of employees who are visible minorities: **37**. Resumes received by their human resources staff in past year: **1,000**. Weeks of vacation their HR manager took last year: **4**. Average employee age: **41**. Years longest-serving employee has worked there: **38**. Car the president drives: **2003 BMW**. Where it's parked in the lot: **with everyone else**.

## *Physical Workplace* — *Rating: A*

L'Union Canadienne's physical workplace is rated as **above-average**. The company's head office is located in beautiful Québec City. Living in one of Canada's most popular tourist destinations, employees enjoy great events throughout the year as well as easy access to ski resorts, golf courses, swimming and even ice canoeing during in the winter.

As part of their recent head office renovation, L'Union employees were asked to provide feedback on the design and selected furniture and accessories for the employee lounge. Employees received a budget to design their own lounge area, complete with TV, music, billiards and an outdoor patio.

**Physical Workplace at a Glance:** Their **employee lounge and rest areas** feature: pool table; television; music; board games; massage room; comfortable couches. For **food and refreshment**, L'Union Canadienne offers: outdoor eating area; barbeque. Nearby **amenities** include: variety of restaurants; major shopping mall; fitness facility; Laval University; park/wilderness area (Plaines d'Abraham); recreation centre (Les Galeries de la Capitale). For **commuters**, L'Union Canadienne offers: nearby public transit; secure bicycle parking; subsidized car parking. Other **work area amenities** include: open-concept workstations; ergonomic workstation design; wireless connectivity throughout office; plant life that is tended professionally.

## *Work Atmosphere & Social* — *Rating: B+*

L'Union Canadienne's work atmosphere is rated as **average**. The company-subsidized social committee organizes events throughout the year. Every fall, L'Union Canadienne brings employees together for a day of fun activities and an evening dinner and dance. In addition, the company provides paid weekend getaways to teams of employees in recognition of exceptional work.

## *Health, Financial & Family Benefits* — *Rating: A*

L'Union Canadienne's health benefits plan is managed by Co-operators Life and is rated as **above-average**. Full-time and part-time employees who work more than 20 hours per week are covered by the plan. There is no waiting period before new employees are eligible for coverage.

**Health Benefits at a Glance:** L'Union Canadienne's health plan includes the following coverage: dental (80% of eligible costs, to $2,500 each year); orthodontics (50% of eligible costs with a lifetime maximum of $2,500); prescription drug; extended health benefits; nutrition planning; massage therapy; physiotherapy; alternative therapies; personal and family counselling.

The company's salary and financial benefits are rated as **exceptional**. To keep pay-levels competitive, L'Union Canadienne participates in outside salary surveys every 6 months. Individual salaries are reviewed every 12 months. The company operates a traditional pension plan where L'Union Canadienne makes a contribution equal to 6.5% of each employee's salary to their plan each year.

L'Union Canadienne offers a unique bonus ($1,200 annually) to employees fluent in both French and English. In addition, travelling employees who choose to fly economy class (instead of business class) can split the savings with the company or invite their spouse or a friend who flies for free — the company pays for the extra ticket.

**Financial Benefits at a Glance:** L'Union Canadienne provides an extensive set of financial benefits, including: life and disability insurance; subsidized auto insurance; subsidized home insurance; profit-sharing plan; performance bonuses; referral bonuses for some employees (to $1,500).

L'Union Canadienne's family-friendly benefits are rated as **above-average**. For employees who take maternity leave, L'Union Canadienne provides a top-up to 100% of salary for the first 6 weeks of their leave. Other family-friendly benefits include: daycare subsidies; flexible start and finish hours; shortened work week (fewer hours); compressed work week (same hours, fewer days).

### *Vacation & Time Off* — *Rating: A*

L'Union Canadienne's vacation and time off are rated as **above-average**. New employees receive 3 weeks of vacation allowance after their first year, which increases to 4 weeks after 10 years of service. The maximum vacation allowance is 6 weeks for long-serving employees. Employees at L'Union Canadienne also receive 3 paid personal days off each year, in addition to their regular vacation allowance.

### *Employee Communications* — *Rating: A*

L'Union Canadienne's internal communications program is rated as **above-average**. To keep employees informed about new developments, L'Union Canadienne publishes an in-house newsletter (called *Le Trait d'union*). The company also has an intranet site, which keeps employees informed about news and human resource policies that affect their work. To solicit feedback from employees, the company operates an email suggestion box. An employee satisfaction survey is conducted by email every 36 months. An outside consultant compiles the survey results for L'Union Canadienne's management team.

### *Performance Management* — *Rating: A*

L'Union Canadienne's performance management program is rated as **above-average**. The company operates a formal performance management program. Once a year, employees and managers meet for review sessions. (Managers receive training in how to conduct effective reviews.) Employees can also provide confidential feedback on their managers' performance to the human resources department. The review process forms the basis for salary increases.

### *Training & Skills Development* — *Rating: A*

L'Union Canadienne's training and skills development program is rated as **above-average**. The company provides tuition subsidies for courses related to an employee's current position (100% of tuition). The company assists employees' career development with: in-house training; reimbursement for professional association dues. Employees who complete particular academic programs and professional accreditations receive automatic salary increases.

### *Community Involvement* — *Rating: A*

L'Union Canadienne's community involvement program is rated as **above-average**. A very good corporate citizen, L'Union Canadienne actively supports a variety of local and national charitable initiatives. Employees take part in the selection of charitable groups assisted by the company. Employees at L'Union Canadienne receive paid time off (1 day each year) to volunteer at local charities.

Employees also volunteer their time to raise money for selected charities and the company follows with matching contributions. In the past, employees have organized fundraising activities for the United Way, the Breast Cancer Foundation, the Canadian Cancer Society and a local children's hospital.

**UNIVERSITY HEALTH NETWORK / UHN**
**190 Elizabeth Street**
**R. Fraser Elliott Building**
**Toronto, ON M5G 2C4**

**Tel. 416-340-3388**
**Fax 416-340-4948**
**uhn.info@uhn.on.ca**
**http://www.uhn.on.ca**

University Health Network
Toronto General Hospital Toronto Western Hospital Princess Margaret Hospital

**INDUSTRY: HOSPITALS**

***Highlights:***

- Work for a healthcare employer with a stellar work environment, including nursing relaxation lounges, a sushi bar and one of the best onsite fitness centres in this book — all the result of employee involvement in their planning process.
- Improve your work-life balance at an employer with onsite daycare, excellent maternity top-up (75% of salary for 25 weeks) and a range of alternative work arrangements.
- Take the anxiety out of your next review at an employer that completely redesigned its annual review process to be more predictable and participatory as a result of extensive employee consultation.

## *Employer Background*

UHN is Canada's largest academic health sciences centre, operating three major hospitals in downtown Toronto. With roots dating back to 1812, the group includes Toronto General Hospital, Toronto Western Hospital and Princess Margaret Hospital. UHN also has a unique partnership with Toronto Medical Laboratories, a private-public sector partnership that provides laboratory services.

UHN is a large employer, with 9,358 full- and part-time employees, 520 physicians and 1,000 volunteers providing care for over 850,000 patients each year. As a major teaching hospital, UHN provides clinical education for 40% of the medical students at the University of Toronto. In addition, the group is one of the country's leading research institutions, spending $100 million on medical research every year.

UHN has built major new facilities over the past few years, including the spectacular new R. Fraser Elliot building at its Toronto General Hospital site and a new wing at Toronto Western Hospital. UHN also established several new healthcare programs last year, including a telehealth initiative to assist patients living in Northern Ontario and a patient education centre to help individuals manage their own recovery programs.

**Workforce at a Glance:** Number of full-time employees: **6,666**. New jobs created in Canada in past year: **207**. Percentage of employees who are women: **76**. Of managers: **55**. Percentage of employees who are visible minorities: **65**. Of managers: **19**. Resumes received by their human resources staff in past year: **25,000**. Weeks of vacation their HR manager took last year: **3**. Average employee age: **41**. Years longest-serving employee has worked there: **46**. Person you should get to know first: **Betty, the Head of OR is an exceptional role model for new nurses (and is fun to be around)**. Car the president drives: **Acura 3.2TL**. Where it's parked in the lot: **with everyone else**.

## *Physical Workplace* — *Rating: A+*

UHN's physical workplace is rated as **exceptional**. The administrative head office is located at the Toronto General Hospital site in the new R. Fraser Elliot Building. The downtown location is near other major hospitals, as well as the University of Toronto and some of the city's most vibrant and livable communities.

**Physical Workplace at a Glance:** Their **onsite fitness facility** features: subsidized memberships; extended hours of operation (always open); treadmills; stationary bikes; stairmasters; rowing machines; weights; basketball court; instructor-led classes; personal trainer and fitness assessment; swimming pool (with scuba lessons); squash and tennis courts; shower facilities; onsite salon and spa; onsite massage therapy clinic. Their **employee lounge and rest areas** feature: comfortable couches; music; television; nursing library with internet access. For **food and refreshment**, UHN offers: outdoor eating area; barbeque; onsite food court (with Tim Hortons, Second Cup, Sushi Bar, Subway, etc.). The group has an onsite cafeteria that features: healthy menu items; special diet menus. Nearby **amenities** include: variety of restaurants; local shops and services; Art Gallery of Ontario; Royal Ontario Museum; park/wilderness area (Queen's Park); recreation centre (Scadding Court Recreation Centre). For **commuters**, UHN offers: nearby public transit; secure bicycle parking; subsidized car parking. Other **work area amenities** include: open-concept workstations; traditional offices; teaching classrooms; access to natural light for all employees; ergonomic workstation design; plant life that is tended professionally.

## *Work Atmosphere & Social* — *Rating: A*

UHN's work atmosphere is rated as **above-average**. Employees at UHN enjoy business casual dress daily and can listen to radio or music while they are working. The group has an on-site concierge service.

Throughout the year, the UHN hosts a variety of social events, including themed parties (such as last year's "*Strawberry Social*" and "*Brazil Night*"), an annual pancake breakfast (served by senior managers), volunteer recognition events, employee length-of-service celebrations and parties to celebrate major holidays.

UHN also operates a unique diversity program that actively promotes a work environment that reflects the unique perspectives and cultural identities of its diverse urban workforce.

## *Health, Financial & Family Benefits* — *Rating: A*

UHN's health benefits plan is managed by Clarica Life and is rated as **above-average**. There is no waiting period before new employees are eligible for coverage.

**Health Benefits at a Glance:** UHN's health plan includes the following coverage: dental (100% of eligible costs, with no annual maximum); eyecare (to $90 every 2 years); extended health benefits; prescription drug; nutrition planning; massage therapy; physiotherapy; alternative therapies; personal and family counselling; employee assistance plan (EAP) for substance abuse/mental health.

The group's salary and financial benefits are rated as **above-average**. To keep pay-levels competitive, UHN participates in outside salary surveys every 12 months. Individual salaries are reviewed every 12 months. The group operates a traditional pension plan, where it matches 125% of employee contributions to the plan.

**Financial Benefits at a Glance:** UHN provides a variety of financial benefits, including: life and disability insurance; discounted products and services (travel, leisure, health and financial services); discounted home computers.

UHN's family-friendly benefits are rated as **exceptional**. Employees with preschool children have access to a subsidized daycare facility located onsite. The daycare facility has 48 spaces and employs 3 childcare workers. For employees who take maternity leave, UHN provides a generous top-up to 75% of salary for the first 25 weeks of their leave. Other family-friendly benefits include: jobsharing; reduced summer hours; telecommuting and working from home; compressed work week (same hours, fewer days); shortened work week (fewer hours); flexible start and finish hours.

To help offset rising tuition costs, the UHN operates a generous scholarship program that awards 20 post-secondary scholarships ($1,000 each) to employees' children.

### *Vacation & Time Off* — *Rating: B+*

UHN's vacation and time off are rated as **average**. New employees receive 2 weeks of vacation allowance after their first year, which increases to 3 weeks after 2 years of service. The maximum vacation allowance is 6 weeks for long-serving employees. Employees at UHN also receive 2 paid personal days off each year, in addition to their regular vacation allowance. (Nursing employee groups start with 3 weeks of paid vacation.) Employees at the group can also apply for unpaid leaves of absence.

### *Employee Communications* — *Rating: A+*

UHN's internal communications program is rated as **exceptional**. To keep employees informed about new developments, UHN publishes an in-house newsletter (called *UHN News/Caring Together*). The group also has an intranet site, which keeps employees informed about news and human resource policies that affect their work. To solicit feedback from employees, the group operates a traditional suggestion box program and an email suggestion box. An employee satisfaction survey is conducted every 12 months. An outside consultant compiles the survey results for UHN's management team. UHN also conducts in-house employee satisfaction surveys to address specific issues.

In an impressive communications initiative, the Hospital's new business plan was developed with feedback from over 700 individuals, including administrative employees, clinical staff, physicians, researchers, volunteers, managers and community members.

***Performance Management*** ***Rating: A+***

UHN's performance management program is rated as **exceptional**. The group operates a well-designed performance management program. Once a year, employees and managers meet for review sessions. (Managers receive training in how to conduct effective reviews.) At the reviews, employees and managers review past performance and establish development goals for the upcoming year. The review process forms the basis for salary increases.

Employees can also provide confidential feedback on their manager's performance through a unique process that includes assessments from other managers and employees. (Many employees were actively involved in the recently re-designed review process.)

***Training & Skills Development*** ***Rating: A+***

UHN's training and skills development program is rated as **exceptional**. The group provides tuition subsidies for courses related to an employee's current position (100% of tuition). Commendably, UHN also offers subsidies for courses not related to an employee's current job (50% of tuition to $1,000). The group assists employees' career development with: reimbursement for professional association dues; mentoring; career planning; in-house training.

The group's in-house training program includes a variety of courses as well as partnerships with local academic institutions. (UHN has a $6.5 million recruitment and retention fund, which is used to support ongoing employee education and training.)

***Community Involvement*** ***Rating: A***

UHN's community involvement program is rated as **above-average**. A very good member of the community, UHN actively supports a variety of local and national charitable initiatives. Every year, employees support the United Way, Christmas toy drives, local food banks and clothing drives for the homeless. Employees take part in the selection of charitable groups assisted by the group.

UHN is active in the community through education projects with local schools. The group is also an active promoter (and developer) of multicultural resources for numerous community-based programs that assist patients and their families.

**URBAN SYSTEMS LTD.**
**286 St. Paul Street**
**Suite 200**
**Kamloops, BC V2C 6G4**

**Tel. 250-374-8311**
**Fax 250-374-5334**
**http://www.urban-systems.com**

**INDUSTRY: ENGINEERING, ARCHITECTURAL & SURVEYING FIRMS**

*Highlights:*

- Work for an employer that's a vacation leader in its industry, offering three weeks of paid vacation allowance to new employees.
- Build your career at a mid-sized engineering firm in the Okanagan Valley that has resisted the takeover craze sweeping its industry by placing more emphasis on stable employment and employee development.
- Make a difference at a community-minded employer that hires disadvantaged young people for one year work terms, providing them with training and even financial support if they decide to pursue a trade or more schooling.

## *Employer Background*

Urban Systems Ltd. is a multidisciplinary firm of engineers, planners and landscape architects serving clients throughout British Columbia and Alberta. Founded in 1975, the firm provides a variety of consulting engineering services, including: water and wastewater treatment; transportation planning and engineering; land development; and general consulting services. Urban Systems works with a range of clients, including land developers, First Nations communities and all levels of governments.

The Kamloops-based firm competes with much larger firms and regularly wins large contracts. Urban Systems works closely with complementary firms to expand its capabilities on assignments where specialized skills are needed. (Their strategy stands in marked contrast to many other engineering firms, which have sought alliances with — or outright acquisitions by — large international engineering groups.) Urban Systems is owned by 36 partners at the firm.

In addition to the Kamloops head office, Urban Systems has four other locations in British Columbia (Richmond, Nelson, Kelowna and Fort St. John) and two in Alberta (Calgary and Edmonton).

**Workforce at a Glance:** Number of full-time employees: **168**. At this location: **55**. New jobs created in Canada in past year: **30**. Percentage of employees who are women: **37**. Percentage of employees who are visible minorities: **4**. Resumes received by their human resources staff in past year: **650**. Weeks of vacation their HR manager took last year: **3**. Average employee age: **40**. Years longest-serving employee has worked there: **27**. Car the president drives: **rumoured to be old Ford Taurus**. Where it's parked in the lot: **not often seen**.

### *Physical Workplace* — *Rating: A*

Urban Systems' physical workplace is rated as **above-average**. The custom-designed head office building was constructed in 1997. Located in downtown Kamloops, the head office location offers convenient access to local shops, restaurants and services as well as parkland along the South Thompson River.

**Physical Workplace at a Glance:** For **food and refreshment**, Urban Systems offers: free snacks (every Thursday is "Donut Day"); free coffee and tea; outdoor eating area; barbeque. Nearby **amenities** include: variety of restaurants; summer farmer's market; fitness facility; park/wilderness area (Riverside Park); recreation centre (YMCA). For **commuters**, Urban Systems offers: limited free parking; subsidized car parking; nearby public transit; secure bicycle parking; shower facilities. Other **work area amenities** include: open-concept workstations; access to natural light for all employees; ergonomic workstation design.

### *Work Atmosphere & Social* — *Rating: A*

Urban Systems' work atmosphere is rated as **above-average**. Employees at Urban Systems enjoy business casual dress daily and can listen to radio or music while they are working. There is also a company-subsidized social committee, called the '*Essence Committee*'.

The committee organizes several events to celebrate holidays throughout the year, including Easter egg hunts, Halloween pumpkin-carving contests and "*shamrock shakes*" on St. Patrick's Day. The company also hosts a Christmas party for employees and their spouses (with a separate party for employees' children), an annual golf tournament, picnics for each office and a year-end celebration with gifts for employees.

### *Health, Financial & Family Benefits* — *Rating: A*

Urban Systems' health benefits plan is managed by Equitable Life and is rated as **above-average**. Full-time and part-time employees who work more than 20 hours per week are covered by the plan.

**Health Benefits at a Glance:** Urban Systems' health plan includes the following coverage: dental (100% of eligible costs, to $1,000 each year); orthodontics (50% of eligible costs with a lifetime maximum of $2,000); extended health benefits; prescription drug; employee assistance plan (EAP) for substance abuse/mental health; massage therapy; physiotherapy; alternative therapies.

The company's salary and financial benefits are rated as **average**. To keep pay-levels competitive, Urban Systems participates in outside salary surveys. Individual salaries are reviewed every 12 months. The company offers a group RSP.

**Financial Benefits at a Glance:** Urban Systems provides a variety of financial benefits, including: life and disability insurance; discounted home computers; low-interest home loans (in some cases); share ownership plan for partners.

Urban Systems' family-friendly benefits are rated as **above-average**. Employees with pre-school children have access to a daycare facility located nearby. For employees who take maternity leave, Urban Systems provides a generous top-up to 70% of salary for the first 25 weeks of their leave. Other family-friendly benefits include: shortened work week (fewer hours); flexible start and finish hours.

*Vacation & Time Off* **Rating: A**

Urban Systems' vacation and time off are rated as **above-average**. New employees receive 3 weeks of vacation allowance after their first year, which increases to 4 weeks after 5 years of service. The maximum vacation allowance is 4 weeks for long-serving employees. Employees at the company can also apply for unpaid leaves of absence. (Recently, one employee took a 6 month leave to travel through Africa.)

*Employee Communications* **Rating: A**

Urban Systems' internal communications program is rated as **above-average**. To keep employees informed about new developments, Urban Systems publishes an in-house newsletter (called *The Pipeline*). The company also has an intranet site (called *The Pulse*), which keeps employees informed about news and human resource policies that affect their work. An in-house employee satisfaction survey is conducted by having employees complete an online questionnaire every 12 months. Urban Systems also operates a unique initiative that lets employees provide feedback directly to senior management. Employees who raise important questions are invited to branch meetings for open discussions with the CEO.

*Performance Management* **Rating: A+**

Urban Systems' performance management program is rated as **exceptional**. The company operates a formal performance management program. Once a year, employees and managers meet for review sessions.

At the reviews, employees work with their manager to develop future training and career development goals. The process assists the company in identifying its future leaders and is an important component in its succession planning process. Employees can also provide confidential feedback on their manager's performance through the annual survey.

Employees can also recognize a co-worker's excellent job performance through a popular program, called "*Spirit Awards*". Recipients receive special gift certificates (to $100) and have their name added to a coveted trophy.

*Training & Skills Development* **Rating: A**

Urban Systems' training and skills development program is rated as **above-average**. The company provides tuition subsidies for courses related to an employee's current position (100% of tuition). The company assists employees' career development with: reimbursement for professional association dues; mentoring; coaching; career planning; in-house training.

*Community Involvement* **Rating: A+**

Urban Systems' community involvement program is rated as **exceptional**. An outstanding corporate citizen, Urban Systems actively supports a variety of charitable initiatives.

The company operates an interesting foundation that helps disadvantaged youth build skills and confidence through work experience and encourages them to pursue higher education. Through this program, the company hires under-qualified candidates (between the ages of 16 and 28) for one year work terms. Urban Systems provides on-the-job training, mentoring, career planning and even subsequent financial support if they wish to continue their education. As part of this program, the company also provides financial support to international organizations assisting disadvantaged youth in other countries.

VanCity

**VANCOUVER CITY SAVINGS CREDIT UNION**
**183 Terminal Avenue**
**PO Box 2120, Station Terminal**
**Vancouver, BC V6B 5R8**

**Tel. 604-877-7000**
**Fax 604-877-8299**
**hr@vancity.com**
**http://www.vancity.com**

**INDUSTRY: CREDIT UNIONS**

*Highlights:*

- Get three weeks vacation allowance in your first year — and purchase additional vacation days by changing your flexible benefits plan.
- Work for an exceptional corporate citizen that offers an amazing $1 million award each year to a local organization that's improving the quality of life in Vancouver.
- Become a green commuter and receive transit subsidies for the city's light rail transit system that runs literally through their head office!
- Work for a financial services innovator that's making a difference with unique financial products, such as discounted car loans for electric hybrid vehicles.

## *Employer Background*

Vancouver City Savings Credit Union (VanCity) is Canada's largest credit union. Founded in 1946, VanCity operates 39 branches across British Columbia's Lower Mainland, as well as in Victoria and the Fraser Valley.

The member-owned credit union provides a complete range of financial services to over 286,000 members. VanCity manages over $8.2 billion in assets, making it one of the largest credit unions in the world.

In addition to being a leading financial services provider, VanCity has a long history of supporting the social and economic development of its members and the community. Last year, the credit union distributed over $11 million (over 30% of its net earnings) in the form of membership dividends and community grants.

VanCity continues to expand, adding more than 10,000 new members and posting record earnings last year.

**Workforce at a Glance:** Number of full-time employees: **1,076**. New jobs created in Canada in past year: **90**. Percentage of employees who are women: **72**. Of managers: **62**. Resumes received by their human resources staff in past year: **11,000**. Weeks of vacation their HR manager took last year: **2**. Average employee age: **37**. Years longest-serving employee has worked there: **38**. Person you should get to know first: **Jeanne bakes birthday cakes for colleagues and has a cappuccino maker at her desk.** Car the president drives: **2001 Audi A6**. Where it's parked in the lot: **with everyone else (when not taking transit)**.

### *Physical Workplace* *Rating: A*

VanCity's physical workplace is rated as **above-average**. The credit union's modern head office is located near downtown Vancouver along the popular False Creek Seawall. The building includes a station for Vancouver's SkyTrain, providing easy transit access for employees. During construction, an employee committee provided feedback on the final design of the interior.

> **Physical Workplace at a Glance:** Their **employee lounge and rest areas** feature: comfortable couches; television; book lending library. For **food and refreshment**, VanCity offers: free coffee and tea (all coffee is fair trade and organically grown); outdoor eating area; lunchroom with vending machines. Nearby **amenities** include: variety of restaurants; local shops and services; fitness facility (with subsidized memberships); park/wilderness area (False Creek Seawall); recreation centre (Vancouver Aquatic Centre). For **commuters**, VanCity offers: nearby public transit; transit subsidies; free onsite car parking (for employees who need their cars); subsidized car parking (for employees who carpool); secure bicycle parking; shower facilities. Other **work area amenities** include: ergonomic workstation design; access to natural light for all employees; plant life that is tended professionally.

### *Work Atmosphere & Social* *Rating: A*

VanCity's work atmosphere is rated as **above-average**. Employees at VanCity enjoy business casual dress daily. The credit union hosts a variety of employee events every year, including an employee recognition dinner, a summer family picnic, a family skating party, service awards celebrations, and a holiday dinner at Christmas.

VanCity also sponsors an employee softball tournament and a dragon boat team, as well as providing up to $500 for employee sports teams that compete in local leagues.

### *Health, Financial & Family Benefits* *Rating: A+*

VanCity's health benefits plan is managed by Maritime Life and is rated as **exceptional**. Their health benefits plan is flexible, meaning that employees can tailor individual plans to their personal circumstances.

> **Health Benefits at a Glance:** VanCity's health plan includes the following coverage: dental; orthodontics; eyecare (to $275 every 2 years); prescription drug; extended health benefits; nutrition planning; physiotherapy; massage therapy; alternative therapies; wellness subsidy (to $200 annually); personal and family counselling; employee assistance plan (EAP) for substance abuse/mental health.

The credit union's salary and financial benefits are rated as **exceptional**. To keep pay-levels competitive, VanCity participates in outside salary surveys every 12 months. Individual salaries are reviewed every 12 months. The credit union offers a group RSP. The credit union also operates a traditional pension plan where VanCity contributes up to 12% of an employee's salary (depending on their age) to the plan every year.

> **Financial Benefits at a Glance:** VanCity provides an extensive set of financial benefits, including: life and disability insurance; profit-sharing plan; low-interest home loans; subsidized home insurance; discounted company products; discounted home computers; discounted products and services (from Microsoft software to Whistler accommodations); referral bonuses for some employees (to $800).

VanCity's family-friendly benefits are rated as **average**. Employees with pre-school children have access to a subsidized daycare facility located onsite. (The daycare facility is used by employees with pre-school children for short-term care.) Other family-friendly benefits include: flexible start and finish hours; shortened work week (fewer hours); compressed work week (same hours, fewer days); telecommuting and working from home.

### *Vacation & Time Off* — *Rating: A*

VanCity's vacation and time off are rated as **above-average**. New employees receive 3 weeks of vacation allowance after their first year, which increases to 4 weeks after 4 years of service. The maximum vacation allowance is 6 weeks for long-serving employees. Employees at VanCity also receive 1 paid personal day off each year, in addition to their regular vacation allowance. Employees at the credit union can also apply for unpaid leaves of absence.

As part of the credit union's flexible benefits plan, employees can purchase up to 5 additional vacation days every year by foregoing other benefits. Employees also receive a bonus week of vacation when celebrating their 10th year (and every subsequent 5th year) of employment.

### *Employee Communications* — *Rating: A*

VanCity's internal communications program is rated as **above-average**. To keep employees informed about new developments, VanCity publishes an in-house newsletter (called *TATS*). The credit union also has an intranet site, which keeps employees informed about news and human resource policies that affect their work. An employee satisfaction survey is conducted every 12 months. An outside consultant compiles the survey results for VanCity's management team.

### *Performance Management* — *Rating: A*

VanCity's performance management program is rated as **above-average**. The credit union operates a thorough performance management program. Every 6 months, employees and managers meet for review sessions. (Managers receive training in how to conduct effective reviews.) As part of the review process, managers and employees establish mutually agreed upon performance goals. Managers are also encouraged to provide ongoing coaching, feedback and recognition throughout the year.

VanCity also operates a unique peer recognition program (called *Mount Kudos*) that allows employees to recognize one another for excellent job performance.

### *Training & Skills Development* — *Rating: A*

VanCity's training and skills development program is rated as **above-average**. The credit union provides tuition subsidies for courses related to an employee's current position (100% of tuition). Commendably, VanCity also offers subsidies for courses not related to an employee's current job (50% of tuition). The credit union assists employees' career development with: reimbursement for professional association dues; career planning; in-house training. VanCity's in-house training program covers a range of subjects, including leadership training, financial services and management training.

***Community Involvement*** ***Rating: A+***

VanCity's community involvement program is rated as **exceptional**. An outstanding member of the community, VanCity actively supports a variety of charitable initiatives. Every year, employees submit their ideas for the the company's annual fundraiser. Last year, employees raised over $86,500 for Family Services of Greater Vancouver through bake sales, barbeques, a mini-golf tournament, a dunk-tank, book sales and potluck lunches.

VanCity also matches employee charitable donations and donates money ($250) to charities where employees volunteer. Employees are also encouraged to volunteer at VanCity-sponsored events throughout the year, including the Vancouver AIDS Walk, the annual Commuter Challenge (over 90 percent of employees participated last year), and the annual Clean Air Day.

VanCity also supports local charitable and community organizations through a unique profit sharing program. Past recipients include the Burnaby Association for the Mentally Handicapped, the Canadian Centre for Educational Development, and the South Burnaby Neighbourhood House.

Impressively, VanCity awards $1 million annually to a non-profit organization working on a significant community project. Past projects include the renovation of a community cultural centre and the construction of a bicycle trail to connect Lower Mainland communities.

**WARDROP ENGINEERING INC.**
**386 Broadway**
**Suite 400**
**Winnipeg, MB R3C 4M8**

**Tel. 204-956-0980**
**Fax 204-988-0546**
**recruitment@wardrop.com**
**http://www.wardrop.com**

**WARDROP**

**INDUSTRY: ENGINEERING, ARCHITECTURAL & SURVEYING FIRMS**

*Highlights:*

- Work for a leader in the engineering industry on world-class projects, such as the International Space Station and the Canadarm.
- Earn cash bonuses that can double your salary.
- Accumulate your overtime (to 160 hours) and take the time off later.
- Recently reviewed and expanded its benefits offerings.

*Employer Background*

Wardrop Engineering Inc. is a multidisciplinary engineering, environmental, information technology and business consulting firm. The firm has completed projects in over 40 countries throughout North America, Latin America, Europe, Africa and Asia. Projects range from developing complex transportation networks in North America to designing hand pumps for clean water in Africa.

Founded in 1955, Wardrop started as a consulting engineering firm working on public works projects and housing subdivisions in Winnipeg. Over time, the firm began to provide consulting services around the world in the pulp and paper, international development, environmental, nuclear waste management and information technology industries. The award-winning firm has worked on such high-profile projects as the International Space Station, the Canadarm, the partial decommissioning of the Chernobyl nuclear reactor in the Ukraine, and the rebuilding of New York's subway line under the former World Trade Center.

Wardrop has recently shifted from a geographic focus to an emphasis on key business sectors in the world economy. These include: health care; nuclear; oil and gas; food and beverage; manufacturing and supply; pulp and paper; transportation; mining and mineral processing; power; and water and waste treatment. Wardrop expects this strategic change to double its employee count over the next five years.

Wardrop has six offices across North America (Winnipeg, Saskatoon, Toronto, Sudbury, Thunder Bay, Minneapolis) and international offices in Nigeria, Ghana and Uganda.

**Workforce at a Glance:** Number of full-time employees: **316**. At this location: **184**. Worldwide: **402**. New jobs created in Canada in past year: **12**. Percentage of employees who are women: **27**. Of managers: **14**. Percentage of employees who are visible minorities: **32**. Of managers: **18**. Resumes received by their human resources staff in past year: **9,298**. Weeks of vacation their HR manager took last year: **2**. Average employee age: **38**. Years longest-serving employee has worked there: **40**. Person you should get to know first: **Barb in Supplies (she knows were to find absolutely everything)**. Car the president drives: **BMW 5 Series**. Where it's parked in the lot: **with everyone else**.

***Physical Workplace*** ***Rating: B+***

Wardrop's physical workplace is rated as **average**. The company's Winnipeg head office is situated near the Assiniboine River, a location with lots of green space and pathways for cycling or lunchtime strolls. During the summer, the area comes alive with pedestrians and street vendors offering a variety of food specialties. At project locations around the world, employees experience a diversity of cultures and work environments.

**Physical Workplace at a Glance:** Their **employee lounge and rest areas** feature: table tennis. For **food and refreshment**, Wardrop offers: free coffee and tea; privately operated cafeteria downstairs. Nearby **amenities** include: variety of restaurants; major shopping mall; fitness facility; park/wilderness area (Assiniboine Riverwalk and The Forks Marketplace); recreation centre (YMCA). For **commuters**, Wardrop offers: nearby public transit; subsidized car parking; secure bicycle parking. Other **work area amenities** include: open-concept workstations; ergonomic workstation design; plant life that is tended professionally.

***Work Atmosphere & Social*** ***Rating: A***

Wardrop's work atmosphere is rated as **above-average**. Employees at Wardrop enjoy business casual dress daily and can listen to radio or music while they are working. There is also a firm-subsidized social committee, which has operated since 1979.

The social committee organizes a variety of events, including a company dinner and dance (with live music) in the spring, a summer golf tournament, a pool tournament in the fall, a holiday wine and cheese party, and a separate Christmas event for employees' children.

Across the company, each Wardrop office operates a social calendar tailored to the interests of its employees. Employees enjoy summer barbeques, holiday celebrations, golfing and other activities. Wardrop also sponsors employee hockey teams at its offices across Canada.

***Health, Financial & Family Benefits*** ***Rating: A***

Wardrop's health benefits plan is managed by Blue Cross and is rated as **above-average**. Their health benefits plan is flexible, meaning that employees can tailor individual plans to their personal circumstances. New employees must wait 90 days before they can enroll in the plan.

**Health Benefits at a Glance:** Wardrop's health plan includes the following coverage: dental (100% of eligible costs, to $1,000 each year); orthodontics (60% of eligible costs with a lifetime maximum of $2,500); eyecare (to $250 every 2 years); prescription drug; extended health benefits; nutrition planning; physiotherapy; massage therapy; alternative therapies; personal and family counselling; employee assistance plan (EAP) for substance abuse/mental health.

The firm's salary and financial benefits are rated as **exceptional**. The firm operates a traditional pension plan. Wardrop contributes 1.25% of each employee's salary to their plan each year.

> **Financial Benefits at a Glance:** Wardrop provides a variety of financial benefits, including: life and disability insurance; share purchase plan; discounted mortgage broker services; discounted home insurance; signing bonuses for some employees; referral bonuses for some employees (from $500 to $2,000); year-end bonuses (to $30,000 for non-executives).

Wardrop's family-friendly benefits are rated as **average**. Other family-friendly benefits include: flexible start and finish hours; shortened work week (fewer hours); telecommuting and working from home; accumulated overtime (up to 160 hours) can be saved for later use.

Wardrop also supports ongoing women in technology workshops to help women advance their careers in non-traditional areas of science, math and technology.

### *Vacation & Time Off* — *Rating: A*

Wardrop's vacation and time off are rated as **above-average**. New employees receive 2 weeks of vacation allowance after their first year, which increases to 3 weeks after 2 years of service. The maximum vacation allowance is 4 weeks for long-serving employees. Each year, Wardrop also provides employees with a paid holiday shutdown from Christmas to New Year's. Employees at the firm can also apply for unpaid leaves of absence. (Recently, one employee took a four-week leave to tour Australia.)

### *Employee Communications* — *Rating: B+*

Wardrop's internal communications program is rated as **average**. To keep employees informed about new developments, Wardrop publishes an in-house newsletter (called *Latest Happenings*), which is also distributed to over 2,800 clients. The firm also has an intranet site, which keeps employees informed about news and human resource policies that affect their work. An in-house employee satisfaction survey is conducted every 12 months.

### *Performance Management* — *Rating: A+*

Wardrop's performance management program is rated as **exceptional**. The firm operates a comprehensive performance management program. Every 3 months, employees and managers meet for review sessions. (Managers receive training in how to conduct effective reviews.) Employees also have the opportunity to provide confidential feedback on their manager's performance through the annual employee survey.

The company recognizes outstanding performance through salary increases, cash bonuses (outstanding employees can earn more than 100% of their salary), and non-cash rewards such as gift certificates for restaurant meals.

### *Training & Skills Development* — *Rating: A*

Wardrop's training and skills development program is rated as **above-average**. The firm provides tuition subsidies for courses related to an employee's current position (100% of tuition). The firm assists employees' career development with: reimbursement for professional association dues; career planning; in-house training; mentoring. The company's mentoring program ensures that each new employee is paired with a senior employee on their first day of employment.

*Community Involvement* *Rating: A*

Wardrop's community involvement program is rated as **above-average**. A very good corporate citizen, Wardrop actively supports a variety of charitable initiatives. Employees take part in the selection of charitable groups assisted by the firm. Employees at Wardrop receive paid time off to volunteer at local charities. Last year, Wardrop's employees volunteered over 843 hours on charitable projects in the community (about 2.7 hours per employee).

Wardrop's charitable support is focused on three main areas: education, international development, and local community support. Last year, the company and its employees supported a variety of interesting initiatives, including: the Monaghan & Portadown Partnership, which provides work experience for young people from Ireland; the construction of a children's health clinic in Kano, Nigeria; and the local United Way and the Christmas Cheer Board in Winnipeg.

THE CITY OF Waterloo

**WATERLOO, CITY OF**
**100 Regina Street South**
**Waterloo, ON N2J 4A8**

**Tel. 519-886-1550**
**Fax 519-747-8511**
**hrinfo@city.waterloo.on.ca**
**http://www.city.waterloo.on.ca**

**INDUSTRY: GOVERNMENT, GENERAL**

*Highlights:*

- Get meaningful feedback about your on-the-job performance from co-workers in your occupational category — an interesting element of this employer's performance management program.
- Enjoy free access (with your family) to this employer's recreational facilities across the city.
- Work for a benevolent employer that provides health benefits to retired employees and operates an innovative matching program that helps people find local charities where their skills are needed.

## *Employer Background*

The City of Waterloo provides municipal government services to the residents and businesses of Waterloo. Incorporated in 1857, the City's 857 full- and part-time employees serve over 104,000 citizens (including 12,300 university students), providing municipal services in public works, recreation and leisure, public safety, development planning and city administration.

The municipality has a diversified economic base, with major employers in the education, high-technology and insurance fields. The region's steady growth and success has led to the development of one of Canada's most innovative local governments.

Besides providing municipal services to existing residents and businesses, City employees are helping build one of Canada's fastest-growing urban areas. Recently, the City completed construction of North America's largest municipal recreation project , RIM Park, which features 500 acres of parkland, trails, recreational facilities and a public golf course.

The City of Waterloo is also redeveloping its downtown area, with two large projects under construction (the Perimeter Institute for Theoretical Physics and the Centre for International Governance Innovation) in the downtown core. As well, the City is playing an important role in the development of a world-class research and development park on the campus of the University of Waterloo.

**Workforce at a Glance:** Number of full-time employees: **555**. New jobs created in Canada in past year: **50**. Percentage of employees who are women: **47**. Of managers: **40**. Percentage of employees who are visible minorities: **4**. Of managers: **5**. Resumes received by their human resources staff in past year: **6,000**. Weeks of vacation their HR manager took last year: **4**. Average employee age: **35**. Years longest-serving employee has worked there: **44**. Person you should get to know first: **Lynne will help you decipher your benefits plan**.

### *Physical Workplace* — *Rating: A*

The City of Waterloo's physical workplace is rated as **above-average**. City employees work in a variety of environments across Waterloo. Almost all of the City's offices are newly built or have been significantly renovated in the last decade. (Employee feedback was solicited when designing work and customer service areas.) The City also has two committees working to ensure safe and healthy working environments. Most employees work at City Hall, which is located in the heart of downtown Waterloo.

**Physical Workplace at a Glance:** Nearby **amenities** include: variety of restaurants; local shops and services; major shopping mall; library; park/wilderness area (Waterloo Park); recreation centre (Memorial Recreation Centre). For **commuters**, The City of Waterloo offers: nearby public transit; free onsite car parking; secure bicycle parking. Other **work area amenities** include: open-concept workstations; wireless connectivity throughout office; plant life that is tended professionally; outdoor eating area.

### *Work Atmosphere & Social* — *Rating: B+*

The City of Waterloo's work atmosphere is rated as **average**. Employees at The City of Waterloo enjoy business casual dress daily and can listen to radio or music while they are working. There is also a City-subsidized social committee, which has operated since 1960.

Each year, City employees enjoy family picnics, golf tournaments, curling bonspiels and skiing trips. The City also organizes employee exchanges with Waterloo's sister cities in Québec and Ohio. Employees also receive free family passes to municipal recreation facilities.

### *Health, Financial & Family Benefits* — *Rating: A*

The City of Waterloo's health benefits plan is rated as **above-average**. Full-time and part-time employees who work more than 17.5 hours per week are covered by the plan. New employees must wait 90 days before they can enroll in the plan. The City of Waterloo's health plan also covers employees in their retirement.

In addition to its health benefits plan, the City offers an interesting program to help employees maintain a healthy work-life balance. The program offers fitness, nutrition and wellness classes to employees, as well as a resource library, an annual health fair and seminars on issues ranging from stress management to financial planning.

**Health Benefits at a Glance:** The City of Waterloo's health plan includes the following coverage: dental (100% of eligible costs, with no annual maximum); orthodontics (50% of eligible costs with a lifetime maximum of $1,500); eyecare (to $300 every 2 years); extended health benefits; prescription drug; nutrition planning; massage therapy; physiotherapy; alternative therapies; personal and family counselling; employee assistance plan (EAP) for substance abuse/mental health.

The City's salary and financial benefits are rated as **above-average**. To keep pay-levels competitive, The City of Waterloo participates in outside salary surveys every 24 months. Individual salaries are reviewed every 12 months. (Union pay levels are set by collective agreement.) The City operates a traditional pension plan.

**Financial Benefits at a Glance:** The City of Waterloo provides a variety of financial benefits, including: life and disability insurance; subsidized auto insurance; subsidized home insurance; discounted home computers; emergency loans.

The City of Waterloo's family-friendly benefits are rated as **average**. Employees with pre-school children have access to a daycare facility located nearby. Other family-friendly benefits include: flexible start and finish hours; compressed work week (same hours, fewer days); telecommuting and working from home.

### *Vacation & Time Off* — *Rating: B+*

The City of Waterloo's vacation and time off are rated as **average**. New employees receive 2 weeks of vacation allowance after their first year, which increases to 3 weeks after 3 years of service. The maximum vacation allowance is 6 weeks for long-serving employees. Employees at The City of Waterloo also receive 5 paid personal days off each year, in addition to their regular vacation allowance. Employees at the City can also apply for unpaid leaves of absence.

### *Employee Communications* — *Rating: A*

The City of Waterloo's internal communications program is rated as **above-average**. To keep employees informed about new developments, The City of Waterloo publishes an in-house newsletter. The City also has an intranet site, which keeps employees informed about news and human resource policies that affect their work. An in-house employee satisfaction survey is conducted every 12 months. Each year, the City holds a unique in-house conference that brings together 60 employees (representing all departments, locations and seniority levels) to determine areas that need improvement. In addition, many staff groups and business units have periodic consultations to identify employee concerns at the unit level.

In an interesting extension of its employee consultation process, the City now surveys Waterloo residents regularly to solicit their feedback on local priorities. This inclusive approach has led to significant public input on several city council committees, future development planning and new environmental regulations.

### *Performance Management* — *Rating: A+*

The City of Waterloo's performance management program is rated as **exceptional**. The City operates a formal performance management program. Once a year, employees and managers meet for review sessions. (Managers receive training in how to conduct effective reviews.) The City of Waterloo uses a 360-degree feedback process to gather additional performance-related information from co-workers, supervisors and employees. Employees also have the opportunity to provide confidential feedback on their managers.

The City uses performance reviews to determine salary increases for all employees. In addition, the City recognizes exceptional performance through informal rewards, such as gift certificates, dinners and pizza lunches.

Going beyond typical performance management programs, the City also encourages peer feedback within occupational categories. (For example, firefighters receive technical and interpersonal feedback annually from other officers in their platoon.) The City and its staff union are jointly developing a similar performance review system for union members.

*Training & Skills Development* *Rating: A*

The City of Waterloo's training and skills development program is rated as **above-average**. The City provides tuition subsidies for courses related to an employee's current position (50% of tuition). Commendably, The City of Waterloo also offers subsidies for courses not related to an employee's current job (50% of tuition). The City assists employees' career development with: reimbursement for professional association dues; career planning; succession planning; in-house training. The City's in-house training program includes a variety of courses, from customer service skills to management training.

*Community Involvement* *Rating: A+*

The City of Waterloo's community involvement program is rated as **exceptional**. An outstanding member of the community, The City of Waterloo actively supports a variety of local and national charitable initiatives. Employees take part in the selection of charitable groups assisted by the City. Employees at The City of Waterloo receive paid time off to volunteer at local charities.

Each year, City employees raise funds and volunteer for a variety of charitable organizations, including the United Way, the MS Society, the Breast Cancer Foundation, Big Brothers, Earth Day, the K-W Sexual Assault Centre and the Christmas Hamper Program, which provides assistance to families in need.

The City also operates a popular placement program to connect local charitable groups with interested volunteers, who work on projects ranging from serving seniors lunch to assisting with minor sports. Over 6,700 volunteers take part in the program, which recognizes their efforts at an annual awards dinner.

**YAMAHA MOTOR CANADA LTD.**
**480 Gordon Baker Road**
**Toronto, ON M2H 3B4**

**Tel. 416-498-1911**
**Fax 416-491-3517**
**careers@yamaha-motor.ca**
**http://www.yamaha-motor.ca**

**INDUSTRY: TOY & SPORTING GOOD WHOLESALERS**

*Highlights:*

- Sign out company products for the weekend, including motorcycles, dirt bikes, snowmobiles and all-terrain-vehicles.
- Outstanding employees are treated to an extra week of vacation plus an all-expense-paid trip to a Caribbean resort each year.
- Get three weeks of paid vacation allowance after your first year, plus four paid personal days off each year.

## *Employer Background*

Yamaha Motor Canada Ltd. is a leader in the leisure vehicle industry. Yamaha Canada is a subsidiary of Japan-based Yamaha Motor Co., Limited.

Established in 1889, the parent company manufactures a wide range of leisure and industrial products, including motorcycles, marine engines, snowmobiles, personal watercraft, all-terrain vehicles, outdoor power equipment automobile engines, electric-hybrid bicycles, industrial robots, heat-pump air conditioners and helicopters. Yamaha operates 60 manufacturing facilities in over 40 countries.

Founded in 1973, Yamaha Canada markets and distributes snowmobile, watercraft, outboard motors, motorcycles, all-terrain vehicles and outdoor power equipment to independently owned retailers across the country. In addition to the Toronto head office, Yamaha Canada has regional offices in Montréal and Vancouver.

**Workforce at a Glance:** Number of full-time employees: **176**. At this location: **147**. Worldwide: **33,158**. New jobs created in Canada in past year: **11**. Percentage of employees who are women: **36**. Of managers: **25**. Percentage of employees who are visible minorities: **23**. Of managers: **17**. Resumes received by their human resources staff in past year: **4,000**. Weeks of vacation their HR manager took last year: **3**. Average employee age: **40**. Years longest-serving employee has worked there: **30**.

## *Physical Workplace* — *Rating: B+*

Yamaha Canada's physical workplace is rated as **average**. Situated on 7 acres of land, the company's head office is also their primary distribution facility in Canada, with over 86,000 square feet of warehouse space.

**Physical Workplace at a Glance:** Their **employee lounge and rest areas** feature: music; television. For **food and refreshment**, Yamaha Canada offers: outdoor eating area. The company has an onsite cafeteria that features: subsidized meals (a turkey sandwich costs $2.50). Nearby **amenities** include: variety of restaurants; major shopping mall; fitness facility (with subsidized memberships). For **commuters**, Yamaha Canada offers: free onsite car parking; convenient highway access; nearby public transit; secure bicycle parking. Other **work area amenities** include: open-concept workstations; ergonomic workstation design; plant life that is tended professionally.

## *Work Atmosphere & Social* — *Rating: A+*

Yamaha Canada's work atmosphere is rated as **exceptional**. Employees at Yamaha Canada can listen to radio or music while they are working. There is also a company-subsidized social committee, which has operated since 1980.

The company hosts a variety of social events throughout the year, including a Christmas Party (with a separate event for employees' children), a dinner and dance to celebrate the arrival of Spring, an employee appreciation lunch (served by managers), a product demonstration day and barbeque, a golf tournament, evenings at the horse races, indoor motocross at Toronto's Skydome, Blue Jays baseball games (the company has season tickets), and an annual party for retiring employees. Yamaha Canada also sponsors employee sports teams that compete in local leagues.

Through a truly unique program, employees can borrow Yamaha products for the weekends, including motorcycles, all-terrain vehicles, dirt bikes and snowmobiles.

## *Health, Financial & Family Benefits* — *Rating: A*

Yamaha Canada's health benefits plan is managed by Maritime Life and is rated as **above-average**. Full-time and part-time employees who work more than 15 hours per week are covered by the plan. There is no waiting period before new employees are eligible for coverage.

**Health Benefits at a Glance:** Yamaha Canada's health plan includes the following coverage: dental (100% of eligible costs, to $1,500 each year); orthodontics (50% of eligible costs with a lifetime maximum of $2,000); eyecare (to $175 every 2 years); extended health benefits; prescription drug; massage therapy; physiotherapy; alternative therapies; personal and family counselling; employee assistance plan (EAP) for substance abuse/mental health.

The company's salary and financial benefits are rated as **above-average**. To keep pay-levels competitive, Yamaha Canada participates in outside salary surveys every 12 months. Individual salaries are reviewed every 12 months. The company offers a group RSP that allows employees to contribute up to 5% of their salary, with matching employer contributions. The company also operates a traditional pension plan.

**Financial Benefits at a Glance:** Yamaha Canada provides a variety of financial benefits, including: life and disability insurance; discounted new and used company products; annual product sale for employees (discounted by 10% to 25%); subsidized home insurance; subsidized auto insurance; discounted CAA memberships; annual clothing allowance for warehouse employees (to $250); year-end bonuses.

Yamaha Canada's family-friendly benefits are rated as **average**. Other family-friendly benefits include: flexible start and finish hours; telecommuting and working from home.

*Vacation & Time Off* **Rating: A**

Yamaha Canada's vacation and time off are rated as **above-average**. New employees receive 3 weeks of vacation allowance after their first year, which increases to 4 weeks after 10 years of service. The maximum vacation allowance is 5 weeks for long-serving employees. Employees at Yamaha Canada also receive 4 paid personal days off each year, in addition to their regular vacation allowance. Employees at the company can also apply for unpaid leaves of absence. (Recently, one employee took a two month leave to visit family in China.)

*Employee Communications* **Rating: A**

Yamaha Canada's internal communications program is rated as **above-average**. To keep employees informed about new developments, Yamaha Canada publishes an in-house newsletter (called *The Yammer*). The company also has an intranet site, which keeps employees informed about news and human resource policies that affect their work. An in-house employee satisfaction survey is conducted every 36 months. Employees can also provide timely feedback through email and traditional suggestion box programs. The company operates a unique program that pays employees (up to $500) when their suggestions are adopted.

*Performance Management* **Rating: A**

Yamaha Canada's performance management program is rated as **above-average**. The company operates a comprehensive performance management program. Once a year, employees and managers meet for review sessions. (Managers receive training in how to conduct effective reviews.) The review program helps employees establish training and development objectives.

In addition to long-service awards, the company operates a generous program to reward excellent performance. Each year, eight employees (and a guest) are given an extra week of vacation and sent on all-expense-paid trip to a Caribbean resort.

*Training & Skills Development* **Rating: A**

Yamaha Canada's training and skills development program is rated as **above-average**. The company provides tuition subsidies for courses related to an employee's current position (100% of tuition). The company assists employees' career development with: reimbursement for professional association dues; in-house training. The company's in-house training program includes a variety of courses, including first-aid, computer training, retirement planning and new product seminars.

*Community Involvement* **Rating: A+**

Yamaha Canada's community involvement program is rated as **exceptional**. An outstanding corporate citizen, Yamaha Canada actively supports a variety of local and national charitable initiatives. Employees take part in the selection of charitable groups assisted by the company. Employees at Yamaha Canada receive paid time off to volunteer at local charities. Last year, the company contributed to approximately 35 charitable groups, including: the Hospital for Sick Children, the Heart and Stroke Foundation, the Canadian Cancer Society, the Kids Help Line, the Children's Wish Foundation and the Ride for Sight charity.

In a thoughtful initiative, Yamaha Canada's cafeteria (and its recycling program) are managed by individuals from the Canadian Mental Health Association. The partnership provides a controlled work environment that helps mentally challenged individuals integrate into the workforce.

Yamaha Canada is also a leading sponsor of the annual Skills Canada competition. Through this program, high school students from across the country have the opportunity to take complete engines apart — and then try to put them back together. The company also donates engine products to educational institutions across the country. For the children of employees (and Yamaha retailers), the company operates an scholarship program.

Water for the World

**ZENON ENVIRONMENTAL INC.**
**3239 Dundas Street West**
**Oakville, ON L6M 4B2**

**Tel. 905-465-3030**
**Fax 905-465-3050**
**hradmin@zenon.com**
**http://www.zenon.com**

**INDUSTRY: OTHER MECHANICAL EQUIPMENT MANUFACTURERS**

*Highlights:*

- Build your career at a growing employer that's become a key player in an industry that promises to revolutionize how people obtain safe drinking water around the world.
- Work in a custom-built facility includes a fully equipped fitness centre, a subsidized cafeteria (with a healthy menu) and 8km of forest trails for walking, running or cycling.
- Believe in your work at an employer that's not connected to the municipal sewer system — 100% of its drinking water is recycled by the company's own treatment equipment!

## *Employer Background*

Zenon Environmental Inc. develops membrane-based filtration systems for drinking water and wastewater treatment applications. The company was founded in 1980 with the modest goal of solving the world's water quality and shortage problems. To meet this mission, Zenon has developed advanced technologies for water purification and wastewater recycling.

At the heart of the company's success is its revolutionary membrane technology (called *ZeeWeed*), which is protected by over 50 patents worldwide. With thousands of installations around the world, Zenon's technology makes it possible for people to have clean, fresh drinking water from unconventional sources.

The company's technology is used in municipal water treatment plants, cruise ships, desalination plants and on remote defence and peacekeeping missions. Zenon's innovative treatment process requires less energy and chemicals to guarantee safe levels of water quality. Zenon's newest product is a small home-based system that ensures safer, better-tasting drinking water directly from the tap.

In addition to its Oakville head office, Zenon has 16 offices in North America, Europe, Asia, Latin America and the Middle East. In the past year, the company signed major contracts to supply new water filtration systems in Singapore, Hungary, Michigan and Kamloops, British Columbia. Zenon's revenues increased to over $145 million last year.

**Workforce at a Glance:** Number of full-time employees: **636**. At this location: **382**. Worldwide: **911**. New jobs created in Canada in past year: **60**. Percentage of employees who are women: **28**. Of managers: **14**. Resumes received by their human resources staff in past year: **1,800**. Weeks of vacation their HR manager took last year: **1**. Average employee age: **36**. Years longest-serving employee has worked there: **22**.

### *Physical Workplace* — *Rating: A+*

Zenon's physical workplace is rated as **exceptional**. Located on a 150-acre site, the company's Oakville head office is remarkable for one unusual detail: the facility is not connected to the municipal sewer system. Instead, Zenon treats its own wastewater and purifies drinking water for the facility. (You really have to believe in the company's technology to work here.) Designed with input from employees, the custom-built facility houses nearly all of the company's Ontario operations.

**Physical Workplace at a Glance:** Their **onsite fitness facility** features: subsidized memberships; treadmills; stationary bikes; stairmasters; rowing machines; weights; basketball court; outdoor beach volleyball court; 8 km forest trail for walking, jogging or bicycling; instructor-led classes; fitness trainer; chiropractor and massage therapist; sauna; shower facilities. For **food and refreshment**, Zenon offers: outdoor eating area; barbeque. The company has an onsite cafeteria that features: subsidized meals (a turkey sandwich costs $3.50); healthy menu items. Nearby **amenities** include: variety of restaurants; major shopping mall; park/wilderness area (Bronte Creek Park); recreation centre (Transley Woods Recreation Centre). For **commuters**, Zenon offers: free onsite car parking; secure bicycle parking. Other **work area amenities** include: open-concept workstations; ergonomic workstation design; access to natural light for all employees; plant life that is tended professionally.

### *Work Atmosphere & Social* — *Rating: A*

Zenon's work atmosphere is rated as **above-average**. Employees at Zenon enjoy business casual dress daily. There is also a company-subsidized social committee, which has operated since 1995.

Employees enjoy a number of fun events throughout the year, including a family summer social (with fresh strawberries and shortcake), a winter dinner-dance for employees and a special Christmas party with gifts for employees' children. Zenon also subsidizes an employee softball team (called the *WetSocs*) and a hockey team, both of which compete in local leagues.

### *Health, Financial & Family Benefits* — *Rating: A*

Zenon's health benefits plan is managed by Canada Life and is rated as **above-average**. Full-time and part-time employees who work more than 20 hours per week are covered by the plan. New employees must wait 90 days before they can enroll in the plan.

**Health Benefits at a Glance:** Zenon's health plan includes the following coverage: dental (100% of eligible costs, to $1,500 each year); orthodontics (50% of eligible costs with a lifetime maximum of $2,500); eyecare (to $250 every 2 years); extended health benefits; prescription drug; nutrition planning; massage therapy; personal and family counselling.

The company's salary and financial benefits are rated as **above-average**. To keep pay-levels competitive, Zenon participates in outside salary surveys every 12 months. Individual salaries are reviewed every 12 months. The company offers a group RSP that allows employees to contribute up to 4% of their salary, with matching employer contributions.

In addition to generous financial benefits, Zenon employees recently received an unexpected bonus when the company's Chief Technology Officer received the prestigious Manning Award for inventing the new ZeeWeed filtration system. Half of the $100,000 award was distributed to the team members who developed the technology, while the other half was distributed to all Zenon employees.

> **Financial Benefits at a Glance:** Zenon provides a variety of financial benefits, including: life and disability insurance; subsidized auto insurance; subsidized home insurance; discounted home computers; discounted company products; share purchase plan; profit-sharing plan.

Zenon's family-friendly benefits are rated as **average**. Employees with preschool children have access to a daycare facility located nearby.

### *Vacation & Time Off* — *Rating: B+*

Zenon's vacation and time off are rated as **average**. New employees receive 2 weeks of vacation allowance after their first year, which increases to 3 weeks after 3 years of service. The maximum vacation allowance is 4 weeks for employees who spend 10 years with the company. Employees at the company can also apply for unpaid leaves of absence. (Recently, one employee took a three month leave to volunteer with a community relief program in South America.)

### *Employee Communications* — *Rating: A*

Zenon's internal communications program is rated as **above-average**. To keep employees informed about new developments, Zenon publishes an in-house newsletter (called *Zenoflash*), which is available online. The company also has an intranet site, which keeps employees informed about news and human resource policies that affect their work. An in-house employee satisfaction survey is conducted periodically.

### *Performance Management* — *Rating: A*

Zenon's performance management program is rated as **above-average**. The company operates a comprehensive performance management program. Every 6 months, employees and managers meet for review sessions. (Managers receive training in how to conduct effective reviews.) Zenon uses a 360-degree feedback process to gather additional performance-related information from co-workers, supervisors and employees. At the reviews, employees and managers evaluate progress and jointly develop a written action plan for the upcoming months.

### *Training & Skills Development* — *Rating: A*

Zenon's training and skills development program is rated as **above-average**. The company provides tuition subsidies for courses related to an employee's current position (100% of tuition). The company assists employees' career development with: reimbursement for professional association dues; monthy professional development courses; career planning; in-house training.

*Community Involvement* *Rating: A+*

Zenon's community involvement program is rated as **exceptional**. An outstanding corporate citizen, Zenon actively supports a variety of local, national and international charitable initiatives. Employees take part in the selection of charitable groups assisted by the company. Last year, the company contributed to approximately 12 charitable groups, including: the United Way, Foodshare, Salvation Army, Halton Family Services, Make-A-Wish Foundation, Easter Seals and the Heart and Stroke Foundation.

In addition, Zenon donates its technology and expertise to help people in need of clean water. The company recently provided water purification systems to a First Nations settlement in Northern Ontario and a village in Vietnam. Employees volunteered their time to design, install and train local residents to operate the new systems.

# TEN BEST EMPLOYERS FOR VACATION & TIME-OFF

1. Suncor Energy Inc.
2. Enmax Corporation
3. Husky Energy Inc.
4. Adacel Inc.
5. KPMG LLP
6. Georgian College
7. BHP Billiton Diamonds Inc.
8. Frank Russell Canada Limited
9. Credit Union Electronic Transaction Services Inc. / CUETS
10. Environics Communications Inc.

*These employers are leaders in offering exceptional vacation allowance and personal days off. All offer at least three weeks of paid vacation allowance for new employees — many provide four weeks vacation in the first year of employment. Most also provide additional paid time off in the form of personal days, shortened work weeks, reduced summer hours and, in some cases, paid leaves of absence to pursue educational and other career objectives. By providing employees with more time for family and personal commitments, these employers attract talented employees who are interested in keeping a healthy work-life balance.*

# TEN BEST EMPLOYERS FOR WORKING CONDITIONS

1. Intuit Canada Limited
2. Crystal Decisions, Inc.
3. University Health Network
4. The Banff Centre
5. Algorithmics Incorporated
6. Telvent Canada Ltd.
7. BHP Billiton Diamonds Inc.
8. Enmax Corporation
9. IBM Canada Ltd.
10. The Great-West Life Assurance Company

*These employers have created wonderful workplaces that offer much more than a desk and a chair. Many have been designed with employee feedback and offer everthing from onsite fitness facilities to relaxation and nap rooms.*

*Honourable mentions go to the Law Society of Upper Canada and Fairmont Hotels & Resorts for their unique workplaces.*

# TEN BEST EMPLOYERS FOR FAMILY-FRIENDLY WORK ENVIRONMENTS

1. University Health Network / UHN
2. Merck Frosst Canada
3. South-East Regional Health Authority
4. IBM Canada Ltd.
5. KPMG LLP
6. Ecotrust Canada
7. Procter & Gamble Inc.
8. Suncor Energy Inc.
9. Sun Life Financial Services of Canada Inc.
10. The Banff Centre

*These employers are the best places to work for people who have young children or significant family commitments. All provide generous maternity top-up payments and offer alternative work arrangements, including flexible hours and telecommuting. Some also offer onsite daycare programs, daycare subsidies and special assistance for adoptive families.*

*Honourable mentions go to: Bank of Montreal, Cascades Inc., Co-operative Trust Company of Canada, Co-operators Life Insurance Company, Ernst & Young LLP, Georgian College, Hamilton Police Service, IKEA Canada, City of Mississauga and Pfizer Canada Inc.*

# TEN BEST EMPLOYERS FOR TRAINING & DEVELOPMENT

1. MacDonald, Dettwiler and Associates Ltd.
2. Bank of Montreal
3. CAE Inc.
4. Dofasco Inc.
5. KPMG LLP
6. OMERS
7. Meridian Technologies Inc.
8. Shell Canada Limited
9. Rogers Communications Inc.
10. PCL Construction Group Inc.

*These employers all place tremendous emphasis on employee training and development. They offer a variety of outstanding career development programs, including tuition subsidies at outside institutions, reimbursement for professional association dues, mentoring, career planning assistance and a range of in-house training courses (both traditional and online). Many operate impressive training facilities and have made ongoing employee development a key part of their competitive strategy. Several of these employers have also created custom training programs with local colleges and universities, which provide employees with a diploma or certificate on the successful completion of each training program.*

*Honourable mentions go to the Canadian Broadcasting Corporation and Cara Operations Limited.*

# TEN BEST EMPLOYERS FOR VISIBLE MINORITIES

1. Frank Russell Canada Limited
2. Matrikon Inc.
3. Algorithmics Incorporated
4. Telvent Canada Ltd.
5. IKEA Canada
6. Amex Canada Inc.
7. University Health Network / UHN
8. Bank of Montreal
9. SAS Institute (Canada) Inc.
10. Wardrop Engineering Inc.

*These employers are truly outstanding places for visible minorities to work and get ahead. At these employers, visible minorities make up 43% to 17% of management ranks. Not surprisingly, employers with strong visible minority representation have had considerable success in their industries. Encouraging diversity in the workplace isn't just about being a "good employer" — in today's competitive labour market, it's essential in attracting the best people.*

*Honourable mention goes to Ernst & Young LLP for its unique "Ethnic Diversity Task Force".*

# TEN BEST EMPLOYERS FOR WOMEN

1. Maritime Travel Inc.
2. Trillium Health Centre
3. Carlson Wagonlit Travel
4. South-East Regional Health Authority
5. Blake, Cassels & Graydon LLP
6. Vancouver City Savings Credit Union
7. Advanced Book Exchange Inc.
8. Law Society of Upper Canada, The
9. L'Union Canadienne, Compagnie d'Assurances
10. Sun Life Financial Services of Canada Inc.

*These employers are excellent places for women to work and advance through management ranks. At each of these organizations, women make up from 97% to 58% of management. (Yes, there really is an employer on this list where 97% of the managers are female!) These employers are leading the march towards gender equality in the workplace, particularly when it comes to promoting women into management positions.*

## TEN BUSIEST HUMAN RESOURCE OFFICES

1. Rogers Communications Inc.
2. IKEA Canada
3. Trillium Health Centre
4. Cara Operations Limited
5. Epcor Utilities Inc.
6. Sun Life Financial Services of Canada Inc.
7. CAE Inc.
8. Pfizer Canada Inc.
9. KPMG LLP
10. University Health Network / UHN

*These employers are the leaders in attracting applicants from across Canada, receiving from 110,000 to 25,000 job applications each year. They are popular and busy places to work — especially for the human resources staff!*

# TEN BEST EMPLOYEE NEWSLETTERS

1. BHP Billiton Diamonds Inc. ("The Diamond Pipe")
2. The Banff Centre ("The Rough Copy")
3. Alias Systems ("WaveLength")
4. Ecotrust Canada ("Notes from the Front")
5. South-East Regional Health Authority ("Vital Signs")
6. Yamaha Motor Canada Ltd. ("The Yammer")
7. Enmax Corporation ("Buzz")
8. Export Development Canada ("Link")
9. Co-operators Life Insurance Company ("The LifeLine")
10. Toronto Transit Commission ("Coupler")

*These interesting in-house newsletters are entertaining and feature among other things: colour photos of employee parties and social events; ads for community events; wedding and new baby announcements; short features on individual employees; comic strips; sports sections on employee teams; short articles by technical staff explaining new products; and even book reviews. While newsletters are increasingly moving from traditional print to online versions, the focus for the best newsletters remains the same.*

# TEN BEST EMPLOYERS FOR YOUNG PUPS

1. BioWare Corporation
2. iAnywhere Solutions, Inc.
3. Mitra Inc.
4. Intuit Canada Limited
5. Blast Radius Inc.
6. Matrikon Inc.
7. Spielo Manufacturing Inc.
8. Crystal Decisions, Inc.
9. Advanced Book Exchange Inc.
10. Recruitsoft, Inc.

*If being around people who are more familiar with the Beatles than Xbox gives you the creeps, these employers are for you. The average age of employees at these organizations ranges from 29 to 33 years old.*

# TEN BEST EMPLOYERS FOR OLD DOGS

1. Georgian College
2. Industrial Accident Prevention Association
3. Neill and Gunter Limited
4. Dofasco Inc.
5. Toronto Transit Commission
6. Seaspan International Ltd.
7. Patheon Inc.
8. Shell Canada Limited
9. General Dynamics Canada, Ltd.
10. Suncor Energy Inc.

*If the sight of another Blackberry-wearing kid in a turtleneck makes you cringe, you might want to think about these employers. The average age of employees at these organizations ranges from 47 to 42 years old.*

*Our new "Branch Office Index" lists both head office **and** branch office locations for each of the employers in cities and towns across Canada.*

## BRITISH COLUMBIA

| | |
|---|---|
| Vancouver | Ernst & Young LLP |
| Vancouver | Export Development Canada |
| Vancouver | Fairmont Hotels & Resorts |
| Vancouver | Great-West Life Assurance Company, The |
| Vancouver | Halsall Associates Limited |
| Vancouver | KPMG LLP |
| Vancouver | Matrikon Inc. |
| Vancouver | Merck Frosst |
| Vancouver | Neill and Gunter Limited |
| Vancouver | PCL Construction Group Inc. |
| Vancouver | Qunara Inc. |
| Vancouver | SAS Institute (Canada) Inc. |
| Vancouver | Sierra Systems Group Inc. |
| Vancouver | Standard Aero Limited |
| Vancouver | Sun Life Financial Services of Canada Inc. |
| Vancouver | Vancouver City Savings Credit Union |
| Vernon | KPMG LLP |
| Victoria | Advanced Book Exchange Inc. |
| Victoria | Great-West Life Assurance Company, The |
| Victoria | KPMG LLP |
| Victoria | Sierra Systems Group Inc. |

## ALBERTA

| | |
|---|---|
| Banff | Banff Centre, The |
| Bow Island | Murray Auto Group, The |
| Calgary | AltaGas Services Inc. |
| Calgary | Amex Canada Inc. |
| Calgary | Bank of Montreal |
| Calgary | Blake, Cassels & Graydon LLP |
| Calgary | Carlson Wagonlit Travel |
| Calgary | Cascades Inc. |
| Calgary | Ceridian Canada Ltd. |
| Calgary | CGI Group Inc. |
| Calgary | Enmax Corporation |
| Calgary | Epcor Utilities Inc. |
| Calgary | Ernst & Young LLP |
| Calgary | Export Development Canada |
| Calgary | Fairmont Hotels & Resorts |
| Calgary | General Dynamics Canada, Ltd. |
| Calgary | Great-West Life Assurance Company, The |
| Calgary | Hewlett-Packard (Canada) Co. |
| Calgary | Husky Energy Inc. |
| Calgary | IKEA Canada |
| Calgary | Intuit Canada Limited |
| Calgary | KPMG LLP |
| Calgary | Matrikon Inc. |
| Calgary | Merck Frosst |
| Calgary | PCL Construction Group Inc. |
| Calgary | Pfizer Canada Inc. |
| Calgary | Procter & Gamble Inc. |
| Calgary | Qunara Inc. |

## SASKATCHEWAN

## MANITOBA



## ONTARIO

Mississauga ..... ATS Automation Tooling Systems Inc.
Mississauga ..... Cara Operations Limited
Mississauga ..... Ceridian Canada Ltd.
Mississauga ..... Ernst & Young LLP
Mississauga ..... Great-West Life Assurance Company, The
Mississauga ..... Hewlett-Packard (Canada) Co.
Mississauga ..... IMS Health Canada Ltd.
Mississauga ..... KPMG LLP
Mississauga ..... Merck Frosst
Mississauga ..... Mississauga, City of
Mississauga ..... Patheon Inc.
Mississauga ..... Pfizer Canada Inc.
Mississauga ..... Qunara Inc.
Mississauga ..... Recruitsoft, Inc.
Mississauga ..... Trillium Health Centre
North Bay ..... KPMG LLP
Oakville ..... TDL Group Ltd., The
Oakville ..... Zenon Environmental Inc.
Orangeville ..... Georgian College
Orangeville ..... Pfizer Canada Inc.
Orillia ..... Georgian College
Oshawa ..... Great-West Life Assurance Company, The
Ottawa ..... Amex Canada Inc.
Ottawa ..... Blake, Cassels & Graydon LLP
Ottawa ..... Canadian Broadcasting Corporation
Ottawa ..... Carlson Wagonlit Travel
Ottawa ..... Cascades Inc.
Ottawa ..... Ceridian Canada Ltd.
Ottawa ..... CGI Group Inc.
Ottawa ..... Ernst & Young LLP
Ottawa ..... Export Development Canada
Ottawa ..... Fairmont Hotels & Resorts
Ottawa ..... General Dynamics Canada, Ltd.
Ottawa ..... Gennum Corporation
Ottawa ..... Great-West Life Assurance Company, The
Ottawa ..... Halsall Associates Limited
Ottawa ..... Hewlett-Packard (Canada) Co.
Ottawa ..... IKEA Canada
Ottawa ..... Industrial Accident Prevention Association
Ottawa ..... KPMG LLP
Ottawa ..... Law Society of Upper Canada, The
Ottawa ..... MacDonald, Dettwiler and Associates Ltd.
Ottawa ..... Merck Frosst
Ottawa ..... PCL Construction Group Inc.
Ottawa ..... Qunara Inc.
Ottawa ..... SAS Institute (Canada) Inc.
Ottawa ..... Sierra Systems Group Inc.
Ottawa ..... Sun Life Financial Services of Canada Inc.
Owen Sound ..... Georgian College
Parry Sound ..... Georgian College
Sarnia ..... Suncor Energy Inc.
Sault Ste. Marie ..... KPMG LLP

Toronto ... Toronto Transit Commission
Toronto ... Trillium Health Centre
Toronto ... University Health Network / UHN
Toronto ... Wardrop Engineering Inc.
Toronto ... Yamaha Motor Canada Ltd.
Vaughan ... IKEA Canada
Waterloo ... Ceridian Canada Ltd.
Waterloo ... Dalsa Corporation
Waterloo ... Great-West Life Assurance Company, The
Waterloo ... iAnywhere Solutions, Inc.
Waterloo ... KPMG LLP
Waterloo ... Mitra Inc.
Waterloo ... Sun Life Financial Services of Canada Inc.
Waterloo ... Waterloo, City of
Whitby ... Patheon Inc.
Windsor ... Great-West Life Assurance Company, The
Windsor ... Halsall Associates Limited
Windsor ... KPMG LLP
Woodbridge ... ATS Automation Tooling Systems Inc.

## QUÉBEC

Boucherville ... Yamaha Motor Canada Ltd.
Bromont ... Dalsa Corporation
Bromont ... IBM Canada Ltd.
Brossard ... Adacel Inc.
Brossard ... Great-West Life Assurance Company, The
Dorval ... Adacel Inc.
Jonquière ... CGI Group Inc.
Kingsey Falls ... Cascades Inc.
Kirkland ... Hewlett-Packard (Canada) Co.
Laval ... Boehringer Ingelheim (Canada) Ltd.
Laval ... Great-West Life Assurance Company, The
Montréal ... Amex Canada Inc.
Montréal ... Bank of Montreal
Montréal ... Blake, Cassels & Graydon LLP
Montréal ... Canadian Broadcasting Corporation
Montréal ... Carlson Wagonlit Travel
Montréal ... Cascades Inc.
Montreal ... Ceridian Canada Ltd.
Montréal ... CGI Group Inc.
Montréal ... Environics Communications Inc.
Montréal ... Ernst & Young LLP
Montréal ... Export Development Canada
Montreal ... Fairmont Hotels & Resorts
Montréal ... Fuller Landau LLP
Montréal ... Great-West Life Assurance Company, The
Montréal ... KPMG LLP
Montréal ... MEI Inc.
Montréal ... Merck Frosst
Montréal ... Pfizer Canada Inc.
Montréal ... Procter & Gamble Inc.

## NEW BRUNSWICK



## NOVA SCOTIA

Halifax ........ KPMG LLP
Halifax ........ MacDonald, Dettwiler and Associates Ltd.
Halifax ........ Maritime Travel Inc.
Halifax ........ Merck Frosst
Halifax ........ PCL Construction Group Inc.
Halifax ........ Procter & Gamble Inc.
Halifax ........ Qunara Inc.
Halifax ........ Sierra Systems Group Inc.
Sydney ........ KPMG LLP
Sydney ........ Neill and Gunter Limited

## PRINCE EDWARD ISLAND

Charlottetown ........ Diagnostic Chemicals Limited

## NEWFOUNDLAND & LABRADOR

St. John's ........ Canadian Broadcasting Corporation
St. John's ........ Ceridian Canada Ltd.
St. John's ........ Ernst & Young LLP
St. John's ........ Export Development Canada
St. John's ........ Fairmont Hotels & Resorts
St. John's ........ Great-West Life Assurance Company, The
St. John's ........ PCL Construction Group Inc.

## NORTHWEST TERRITORIES

Yellowknife ........ BHP Billiton Diamonds Inc.
Yellowknife ........ Canadian Broadcasting Corporation
Yellowknife ........ PCL Construction Group Inc.

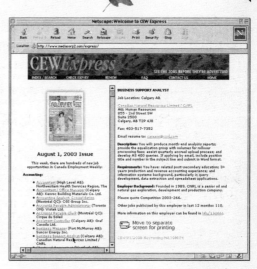

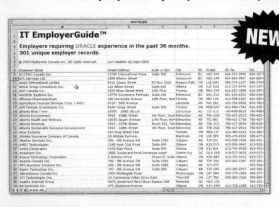

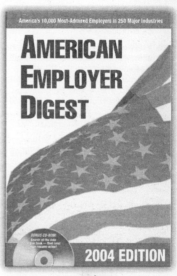

## *COMMENTS & CHANGES*

If you would like to suggest an employer we should research for the next edition of *Canada's Top 100 Employers* (or would like to make comments on any included in this edition), please write. You can send this form to the address listed below, or email the information to ct100@mediacorp2.com.

NAME OF EMPLOYER

SUBMITTED BY (OPTIONAL)

DATE TELEPHONE EMAIL ADDRESS

***Send completed form to:***

**Canada's Top 100 Employers, Mediacorp Canada Inc.**
**21 New Street, Toronto, ON M5R 1P7 • Tel. (416) 964-6069 • Fax (416) 964-3202**

# Four Easy Ways to Order:

Rapid Order Form

- Call us toll-free at **1-800-361-2580**
- Order online at **www.mediacorp2.com**
- Fax this order form to us at **416-964-3202**
- Mail this order form to us at: **Mediacorp Canada Inc., 21 New Street, Toronto, Ontario M5R 1P7. Tel. 416-964-6069. info@mediacorp2.com.**

| QTY. | PUBLICATION | PRICE | TOTAL |
|---|---|---|---|
| | WHO'S HIRING 2004 — *Includes CD-ROM* | $ 41.95 | $ |
| | THE CAREER DIRECTORY (2004 ED.) — *Includes CD-ROM* | $ 34.95 | |
| | CDN. DIRECTORY OF SEARCH FIRMS (2004 ED.) – *Includes CD-ROM* | $ 69.95 | |
| | CANADA'S TOP 100 EMPLOYERS (2004 EDITION) | $ 22.95 | |
| | AMERICAN EMPLOYER DIGEST 2004 — *Includes CD-ROM* | $ 39.95 | |
| | CANADA EMPLOYMENT WEEKLY (NEWSPRINT) — *12 issues inside Canada* | $ 69.95 | |
| | CANADA EMPLOYMENT WEEKLY (NEWSPRINT) — *50 issues inside Canada* | $ 291.46 | |
| | CANADA EMPLOYMENT WEEKLY (INTERNET) — *12 issues sent anywhere* | $ 49.95 | |
| | IT EMPLOYERGUIDE – *Specify language(s):* ________________ | $ 49.95 | |
| | Shipping Charges — Book orders only *(Canadian residents: add $4/order + $1.75/book)* | | $ |
| | **Sub-Total** | | $ |
| | GST *(Canadian residents add 7% of Sub-Total. NS, NB & NF residents add 15% HST. GST/HST#134051515)* | | $ |
| | **Total Order** | | $ |

**PAYMENT INFORMATION**

☐ Visa
☐ MasterCard
☐ Amex
☐ Cheque Enclosed
☐ PayPal

CREDIT CARD NUMBER ________________ EXPIRY ________

CARDHOLDER NAME ________________ SIGNATURE ________________

☐ P.O. #: ☐ Make this a **Standing Order** and save 15% on future editions

**YOUR SHIPPING ADDRESS**

YOUR NAME ________________ COMPANY / ORGANIZATION ________________

ADDRESS ________________ CITY ________________ PROV ________

EMAIL ADDRESS ________________

TELEPHONE ________________ FAX ________________